THE POLITICS
OF RAILROAD
COORDINATION

1933–1936

THE POLITICS
OF RAILROAD
COORDINATION

1933–1936

EARL LATHAM

Joseph B. Eastman Professor of Political Science
Amherst College

HARVARD UNIVERSITY PRESS
Cambridge, Massachusetts · 1959

Distributed in Great Britain by
Oxford University Press London

This book has been aided by a
grant from the Ford Foundation.

Library of Congress Catalog Card Number 59-9279

Printed in the United States of America

To
Peter and Susan

PREFACE

Although this volume is an analytical study and not a testimonial, a biographical note about the principal figure may not be amiss. Joseph Bartlett Eastman, born in Katonah, New York, June 26, 1882, was graduated from Amherst College in 1904, and served as a member of the Interstate Commerce Commission from 1919 until his death on March 15, 1944. A lifetime of public service began when he joined the South End House in Boston after his graduation from college. He was soon drawn into more active public affairs when he left settlement house work to become secretary of the Public Franchise League. Here Eastman came under the compelling influence of Louis Dembitz Brandeis, forming an association that was to help shape both his philosophy and his career.

From the Public Franchise League, Eastman was appointed to the Massachusetts Public Service Commission in 1914 at the suggestion of George W. Anderson, a resigning member, and with the endorsement of Brandeis. When a vacancy occurred in the Interstate Commerce Commission in 1918, Brandeis brought Eastman's name to the attention of President Wilson who appointed him to the position in 1919 in which he was to serve with great distinction for the next two decades and a half. Eastman's name deserves to rank with that of the famous Judge Thomas M. Cooley, the first chairman of the Interstate Commerce Commission, as one who exercised decisive and lasting influence upon the development of the practise and the administrative law of the Commission.

While a member of the Commission, Eastman was given two important special assignments by President Roosevelt, first as Federal Coordinator of Transportation in 1933, and second as Director of the Office of Defense Transportation in 1942. He served as Coordinator until his authorities lapsed in 1936; and served as Director until his death.

Eastman's papers are in the custody of the Joseph B. Eastman

Foundation of Amherst College, to which the author makes grateful acknowledgement for time, materials, and research assistance. All unpublished sources cited in this book are to be found in the Foundation, unless otherwise specified.

Thanks are owed to Mr. Robert V. Fletcher of the Association of American Railroads for his kindness to the research enterprise, and to the late Commissioner Patterson and former Charles D. Mahaffie of the Interstate Commerce Commission for aid and counsel. Acknowledgements are also owed to Hon. Frances Perkins, former Secretary of Labor, Robert E. Freer, former Chairman of the Federal Trade Commission, former Senator Burton K. Wheeler of Montana, Adolph Berle, Jr., Donald C. Richberg, former counsel to the Railway Labor Executives Association, former Congressman Clarence Lea, who was head of the House Commerce Committee during the period of the Federal Coordinator, and to the late Elizabeth Eastman of Washington, D.C. Professor George Goodwin, Department of Political Science, University of Massachusetts, performed valuable research assistance.

Special thanks are owed to Dr. Charles S. Morgan, formerly of the staff of the Interstate Commerce Commission, for important services of review, comment, information, and advice.

All errors are the responsibility of the author.

EARL LATHAM

Amherst, Massachusetts
November 1958

CONTENTS

THE POLITICS
OF RAILROAD
COORDINATION

1933–1936

I. A NOTE OF INTRODUCTION

"The true history of the United States is the history of transportation . . . in which the names of railroad presidents are more significant than those of Presidents of the United States." Philip Guedalla

This is a study of the politics of administration in which the focus is the effort of the federal coordinator of transportation to "coordinate" under the Emergency Railroad Transportation Act of 1933. The federal coordinator is regarded as the center of one group (the agency established by statute) inhabiting an environment of groups, official and private, each an active center of power capable of bringing pressure against him, or of cooperating or refusing to cooperate with him in the fulfillment of his mandate under the statute. He was supposed to "coordinate" the complex of railroad groups. He eventually concluded that it was necessary and desirable to coordinate all of the groups in the transportation field. He effected little coordination of the railroad groups because they would not let him. He did little coordination of the others because he lacked the authority.

After an analysis of the group struggle that led to the passage of the 1933 statute, the study deals with Eastman's concept of coordination, the instrumentalities at his disposal for producing the required alignment of power centers in the railroad industry, the relations between the coordinator and the official agencies of which he was a part, the alliances and cross alliances of private and official groups in a changing pattern of check and countercheck against the coordinator, the "co-optation" of the function of coordination by the carriers through a private mechanism of leadership and control (the Association of American Railroads), one of the objects of which was to nullify and vitiate the coordinator's office, the changing roles of the carriers and the unions, and the eventual withdrawal of support by both the carriers and the unions when they, by treaty, made temporary peace with each other and then deserted the coordinator. Although the coordinator hoped to make the function of coordination a permanent one, his authorities were allowed to lapse by inaction in 1936 when Congress failed to renew the Emergency Railroad Transportation Act. There was no fight about such renewal. The coordinator simply did not have any affirmative support, or none that could be mustered, among the official groups or in the structure of private associations with which he had been dealing since 1919 as a commissioner of the Interstate Commerce Commission.

The experience of the coordinator supports certain political propositions. Top administrators often have to organize and concentrate the power which they administer. In a political system as strongly pluralized as that of the United States, the political parties do not accumulate and organize sufficient power to permit the administrator to concentrate upon the professional aspects of his work, as is the case in England and in other places. The relation of a President to his administrative heads and cabinet officers is normally not such that he can delegate to them the necessary power which a clear mandate in a parliamentary system provides. The programs of the agencies are developed in great part by the agencies themselves out of the interactions of groups, official and otherwise. An agency goes forward with a program when its power base is strong and firm. And its power base may have its strongest points of support outside the hierarchy of the official groups of which the agency is a part.

The administrator's problem of organizing his own power base is difficult enough when the program he seeks to administer is one that does not require the active cooperation of the groups to be regulated but merely calls for a suppression or deferment of active hostilities. How much more difficult it is when the program requires active cooperation, an initiative by the constituent groups to proffer sustained and active contribution to the development of the administrator's program. Such cooperation was of the essence of the coordinator's program. He was supposed, among other things, to coordinate; that is to say, to align and rationalize the self-generated actions of the constituent parts of the railroad industry towards the elimination of waste and preventable expense. By nonaction the constituent groups could veto the program. Although he was given an authority to initiate or require action, the power needed to move an unmoving object is greater than the power needed to deflect it from its course when in motion. Automobile wheels are easier to turn when a car is being driven than when it is standing still. The authority of a statute unsupported by the power of groups that stand to gain advantage from its enforcement against rival groups that stand to lose advantage, leaves the administrator with only the sanctions of the official agencies, including the courts. These sanctions may be evaded or prolonged to a point where they represent no effective coercion or control at all. And when the rival groups which have a stake, respectively, in the enforcement and nonenforcement of a statute combine with each other against the administrator, he can lose his office before the courts can support his authority.

The prudent administrator clearly recognizes the difference between authority and power. The first is the right to wield power and the second is the actual exercise of power. If he has authority merely, he will refrain from trying to act as though it were power; for the inevitable consequence is that he will lose authority also in the showdown. It was so with the federal coordinator of transportation. He had the right to give orders — he had "authority" — under the Emergency Railroad Transportation Act of 1933. For the first two years of his official life he refrained from trying to exercise this authority, with certain few and minor exceptions which are noted in the study. In his third year he set out to wield authority as though it were power. The principal combinations of constituent groups in the railroad field joined against him. His third year was his last because, as has been said, his authority was not renewed.

A chess player confronted with an impasse which can have only one result, however long it may be deferred, resigns and starts a new game. Some military actions are conducted on the chess principle. The civilian administrator may always hope to reorganize his power base in such a way as to build superior influence in his favor. The chess player cannot borrow the pieces he needs from another game that may be going on. Nor can the military commander normally wish into being the troops and guns he requires to make his force the superior one. But the administrator has other courses of action, however hopeless his cause. His statute usually gives him several activities to administer and he is likely, if frustrated in one, to augment another. Thus it was with the federal coordinator of transportation. He was not only required to coordinate the carriers to eliminate waste and preventable expense; he was also required to "investigate and consider means . . . of improving transportation conditions throughout the country" (Section 13). And this he did with great distinction. For the life of the statute, at least, he was in complete control of a research staff that reported to him directly, both those hired and paid by him and those borrowed from the Interstate Commerce Commission. This activity he could command and direct himself, without let or hindrance from the constituent groups that made up the railroad industry. Chapter IX discusses the research and reporting activity of the coordinator and points out the theme that runs through all the reports, namely, the need for an increasing encompassment of the groups to be coordinated, with some account of the resistance experienced from the groups to which coordination applied.

The federal coordinator of transportation was alive to the changing make-up of the transportation industry and to the shifting alignments of group support that technology had brought into being. And he attempted more than once to reorganize the Interstate Commerce Commission to make it more "representative" of the configuration of groups in the transportation industry. This he was not able to do, however, and it is possible that the Interstate Commerce Commission today suffers from the difficulties that he was able to foresee but against which he was unable to forfend.

A word may be said about the method of the study. The principal materials are documentary materials, in the public and private records. This means that the conclusions are limited to the data, but that the totality of the data was never developed to make it easy to answer the questions of academics, which are not the same thing as academic questions. Many data that would be relevant to an inquiry into the relations of the coordinator with the railroads, the White House, the Interstate Commerce Commission, and so on simply do not exist. The coordinator did not live his life with the requirements of researchers long after the event in mind. The student of these subjects therefore is bound by and restricted to the materials which were created for other reasons than his interest and convenience.

The research of things past also suffers from the limitation that it often is impossible to create materials that are needed to fill gaps and to supply information. Interviews are relatively useless because the memory of most men is wildly fallible, especially about events in which they have had a part. Conversations have been had with individuals who worked with the coordinator, and what is remembered is his personality and the relation of the narrator with that personality, which tells something, to be sure, about the personal relationship but little or nothing about the event.

These matters are mentioned not because it is felt that there is any gravely serious loss to the account in having to rely solely on such public and private records as are available, but because reliance upon such records is regarded by some students of political behavior as unsophisticated. Those who feel more confident than the author about the immediate development of a "science" of politics prefer to concentrate upon small-group research and upon the discovery of whatever can be counted in simple controllable interpersonal relations, admitting the study of larger political structures only if extraordinary access is permitted to the personalities, subgroups, and factions that move and function within these structures.

The development of politics as a discipline, however, is not so well advanced that one can say with strong assurance that there is general agreement upon either the basic concepts of the subject or upon the methodology according to which they should be manipulated and employed. Until the arrival of a systematic theory which relates to each other the current miscellany of metaphysics, ethics, juristic systems, institutional descriptions, and small-group experimentation, the student of political behavior may be permitted to explore the material that interests him with such tools as he possesses or can fashion for the purpose. The public and private record, although incomplete and imperfect in many respects, is nevertheless a prime body of data. And if the paleontologist finds it impossible to interview the inhabitants of the Neolithic Age, he can discover a lot about them from what they left behind.

One final word is perhaps in order. The federal coordinator of transportation was Joseph B. Eastman, a man who has the reputation of having been the perfect public servant, selfless, devoted to his work and position, above the petty partisanship of the group struggle, without ambition for gain, and loyal, above all else, to the highest concepts of the public duty and his obligation to serve the public interest. Public service has few heroes, for it is in the nature of the positions that administrators occupy that there is no self-serving group that is bent upon creating hero myths about them. The medical profession has a hagiology, a catalogue of the saints of the profession, as does the law, the military vocation, and business. All of these callings have a pantheon of the great and the near great, whose images are metaphorically exhibited on the feast days of the craft. Even the politician, that marginal broker of the public power, observes the birthdays of those in whose name he contrives results that they might be the first to reject.

Public administration, alas, has few heroes. The public service has not been able to develop in the United States the degree of professionalization that it has reached and enjoyed in other political systems. It has not become so socially rooted as to cultivate a group consciousness, interested in perpetuating symbols of its idealized role in the society. The lawyer-hero is a man who has displayed egregious mastery of the tools of the craft, like Webster who made the New Hampshire judges weep in the Dartmouth College case; or who, like Lincoln, used the lawyer's simple guile to do justice, as in the case of the mendacious witness whose perjury was exposed by the almanac. The medical heroes seem to be distinguished by qualities of personal sacrifice, like the victims of the tsetse fly or the anonymous country doctor who works the clock around. Soldier heroes are the epic champions and defenders. And business heroes are the great producers.

In the folklore of the day and place, however, the public servant is not venerated because he has no stable group or class base to support him but rather is the object of the antagonism of those who possess such a base and who feel that it is to their advantage to prevent him from developing his. In this view the public servant is a suspected mediocrity who goes about eating up the liberties of the people when he is not arbitrarily interfering with the economy. This caricature helps to move the bright and gifted young steadily into the law, medical, and business schools, where they can do justice, help the sick, bring bounty to the people, and make a lot of money at the same time.

Eastman's great reputation as a public servant is all the more astonishing then, not because he did not deserve it, because he did, but because he was and has been allowed to keep it. It is a mild miracle that Eastman, who once had strong views in favor of government ownership of the railroads, should be spoken of in terms of admiration, loyalty, and personal affection by men who opposed his views hotly. Union leaders have expressed great respect and admiration for him even as they were joining with the carriers to take away his authorities. He was close to the desperate struggle of group interests in the railroad industry for much of his adult life, but he seems never to have become a partisan of any of the partisans, and yet was able to hold their genuine and undoubted respect. In these respects and in his deep dedication to his work, which was without let, his reputation as a public servant is unparalleled.

II. THE SALT LAKE CITY LINE

"I have very little hope that it will be possible to deal fundamentally with the transportation problem without resort to some form of public ownership and operation or, shall I say, direct Government responsibility for transportation."   Joseph B. Eastman to Felix Frankfurter

The railroads in 1933 were a sick industry in a staggering economy. Between 1929 and 1933, the roads had suffered a 50.8 per cent reduction in revenue from operations which they had counterbalanced with a nearly equal cut in expenses (50.1 per cent). Jobs were down 41.5 per cent from the 1929 level, and compensation to workers had fallen by 51.6 per cent. Dividends fell 71.7 per cent. Interest currently accrued on funded debt, however, showed no such decline, and in fact was higher in 1933 than in 1929.[1] In his report to Congress in January, 1934, Joseph B. Eastman, the federal coordinator of transportation, said that the volume of freight and passenger traffic between 1926 and 1932 had declined by about 50 per cent, and that railroads operating 42,340 miles were in receivership or in the hands of the courts under the Bankruptcy Act.[2]

The desperate condition of the railroad industry set off a fever of activity to prescribe for its ills; and in a time when relief, recovery, and reform were the three legs of new public policy, the railroads, if not at the center of utmost concern, at least were not neglected. One of the principal lines of policy was to evolve from the speech on transportation problems made by presidential candidate Franklin D. Roosevelt in Salt Lake City, Utah, on September 17, 1932; but before this line delivered the Emergency Railroad Transportation Act of 1933, the case for cartelization was stated, the case for government operation was tested, and immediate action was taken to reform reorganization procedures.

The Salt Lake City Speech

Because it was central to so much that was to occur later, the Salt Lake City speech may be mentioned first.[3] Circulated widely as a campaign tract, the speech was a brief primer on railroad conditions as well as a prospectus of reforms to come. The speech was "understood" by the *New York Times* to have been approved by railway presidents and railway labor executives.[4] And, in fact, it was praised rather warmly by the presidents of the Delaware and Hudson, the New York Central, and the New Haven.[5] A certain amount of mystery, however, shrouds the writing of the speech, and its authorship is by no means clear. The early brain-trusters — Raymond Moley, fresh from the classrooms of Columbia University, and Adolph A. Berle, former Harvard Law School prodigy and a brilliant member of the bar — had a hand in its drafting, although the recollections of each some time after the event are not exact with reference to the parts played by the other.[6] The initial task of preparing the Salt Lake City speech seems to have been given by Roosevelt to Moley. A Roosevelt speech, typically, was built up by numerous small accretions, with many participants adding some bit of phrase or fragment of thought, and the Salt Lake City speech was not different from the pattern. Donald Richberg, at the time counsel for important railroad unions, also had a hand in the potpourri.[7]

There is slight evidence that Eastman had any part to play in the drafting of the speech, although it is possible that he might have been consulted.[8] Certainly there is no warrant for the view expressed by some that the speech was his work.[9] In fact, there is negative evidence to the contrary, since Eastman in a memorandum to Roosevelt in 1936 on the progress of the railroad reform said of one important portion of the Salt Lake City speech, "I cannot say that this recommendation has been carried out, because I am not sure what was meant." [10] This is not the voice of authorship.

There were six principal recommendations in the speech. First, voluntary financial reorganizations by the roads were to be encouraged in return for promised financial help from the federal government. This was not too realistic a proposal since such voluntary reorganizations require the consent of a large percentage of the security holders, who commonly are many in number and widely scattered, and there always are those who dissent or refuse assent.[11] Second, Roosevelt also proposed a thorough overhaul of the federal laws affecting railroad receiverships, saying that these laws "as they now stand" suggested "Mr. Dooley's famous dictum that they are arranged so that every member of the bar may get his fair share of the assets." This proposal was calculated to appeal to the security holders "against irresponsible or self-interested reorganization managers." The third proposal recommended the regulation of motor carriers by the Interstate Commerce Commission in addition to railroads, and further recommended that railroads be permitted to acquire motor carriers under controlled conditions. This proposal was eventually enacted into law by the Motor Carrier Act, 1935.

The fourth recommendation, based upon the belief that "the policy of enforced competition between railroads can be carried to unnecessary lengths," suggested that the Interstate Commerce Commission should be relieved of the duty of requiring competition where traffic was insufficient to support competing lines — a proposal to permit the moderation of the antitrust laws, so long as the elimination of such competition did not lead to abuses of monopolistic power. Actually, the ICC already had power to bar the operation of the antitrust statutes in approving pooling arrangements and various forms of railroad unification; and it also had the authority to authorize the abandonment of nonpaying mileage, another proposal in the Salt Lake City speech. But the manifest intention to reduce wasteful competition and to promote cooperation and coordination of the railroads which was expressed in the speech eventually led directly to the enactment of Title I of the Emergency Railroad Transportation Act of 1933 and indirectly contributed to the establishment and organization of the Association of American Railroads.

In the fifth recommendation, it was said that proposed "consolidations of railroads which are lawful and in the public interest, should be pressed to a conclusion." The ICC had been given authority in the Transportation Act of 1920 to approve such consolidations but the program had encountered difficulties.[12] The last of the six principal recommendations proposed that the railroad holding companies should be definitely put under the regulation and control of the ICC in like manner as the railroads themselves. This recommendation was to be largely carried out in Part II of the Emergency Railroad Transportation Act of 1933 which brought *future* acquisitions of railroad securities by railroad holding companies under the effective control of the Commission. Existing railroad holding companies were not brought under such control, however, except with respect to future acquisitions, and Eastman said that he "was probably responsible for this omission, thinking that such recognition might impair possible proceedings against these companies under the Clayton Act."

There were other recommendations but the principal six contained the gist of the proposals which Roosevelt in September, 1932, was prepared to support. The secretary of labor, William N. Doak, commented tartly on the speech, asserting that it offered nothing new. Indeed, it had done little more than to adopt the essentials of the Hoover policy towards the railroads. Said the secretary of labor, "While Roosevelt talks, Hoover acts." The country did not share the opinion of the Secretary of Labor and, the election being over, the new President-elect set about formulating the programs which he proposed to offer to the new Congress in the following March.

The Coolidge Committee

While it was necessary for Roosevelt to get himself elected before he could put into law any of the proposals he was prepared to make, other groups worked in the fall of 1932 and the winter of 1933 to produce their own proposals for the reconstruction of the seriously distressed railroads. One of these groups was the National Transportation Committee, which came to advocate a form of cartelization of the railroads. Mention of this group is deserved, not because it was influential in the development of the Emergency Railroad Transportation Act of 1933, but because it shows how far railroad creditors were prepared to go to save their investments.

The National Transportation Committee was headed by former President Calvin Coolidge, nominally, at least, and consisted of Bernard Baruch, New York financier and prominent adviser to presidents since World War I; Clark Howell, the editor of the influential southern newspaper The Atlanta Constitution; Alexander Legge, president of the International Harvester Company; and Alfred E. Smith, former governor of New York and disappointed candidate for the Democratic presidential nomination in 1932. The motive force behind the appointment of the Coolidge

Committee was generated by a large group of insurance companies interested as creditors of the railroads in saving their investments by reducing competitive wastes in railroad operation and in other ways. The railroads were not in a mood by themselves, even at this time, to undertake cooperative projects for the reform of the industry. Jealousy, suspicion, and an unwillingness to submerge private interests for the common good of the industry prevented this.[13] The insurance companies were joined in their concern for the railroad industry by Harvard, Yale, Columbia, and Chicago universities, also holders of railroad securities. The Coolidge Committee of course did none of the staff investigation of the railroad industry but it did engage the head of the Brookings Institution, Harold G. Moulton, to make a survey, held open hearings of its own, and used studies by other investigating bodies, memoranda, briefs, and specific suggestions. The staff under Moulton also made independent studies, received the recommendations of many of the interested groups in the transportation industry, took advice and counsel from many official and unofficial sources, ignored the labor unions, and produced a good-sized volume, issued by Brookings, under the title *The American Transportation Problem*.

This busy concern with transportation policy may have set in motion other efforts to clarify ideas and to state positions. Thus, the Association of Railway Executives, a predecessor of the Association of American Railroads, joined with the National Highway Users Conference to create a committee headed by Alfred P. Sloan, Jr.[14] This committee delivered a report to the National Transportation Committee recommending that motor common carriers be required to obtain certificates of public convenience and necessity, but they failed to agree on the question whether trucks and busses in interstate commerce should be subjected to rate regulation.[15]

Eastman followed the work of some of these groups in the great deliberations over transportation policy with keen interest. He was in touch with Moulton, for example, and made available to him his (Eastman's) views about developments from time to time.[16] On one occasion, at least, he brought to the attention of the research director for the National Transportation Committee an eastern trucking operator who wanted a conference with Moulton's group.[17] Eastman himself had an interest in bringing to the attention of Moulton his own plan for the voluntary transfer of railroad properties to the federal government, of which more will be said presently. In one of his letters to Moulton, he said of his plan, "It is only a skeleton — mere food for thought, and I am by no means committed to it myself. It would need to be tested out in a great many ways for which I have as yet had no time. I think it may have germs of possibilities in it, but again it may not. It would, I assume, be too radical for your crowd. Please treat it confidentially, because I do not yet wish to father it." [18] Eastman's government ownership "skeleton" was not to rattle in the closet of the National Transportation Committee, however, although the committee, in other respects, relied upon him for needed material.[19]

The National Transportation Committee began its business in October, 1932, and produced its awaited report with recommendations for the reform of the transportation industry on February 13, 1933. It contained emergency recommendations for a revision of bankruptcy procedures, the repeal of the recapture clause of the Transportation Act of 1920 that had also been recommended by Roosevelt in his Salt Lake City speech, a revision of the statutory rule for rate-making, and a more liberal definition of "adequate security" in the lending procedures of the Reconstruction Finance Corporation as applied to the railroads. The principal recommendations for permanent reform of transportation and its regulation sought to advance the public interest, although the result in some respects would have been to protect the railroads from competing forms of transportation. It was said that there was no need to foster competition among the railroads because regulation defends against monopoly and because there was increasing competition between railroads as a group and other forms of transportation. Regional consolidations should be hastened and, where necessary, enforced; and unprofitable railroad service should be replaced by cheaper alternative methods. The railroads were to be permitted to own competing services, government should refrain from subsidizing competing forms of transportation, motor carriers should be regulated to the extent necessary for public protection, and they should be taxed their "fair share." There was no recommendation about pipe lines. Air services were to be supported at public expense only in the development phase.

The railroads, in turn, were urged to look inward upon themselves and to undertake a stiff and stern course of self-improvement. They were advised to cooperate with each other to reduce unnecessary expenditures, to abandon unnecessary services, to consolidate terminals, and to stop circuitous haulage. They were warned to improve the financial management of railroad properties and to bring their transportation methods and equipment up to date and in line with the best modern developments. The machinery of regulation was also to be overhauled, for the committee proposed that regulation be extended to all forms of transportation to the extent necessary to protect the public interest, and that the Interstate Commerce Commission be reorganized, without expansion or increase of expense. The principal reform urged was that the executive, legislative, and judicial functions of the Commission be separated with a chief at the head of each, a separation of powers that the later Administrative Procedure Act of 1946 extended in principle, although not in detail, to all of the regulatory agencies of the federal government.

Alfred E. Smith could not go all the way with the other members of the committee and did not sign the report. He said that there was need for caution in extending regulation to other forms of transportation. They did not offer much competition although the potentialities of motor transportation were acknowledged. Motor carriers should be regulated only so far as necessary for the public safety. With the unhappy O'Fallon case fairly recently in mind, Smith urged that a new principle of valuation be employed, presumably one that worked more favorably to the users of railroad services than a formula in which reproduction cost new less depreciation received considerable weight. He did not propose to wait for necessary railroad consolidations but urged that they be put into effect upon a large scale, by force if necessary. Nor did he temporize with what he considered to be the shortcomings of the Interstate Commerce Commission. He proposed the abolition of the Commission and the creation of a new Department of Transportation or a bureau of transportation in the Department of Commerce to carry out and enforce the regulatory statutes.

Although it somewhat overstates what was recommended, it is not entirely unfair to say that the National Transportation Committee set out the case for the eventual cartelization of the railroads. Regional consolidations, the committee thought, should be hastened and, where necessary, enforced, looking eventually to a single national system. The railroads were ultimately to be thought of as a single business and not as a special interest or set of special interests. This aspect of the report of the committee drew favorable comment in *Business Week,* which observed, nevertheless, that there was small consolation for the railroads in a report which recommended that the rate-making rule should allow the roads to make a reasonable profit based upon the costs of efficient operation.[20] The *New York Times* said that "little or no progress has been or is likely to be made along the lines of voluntary consolidation . . . if our railroads are to be consolidated, compulsion is plainly necessary." [21] In a letter to the Hon. George W. Anderson, a former Interstate Commerce Commissioner, Eastman said of all this, "I suppose you have seen the report of the National Transportation Committee. It did not impress me as being a document which is likely to have much effect. However, I am inclined to agree that the way to secure maximum harmony in railroad operation is to operate them as a single unit for the entire country, but if that should be done I think public ownership will be inevitable." [22]

Reorganizing the Commission

One part of the report of the National Transportation Committee — the recommendations for the reorganization of the Commission — did not catch Eastman unawares. In fact, he had taken steps to interest the Commission in reorganization before the report was issued in order to make it ready to assume any new functions of regulation and control that might be imposed upon it. Under date of December 2, 1932, Eastman sent a memorandum to his fellow commissioners bringing to their attention the desirability of making internal improvements in the work of the Commission.[23] He said that consideration of the "present transportation situation" was bound to lead either to a curtailment of federal regulation and supervision, or to an extension of both, and that he thought the latter was the more likely alternative. If so, then either new agencies would be established or the jurisdiction of the Commission would be increased. It was his "guess" that the authority of the Commission would be increased, "provided the Commission can be so organized as to perform the work efficiently and without delay." He laid suggestions before them for a clearer division of duties within the Commission and for the delegation of work to boards of employees. A group within the Commission was designated to consider the question of reorganization, and it reported to the Commission on December 30. The report did not please Eastman and he ventured the observation that he had not made himself clear earlier in the month.

With painstaking care, therefore, he undertook in a massive memorandum to the Commission, dated January 3, 1933, to make himself clear.[24] He forecast the possible enactment of legislation for comprehensive regulation of all forms of transportation, communications, and power through a Transportation Commission, a Communications Commission, and a Power Commission respectively. The ICC was the likely nucleus for a Transportation Commission. He then reviewed some of the administrative shortcomings of the Commission as tactfully but as clearly as possible. The Coolidge Committee was certainly in his mind, and he referred to it more than once. His principal suggestion for reform was further delegations of the work of the Commissioners, and he invited his colleagues to consider the most feasible ways of accomplishing this change.

In the meantime, a bill had been introduced in Congress to empower the Commission to delegate its powers internally, and Eastman lent his support to the measure. He appeared before the House Committee on Interstate and Foreign Commerce on January 18, 1933, and was gratified to find that the measure was viewed favorably and opposed by none. To the contrary, it was supported by the Association of Interstate Commerce Commission Practitioners, the National Industrial Traffic League, and the American Short Line Railroad Association. Eastman helped the measure on its way in the Senate by writing to Senator James Couzens to bespeak its support, citing in its favor the lack of opposition, the positive endorsements it had received among the transportation groups, and the adoption of the measure in the House by unanimous consent.[25] Because he feared that the recommendations of the National Transportation Committee with respect to the Commission might be in conflict with the congressional measure (as, indeed, they were), he took the precaution of preparing an unfavorable analysis of the Committee's recommendations and sent it along to Senator Couzens and to Congressman Rayburn, although the latter precaution was unnecessary since the House had already approved.[26] In the letter of transmittal to Congressman Rayburn, Eastman asked him not to make the analysis public "because I see no reason for entering a public defense against suggestions of the National Transportation Committee with respect to the work of the Commission, unless there is reason to believe that there is need for such a defense." [27] No such need occurred.

Eastman on Federal Operation

Eastman had said of the report of the National Transportation Committee that the possible eventual organization of the railroads into a single national unit would probably make public ownership inevitable. As was said earlier, he was himself interested at this time in gauging the prospect of government operation. To test the possibility, he quietly floated a trial balloon to see whether there was any serious support for the voluntary transfer of the railroads to the federal government, which would run them as a government enterprise. Mention is made of government ownership in a letter Eastman wrote to Charles D. Mahaffie, his friend and colleague on the Interstate Commerce Commission, early in January, 1933. Accompanying the letter was a memorandum "suggesting a possible program on which we may be able to agree, if it so happens that we are summoned to confer with the President-elect." [28] Such a meeting was in the wind, for Robert W. Wooley, a former member of the Interstate Commerce Commission, had seen Franklin Roosevelt in December and suggested that a meeting be held to discuss railroad problems.[29] Felix Frankfurter, two days after Eastman's letter to Mahaffie, told Eastman that Roosevelt had told him he would call Eastman and Mahaffie to a meeting. To this news, Eastman telegraphed, "Do not anticipate visiting New York unless summoned." [30] On January 7, Eastman received a letter from Marvin H. McIntyre, one of Roosevelt's secretaries, inviting him to a conference with the President-elect, and Eastman accepted for himself and Mahaffie.[31]

The agenda that Eastman proposed to Mahaffie for consideration was in two parts, "Suggested Emergency Measures" and "Suggested Normal Measures." Included in the first were three questions dealing respectively with the Reconstruction Finance Corporation, legislation concerning railroad reorganizations, and preparation for government operation. All of the "normal" measures were eventually adopted, although not at the same time: Federal regulation of motor and water transportation; certain rate reforms; and the delegation of work within the Interstate Commerce Commission. The proposals Eastman offered as a basis for discussion of government operation were set out in some detail. The government was to manage the railroads but not own them. It was to acquire control through voluntary transfer without exercise of the power of eminent domain. No government bonds were to be issued for the purpose. The transfer would incur minimum financial responsibility, a responsibility which could probably be sustained through railroad earnings alone. It was expected that this responsibility would be taken care of by the increased market value of the bonds accruing from government management and the justified expectations of stockholders in increased earnings. In short, government was to operate the railroads and some of the cost of the transfer would be paid for out of the increased private values of railroad securities that this would produce. Financial policy under government management would look towards the financing of railroad bond maturities on the most favorable terms and a gradual reduction of railroad debt.

The political side of government railroad operation required certain precautions. Eastman suggested that the actual functioning of the roads be entrusted to the hands of the most capable railroad men in the country and that safeguards be erected to prevent political interference in management. The nature of some of these safeguards was developed by Eastman in his *First Report* to Congress as federal coordinator of transportation, and they were designed in the main to prevent the appointment of political hacks as trustees in charge of the public interest.[32] The railroads under federal control would continue to pay all taxes, although protections would be designed against uneven and unfair state taxation. It was Eastman's thought that the roads would and should be relieved under government operation of many of the burdens of regulation "now necessary." One favoring effect would be the better coordination of rail, water, and motor transportation that Eastman urged.

These were not measures that Eastman was actively urging but proposals that might provide focus and centrality to discussions about new railroad policy. Although he was not an active and actual advocate of his scheme for government operation, he certainly at this time did not look upon government operation with an unkindly eye. To the contrary, in fact, in his letter to Mahaffie of January 3, he expressly pointed out that the then current difficulty of the railroads was reaching emergency proportions and that something fairly drastic, such as government operation, might be necessary. This was an old concern of Eastman's. In the debates over the Plumb plan in 1919 and 1920 he had been clearly sympathetic with the idea of government ownership or operation as the ultimate policy for the railroads. After watching his trial balloons blow this way and that without really soaring high and far in 1933 and 1934, Eastman came to the conclusion in 1935 that this policy just was not feasible, given the existing context of groups and interests in the railroad industry and the government.[33]

Eastman wrote to Felix Frankfurter of the Harvard Law School after he had received the invitation from Marvin McIntyre to attend a meeting in New York with Roosevelt. He brought Frankfurter up to date on various legislative activities concerning railroad reorganization, and indicated that he had been working with A. A. Berle on the matter.[34] He informed Frankfurter of the letter from McIntyre and expressed willingness, while in New York, to see "your friend Lowenthal," a lawyer interested in railroad reorganization, a friend of Frankfurter's, and the author of a book on the reorganization of the Chicago, Milwaukee, and St. Paul that appeared in June, 1933. Max Lowenthal later worked closely with Senator Harry S. Truman of Missouri in committee investigations and, according to the common report, became one of the few "intellectuals" President Truman liked during his terms in the White House.

The meeting of Eastman and Mahaffie with Roosevelt took

place on January 11, 1933, in the Roosevelt home in New York City, and was attended by numerous persons who later became known to the general public as the "Brain Trust." Among them were Rexford Guy Tugwell and Raymond Moley, both of Columbia University. Reports of the meeting indicate that Eastman spent most of the time he had with the President-elect in talking about federal operation of the roads. The critical matter of the moment, however, was the financial plight of the railroads, which will be discussed presently, and, although Eastman managed to talk about some matters on the agenda he had given to Mahaffie, he did not get to talk about them all. The subsequent meetings which grew out of the January 11 session concerned themselves with ways and means of dealing with railroad finances, and Eastman took his proposals for federal operation to the attention of others.

He sent a copy of the plan for voluntary transfer of the roads to the federal government to George Foster Peabody and said of it, "The plan needs much further study, and I am by no means committed to it. I merely put it on paper as something to shoot at for purposes of discussion, and have given it no general publicity." [35] On January 24, he sent the papers he had worked up for the meeting with Roosevelt to his friend Felix Frankfurter, and said,

You may be interested, for your confidential information, in reading a memorandum which Mahaffie and I drew up for the purpose of our conference with the President-elect. We had no opportunity to discuss most of the matters covered by this memorandum but I think it will interest you. The suggested plan for the voluntary transfer of the railroads to the Federal Government I prepared and Mahaffie thinks much less well of it than I do. I am by no means committed to it and realize that it is probably full of defects. I drew it up principally as something to shoot at.[36]

A few days later he had occasion to reply to a request made to him by William G. McAdoo, the former Director-General of Railroads during World War I. McAdoo was under the impression that Eastman had prepared a recent memorandum on government ownership of the railroads, but Eastman dispelled the idea. The grapevine was obviously at work when McAdoo in Los Angeles could hear, in however garbled form, a rumor that Eastman in

Washington was concerning himself with government ownership. In his reply to McAdoo, Eastman sent him his plan for the voluntary transfer of the railroads to the federal government and an article written by Eastman on the subject in 1931.[37] In his letter, Eastman said of the railroad problem,

I have felt very strongly that the remedies which have been and are being applied to that situation are merely temporary palliatives and I doubt very much whether it is going to be possible for the railroads to continue to operate successfully through the medium of private enterprise and private credit unless economic conditions improve very materially and rapidly, which seems unlikely. It is quite possible, therefore, that the Government will have to assume direct responsibility in some form for the railroads and perhaps for the transportation situation in general.[38]

Although the report of the National Transportation Committee was not at the time publicly available, Eastman was well aware that one of the many alternative policies for the railroad industry was operation of the roads as a single unit. Said he to McAdoo, further,

There seems to be a distinct trend of opinion among disinterested students that operation of the railroads as a single unit may become desirable, and I do not personally believe that the country will agree to that unless the Government has a very strong degree of control over the entire situation. For these reasons I have been urging that thought should be given to possible methods of providing for direct government responsibility for the railroads in order that we may be prepared for action if such a move becomes necessary.

He had no objection to the operation of the railroads as a single unit; in fact, he thought, at this time at least, that the ills of the railroads could probably not be cured by any remedy less fundamental than their operation as a single system. But it was not for private managers to do this. If the railroads were to be run as single industry, it was not to be by private managers; the responsibility for their operation would have to be vested in the federal government.

The entire rationale underlying this view was well and earnestly expressed in a long letter to Felix Frankfurter. Frankfurter had sent Eastman a memorandum under date of January 20 of which

Eastman said, "Like everything which you write, it is both thoughtful in itself and also stimulates thought." [39] The stimulus to thought was a series of suggestions to increase the power of the Interstate Commerce Commission to regulate the affairs of the railroad industry, including proposals that the Commission be empowered to order the elimination of competitive wastes and prevent uneconomical operation, whether because of competition or lack of competition. These proposals raised fundamental issues. At the outset, Eastman said he wanted it understood that "I have very little hope that it will be possible to deal fundamentally with the transportation problem without resort to some form of public ownership and operation or, shall I say, direct Government responsibility for transportation."

The proposals regarding Commission power to order the elimination of competitive wastes and prevent uneconomical operation ran

directly counter to the theory of entrusting railroad operation to private operation. The essence of that theory is that the desire for profit on the part of the private owners of the railroads will impel them to select efficient managements and insist on economical operation. A further stimulus is provided by the existence of competition. Disinterested students know that the theory is to a very considerable extent fallacious, and the results are not what they should be.

What did Frankfurter's proposals undertake to do? What was his remedy for the failure of the profit system in the railroad industry to produce economical operation and efficient management?[40] As Eastman saw it, Frankfurter's remedy would

build up a duplicate management sponsored by the Government superimposed over the private management. As I see it, this violates sound principles of administration. It means division of responsibility, lost motion, and waste. It would be bad enough if the Governmental management could function in a direct, administrative way; but that is precisely what it cannot do. It must function through the tedious, time-consuming processes of judicial procedure, with the building up of a "record" and incredible waste of time by lawyers.

It could be no solution of the ills of the railroad industry to increase the powers of the Interstate Commerce Commission to regulate it when the fundamental shortcoming was not a lack of

Commission power. The fundamental relation between railroads and government would have to be altered. In fact, said Eastman, "if a Governmental commission can be trusted to do all that you want it to do, then a body of Governmental trustees can be trusted to operate the properties directly in a way which would be consistent with principles of sound administration."

The force with which Eastman stated his views on the subject of railroad policy to Frankfurter and the care he took to see that his plan for voluntary transfer of railroads to the government was placed among his friends and others are signs that measure the depth of his conviction at this time. Although he warned those to whom he proffered his plan for voluntary transfer that it was merely an alternative to be considered along with many others, the evidence of his correspondence in January, 1933, shows Eastman to have been an advocate of root-and-branch reform of the roads. His immediate interest derived from the desperate plight of the railroads in the depression, perhaps, but his judgment evidently had deeper and earlier sources. This is well illustrated in still one other passage in his letter to Frankfurter of January 30. He said,

For a long time I wavered in my views upon competition. There are impressive evidences that competition is a stimulus to alert, aggressive management, while monopoly may lead to an indifferent and unprogressive management. However, I am now convinced that the evils and wastes of competition outweigh its advantages, and I believe that a monopolistic management can be saved from dry rot. This points to the conclusion that competition among railroads should be eliminated and that they could be operated as a unit. But I do not believe the country will stand for that without Government ownership, and it is also clear that this is the simplest road to unification.

By early February, the crumbs of suggestion that Eastman had been casting upon the waters began to return to him in the forms of loaves of commendation and advice about his "plan" to transfer the railroads to the federal government. George Foster Peabody had been trying to show the President-elect, with whom he was on terms of friendship growing out of past association, the importance of giving consideration to possible radical steps in connection with the railroad situation, and Eastman told him that he was glad to know this, adding, "If conditions do not improve materially and rapidly in the near future, I feel quite sure that some plan for their unified operation under government auspices will be necessary." [41] George Creel, the head of the Committee on Public Information during World War I, wrote to Eastman about using certain quotations by Eastman in some articles Creel was preparing, but Eastman drew back somewhat. He said that he hesitated to permit himself to be quoted in public places on the voluntary transfer of the roads to the federal government because the plan was not yet perfected. Although he felt that it was sound in outline and principle, there were many details to be worked out. Another reason, and this was perhaps even more important than the first, was Eastman's doubt whether he ought to be the man to launch such a proposal officially and in public. Said Eastman, "For a long time now I have been regarded as an advocate of public ownership and management of railroads and public utilities, and for that reason it is likely that any plan of this character that I might suggest would be discounted considerably in the public mind." [42] Eastman then told Creel that he had "been trying to interest various people in the plan and particularly to convince the new administration that it ought to have some such plan carefully studied." Eastman's judgment about the timeliness of the plan was based upon his estimate of the forces, interests, and groups that would be concerned in its outcome, groups whose consent would have to be won in advance. He confessed that he had always doubted whether such a plan could be made effective "until the more conservative interests of the country are convinced that it is necessary." The state of the nation, however, was growing so desperate so rapidly that Eastman believed that "the time will soon be ripe for such a plan, if economic conditions do not improve materially and rapidly."

Although Eastman wrote in somewhat similar fashion to others whose interest in voluntary transfer had been sparked by the considerable private notice he had given to it, the Commissioner was most greatly involved during the rest of February and the first part of March, 1933, with the legislation dealing with railroad reorganizations that was moving through the Congress.[43] A week after the inauguration of President Roosevelt, Eastman was still talking about voluntary transfer of the railroads as a possibility, but the tone of his discussion had by now changed somewhat. In a letter to Daniel Willard, the president of the Baltimore and Ohio Railroad, he seems to have been less enthusiastic than he was in his correspondence with Frankfurter and Creel the month before. It may be that he felt it prudent to be circumspect in discussing his plan with an important railroad president. Whatever the reason, he was at some pains to belittle his brain child, about which he said that he was "convinced that it is imperfect in various respects and would require considerable modification even if it were to be accepted in principle." [44] He also made a point of denying that it was "my plan for the railroads" and said of it that it was only a vehicle to help in formulating such a plan if one should become necessary or desirable.[45] The need for further consideration was made more specific in a letter dated March 20, 1933, to Senator Clarence Dill, member of the Senate Committee on Interstate and Foreign Commerce. He sent to Senator Dill, at the latter's request, a copy of the plan for voluntary transfer of the railroads which, Eastman said, "I submitted to President Roosevelt last January." [46] But, said Eastman, "Since that time I have given additional thought to the matter and believe that if any such plan were to be adopted the method of determining the initial guarantee of net railway operating income would have to be modified materially." By the end of March he was already being considered for the position of federal coordinator of transportation and his attention thereafter was preoccupied with shaping the policy that the administration was going to support rather than a policy that he thought it might consider.[47]

Although the proposal for a voluntary transfer of the railroads to the federal government was set aside by the decision of the administration and the course of legislative events, Eastman kept the possibility in the back of his mind. The time (to use his cliche) was not "ripe" in March, 1933, and the tremendous sweep and force of the numerous programs being fostered by the new occupant of the White House could possibly have appeared to Eastman to hold some promise that improved economic conditions would remove the immediate basis for considering the plan. He was well disposed towards the New Deal in its early days, and there is no evidence that he did not continue to regard its aims with approval.[48]

Railroad Reorganization

Although the case for cartelization had been stated and the case for government operation tested, both with negative results, it was the preparation of immediate measures for the relief of the railroads that was the vital business of Roosevelt's advisers in the weeks just before the inauguration.

One of these advisers, A. A. Berle, has said of this period, "The brain trust, fearing a wreck when FDR took office, tried to introduce as much legislation as possible in the post-election 1932 Congress, so that hearings would be out of the way when Congress met in 1933. Thanks to the leadership of Thatcher and LaGuardia, the Bankruptcy Act and housing legislation were passed in 1932, and much work was done on the transportation legislation." [49] The principal work done on transportation was the making of new rules for railroad reorganizations. It will be recalled that President Roosevelt in his Salt Lake City speech in the preceding September had urged that measures be taken to regulate railroad reorganizations somewhat more to the advantage of railroad security holders and somewhat less to the profit and advantage of the lawyers. Some of the railroads, with their large and often unacceptably inflated degree of capitalization, their heavy fixed indebtedness, the high cost of operation because of inefficiency of management and administration, and the low rate of return because of declining traffic, were frequent candidates for receiverships, out of which the existing managers and legal counsel could sometimes make careers, much like the lawyers in *Bleak House*.[50] A critic of the practices of the railroads, Max Lowenthal, listed, in 1933, the following abuses in railroad reorganizations: "control of receivership administration and of reorganization by men who controlled the property prior to its formal acknowledgement of insolvency; inadequate administration of the property and affairs of the railroad pending reorganization; inadequate supervision by the regulating authorities of receivership and administration; undesirable practises of committees and managers; confusion of trusteeship duties with self-interest of the trustees; preparation of plans without hearing; control of the voting machinery by a few, to the exclusion of the body of the security holders; depriving the latter of a vote on the reorganization plans; fees and expenses disproportionate to the services rendered and the results achieved." [51] Somewhat similar criticisms of reorganization procedure were made in the Brookings staff studies for the National Transportation Committee.[52]

The increasing intensity of the depression posed a threat to the solvency of all the railroads. Eastman said, "In 1932, railroads operating nearly 74 percent of the total class I mileage failed by $250,000,000 to earn their fixed charges." [53] The Reconstruction Finance Corporation, which had been created in 1932 to help "prime the pump," had granted loans to railroads (up to December 31, 1932) in the amount of $337,200,000.[54] It was the hope of the National Transportation Committee that the RFC interpretation of the requirement that borrowers put up "adequate security" be extended to include an expectation of earnings as well as collateral, but Alfred E. Smith dissented from this recommendation. The ever-growing crisis called for strong measures if existing railroad companies were to survive, and a reform of the procedures of reorganization if they were to be made both efficient and solvent.

Steps in this direction had been started in mid-1932. On June 15 (calendar day June 21), Senator Hastings of Delaware introduced a bill in the Senate to deal with the general subject of corporate reorganizations. This bill, S.4921, which amended the existing bankruptcy legislation in order to provide a better system for the voluntary reorganization of corporations, including railroad corporations, did not substantially enlarge the powers of the Interstate Commerce Commission, which had a rather indirect influence on reorganizations through its authority to approve or disapprove the issuance of new railroad securities. Corporate reorganizations usually provided for the issuance of such new securities. The Hastings Bill was sponsored, in large part at least, by the Solicitor-General of the United States.

Since the bill did involve the railroads, which were prepared to support it with certain amendments not necessary at this place to discuss, it was normal for the Senate Committee on Interstate and Foreign Commerce to refer it to the Interstate Commerce Commission for an opinion. Eastman anticipated the committee action and took steps to obtain learned opinion before the Hastings Bill actually was transmitted. On December 16, 1932, he wrote to his friend Felix Frankfurter at the Harvard Law School and sent him a copy of the measure, telling him that the Commission would soon be called upon for an opinion. He said, "I find it a very difficult question because there is a great deal of law involved upon which I am very imperfectly informed up to the present time." [55] Specifically, he wanted to know what Frankfurter thought of the Hastings Bill and, if he disapproved, what "scheme of legislation with respect to receiverships and reorganizations you think ought to be substituted." At the same time, Eastman wrote to Louis B. Wehle for similar advice.[56] Before he could have had time to hear from his advisers, a new version of the Hastings Bill had been prepared containing "certain amendments which are desired by the railroads" and Eastman sent some copies of the revised bill along to Frankfurter,[57] and to Wehle.[58] When Senator Couzens informally requested Eastman's personal views on the developing measure, Eastman widened his field of advisers to include Professor James C. Bonbright, a Columbia professor of economics and an authority on corporate finance. In his request to Bonbright, Eastman suggested that he might consider the matter "in consultation with your colleague Professor Berle," who, of course, had been close to the developing legislative program of the President-elect and was one of the authors of the Salt Lake City speech.[59]

Eastman's thought on the subject of railroad reorganizations had matured enough by the first of the New Year to permit him to speak trenchantly of it in his memorandum to Mahaffie, the Commission expert on finance. This memorandum formed the basis of the January 11 conference with President-elect Roosevelt and his advisers. In the Mahaffie memorandum, Eastman pointed out that the existing procedures provided no means short of receivership and judicial sale of railroad properties for the reorganization of the financial structure of a railroad in order to reduce the burden of fixed charges too heavy to be carried ordinarily. In Eastman's view there were two main objections to this procedure, the expense in time and money and the control and domination of the reorganization "by bankers associated with the property in the past." Of them Eastman said further, "The bankers do not represent the public interest, they ordinarily represent the interests of the security-holders very imperfectly, and the chief interest they represent is their own." The control over the reorganization process available to the Commission was imperfect, for it was

limited to the approval or disapproval of new securities that might
be proposed as part of the reorganization plan. Eastman thought it
urgent to correct this situation by legislation "and the sooner it
can be enacted the better."

Eastman thought that the bill pending in the Senate would
undoubtedly expedite reorganizations and make them possible
without receivership proceedings, chiefly by decreasing the opportunities of dissenting security-holders to obstruct, and he believed
that expedition was desirable and that it would save considerable
expense. As indicated, such reform had the sponsorship of the
Solicitor-General and the support of the railroads and the bankers.
Eastman pointed out, however, that the bill would permit reorganization managers and committees representing security holders to be selected as they had been heretofore. More than that,
the collection of the charges that these functionaries would demand would be facilitated by the proposed bill under which they
might become charges on the property being administered. This,
Eastman thought, was objectionable. "It would allow these managers and committees and their lawyers to attach themselves to a
property and make claims on its assets without any prior limitation or authorization by the court or by anybody else." What was
really missing was some way to protect the public interest in railroad reorganizations. Since the approval of the Commission for
the issuance of new securities was necessary, it was only "logical
that the Commission should be the body brought in to represent
the public interest during the formulation of the plan." If this
were to happen, the appropriations of the Commission would have
to be increased to permit it to engage new assistants with the
appropriate legal and financial experience.

The belief of Eastman that the role of the Commission in railroad reorganizations should be enhanced was shared by Felix
Frankfurter, who recommended this policy in the memorandum on
the revised draft of S.4921 that he sent to Eastman on January 5.
Eastman told Frankfurter that he believed him to be right in
principle but that, as a practical matter, it would be necessary for
the Commission to have increased staff and funds if it were properly to function in railroad reorganizations.[60] In the meantime,
Berle had been bestirring himself on the Hastings Bill and had held
conferences with Solicitor-General Thatcher and with a member

of the firm of Paul D. Cravath, which had had something to do with the writing of the Hastings Bill. Eastman thought it likely that Berle's conferences would produce some changes in the bill.[61] He ventured to facilitate the process of rewriting the Hastings Bill by asking Frankfurter for permission to show the latter's memorandum on railroad reorganization to Congressman Oliver of New York.[62] One whose advice seems to have been influential in helping Eastman make up his mind was Mr. Harold Palmer of New York, who sent the Commissioner an analysis of the Hastings Bill and drew the comment that "you have done a public service in putting so much time without compensation on this matter." [63]

The work done by Eastman, Berle, Palmer, LaGuardia, and others on the Hastings Bill resulted in its introduction into the House of Representatives in a new version (H.R. 14110) known as the LaGuardia Bill. It now represented a compromise of the views of more of the principal parties in interest and was no longer so exclusively a measure fulfilling the desires of the railroads and the bankers. Eastman felt that the bill in its revised form "represents a compromise which is probably the best thing that can be done at the present session. It brings the Interstate Commerce Commission in very completely *at the end,* and in the beginning so far as the appointment of trustees is concerned." [64] Even in its improved form, it did not seem to Eastman to go far enough in protecting the public interest in railroad reorganizations. It left reorganization managers to be appointed and to function, with their attendant committees, along the old lines. It did, however, improve things a bit, for it put the Commission in a place where it could "inject itself into the situation to a sufficient extent to do some good."

Eastman worked directly with Congressman LaGuardia and with Chairman Somers of the House Judiciary Committee in an effort to improve further the already improved version of the original Hastings Bill.[65] His conferences with the two congressmen left him hopeful that the Commission's role in reorganizations would be enhanced further, and that there would be full hearing and investigation of any proposed reorganization before security holders would be asked to take any action. Judges would be in a position to disapprove of plans accepted by the Commission but they would not be able to approve plans which the Commission thought should be rejected. Eastman was permitted to draft his views in the form of amendments to the LaGuardia Bill, which the House Judiciary Committee accepted.[66]

Having succeeded in getting amendments to the Hastings Bill which improved it in the LaGuardia version, and then having succeeded in drafting amendments to the LaGuardia version which the House Judiciary Committee accepted, Eastman then proceeded to draft a report to the Senate committee in regard to the reorganization measure (the House bill was reported out as H.R. 14359), with suggestions for further improvement.[67] As he said to his friend Frankfurter, "While I had something to do with the amendments which were made in the House Bill at the eleventh hour, I had a very short time to work in and I think that the bill can be made a much more finished document than it is at present." Eastman was well in command of his own views and opinions by this time. He told Frankfurter that he had "had a letter from your friend Lowenthal and he says that any Wall Street lawyer could drive a team of horses through the House Bill as it has been reported out." This criticism did not perturb Eastman, who remarked, "I am not persuaded that the bill is as poor a product as he thinks."

Eastman's report to Senator Hastings was a carefully detailed exposition of the House bill and the Senate bill (LaGuardia and Hastings respectively),[68] with specific recommendations for the further amendment of the House bill. He described with some care the procedure by which railroads, through voluntary receiverships brought about with the aid of friendly judges, went through reorganizations under the eyes of the "New York bankers" who were often appointed as reorganization managers and who had a strong and special interest in the properties of which they were the creditors. The receivers of the railroads were frequently the existing managers so that the reorganization was entirely in the hands of the individuals, groups, and interests responsible for the financial difficulties in the first place. The reorganization managers, because of their connection with the railroad management had "a closer relation to its stockholders than to its creditors, but they may have a direct interest in some classes of its indebtedness, and also an indirect interest because of the fact that they marketed the bonds." [69]

One of the first steps they take, Eastman said, is the appointment of committees to represent each class of security holders. The result is a combination of interested groups who work together, sometimes to defeat the interest of others. At every step there are opportunities to distribute patronage in the form of fees and charges for engineering and legal services so that the result is not unlike that referred to by Roosevelt when he quoted Mr. Dooley in the Salt Lake City speech. There is no custodian of the public interest in any effective place in the process of reorganization. The judges are incapable of discharging this role effectively. Eastman appended to his memorandum an article by William Howard Taft when he was a lower federal judge, printed in the *Reports* of the American Bar Association in 1895, which discussed the inadequacies of the courts in reorganization cases.

Eastman felt that certain principles should be observed in the conduct of reorganizations, the first of which was that "the public interest should be adequately represented, not in the final stage only, but from the beginning." Bankers and lawyers should assist in the plan but they "ought not to dominate its preparation." The committees chosen to represent the interests of various classes of security holders ought not to be appointed *in camera* by the reorganization managers or outside volunteers but should be selected "at meetings of the security holders called for the purpose." Reorganization managers should be wholly impartial and should not be affiliated with any group of security holders nor with any particular group of bankers. The reorganization plans should be submitted to the Interstate Commerce Commission before being presented to the security holders and an opportunity should be present for public hearings to air any protests against them. Finally, there should be no divided jurisdiction and the courts should not be required to pass upon questions determined by the Commission, or vice versa.

After a comparison of the points of similarity and difference in the Senate and House bills, Eastman indicated that the House version was preferable, although it too could be further improved even at the late stage in which it then existed. Specific recommendations were made for the improvement of the House bill. Eastman did not have his way entirely but there is no doubt that he was influential in the form that the legislation finally took, emerging as Section 77 of the Bankruptcy Act. Under the new procedure enacted by Congress, railroads in financial difficulty could, as before, go into voluntary receivership. The judge to whom the petition of bankruptcy was made then was permitted to appoint trustees to handle the affairs of the straitened road from a panel of trustees prepared by the Interstate Commerce Commission. This requirement brought the Interstate Commerce Commission into receivership proceedings at an early stage, as desired by Eastman. The Commission then was authorized to hold hearings on proposed reorganization plans and to recommend a plan among those proposed, or a plan of its own, to the creditors and security owners. Approval of a reorganization plan required the consent of the Commission and of the owners of more than two-thirds of the affected securities and claims, after which it could be submitted to the judge for hearing. After hearing, the judge could accept or reject such reorganization plans. When a plan was accepted by him, it was then to bind all of the security holders and claimants against the railroad. Some exceptions from this provision were permitted under Section 77.

Thus, one of the principal contentions made by Eastman was met. The public interest was represented at a much earlier stage than had been possible under the older method. The device of selecting trustees chosen by judges from panels prepared by the Commission went far towards meeting Eastman's objection to the domination of railroad reorganizations by bankers, lawyers, and railroad managers. The provisions for Commission hearings on reorganization proposals protected the security holders from being confronted with Hobson's choice by reorganization managers and, in fact, enabled them, through the hearing process, to participate somewhat in the formulation of reorganization plans.

Eastman kept his friend Frankfurter informed of the proceedings of the legislation through its various stages and relied here and there upon his advice, although the amendments he proposed to the Hastings committee in the Senate were the result of his own reflections and labors.[70] He acknowledged the help of Professor Bonbright, also, and the considerable effort of A. A. Berle, who labored hard and skillfully "to secure an agreement of interested parties upon a proper bill." [71] Eastman himself assisted in the formulation of an understanding of interested parties concerned with the plight of the railroads, and there is a record in his correspondence of arrangements for at least one dinner meeting of such parties at the Mayflower Hotel. He thought that Daniel Willard of the Baltimore and Ohio Railroad ought not to be invited to this dinner because his presence would give the affair too much of a "Business Aspect," whereas what was needed was "talk over the railroad situation from the point of view of the public interest." [72]

The new bill became law on March 3, 1933, the day before the Hoover administration left office. The work on the provisions dealing with railroad reorganizations had been somewhat hasty. There was disappointment in the legislation among some, such as Frankfurter, who had hoped for more thoroughgoing reform. Indeed, it was suggested that some effort be made at the eleventh hour to seek to prevent the passage of the reorganization provisions, in the hope that the new Congress taking office with President Roosevelt might adopt legislation closer to the reformist ideal. In resisting this suggestion, Eastman preferred the slow gradualism of piecemeal reforms and exhibited a disposition to hold on to small gains rather than to try for larger gains at the risk of having none. On this issue, as on many others, his independence of judgement was proof against friendly influence. Unlike Frankfurter, Eastman felt that the improvements in reorganization procedure represented by the new legislation were not inconsiderable and he concluded one letter with the words, "I am sorry that you feel as you do about the bill, but you may be sure that I used the best judgment that I had, be it good or bad." [73]

III. THE COMPROMISE OF GROUP INTERESTS

"Plans for greater cooperation or coordination in railroad affairs meet resistance because they are foreign to certain habits of thought which are the growth of many years. There are various other influences which are antagonistic to greater railroad cooperation and coordination, for one reason or another, and have an effect upon the managements. Labor is hostile, fearing loss of employment, and there are railroad officers, both major and minor, who have similar fears. Various communities fear that they will be adversely affected. Various supply companies are not friendly to collective railroad action in such matters as scientific research and purchases. Various large shippers are accustomed to play one railroad against another to their own advantage and do not like to see such opportunities reduced. Shippers are particularly antagonistic to increases in the charges for accessorial services."

Fourth Report of the Federal Coordinator, pp. 37–38

Although much work was done on various phases of the railroad problem before the inauguration of the new President in March, 1933, it was, aside from the enactment of Section 77 of the Bankruptcy Act, tentative, piecemeal, and incomplete. No full scale attack upon the depressed condition of the railroads could be made without a similar attack upon other fronts of the economy. President Hoover was without influence in the Congress, which, with him, had been repudiated in the national elections the preceding November. And, as the depression pulled down the banks, increased unemployment, provoked violence among farmers whose mortgages were being foreclosed, and shut the doors of plants and factories, the country awaited the leadership and energy of the new administration.

As early as February 4, 1933, the President-elect announced in Warm Springs that he had plans for the regulation of all forms of transportation, and there had been rumors even before this time that he contemplated unified regulation of railroads, trucks, buses, pipe lines, waterways, and air transport.[1] Eastman, of course, had been thinking along the same lines and had invited the attention of his colleagues to the question of internal organization that would be raised by the accession of new and important powers.[2] A more specific matter, however, received first attention. Between the Roosevelt press conference at Warm Springs in the first week in February and the following June, a great and busy effort was applied to the formulation of what became the Emergency Railroad Transportation Act of 1933. Government officials, bankers, congressmen, security holders, railroad managers, presidential brain-trusters, shippers, labor unions, and volunteer advisers all lent a hand. The Emergency Railroad Transportation Act, like Section 77 of the Bankruptcy Act, was the product of this criss-cross of groups, some well organized, others less well organized, struggling with each other to write the new rules to their advantage or, at the least, to avoid disadvantage. Out of the welter of conferences, caucusses, committees, notes, plans, memoranda, draft proposals, messages, letters, and replies six principal coalitions of interested groups emerged and the final product was the result of their mutually influential activities. These were the bankers, investors, shippers, railroad managers, railroad unions, and government officials.

Among the private interest groups, the stake in the struggle was the security of the group in a tense economic environment. Among the official agencies, one of the prizes was the expansion of authority and influence that would accrue if the entire transportation complex should come under central regulation. In this matter, the secretary of commerce, Daniel C. Roper, was a leading candidate to administer the empire that he and his aides thought might be built. Given authority by President Roosevelt to consider various proposals for the regulation of transportation, Secretary Roper appointed a first and then a second committee to receive suggestions, harmonize conflicts of interest, develop an acceptable program for regulation, and draft proposed legislation. Something considerably less than centralized regulation of the entire transportation net emerged from the deliberations of the two Roper committees, however, and any notion that the Commerce Department might become the power in transportation was disappointed. In shaping up their policies, the Roper committees had available the plans of various group interests in the railroad industry that had been devised for their self-protection.

Hearings of the First Roper Committee

The views and interests of the public officials in the framing of the Emergency Railroad Transportation Act appear in part in the course of events which began when the new President turned over to his new secretary of commerce, Daniel C. Roper, the responsibility for framing some recommendations for the regulation of transportation which could be submitted to the Congress. The Secretary of Commerce was one in an undistinguished line of secretaries in a department which, with the possible exception of Herbert Hoover, has not been noted for the quality and caliber of its leadership.[3] The appointment of the first Roper committee was one fruit of a conference held by President Roosevelt shortly after his inauguration with Eastman, Mahaffie, and Porter of the Interstate Commerce Commission. The first Roper committee consisted of Eastman, chairman, E. Lane Cricher, head of the transportation division of the Department of Commerce, and Walter M. W. Splawn, adviser to the House Committee on Interstate and Foreign Commerce. This committee met daily for two or three weeks. Berle and Moley sat in as it listened to the presentation of many different proposals — the Prince Plan, the ARE proposals, the investors' suggestions, and others, including some notions that Splawn had developed as adviser to the House Commerce Committee, and bills which had been introduced in the House of Representatives by Samuel Rayburn of Texas. These were bills[4] to repeal the recapture provisions of the Transportation Act of 1920 and to facilitate voluntary consolidations without penalty under the antitrust laws.

The Prince Plan   The interest of bankers in railroad regulation and reform was represented for a time by the proposal called the Prince plan. The Prince plan for the consolidation of railroads was drawn up by John W. Barriger,[5] a railroad analyst for Kuhn-Loeb. It was backed by Frederick H. Prince, a Boston banker and financier, former president of the Pere Marquette and connected in 1933 with Armour and Company.[6] Mr. Prince had earlier come to the unfavorable attention of the Interstate Commerce Commission, which at one time had disapproved of Prince's financial operations in the railroad business. The Prince plan proposed widespread consolidation of the railroads and was both simple and dramatic in its sweep. It reflected the understandable desire of the bankers to eliminate as much competitive waste as possible in railroad management and operation, a point of view which had also been put forward by the Brookings Institution in the research it performed for the National Transportation Committee. An early New Deal adviser, Raymond Moley, has said that he thought the Prince plan was originally attractive to the new President because it was novel, and Franklin Roosevelt was "interested in anything novel." [7] Indeed, the new President had to be protected from people who had novel ideas, according to Moley. At one time Roosevelt was said to be interested in a scheme to convert man-hours into currency. George M. Harrison, president of the Brotherhood of Railway and Steamship Clerks, a member of the Railway Labor Executives Association, and vice president of the American Federation of Labor, said that Barriger had convinced Prince that the Prince plan was one with which its sponsor "could make a killing." [8]

The Prince plan proposed the voluntary consolidation of the railroads of the United States into seven systems, to be brought about with the aid of the public treasury. Congress was to adopt legislation vesting general supervisory power in the federal government to oversee the consolidations. Provision was made for various grants, powers, funds, and other facilities to transform existing methods of handling railroad traffic. This medicine was too drastic, even for a patient as sick as the railroad industry, and the first Roper committee therefore made a strong recommendation against the Prince plan, on the grounds that it called for an "extraordinary change" in railroad transportation, a change "which might well be called revolutionary," promised uncertain economies, was fraught with serious social consequences to the communities served by railroads and to railroad employees, and involved grave political risks. It was also felt that Congress would never accept such a proposal without long and extensive hearings, and the amount of government financing required would "in itself be a serious obstacle." Eastman was also opposed to the Prince plan, which he later subjected to a searching analysis in his *First Report* to Congress as federal coordinator in 1934.[9]

The Prince plan took little account of the political elements in any economic reform of the railroad industry. Consolidations on the scale proposed would have aided the competitive position of some communities and their businessmen, their tributary farming areas, and their workers, and would have injured others. That the Interstate Commerce Commission had had such difficulty with consolidations under the Transportation Act of 1920 is a testimonial to the strength of position of the carriers, who sometimes speak of themselves as hopeless victims of big government. Consolidations on the scale proposed in the Prince plan would probably have required massive pressure, which the administration was not prepared to apply, to outmatch the capacity of the carriers to resist and to overcome the reluctance of the unions to be "consolidated" out of work. There would also have been shipper and community interests to hear from. And as the carriers perfected their central organization in the Association of American Railroads and the unions increased in power and influence under the New Deal, the prospect for "revolutionary" reform on the Prince model grew less, not greater.

The Railroads   With the talk of railroad reform widespread in the late winter and spring of 1933, the railroad managers were understandably on the alert to represent their special interests as clearly and as skillfully as possible in the great debate. The central body of managers, then organized as the Association of Railway Executives, early established a "contact committee" consisting of C. R. Gray of the Union Pacific, F. E. Williamson of the New York Central, and J. J. Pelley of the New York, New Haven, and Hartford. Just as the Prince plan was a program devised by financial groups for the protection of the investments of financial groups, so the managers proposed a plan to insure the security of the managers. The Prince plan was released on March 15 and the railway executives were ready with theirs a little more than a week later. The "contact committee," which had met with Roosevelt, reported its suggestions to the ARE and, according to the *New York Times*, the discussion between the contact committee and the ARE centered upon the question whether one man should be appointed as "dictator." Some attention was also given to the question whether the railroad industry should not move in the direction of greater unity organizationally. This step was taken a year later in

the establishment of the Association of American Railroads.[10]
Business Week reported that Roosevelt was considering "federalizing" the roads and said that railroad executives, usually deliberate,
were scrambling into conferences to try to reach agreement on a
program that would either meet Roosevelt halfway or forestall
him.[11] Bondholders were said to be looking on approvingly at this
surge for self-redemption.

But it is of special interest that the idea for the proposals that
the ARE drew up for consideration by the first Roper committee
seems to have come from *that* committee, perhaps from its chairman, Joseph B. Eastman. Robert V. Fletcher, the learned counsel
of the ARE, has said that Eastman suggested that he (Fletcher)
try his hand at drawing up a "coordinator bill" and that he did
so. A. A. Berle, who attended the meetings of the first Roper committee with other experts and specialists, proposed that Fletcher
help him in drawing up a bill along the lines indicated by the
committee. Fletcher then hurried back to his office and went without supper so that he could have his thoughts down on paper before Berle joined him in the evening.[12] Berle recalls the incident
and corroborates it.[13] The inspiration for the ARE plan then
seems to have come from the first Roper committee, of which Eastman was chairman, although the plan was later generally referred
to as the proposal of the railroad executives themselves. It is not
implied that the details of the plan were influenced by the committee; indeed the opposite is the case, since the committee rejected the specific suggestion made by the ARE as too favorable to
the carriers and worked out a much more balanced scheme.

The proposal of the railway executives did, however, mark out
lines along which the eventual enactment was to travel. The proposal was in three parts. The first part provided for exemptions
from the antitrust laws and for the establishment of a system of
regional coordinating committees. The members of these regional
coordinating committees were to be selected by the railroads and
were to be clothed with the official power of the federal government. The regional coordinating committees were to be assisted
by a federal coordinator of transportation to be appointed by the
President for a term of four years. With the approval of the federal
coordinator, the regional coordinating committees were to be empowered to issue orders and directions to the railroads looking

towards the avoidance of unnecessary expenses and towards the establishment of pooling arrangements. Provision was to be made for an appeal to the federal coordinator by any road disaffected by such an order, but such orders were not to be suspended pending a hearing. Failing to move the coordinator on appeal, the disaffected railroad was then to be permitted to appeal to the Interstate Commerce Commission. A second part of the proposal of the railway executives requesting the repeal of the recapture provisions of the Transportation Act of 1920 had been suggested by Roosevelt himself in the Salt Lake City speech. The third part suggested the amendment of the Reconstruction Finance Corporation Act to permit railroads to borrow money on easier terms.

In the proposals made by the railway executives, the entire initiative in the exercise of power over the roads would have been in the executives themselves. From one point of view, the proposal would have endowed self-chosen railroad managers with a power to coerce the industry. As the record of the attempts to create institutions for the self-government of the railroad industry shows, the habit of vested independence was strongly ingrained in its history, inherited perhaps from the time when the roads were in their early days. Conditions then favored anarchic competition, with the prizes of big money and big power going to those who were most aggressive, most clever, most unscrupulous.[14] Even though the ARE could agree to establish an authority to direct needed reforms, the authority would have been split and decentralized, for the centers of the new pattern of power were to have been in the three regions: East, South, and West. The suggestion that private individuals be vested with the powers of the federal government was not too astonishing in the context of the times, since this approach was not uncommon. Indeed, it was institutionalized in the National Industrial Recovery Administration. Critics of the New Deal who accused it of leftist designs were quite wide of the mark, since the codes represented a typical rightist solution for economic ills: control of supply, price fixing, and governmental sanctions for violation of private rules. But the carriers were not applying for a place in the National Industrial Recovery Administration. Indeed, their plan was intended to provide a form of self-regulation quite outside the code structure.

The first Roper committee heard the contact committee on its proposals and reviewed the recommendations of the railway executives, as it had done the Prince plan. It then discarded the draft legislation that had been prepared by the contact committee and the new counsel for the ARE, Robert V. Fletcher, because it felt that the power of the government was not sufficiently detached from the carriers. Eastman agreed with this disposition of the ARE proposal. At this time, his correspondence with his friend Frankfurter on a distantly related issue illuminated his attitude towards the ARE plans. In the establishment of panels of persons, nominated by the Interstate Commerce Commission as possible trustees for railroads in receivership under the new arrangements provided by Section 77 of the Bankruptcy Act, the question was raised whether the chief executive officer of a carrier ought ever to be allowed to serve as such a trustee.[15] Frankfurter made out a strong case against the proposition that such officers should ever be trustees but Eastman was inclined to disagree, feeling that the important thing was that the Commission should have control of the reorganization plan, which it did get. It was one thing for a private railroad official to serve as an agent of the Commission and the courts, and quite another for Congress to endow him with public power to issue orders and directions for others in the industry. Eastman thought well of the first arrangement and ill of the second.

The proposals of the railway executives drew part of the new design of regulation which many more conferences and discussions were to fill in. First, the theory of the new controls was to be coordination. Second, a new functionary called the federal coordinator of transportation was to be appointed. Third, he was to operate through three regional coordinating committees. Fourth, a power of ordering and directing was to be lodged somewhere in this new administrative structure. The proposals also supplied the basis for speculation that Eastman would be appointed to an important position in any new system of controls, for news flies fast in Washington, and rumors fly faster. Mention of the federal coordinator idea was made in the *New York Times* of March 25, and the name of Walker D. Hines was noted as a likely candidate for the new post, if one was to be created. Hines had succeeded William G. McAdoo as director-general of railroads during and for a time after World War I. But, at the same time, Eastman's name was being discussed, for on March 31, a few days after the ARE had made its proposals, he wrote to his friend Col. Henry W. Anderson, receiver for the Seaboard Air Line, "I appreciate very much indeed your kind letter of March 28 in regard to the possibility that I may be asked to become a Federal coordinator of transportation, if such an office should be established by act of the present Congress. It is, of course, very possible that I may never have occasion to make a decision with respect to this matter, and I hope that it will not be necessary for I know that I shall have difficulty in deciding what I ought to do." [16]

Investors and Shippers   The investors in railroad securities gave earnest attention to developments affecting their holdings and actively moved some of these developments through organizations of their own. It will be recalled that the principal sponsors of the National Transportation Committee had been the insurance companies.[17] Much of the burden of representing the investors in the early months of 1933 was assumed by Henry Bruere of the Bowery Savings Bank. He had known Roosevelt as governor of New York and, indeed, had been appointed by him as chairman of the New York State Committee on Stabilization at the suggestion of Miss Frances Perkins. Bruere was known to Eastman also through his work as chairman of the Railroad Committee of the Mutual Savings Banks Association. Working with Bruere at the time of the formulation of the Emergency Railroad Transportation Act of 1933 was Philip Benson, chairman of the Security Owners Association. Both Bruere and Benson employed Fred Oliver as legal adviser, and all three spent a good deal of time in Washington.[18] Oliver later became president of the Security Owners Association. The investors had been on the firing line for the railroads with some frequency. At the least, they had taken an active part in bringing about a lowering of railroad wages in the early thirties and they were busy in support during the drawing up of the Emergency Railroad Transportation Act of 1933.

The investors had no specific set of proposals to throw into the big debate unless those of the National Transportation Committee be so regarded; and there is no evidence that the recommendations of this group were influential in the deliberation, although the final enactments dealt with some issues, such as the repeal of the recapture clause, in the manner which the committee had urged.

Bruere and Oliver worked effectively in behalf of their clients, however, in the slow and patient work of developing a central line of legislative policy. They did not oppose the idea of a federal coordinator of transportation and in fact supported it well. They did not find the ARE version of the federal coordinator acceptable, however, and urged a somewhat different relation between the coordinator and the industry. In the opinion of many, the ARE proposal would have made the coordinator a fancy front and a dignified but inferior vassal to the railroads operating through the regional committees. Bruere and Oliver wanted to give the coordinator more authority over the industry than the industry thought that it was prepared at the time to accept. The investors, as represented by their spokesmen in the deliberations of the first Roper committee, were by no means antagonistic towards the managers, but they did feel that the managers could stand somewhat more supervision and direction in the public interest than they had endorsed.

Like the investors, the shippers had relatively little to do with the actual development of the legislation but they did lend their influence to the result. The main spokesman for the shippers was the National Industrial Traffic League. In general, the shippers were opposed to railroad consolidation which, in some form or other, was the prescription of the savings banks, the insurance companies, the organizations of security holders, important public officials, and some of the railroad managers themselves. On the issue of consolidation, the shippers believed that their interest lay in maintaining competition. The banks, insurance companies, and security holders were keen on eliminating what they called "competitive wastes." The Prince plan went so far as to raise serious questions of community service and municipal planning. But consolidation that improved the financial position of the roads and increased their profits would not necessarily supply the optimum service to shippers and local communities. The managers did not want to be eliminated in any consolidation; the shippers did not want to lose either local service or the advantages of competitive rates. The representatives of the National Industrial Traffic League were lukewarm towards the proposal to establish a federal coordinator of transportation and they specifically suggested that, if such a functionary were to be appointed, he should be given the power to issue orders only when requested to do so by the regional committees. They, like the managers, correctly calculated that their influence in regional committees would be greater than their influence in an office of a remote functionary in Washington.

The Unions The most active union group was the Railway Labor Executives Association, comprising the chief executives of twenty-one national labor unions of railway workers, and led by George Harrison and B. H. Jewell. The principal legal adviser was Donald Richberg, who later became administrator for the National Industrial Recovery Administration. The general position of the railroad union executives was that transportation legislation should seek to improve labor relations and working conditions and should not lead to an increase in unemployment. Harrison, Jewell, and Richberg proposed that labor boards corresponding to the regional coordinating committees be set up to handle coordination proposals that might lead to the loss of jobs. No economy action was to be taken if the labor boards disapproved, unless the coordinator should find that such action was in the public interest, in which case provision should be made for displacement compensation.

More will be said presently about the activities of the unions in the enactment of the Emergency Railroad Transportation Act of 1933. It is to be noted here that the unions did not have a complete plan of railroad reform as did Barriger and Prince, or the Coolidge committee, nor were they invited to formulate one, as were the railroad managers, through Fletcher. This is not to say that the unions were hesitant about prescribing for the entire industry, for it had been the unions that sponsored the Plumb plan in 1919 and 1920, which would have established government ownership of the roads. In 1933, however, they were not invited by the first Roper committee to propose a plan and they had none of their own. From the union point of view, the chief matters of interest were jobs, wages, hours, working conditions, and labor relations on the roads. Their role was to be that of critics, not originators, for the development of the Emergency Railroad Transportation Act was in the hands of the public officials and the more conservative elements of the industry, just as the formulation of the codes and the enactment of the NIRA were the work of the public officials and the business elements throughout the country.

Report of the First Roper Committee

The first Roper committee followed none of the many proposals submitted to it for consideration, but presented a plan of its own to the Secretary of Commerce. But, although it did not imitate any of the existing plans, the plan of the first Roper committee resembled that of the ARE in many respects. The new plan proposed legislation to establish in Washington an office of federal coordinator of transportation to be appointed by the President, possibly from among the membership of the Interstate Commerce Commission. The President was to be empowered to fix the salary of the coordinator unless he were a commissioner, in which case he was to receive the established salary fixed by law for his office. The coordinator was to divide the railroads into three groups: Eastern, Southern, and Western, each of which was to be headed by regional coordinating committees elected by the component carriers from among their members. The franchise for voting for members of these committees was to be based upon mileage, with the carriers having the longest mileage wielding the largest vote. It was to be the function of these regional coordinating committees to encourage and promote action on the part of the carriers that would eliminate unnecessary duplication of services and facilities and permit the joint use of terminals; that would control allowances and other practices affecting service, operations, or revenue; or that would eliminate waste, undue expense, or unreasonable disturbance of rates. The coordinator was to further just pooling arrangements as needed, wherever the carriers should fail to do so.

It was realized that the coordinator would merely have a function of kneeling and praying with the carriers in an effort to get them to comply with the purposes of the proposed act unless he were given independent authority to require compliance. And so it was proposed that the coordinator have such a power to issue orders to accomplish just and equitable coordination arrangements, with possible review of these orders by the Commission. Other proposals of the expert committee provided for representation of the views of railway labor organizations before the issuance of orders affecting employees; for exemption of carriers from the antitrust laws in certain cases; and for the punishment of carriers which failed to comply with the proper orders of the coordinator, upon prosecution under direction of the Attorney-General. All of these provisions dealing with the authority of the coordinator to issue enforceable orders were evidence of the opinion of the experts that he would need such powers if he were to exercise leadership in the formulation and development of plans for eliminating waste and improving efficiency through changes in railroad facilities and services. At the same time it was recommended that the coordinator be required to study and plan further for the improvement of the stability and efficiency of the railroad industry and to report his recommendations for the comments of the Commission and the information of the President and the Congress.

The recommendations of the first Roper committee were proposals made by an expert group for a temporary emergency. No one was more aware than they of the shortcomings and dangers involved in even the sketch of the new railroad policy which they were to propose to the President. The statement was subject to comment and revision, some of which they supplied as a kind of appendix. For example, the first Roper committee accepted the suggestion of Donald Richberg, counsel for many railroad unions, that labor unions be consulted by the coordinator on matters affecting them. It was recognized by the committee that the establishment of a coordinator might complicate relations with the Commission, because the jurisdiction of both would cover the same subject matters,[19] would tend to divide responsibility, create confusion, add expense, and diminish authority. It was felt, however, that the emergency and temporary nature of the proposed legislation justified the risks. The report of the first Roper committee was made in the full knowledge that very extraordinary powers were being vested in the coordinator, and that the exercise of these powers entailed risks to the interests of shippers, carriers, and others. But it was felt that arbitrary action by the coordinator was provided against in the establishment of a line of appeal and review from the orders of the coordinator to the Commission.

One matter of significance may be emphasized at this point. The first Roper committee had no difficulty putting the Prince plan to one side, which it did with the suggestion that it needed further study. Its report was almost entirely devoted to the Fletcher plan, whose preparation Eastman had initiated, but which the committee declined to accept in the form submitted because it gave too much power to the railroad executives. The tentative bill suggested by the committee retained some of the basic features of the Fletcher plan which it considered sound, but made changes to protect a little more obviously and to provide some voice to the labor unions. In so doing, the committee was endeavoring to harmonize the claims and interests of various competing groups, much as a committee of Congress does in hearings on legislation or a national political party does in its choice of platform and candidates. Unlike the national parties, however, the committee had no recommendations for the all-important appointment to the post of coordinator, although eventually no one except Eastman was seriously to be considered.

The Second Roper Committee

President Roosevelt held a conference of interested parties on April 1, 1933, to consider the plan of the first Roper committee. Among those present were Berle, Bruere, Eastman, Gray, Jackson, Moley, Pelley, Perkins, Prince, Richberg, Roper, Splawn, Stockton, Whitney, and Williamson. The interests represented by this assemblage included government officials, the railroads in the persons of the presidents of the Union Pacific, New Haven, and New York Central, securities owners, banks, federal and Democratic party officials, and railroad labor executives. This group worked over the proposals of the first Roper committee in an effort to develop a draft act which could be submitted to the Congress. The pressure upon all of the participants to come up with something to submit to Congress was great, since the desire of the White House to move affirmatively was urgent. It was reported in *Railway Age* that Congress was to be held in session until the important emergency legislation was enacted.[20] This extraordinary group of advisers, counsellors, and representatives of parties-in-interest in railroad legislation produced and developed a draft act out of a welter of proposals, which was then submitted by the President to his cabinet for discussion.[21]

With these clearances made, the President then suggested that a second committee be appointed to iron out certain details of the proposed legislation, and to discuss strategy in getting the measure through the Congress. Thus the second Roper committee was appointed. It consisted of the secretaries of Commerce and the Treasury, Roper and Woodin, respectively; Eastman and Splawn; and the two principal congressional leaders, Rayburn of Texas and Clarence Dill, chairmen of the respective House and Senate committees that would handle the legislation. It is a measure of the speed with which the Congress of the Hundred Days performed its function that there were complaints that Roosevelt was acting too slowly in presenting a railroad proposal to the legislature. It was remarked, for example, that "progress in completing the details of such legislation has been slower than had been hoped for and the numerous complications which the planning has encountered have afforded an opportunity for opposition to develop from several directions while it was still in the formation stage." [22] This was the view of the journal bespeaking the interests of the carriers and their managers and suppliers, and the opposition referred to was that of the labor unions and shippers, of which more will be said presently.[23] An explanation of their anxiety to get on with the legislation and a clue to the reasons for their impatience were provided by a comment in *Business Week*,[24] which observed that Roosevelt would deal as vigorously with railroads as with banks. It speculated that he would appoint a chief over the roads who would compel the carriers to reorganize, consolidate, trim expenses, and share rather than compete for traffic. It suggested that the carriers, usually deliberate, but sensing the President's firm attitude, were hurrying into conferences to try to reach agreement on a program for the purpose of meeting Roosevelt halfway or forestalling him.

The union representatives were given an opportunity to express their views more fully in conference on April 3 [25] and the United States Chamber of Commerce later sent an advisory note to the President setting out the views of its directors as to the principles to be observed in the formulation of new railroad policy.[26] Alfred P. Sloan, Jr., president of General Motors Corporation and chairman of the National Highway Users' Conference, led a delegation of representatives of that organization to Secretary Roper to ask to be included as participants in the formulation of the government's transportation program. They had no detailed plan but offered their cooperation in formulating national plans.[27] Thus the news about the impending new legislation drew in groups other than those originally consulted by the first Roper committee, and the mild apprehension expressed by the carriers over the delay in producing and submitting new legislation to Congress was not without foundation.

That this apprehension was somewhat shared by others closer to the Interstate Commerce Commission and the White House is evident in a written statement by Eastman, dated April 14, 1933, a copy of which was sent to Secretary Roper. In it he reported, "The Secretary of Commerce, Senator Dill, and Congressman Rayburn have grave doubts in regard to the political wisdom of pressing this proposed bill at the present time. This question is outside of my field. It is true, I think, that the bill will be vigorously opposed by railroad labor and that railroad shippers will, at best, not be enthusiastic. It should be well received by railroad security holders and, in general, by the railroads." [28] The bill to which Eastman referred was the final result of the deliberations of the second Roper committee and represented the text of the proposal which the President was to release to the public on April 18. Of this measure, Eastman further said that it would not solve the railroad problem and was "only a step toward solution," although the "only feasible emergency action with respect to railroads at the present time." Eastman felt that the choice was between "some such bill and no bill at all" and ventured the opinion that it "is wise legislation, if introduced by a message which does not raise false hopes, but adequate opportunity for canvassing the doubts which have been raised seems desirable." It is of more than passing interest, in view of the subsequent history of the federal coordinator's office, that Eastman felt, as early as April, 1933, that the most important part of the new bill was one "which provides for an intensive study of other means of improving transportation conditions." He confirmed this estimate of the proposed railroad legislation in a letter to George Foster Peabody in which he said that the measure would "only be a stopgap but that it may pave the way to a more thoroughgoing treatment of the railroad problem." [29]

It was widely assumed that Eastman would become the new federal coordinator of transportation, and much of his mail at this period consisted of letters to the many who prematurely congratulated him on his possible appointment, his expected appoint-

ment, or his assumed appointment. Others, like Bernard Baruch, awaiting the outcome of events still undecided, offered their promise of cooperation.[30] Indeed, the measure had not yet even been sent to Congress, as Eastman reminded Mr. Samuel Untermeyer in a letter in which he suggested that the long-run solution for the ills of the railroad industry might be "some form of public ownership and operation, direct or indirect." [31] On one delicate matter of relationships, that between the proposed coordinator and the Interstate Commerce Commission, Eastman, speaking of himself as the possible appointee to the coordinator's position, said that he would accept the appointment only as a temporary matter and, further, only on condition that he be permitted to remain a member of the Commission but relieved of other duties for the time being. He felt it necessary that final authority should be in the hands of the Commission.[32]

This matter of relationship between the coordinator's office and the Commission was particularly delicate at this time because consideration was being given to a drastic alteration in the place, function, and role of the Commission in the field of railroad regulation. The secretary of commerce, Daniel C. Roper, with whom Eastman had formal working relations without cordiality,[33] assumed the task of preparing some recommendations to the President which involved the fate and fortunes of the Commission. Roper had been an assistant postmaster-general under President Wilson, and Eastman felt that his principal aim was to build up an empire in the Department of Commerce. During the entire time that the details of the federal coordinator bill were being worked out, Roper was busy developing proposals for the partition of the Interstate Commerce Commission and for the transfer of the separated parts to the Department of Commerce. These proposals received some notice in the trade press where, with a certain amount of humor, it was said, "There is, or has been, under consideration, another plan for un-coordinating the ICC by executive order of the President. The commission's organization and others interested in the regulatory problems have been agitated during the past week by a circumstantial but unconfirmed report that the plan . . . submitted by Secretary Roper to the President for his approval provides for the amputation of the Bureau of Valuation . . . and for the division of the remainder between an independent tribunal and a Bureau of Transportation in the Commerce Department." [34]

This was not to be the last time that proposals for the reorganization of the Interstate Commission were to be made. A plural body, which over the years had developed a somewhat courtlike procedure, it was considered by some not a very serviceable instrument for carrying into effect a consistent administrative program, such as the advancement of safety, with energy or single-minded purpose. The President's Committee on Administrative Management in 1937 later recommended that the Commission, along with other quasi-judicial agencies, be brought directly under the control and direction of the President, and that some of its administrative as contrasted with its quasi-judicial functions be lodged either in the Department of Commerce or in a new Department of Transportation. The Hoover Commission was not quite so bold in its recommendations twelve years later, but even it recommended that the straight administrative functions of the Commission be transferred from the Commission to the Department of Commerce or to a new Department of Transportation.

Eastman, however, had very strong views on the need for maintaining the independence of the Commission and the undesirability of bringing it under the direction of the President. To this basic conception of the place and function of the Commission must be added Eastman's lack of respect for Roper and his ambitions. There is little doubt that Eastman was out of sympathy with the schemes of the Secretary of Commerce. They eventually faded from consideration.[35] But at the time the proposed Coordinator Bill was released to the public, members of the Commission and the trade generally were not sure that a fairly drastic shake-up of the Commission might not be forthcoming. Hence, as stated, the relation between the coordinator and the Commission was one of considerable delicacy.

The text of the proposed bill was released to the public on April 28, 1933 to elicit comment. The Railway Labor Executives Association was meeting in Washington on that day, and George Harrison, acting chairman of the Association, went to the President immediately to protest the bill. He has since said that he then told the President that the latter had agreed to include special protections for labor in the bill but that none had appeared in the public version just then released. The union leaders opposed the bill because they could see "no justification for drastic reduction of essential transportation services in order that unearned interest may be paid on idle capital." [36] It was argued that the reduction of "adequate and competitive rival transportation" would depress communities further and throw thousands of railroad workers out of work. Communities, shippers, and railroad workers were encouraged to "prevent the passage of the law as now proposed." The unions felt that the measure had, in the main, been written by carriers and investors with their own interests in view, and they felt further that labor interests not only had been insufficiently represented in the formulation of the bill, but that the representations they had actually made had been ignored. Suspicious of the measure from the start, the unions continued throughout the official life of the federal coordinator to be suspicious of his office and of its influence over the fortunes of railroad workers.

The trial balloon therefore drew fire, which is the purpose of floating trial balloons, but the nature of the opposition from the unions was such that the administration leaders felt that they could risk the trip to Congress. It was not that they expected to be able to defeat unions and shippers if these groups should pressure for defeat of the measure, nor did the administration want to. It was rather that they thought that arrangements could be made more obviously and publicly to protect the interests of workers. There was political value in this tactic but, by following it, the administration leaders seriously delimited and curtailed the area within which the coordinator was to be permitted to function, at least at the outset.

Although the bill was not sent to Congress until May 4, Eastman started to prepare for its passage and his appointment as federal coordinator the day it was released for public information. On April 28, he sent a memorandum to the Director of Valuation in the Commission telling him that the measure might be passed and that he (Eastman) might be the coordinator. Although he warned that the appointment was only a possibility he nevertheless felt that he should be prepared for the eventuality. Foresighted planning for likely eventualities was one of Eastman's strong points. It will be remembered that early in January he had caucussed with his fellow commissioner, Charles D. Mahaffie, and others against the time when he might be called upon to make recommendations about new railroad reorganization legislation. His request to the Director of Valuation was for information about preventable waste in the railroad industry, and he listed fourteen practices that he thought might usefully be controlled or curbed, including unnecessary duplication of services and facilities, unduly circuitous routing, wasteful solicitation of freight, undue maintenance of equipment expense, and so on. His principal search was for opportunities to cut down the wastes of competition through the joint use of terminals, lines, and facilities, pooling arrangements, the joint use of shops, and the abandonment of others, and the combined use of ticket offices. He also asked the director to have his staff submit separate rather than combined reports so that he, Eastman, could appraise the men as well as their reports. A similar memorandum was sent to the Director of Service, with whom Eastman said he expected to work closely if the proposed bill should become law and he should be appointed federal coordinator of transportation.

The emergency railroad bill was sent to the Congress by the President on May 4, 1933, with a very short message of transmittal. The President said that the "broad problem" was to coordinate all agencies of transportation so as to maintain adequate service, but that he was not ready to submit to the Congress a comprehensive plan for permanent legislation. Pending such a program, he said that three emergency steps could be taken: repeal of the recapture provisions of the Transportation Act of 1920 (called Interstate Commerce Commission Act in the message) ; placing railroad holding companies under the control of the Commission in like manner as the railways themselves, a step which Eastman had advocated many times in the past; and the creation of the office of Federal Coordinator of Transportation. Said the President, "I suggest the creation of a Federal Coordinator of Transportation who, working with groups of railroads, will be able to encourage, promote, or require action on the part of carriers, in order to avoid duplication of service, prevent waste, and encourage financial reorganizations. Such a coordinator should also, in carrying out this policy, render useful service in maintaining railroad employment at a fair wage."

The bill sent to the Congress was altered somewhat from the

trial version that had been released on April 27. Some of the changes were editorial but one was material. The earlier version gave the coordinator authority over "owned or partly owned air lines, bus lines, or trucks," among so-called accessorial railroad services within his jurisdiction. The version of the bill submitted to Congress omitted this authority.[37] The bill was simultaneously introduced by Senator Joe Robinson, majority floor leader in the upper chamber (rather than Senator Dill) and by Congressman Rayburn in the House.[38] Bills providing for the repeal of the recapture provisions and for bringing holding companies under the Commission had been previously introduced and hearings held. These were incorporated with the proposals of the President to create a federal coordinator and thus the principal parts of the Emergency Railroad Transportation Act of 1933 were joined.

IV. THE CONGRESSIONAL LIMITED

". . . this is the most constructive piece of legislation that this House has been called upon to enact during this extra session of Congress."

Lloyd of Washington

"As a relief measure I cannot escape the conclusion that title I is just about as near nothing as could be observed under a microscope."

Huddleston of Alabama

Although more than a month elapsed between the President's message and the final acceptance by both Houses of the conference report on the details of the Emergency Railroad Transportation Act, there was no really serious doubt that the measure would pass. This is not to say that there was no adjustment or compromise, or that the measure went through Congress as the second Roper committee had fashioned it. One serious amendment was added to the bill, and it was amended in many minor particulars. The serious amendment was the restriction, in what became Section 7(b) of the act, of the extent to which coordinations adopted pursuant to the act might reduce railroad employment. The time allowed for consideration of the measure in the Congress was relatively short; the mood of the Congress was a desire to get something — almost anything — done that showed some promise of alleviating the economic stringency of the railroads; the carriers, despite the fact that the bill was intended to help them, were unenthusiastic; the unions, sure that the bill was going to pass, made no serious effort to revise it comprehensively, but contented themselves with the promotion of somewhat sweeping amendments, one of which, as has been said, was written into the law. As *Railway Age* summed it up, "An absence of enthusiasm greeted President Roosevelt's emergency railroad bill at the hearings last week and this week before Congressional committees. The most hopeful expressions as to the possibilities of the plan . . . were those of the men who had drafted the bill for the President." [1] "Absence of enthusiasm" does not quite describe the whole range of feeling, however, for the unions and the shippers displayed negative feeling in their serious concern over what seemed to them to be a threat to their interests. The unions were of the opinion that the bill was a "carriers' bill," that it undertook to retrench and cut costs at the expense of the workers, that it would throw thousands more out of jobs, that it represented, in short, the characteristic right-wing remedy for the ills of industries — deflation without regard to the human and social cost. Shippers were worried about threatened reductions of services and a possible increase in rates.

Hearings on the bill were held simultaneously before the Senate Committee on Interstate Commerce and the House Committee on Interstate and Foreign Commerce, under the guidance of the chairmen of these committees, Dill and Rayburn respectively. The Senate hearings were begun on May 9 and concluded on May 12 under constant pressure from Senator Dill to "avoid time-wasting arguments on side issues." [2] The House hearings were begun on May 8 and took twelve days. By and large the same witnesses appeared before the two committees and made the same statements. The difference between the records of the two hearings consists almost entirely of differences in the questions put to the witnesses. The more aggressive and provocative inquisitors were perhaps those on the Senate committee, among them being Brookhart of Iowa, Couzens of Michigan, Huey Long of Louisiana, and Burton K. Wheeler of Montana.

The Pattern of Interest

The composition of economic interests appearing before the House Committee on Interstate and Foreign Commerce is a useful index to the pattern of power in interaction with the Congress. Among the carrier groups, the big railroads were represented by Carl Gray, president of the Union Pacific. A. L. Burford, counsel for the Louisiana and Arkansas Railway Lines (two small unaffiliated lines) bespoke the concerns of the little independents. E. J. Jones represented the American Short Line Railroad Association, an organization of the many railroads outside the Class I category. A. K. Barta, speaking for the American Transit Association, represented the special interests of the "greater part" of the electric railways. Supplementing this representation of the principal carrier interests was the appearance of counsel for the Association of Railway Executives, a predecessor of the Association of American Railroads. All steam railroads were therefore covered by this representative assembly of primary business groups.

These primary structures of economic power and influence moved within an area of secondary interest groups which promoted the interests of clienteles which used or competed with the railroads. R. C. Fulbright, for example, represented the National Industrial Traffic League, composed of thousands of shippers, and two other shippers' organizations, the Southwestern Industrial Traffic League and the Texas Industrial Traffic League. J. R. Van Arnum spoke in behalf of a special interest within the shippers' coalition, the National League of Commission Merchants, a trade organization of associations and individual producers and distributors of fresh fruit and vegetables. William E. Lamb spoke in behalf of the Wisconsin and Michigan Transportation Company, a lake line operating between Milwaukee, Wisconsin, and Grand Haven and Muskegon, Michigan. Charles E. Cotterill spoke for fourteen water carriers and the American Highway Freight Association. Apparently the interests of the water and highway transportation groups were considered to be closely affected by the outcome of any new policy for the regulation of rail transportation. These secondary interest groups may be classified as direct, since they were immediately and directly concerned, either as competitors or dependents, with some phases of the proposed legislation and with the economic situation of the railroads.

Another kind of secondary interest was, however, represented. It may be classified as indirect, since the economic position of the members in this category did not in any way directly depend upon the economic situation of the railroads. Reference is to the organized regulatory group, represented by the National Association of Railroad and Utilities Commissioners. The membership of the NARUC is made up of the state railroad and public utilities commissioners, who use their association to promote their concern in the area of regulation, to exchange views, and to represent the interests of the states not only with relation to the railroads they regulate but to the national regulatory officials with whom they share in some respects a common jurisdiction, and in others a competing jurisdictional interest. It may be said at this point that Eastman did not represent the Interstate Commerce Commission, but appeared as an individual. As an expert with a profound knowledge of the subject matters and the wisdom of a long experience in the field of railroad regulation, he was an important witness.

Finally, appearances were made by what may be called the tertiary bloc of interest groups concerned with the railroad legislation. The tertiary bloc represented general rather than specific economic interests at stake. Such, for example, were the Citizens National Railroad League, represented by its president, Nathan L. Amster of New York City; the People's Lobby, which was not given a chance in the House committee to present its views; and the United States Chamber of Commerce, which made no appearance but sent a communication to the House committee. In a sense, these organizations represented the somewhat inchoate and unstructured interest of the business community in economic policies in conflict or contemplation, which could have effects beyond the immediate field of primary and secondary group interaction. It is sometimes true, of course, that what is represented to be an issue of general interest is a matter of special importance to affected primaries, and primary interest organizations are not above creating tertiary organizations as "fronts." This has been especially true in the representation of big business primary groups, which sometimes present their case through organizations professing to represent the interests of small business primaries.[3]

The principal labor organizations to appear before the committees were the craft unions in the railroad industry, represented collectively in the Railway Labor Executives Association, an association of twenty-one standard railway organizations. The spokesman for this coalition was Donald R. Richberg, who made the strongest attack by any witness upon the proposals submitted by the President. Constituent organizations in this major labor coalition made no appearances but some sent communications to the committees. Among these were the American Train Dispatchers Association and the Railroad Brotherhood's Unity Committee.

The Case for the "Carriers' Bill"

The case for what the unions called the "carriers' bill" was presented first by Secretary of Commerce Roper, who read to the committee the President's letter of May 4, reminded them of the broad purpose of the proposed bill, namely, "to coordinate all agencies of transportation so as to maintain adequate service," and outlined the three steps by which this objective was to be achieved: repeal of the recapture provisions of the Interstate Commerce Commission Act; regulation and control of railroad holding companies by the Commission; and the creation of a federal coordinator of transportation who "will be able to encourage, promote, or require action on the part of carriers, in order to avoid duplication of service, prevent waste, and encourage financial reorganizations." The federal coordinator of transportation was also to help maintain railroad employment "at a fair wage." Sensitive to the criticism that the measure had been called a "carriers' bill," Roper said that after he had become secretary of commerce, he had received plans and proposals from many sources for the further control and regulation of transportation. He therefore organized a committee (the first Roper committee) to examine one of the plans (the Prince plan) and report to him. This committee had recommended that the plan be further studied. Meanwhile, a draft of a bill to relieve the railroads had been submitted by three railroad executives (Gray, Williamson, and Pelley) but was rejected by the first Roper committee on the ground that it placed "too much authority of government in a group of railroad executives." Thereupon the committee drew up a bill of its own. It was modified as a result of suggestions from interested parties invited to attend conferences on the draft. Finally, a committee of six (the second Roper committee) was appointed by the President to prepare the bill for submission to Congress. The bill, in short, was the product of administration officials, although some of the provisions resembled suggestions made by the railroad executives.

After Roper, Eastman testified, and his testimony is especially interesting because it reflects the conception he entertained of the job he was to undertake. After speaking of the features of the proposed act he said,

It will be seen from this summary of the provisions of the act that the coordinator is in no sense to be a czar of the railroads. He is to be an administrative officer of the government whose principal duty shall be to aid and promote and, if necessary, require, the cooperation on the part of the carriers which it is believed the emergency demands and which it is difficult, if not impossible for those companies with their jealousies and intense rivalries and individual interests and present legal inhibitions to accomplish without outside, disinterested help and the aid of the government. The coordinator is given power, appropriate to the emergency, to act without the long delays of judicial procedure. On the other hand, in view of the fact that the orders of the coordinator may override the prohibitions and restraints of many existing laws, State and Federal, the bill recognizes the need for an opportunity of review, after public hearing, by a public body experienced in these matters and knowing the reasons for these laws. This is essential, not only in the general public interest, but from a legal standpoint, for property rights will be involved, and if there is no opportunity for review of the facts by the Commission, such an opportunity will be afforded by the courts. The Commission is not required to grant such a review, if the circumstances do not warrant it, but the opportunity will be there. From this standpoint, the coordinator assumes the role, not of a czar, but of a glorified examiner of the Commission.[4]

The specific disclaimer that the coordinator was to be a "czar" is of special interest in an exchange that Eastman was later to have with Paul Y. Anderson, of which more, below.

On certain other matters which were then in dispute or which were to become controversial, Eastman was equally clear. He believed that it was sound practice to assess the cost of regulation under the act on the railroads themselves, a burden he felt they should be required to assume. As to the effect of the measure on railroad workers, he said that "economies in operation and service mean reduction in labor and there is no escape from it." [5] He was asked whether he had any objection to certain amendments which had been proposed by others. The American Short Line Railroad Association wanted representation of the short lines on the committees under the coordinator when matters were under consideration in which they had an interest. Eastman agreed and the provision was included in the final draft of the legislation. He agreed also to amendments providing for a twenty-day notice between the issuance of a coordinator's order and the time it went into effect, and to an amendment requiring that appeals to the courts be made in the same manner as appeals with respect to orders of the ICC, a procedure set out in the Urgent Deficiency Appropriation Act of 1913. Both procedural changes were incorporated into the final legislation.

The theory and concept underlying what may be called the political aspects of the regulation — those dealing with the structure of the power of the coordinator and of the organizations to be coordinated — were further developed by W. M. W. Splawn, special counsel to the House Committee on Interstate Commerce, who had been a member of both Roper committees. Huddleston of Alabama sought to get Splawn around to the view that the chief weakness of the carriers was lack of business and that, therefore, the bill should provide for some method of increasing business, principally by reducing rates. The rate level was then under investigation by the Commission.[6] Splawn made it clear that the purpose of the bill was not to increase traffic but to enable the carriers to conserve revenue. The distribution of savings accruing by measures of conservation then becomes an interesting question, and Cooper of Ohio asked whether such savings would be passed on to the shippers and workers. Splawn said that if the savings were substantial they would be shared by all, but that if they were small it was doubtful whether they would be shared by all. When asked then who would get them he replied, "the bondholders." It was made clear by Splawn that the bill did not require all or any railroads to go through the wringer of reorganization. He pointed out that there was no power in the coordinator to make the railroads reorganize, although he could encourage them to reorganize under the Bankruptcy Act.

As Roper, Eastman, and Splawn explained the measure, it clearly premeditated a small and carefully contrived effect. It was not, as Eastman more than once said it was not, a bill to accomplish any radical or thoroughgoing reform of the American transportation system, and the title of the coordinator — the federal coordinator of transportation — somewhat exaggerated his authorities under the act. It was emergency legislation, enacted for a year and designed to make a beginning towards economic improvement until more thoroughgoing measures became possible. This circumstance may throw some light on what to many seemed to be an egregious oversight on the part of the planners who had worked up the measure. Why were the labor unions left out? Why were they not only encouraged to share in the formulation of the bill, but indeed to assume an active participating role in the work of the coordinating committees? It was loudly evident that the unions felt that Roosevelt had not taken care of them in the bill, as they assumed he had promised he would. Congressman Wolverton of New Jersey asked what the effect of the bill would be on railroad labor and Splawn replied as Eastman had. Part of the economies contemplated under the act would result in a loss of jobs.

In view of the possibly adverse effect of the bill upon railroad workers, was there any case for giving the unions representation upon the coordinating and other committees to be established under the bill, to afford them a voice in actions affecting them so closely? Splawn said, in response to questions put to him by Congressman Cole of Maryland, that the exclusion of union groups from a participating role in the administration of the act was a matter of deliberate policy — that up to that time, workers, organized or not, had not been given a voice in management, and the bill had been drawn in accordance with the assumption that "coordination" was primarily a management concern. Chairman Rayburn not only concurred with this explanation, but asserted that there was no more reason for giving labor representation on the coordinating committees than there was to give shippers such representation.

In concept, then, the bill, according to its principal framers and advocates, was in truth a carriers' bill, certainly in the sense that it provided a method to enable the carriers to effect economies through unifications of facilities and services. The regional coordinating committees were to represent the primary groups in the railroad field, to wit, the carriers themselves, but they were not to represent other groups in the transportation industry. The exclusion of the secondary business groups and the labor groups from the coordinating committees required these interests to look outside of and beyond the office of the federal coordinator for the protection of their interest and for the conciliation of group tension and conflict — to the Congress, for example, to the White House, and to the bargaining table.

The Scramble for Group Security

Groups excluded from organized and routine representation on the regional coordinating committees made strong appeals to the congressional committees for protection of their interests from adverse action by the regional committees and the office of the

coordinator. The leading members of the congressional committees, however, were prepared for such pleas. In this early period
of the New Deal, their fortunes, as indeed those of the entire
Congress, were pledged to White House direction to a degree never
again to be experienced by President Roosevelt. The pleas of the
special groups in interest did not then fall upon deaf ears, exactly,
but they fell upon ears capable of identifying sounds outside the
committee room, down Pennsylvania Avenue, for example, and
even into the Main Streets of the nation.

The House committee was evidently prepared to promise any
special group that it could have representation on committees
when a matter affecting it directly was in issue, but not permanent
and organized representation. Section 9 of the Emergency Transportation Act of 1933 made such limited and ad hoc representation possible. The spokesman for the National Industrial Traffic
League, however, sought to persuade the House committee to make
fairly fundamental changes in the bill, beyond the simple ad hoc
representation of special interests. He wanted to make sure that at
least one member of each of the coordinating committees was
familiar with the traffic problems of the roads, the traffic problems
being those of particular concern to shippers. He wanted the authority of the coordinator to issue orders to be radically reduced
by depriving him of power to issue orders when a majority of the
interested carriers should disagree on the necessity of the order.
He also suggested that railroad workers be refused the right to
confer with the coordinator before any action affecting them could
be undertaken. He asserted "the employees are amply protected
under the broad provisions of the Railway Labor Act." [7] It was
not clear from what the workers were amply protected unless it
was the right not to be discriminated against when they were discharged, for the Railway Labor Act of 1926, at the time considered
a model piece of labor legislation, did not provide the job security
that the unions sought. He also urged that the orders of the federal
coordinator be delimited in some vague fashion, and urged that
they not be permitted to continue indefinitely. The sharp interest
of the shippers in the legislation was of course economic because
their spokesmen felt that shippers might lose money or service or
other pecuniary advantage. As Mr. R. C. Fulbright, spokesman for
the National Industrial Traffic League and other shipper organi-

zations put it, "The economies which are to be achieved in this legislation will, in the first instance, come out of the shippers, in part, and out of the employees, in part." [8] None of the fundamental changes proposed by Mr. Fulbright was adopted in the final legislation.

Other groups were as successful as the unions, the shortline railroads, and the shippers in getting ad hoc attention when their interests might be affected by issues before the regional coordinating committees. The spokesman for the American Transit Association also sought representation on the regional coordinating committees "whenever the committee is considering matters which will affect our electric railway properties." [9] The general solicitor of the National Association of Railroad and Utilities Commissioners complained that the bill in no way recognized the state commissions, or their existence, or the existence of the states.[10] He proposed that the bill be amended to give state commissioners the right to confer with the coordinator before the issuance of any orders overriding state laws, and to include state commissions and governors as interested parties with the right to appeal an order. He further proposed that all orders of the coordinator expire with the expiration of his office, if in conflict with state laws or future state laws. All of these amendments were incorporated in the final bill.[11] When the president of the United States Chamber of Commerce asked that the shippers be "informed of" and be permitted to "make known their views upon any proposed changes," provision was made for so doing.[12]

In the scramble for group security under the "carriers' bill," water and motor transportation spokesmen were even prepared to argue that they should be brought under the bill. The representative of fourteen water carriers and the American Highway Freight Association, Charles E. Cotterill, suggested that all water and motor carriers be brought under the wing of the coordinator, along with the railroads. That is to say, the coordinator should be empowered to investigate the conduct of these industries, and they were ready and willing to pay their share of the coordinator's expenses.

This position at first blush might seem like an act of pure altruism. The American public had been long conditioned by the propaganda of the business community to regard regulation of private enterprise as an essentially bad thing, to be permitted under only the most extraordinary conditions and circumstances. It was, however, the policy of the Roosevelt administration in the early days to exempt industry from the antitrust laws, to encourage cartelization, and to permit "self-regulation" by industry. This was the basis of the National Industrial Recovery Administration and of the Emergency Railroad Transportation Act of 1933. What the rail carriers were being permitted to do under the latter act, the water and motor carriers wanted to be permitted to do also. Indeed, their sectors of the transportation industry were perhaps under as much pressure to eliminate competition or to find some viable way of managing this competition as were the railroad carriers. For the investment of water and motor carriers per dollar of operating revenue was less than that of the rail carriers; consequently, it was easier to get into and out of the industry, and competition was very keen, particularly in the case of motor carriers.

It was to abate the rigors of unbridled competition in a time of economic stringency that some of the water and motor carrier people sought relief from their condition by appeal to the House Committee on Interstate and Foreign Commerce. They wished to avail themselves of the extraordinary privilege under the Emergency Railroad Transportation Act of 1933 of being exempt from the antitrust laws. The case made in their behalf by Charles E. Cotterill was a moving one but the committee declined to amend the act in so radical a respect. The proposals made by this spokesman for the carriers anticipated part of the public policy as it was to develop eventually, but the time was not yet.[13]

The differential position of the railroads before the House committee as compared with that of the secondary and tertiary business interest groups is illustrated by the nature of the proposals made by them, respectively, to the committee. All of the groups of the second and third rank had suggestions for amendment of the proposed bill, with a desire to include themselves in the processes of the coordinator's office, a minimum request. The carriers, on the other hand, wanted no serious amendments. Carl Gray, the president of the Union Pacific system and one who, with Williamson and Pelley, had presented a plan for a federal coordinator to the first Roper committee, said that "the railroads will give loyal support to this bill. They want to call attention to the fact, however, that it can easily be amended so as to have no practical value." [14] The body of Gray's statement dealt with various amendments that had been suggested by other interested parties (particularly by labor). He attempted to show that most of them were unnecessary, impracticable, or unworkable. Although most of the amendments to which Gray objected were included anyway, his opposition to change by amendment indicates how closely the proposed bill had been tailored to suit the needs of the carriers as they conceived those needs. Not that they were satisfied with all of the provisions or the details. The first proposal of Gray, Williamson, and Pelley clearly indicates that they had in mind a greater degree of autonomy in the railroad carriers than the bill as it emerged from the second Roper committee eventually provided. But they had enough of their desire fulfilled to make them wish to have the measure enacted without change.

R. V. Fletcher, general counsel for the Association of Railway Executives, echoed Gray's warning about changes in the bill when he said that "any amendments to this particular bill would be most unfortunate . . . if the effect of those amendments is to prevent the railroads from doing themselves voluntarily what they desire to do in the way of bringing about these economies and eliminating these economic wastes." [15] Although the measure gave the federal coordinator the authority to issue orders and to require responsive action by the carriers, Fletcher said that he believed that the coordinator would be "a liaison officer as between the Government on the one hand and the railroads on the other." This language was somewhat curious. It is in the nature of a liaison officer that he conducts relations and does not give commands. It is also somewhat curious that the coordinator should have been referred to as a liaison between the *government* and the railroads. He was a part of the government; indeed, he *was* the government so far as his responsibilities under the Emergency Railroad Transportation Act were concerned.

Although the biggest railroad carriers were on the whole satisfied with the bill as it was drafted, and opposed to any material change, not all of the primary groups were equally satisfied. Mention has already been made of the desire of the short lines to be included in any committee discussions that affected the interests of the short-line railroads. A. L. Burford, general counsel for the Louisiana and Arkansas Lines, went somewhat further. He approved the bill but felt that the interests of Class II, Class III, and small independent Class I roads were not "properly safeguarded." [16] He therefore suggested an amendment that would direct the coordinator to give consideration to smaller independent roads in carrying out the purposes of the proposed legislation. The substance of this amendment was included.[17] The few proposals of primary groups were heeded, but all marginal decisions were made against suggestions for change, as in the case of the spokesman for the Wisconsin and Michigan Transportation Company, a lake line, who wanted lake lines put in the same class as railroads and under the application of the act. The stated purpose was the avoidance of competition which engenders waste. His proposed amendments were not accepted.

The most successful achievement of group security was won by the labor unions, after strong criticism of the original bill in the Senate committee on the ground that it did not meet the anxiety of workers about loss of jobs. As W. W. Royster, the spokesman for the Railroad Employees National Pension Association, said, "This bill does not afford labor any means of protecting itself. We are simply a pawn in the game of high finance. We work our lives out in competition with our fellow workers, and in the end are thrown on public charity to continue our miserable existence." [18] Before the House Committee, Donald Richberg said, "The organized railway employees oppose the program embodied in H. R. 5500 because it provides a mechanism of false economy which will seriously reduce transportation service for the public, will deprive from 50,000 to 300,000 employes of work, will not permanently improve railroad operations or railroad credit, will retard economic recovery, and will promote policies that work infinite harm to the public interests." [19] The unions therefore proposed a wide range of far-reaching amendments in the effort to transform the bill somewhat from its pristine purpose — to rationalize in some respects the management of a disorderly industry — into a relief measure for the succor of displaced workers.

These amendments can be understood best in terms of the concept that animated and informed them. Richberg rejected the basic orientation of the measure — improvement of carrier revenues by coordination and elimination of waste — and said instead, "I think . . . we constantly look at this whole industrial picture upside down in thinking of the product of an industry before we think of the fact that the fundamental purpose of industry is to give people a livelihood. That is the reason men start to work." [20] And further, "if such a law is to be enacted, we think it perfectly clear that there ought to be some consideration and very careful consideration given to the interests involved besides those of profit-making." [21] This was a greatly oversimplified view of the purpose and effect of the proposed measure but perhaps inevitably so. For the economy in modern times is such a mesh of interdependent parts that few really comprehend its structure except in terms of the immediate pressure it brings to bear upon them. It was so with the carriers as it was with the unions. The carriers were content to believe that the prosperity of the workers depended upon the prosperity of the companies, and that the first should wait upon the second. The unions tended to argue that the prosperity of the companies depended upon the prosperity of the workers, and that the melioration of the second would improve the prosperity of the first.

Perhaps the best way to illustrate the range of suggestions made by Richberg to introduce labor relief concepts into a carrier relief bill is to list them briefly, and to indicate those that the committee accepted. In summary, Richberg proposed that: (1) the powers of the coordinator should be extended to include other forms of transportation than railroad carriers; (2) the act should include measures and provisions designed "to improve labor relations and to stabilize employment"; (3) provision should be made for the participation of labor representatives in "planning and carrying out industrial operations"; (4) the coordinator should be given power to enforce the Railway Labor Act; (5) if the government displaces workers through the administration of the act, the government should provide for the support of the workers so displaced; (6) the coordinator should be given the power to direct a program of railroad rehabilitation and improvement to increase the total volume of employment; (7) it should be a duty of the coordinator to require the railroads to retire property no longer in use; (8) the coordinator should be given the power to compel financial reorganizations where necessary; and (9) if such an

emergency bill is necessary, why not go all of the way and establish complete government control of the railroad industry during
the period of the emergency.

Of these proposed amendments, the Committee rejected 1, 5, 6,
7, 8, and 9. The substance of 2, 3, and 4 was incorporated into the
final bill.[22] In most respects, the Senate and House committees
held the line on the bill which had been laid down by those who
formulated it, and nullified attempts by labor union representatives to change it radically from its intended purpose as a measure
for the improvement of the desperate economic position of the
carriers. That is to say, the committees did so in all respects save
one, which will be described presently.

That others were aware of the basic conflict of theory and concept over the bill is evident in the statement of H. Shaw, the editor
of the *Unity News,* on behalf of the Railroad Brotherhoods Unity
Committee. He said, "Regardless of the power of the coordinator,
the very essence and purpose of the bill is to increase the income
of the stock and bond holders at the expense of from 100,000 to
250,000, or even more, railroad workers. Therefore, unless the
very purpose and essence of the bill is to be done away with, there
is no use proposing amendments to the bill." [23] It was Shaw's con-
tention that before the government put itself back of any measure
which would deprive workers of their livelihood, it must first
assure those workers an adequate means of existence. In his proposals for assuring the support of railroad workers he recommended that the salaries of railroad executives be cut and that
dividends be reduced. As to the second, since few of the railroads
were earning any dividends, the suggestion did not seem to promise much in the way of relief.

Shaw's suggestion is interesting, however, because it involves
not only a conflict of opinion as to whether the Emergency Railroad Transportation Act should focus on the relief of carriers or
of workers or of both, but because it represents a generally prevailing point of view in the 1930's. The depression of 1929 had
deflated more than the economy. It depressed and deflated the
sanguine belief that domestic expansion of the economy was limit-
less. It turned the thoughts and attention of enterprisers and
workers alike to the conservation and husbanding of what they
had. It was seemingly impossible to count on an expanding econ-

omy to augment the shares of all. It became important, then, for each interest group to increase the size of its individual portions. Although orators of the Democratic Party were later to assert their invincible faith all along in the gospel of perpetual increase, the fact is that the administration in the early days was fully committed to the proposition that the way to restore prosperity was to retrench, rationalize, conserve, and reduce. This is what business men were doing when they shut down the steel mills and turned workers away. The difference between government and business in this respect is that government undertook to provide relief for those turned away, and business was incapable of doing so except through the government, and then with some reluctance.

So, Mr. Shaw's suggestions about reducing the income of stock and bond holders and the salaries of railroad executives in order to provide wages to railroad workers was expressive of the depression mentality. If all salaries had been cut in half and all dividends repudiated or deferred, it is doubtful that the workers would have been much better off than before, for the ills of the industry were not to be cured by any such simple nostrum. But the symbolic value of such actions was no doubt great, and the pressure was strong for some gesture of this sort. Certainly to the union spokesmen it seemed cold-blooded if not avaricious for the railroads and allied interests to be so seemingly indifferent to the cries of the unions.

Although, as has been said, the congressional committees limited the efforts of organizations to establish group security by amendments to the bill, the Senate committee did make one provision for railroad workers that was material. In the form in which it finally appeared in the statute, this amendment provided,

"The number of employees in the service of a carrier shall not be reduced by reason of any action taken pursuant to the authority of this title below the number as shown by the pay rolls of employees in service during the month of May 1933 after deducting the number who have been removed from the pay rolls after the effective date of this Act by reason of death, normal retirement, or resignation, but not more in any one year than 5 per centum of said number in service during May 1933; nor shall any employee in such service be deprived of employment such as he had during said month of May or be in a worse position with respect to his compensation for such employment, by reason of any action taken pursuant to the authority conferred by this title." [24]

When it made this amendment at the request of the unions, the Senate committee was aware that the original purpose of the act — to permit the carriers to rationalize some of the waste and unnecessary expense in the industry under the supervision of the federal coordinator — was being seriously modified. In its report on the measure, the Senate committee pointed out that it had given "the most careful consideration to the proposals of the railroad labor executives" who had insisted that the economies secured by the operation of the act should not result in the additional dismissal of railroad workers, some 750,000 of whom had been dropped from the payrolls during the "hard times period." [25] Said the report of the committee, "Your committee believes that the people as a whole and particularly the railroad employees still in service, should be assured by the terms of the law itself that there will be no wholesale dismissals by the coordinator or the regional committees. For these reasons your committee amended the bill so the coordinator cannot dismiss employees, but his orders may result in reducing the number of employees each year by making it unnecessary to fill vacancies caused by death, retirement, or resignation."

This provision fell short of the desire of the spokesmen for the railroad unions, who hoped to obtain dismissal compensation. But it was the next best thing. Workers could not be separated from the railroad service by reason of any action taken pursuant to the Act, except in the small measure permitted. Time had been gained by the unions during which they could negotiate with the railroads for rules covering dismissals and possibly dismissal compensation. The unions worked assiduously on this project and succeeded in 1936 in securing the Washington Agreement. The unions were not unwilling to support the act with its saving clause in behalf of labor, so long as there was no prospect of improving their position by direct negotiation. When the Washington Agreement gave them what they really wanted, they joined with the carriers in scuttling the federal coordinator.

In the Senate debate on the bill, discussion centered on the labor provisions which had been added to the measure by amendment of the Senate committee. The most serious was Section 7b, which, as has been said, provided that the number of employees could not be reduced below the level of May 1933 except for removal by death, normal retirement, or resignation, not to exceed 5 per cent in any one year. This amendment, originating with the railroad labor unions, was the price they exacted for support (if not advocacy) of the measure. Congressional leaders and the White House were warned that the bill could not be enacted unless it contained this guarantee of group security. A White House conference took place on the issue on May 31 and was attended not only by the committee which had drafted the bill (Rayburn, Dill, Eastman and Splawn) but by A. F. Whitney, George Harrison, and Donald Richberg, all of the Railway Labor Executives Association. The railroad executives "contact committee" had discussed the issue earlier with the President. The President acquiesced in the demand of the railroad unions, and it became party strategy in the House and the Senate then to retain this all-important worker relief provision.[26]

The Senate debated the bill two days, May 26 and May 27, and then passed the measure without a record vote. But before it did so, the intervention of the White House was once again necessary, and again on a labor issue. Senator Hugo Black of Alabama at the time was strongly interested in having the Congress enact legislation establishing the work week at thirty hours as a means of sharing the work. Congress did not enact such legislation but it was one of many such schemes rife at the time, designed to afford relief to workers. He offered an amendment to Section 7 of the Emergency Railroad Transportation Act (the labor section) authorizing the payment for a six-hour day of the same wages as for an eight-hour day.[27] Black's effort to make the "carrier bill" provide worker relief had the support of Senator Burton K. Wheeler of Montana who, in the course of some strong criticisms of the measure, liberally buttressed with quotations from Donald Richberg, said, "I am going to vote against the bill unless it contains a provision for the six-hour day."

Actually, Black apparently was not working very closely with the unions on the matter, for they had not suggested such an amendment nor did they feel, publicly at least, very enthusiastic about this one. A day was allowed to pass without action by the Senate on Black's amendment, during which Dill, who led the floor action on the bill, got in touch with both the unions and the White House. On May 27, when the Black amendment again came up for discussion, he was able to report that he was authorized to speak for the White House and to say that the President considered the amendment "unworkable as it would be applied under this emergency legislation and ruinous to the purposes of the bill." [28] Dill said also that the railroad unions were not anxious to push the matter at the present. Black said that he disagreed with the President's opinion as to the effect of his amendment on the bill, but he withdrew his amendment.

The rest of the Senate debate was interesting primarily because of the range of opinions it supplied about the value of the bill. The bill as worked out by the second Roper committee, it will be recalled, contained three titles, of which only one (Title I) dealt with the office of the federal coordinator of transportation. The others provided mainly for the repeal of the recapture clause and the subjection of railroad holding companies to the authority and jurisdiction of the Interstate Commerce Commission. Neither of these two titles is of particular significance to this study of the federal coordinator. The Senate debate changed the bill in no appreciable respect but it did provide senators with an opportunity to express their views about railroads, unions, the depression, the state of the world in general, and the needs of their constituencies and clienteles in particular. Senator Wheeler made a harsh attack upon the bill, which he said was attempting to accomplish the impossible, to wit, furnishing less transportation service while making more money. The blame for the plight of the railroads he assessed as follows, "If the railroads had not paid out unjustifiable sums in dividends in order to maintain the prices of their stocks upon the stock market, there would not have been any necessity to throw railroad workers out of employment and cut down on the service rendered to the people." [29] Senator Henrik Shipstead, like Wheeler, a modern day Populist, thought that nothing short of outright ownership by the government would meet the problem presented by the railroad industry. He said, "I think it is possibly twenty years too late to expect to get any reduction in the capital structure with the railroads in the hands of private corporations. I do not think there is any remedy except for the government to take them over, under condemnation proceedings, and pay the holders a fair price. . . ." [30] Senator Borah of Idaho said that he would vote against the bill because it provided for exemption of the railroads from the antitrust laws, and Senator Huey Long of Louisiana tried to prevent the abandonment of any route then existing, except with the consent of the coordinator or of all of the participating lines. Senator Dill approved this amendment and the Senate accepted it, one of the few amendments to the committee bill that the Senate did accept.

Before the Senate enacted the measure, without record vote, Senator King of Utah voiced a caution which the event was to prove sound. He disapproved of the bill and said, "With reference to the bill under consideration, I have reached the conclusion that the situation does not require its passage. That there should be legislation dealing with the problems of transportation there can be no doubt . . . But the measure before us is a makeshift, and I fear that it will prove embarrassing when we come to deal in a broad and comprehensive way with the railroad situation." [31] But having so carefully defined the nature of the bill and having so shrewdly anticipated that it might contain the seeds of obstruction and embarrassment, Senator King somewhat spoiled the effect by asserting that it was a step in the direction of government ownership and operation of the railroads of the United States. Others, Shipstead and Wheeler, for example, were of the opinion that what was wrong with the bill was that it did not lead towards government ownership and operation of the railroad industry of the United States.

The bill passed the Senate, then, in much the same form as it had emerged from the committee, including the controversial provision freezing employment in the railroad industry generally at the levels of May, 1933, with some modifications.

Much of the action on the floor of the House of Representatives in the debate on the measure represented efforts to restore in the House the version of the bill as it emerged from the House committee. The House committee stayed close to that version of the bill which had originally been presented by the second Roper committee, and refused to accept the Senate committee variations of the original. But no effort was made to eliminate the controversial labor provision, and the attendance of members of the House during the discussion of the bill was, on the whole, small.

In his presentation of the bill to the House, Congressman Rayburn told the members that he had conferred with representatives of the unions and that they had expressed acceptance of the labor provision, including, of course, the proposal to freeze employment to the extent possible. Perhaps the closest expression of the mood of the House was provided by Cooper of Ohio, who said, "I have my doubts that either the general public, the railroads, or the employees will receive any material benefit from the provisions of title I of the bill. However . . . this is a period of national economic crisis. I shall support the bill, and I hope that material benefits will be passed out through the passage of this bill to the general public, the railroad employees, and railroad managements." [32] Like the famous prescription for buttering the baby's heel, it would not do any harm and might possibly do some good. Cooper was especially sensitive about a statement made in *Labor,* the journal of the railroad brotherhoods, that he was opposed to the labor provisions of the bill, which he denied, saying, "I think that the labor provision of section 1 is a mistake . . . I sympathize as much as anybody else with the railroad employees, but they first ought to help the railroads into good working order so that they themselves will be more secure in their employment." [33]

Congressman Huddleston of Alabama expressed the view which Eastman had earlier presented, that the chief value of Title I was the provision for study of the transportation situation. As a relief measure, Huddleston thought that Title I "is just about as near nothing as could be observed under a miscroscope." [34]

Among the amendments to the bill that were rejected by the House was one put forward by Congressman Mapes of Michigan. He wanted a provision requiring the coordinator to hire all staff, except experts, under the civil service regulations and the Classification Act of 1923. Rayburn opposed this suggestion, saying that the House committee had considered such a proposal and had turned it down by an "overwhelming majority." In the course of his remarks, Rayburn further said,

"It has been stated in various press reports that Commissioner Eastman will be . . . made the coordinator. I doubt if his appointment would be displeasing to anybody, because he is a man of outstanding ability and has the confidence of the shippers and the public in general, as well as of labor and the railroads, as few other men in his position over the years have had.

"One of the things that Mr. Eastman was very definite about was that among those whom the coordinator would call around him would be men who should be of the highest technical skill that he could get, and he thought it would greatly cripple the efforts and the accomplishments of the coordinator if he had to go to the Civil Service rolls to get these employees." [35]

Other proposed amendments were dealt with in more or less summary fashion, and the House passed the bill by a voice vote. Since it had been passed in different form from that in which it had passed the Senate, it was necessary for the two bills to go to conference. The differences were on details, for on the most crucial question, the labor provisions freezing employment at the May 1933 levels, the House and the Senate were in agreement.

Not everybody, however, was happy with the labor provisions. After the House committee had reported the bill to the whole House, the Railway Labor Executives Association issued a statement expressing approval of the position taken by the President on the issue. But the president of the United States Chamber of Commerce wrote to the members of the House committee expressing strong disapproval of the labor provisions, and the action of the whole House in accepting them was said to be a disappointment to him. That these provisions were crucial is evident in the action of the conferees on the bill. Representatives of the House and the Senate held a preliminary meeting on the labor provisions of Section 7 before holding later meetings on the other differences between the House and Senate versions of the bill. At the first meeting on the labor provisions, the group consisted of certain House and Senate members appointed by their respective chambers, and Eastman and Splawn. The latter, therefore, were in on all of the stages through which the measure passed before being enacted into law. It was agreed at this meeting to accept the House version of the labor provisions. With the most vexatious provisions taken care of, subsequent consultation worked out the remaining differences in a day.[36]

The legislative history of the identical Robinson and Rayburn bills may be examined in a degree of detail into which it has not been necessary to go in a discursive narrative.[37] The legislation went through the Congress with the speed of an express. The measure had been introduced simultaneously in House and Senate and referred to the appropriate committees which then held hearings. Each house passed a somewhat different version of the bill and sent it to the other house, which refused to accept the measure. It was necessary, therefore, to create a conference committee to conciliate the differences between the two bills. The conference committee then reported its recommendation to both houses in the same form and both houses accepted these recommendations. With the differences between the two bills thus conciliated, the enrolled bill was then sent to the President for approval. At this point, the Emergency Railroad Transportation Act was actually recalled from the White House by the Congress because two words had been inadvertently omitted, so great was the haste to get the measure through. When the corrections had been made, the bill was again sent to the White House and signed by the President on June 16, 1933. Of the six weeks elapsed time for the round-trip journey of the President's proposal of May 4, only about two weeks were required for introduction, hearing, debate, conference, and enactment.

The act as it emerged from the tortuous processes of consultation, compromise, and consideration provided, first, for the creation of the federal coordinator of transportation, who, through regional coordinating committees, was to encourage the enactment by the carriers of policies for the reduction of waste,[38] such economies to be put into effect, however, without reducing railroad employment, below the allowance for attrition. The carriers were given relief from certain legal restrictions which tended to promote duplication and needless expense. Second, the act supplied a method for forcing financial reorganizations of railroads needing loans from the Reconstruction Finance Corporation. Third, the coordinator was to begin the study of the entire transportation problem with a view towards the possible later enactment of comprehensive reform in the field of transportation regulation. Fourth, the recapture clause and certain rules governing rate-making were repealed.[39] Fifth, the ICC was given jurisdiction over railroad holding companies and other forms of acquisition of control of railroad properties. Sixth, certain improvements were made in the handling of railroad valuations by the Commission. In a summary of the provisions of the Emergency Transportation Act of 1933, the conservative *Railway Age* said that "It is understood that the railroads are relying more on the increase in carloading that has begun in recent weeks to help them to earn their fixed charges for 1933 than upon the economies to be effected in the near future by co-ordination." [40]

Reactions to the Measure

The feelings of some of the parties in interest after the passage of the act were somewhat tart, if one may gather an impression from their comments about "who won" in the struggle of groups to write rules that would favor themselves. Again to quote *Railway Age,* the voice of the carriers, it seemed "President Roosevelt's plan of having bills which he desires passed drafted by his own advisers and submitted to Congress does not appear to have turned out particularly successful in this instance." [41] It was said that a committee appointed by Secretary of Commerce Roper had worked for several weeks on the railroad bill "consulting with representatives of the railroads, labor organizations, security holders, shippers and state commissions and conferring frequently with the President." But all of the work done in advance, it was felt, had not prevented the Senate from rewriting most of the emergency title of the bill. Not only did the carriers mourn that the original bill had been amended, but the same unhappiness was expressed by the shippers. *Traffic World,* for example, said in one of its issues, "Organized railroad labor, the railroads, and the state commissions fared better than the shippers in the revision of the Roosevelt coordinator bill made by the Senate interstate commerce committee which reported the revised measure this week to the Senate for passage." [42] The common note sounded by the carriers and the shippers is in strong contrast to the accusations that were later frequently to be made in the heat of political campaigns. The Congress had *not* been entirely a rubber stamp Congress in the enactment of the Emergency Railroad Transportation Act of 1933. The carriers and shippers seemed to be somewhat downcast that it had not been.

As the record of the passage of the act through Congress amply shows, there were few who had any great illusions about the act or about the role, place, or function of the federal coordinator. Some thought the economies would be slight; some thought that the study provisions were the most important; some felt that the bill was loaded in favor of the carriers; some thought that it had become a bill for the relief of the railroad workers; some thought that it would provide no relief for railroad workers. No one in the Congress, so far as the public record shows, thought that the new federal coordinator was going to rule the railroad industry as William G. McAdoo had in World War I and for a short time thereafter.

But one man, Paul Y. Anderson, a prominent reporter and commentator for the *St. Louis Post Dispatch,* undertook to criticize the act on a ground of his own and to characterize the measure in such a way as to draw an unsolicited letter of rebuke from Eastman, a copy of which he sent to Donald Richberg because he was mentioned and Eastman "thought you ought to see it." [43] The Eastman letter to Anderson supplies the best evidence of Eastman's conception of himself and of the bill he was to administer. Said Eastman, after a salutation to Mr. Anderson:

"I have read your comments in the *Nation* on the railroad bill, and am moved to write you about them. The Coordinator idea did not originate with me (nor do I think that it originated with the railroads), and I have never regarded the bill as more than a useful interim measure which might pave the way for a more radical and thoroughgoing treatment of the transportation situation. That was the substance of my advice to the President. However, your strictures upon the bill, as I see it, are neither discerning nor fair, and that is what I want to make clear to you. The letter is not written for publication, but because I believe you want to be fair and because also, I think that the chief weakness of liberals, and one that they should guard against, is a tendency to hasty and prejudiced judgments. Probably it is unnecessary for me to tell you that I have no overwhelming personal desire for the job of Coordinator, and from that point of view am indifferent as to the fate of the bill. I would not accept any increase in income from the job; and chances that I would gain more credit than discredit would not be better than even; and the chances of sapping health from work and strain would be very good indeed. There would be a momentarily flattering increase in notoriety, but the only real attraction would be the new work." [44]

Eastman thus made clear, what those who knew him well respected greatly in his character and personality, a selflessness in his work in which nothing of the more obvious appearance of ambition or desire for personal gain was allowed to intrude, because the impulses that move these animations did not exist.

The body of the letter dealt with specific points of comment or objection made by Anderson. Of the assertion that the new act nullified some 1500 state regulatory statutes (Anderson borrowed this dubious information from Richberg's testimony) Eastman said, "That, to speak bluntly, is pure bunk." Anderson also said that the bill would "establish a federal 'coordinator,' but would place the real power in the hands of three regional committees composed of railway executives, so that instead of having a federal czar over the railroads, we should actually have a baby czar under the regency of railroad managers." Of this Eastman said, "There is wit but not wisdom or fact in this statement." He agreed that the bill did not establish a federal czar but not for the reason asserted by Anderson. The ultimate authority under the act would be in the hands of the Interstate Commerce Commission. The regional coordinating committees would have no authority that committees voluntarily established outside the proposed legislation would not have. They would have no more power than the then existing Association of Railway Executives. "The minute that anything more was needed or desired," said Eastman, "an order from the Coordinator would be necessary, and that in turn would be subject to the final authority of the Commission. The Coordinator would also have full initiative, regardless of the committees."

This point is of special importance. The curious paradox of administration and politics which the experience of the federal coordinator of transportation supplies is that of an official who was given ample authorities within the power of the Congress to grant and convey. He could make orders. He did not have to seek any fresh authority for his orders. They were technically subject to review by the Interstate Commerce Commission, but he was also a member of the Commission and one of its best two or three people. If Anderson's thesis were entirely correct, there would have been no astonishment at all in the ultimate fate of the federal coordinator.

The union representatives who appeared before the Senate committee had made various estimates of the numbers of people likely to lose their jobs because of economies effected under the act. Anderson repeated the more conservative of these estimates, and said that the coordinator act "would abolish the jobs of 80,000 to 300,000 rail workers without making any provision for their future." As a stickler for statistical accuracy where accuracy was possible, Eastman found this plagiarized estimate unacceptable. He said, "So far as these numbers are concerned, 300,000 might lose their jobs under the Prince Plan, if the contentions of its advocates are correct (which I greatly doubt), and they might under a plan of unified public operation; but this would be utterly impossible under the Coordinator bill. If the number got up within gunshot of 80,000, it would greatly surprise me." Anderson's article was written a few days before the Congress enacted the coordinator bill in its final form, and the labor provisions inserted at the behest of the Railway Labor Executives Association were not yet officially a part of the text. But his assertion that no provision was made in the bill for the relief of workers who might be discharged as a result of economies effected by the coordinator was of course just as true at the time he wrote his criticism as at the later time when the statute was formally on the books.

The Anderson point of view about the act was fundamentally different from that of Eastman and not merely because Anderson was rewriting Richberg for the subscribers of the *Nation*. Out of his knowledge of the way men work and act, each entertained different expectations as to what was likely to befall. Eastman was aware of this fundamental difference in point of view when he said to Anderson,

You and Richberg visualize the results of the bill very differently from what I do. My conviction is that so long as the railroads continue in the ownership of many individual companies (a situation which the bill would not change), it will be very difficult to accomplish the economies which would come from the elimination of economic waste. Instead of conceiving of these regional coordinating committees as champing at the bit eager to put such economies into operation, I believe that it will be very hard for them to agree among themselves, to say nothing of bringing other executives into line. A good many of the executives will more likely be interested in proving that the economies are impracticable than in promoting them, because they will fear the loss of some competitive advantage. This is a situation which I think I know much more about than do you and Richberg.

Of the effect of the statute on jobs, Eastman voiced wonder at the somewhat selective sympathy Richberg and Anderson displayed. From a long-range point of view, Eastman said that he considered it indisputably important to the interest of the railroad worker that the railroads be operated as economically as possible, having in mind the competition "which they face from other transportation agencies," the need for reducing rates, and for developing good railroad credit to support the improvement and modernization of their properties. From the short-range point of view, of course, the loss of jobs to people who had spent their lives railroading and knew nothing else was a great tragedy. But, said Eastman, "it is no more serious for railroad labor than the loss of jobs by Government workers from the present economy program, or the loss of jobs in other industries from programs of greater economy and efficiency. It has been hard for me to understand why all the sympathy should be expended on railroad labor and why no one has anything to say in behalf of Government labor. In our own small department, over 500 employees will go on the street next July, although they are trained and needed for useful Government work; but I have heard no plaints from liberals in their behalf." He then pointed out that the government had plans for the relief of workers, including railroad workers, although none for railroad workers as a special class.

The rest of the long letter to Paul Anderson discussed various points raised by Anderson (and Richberg, whose material he was using) in the light of the facts that Eastman was able to command from his experience. Having concluded an extremely long lecture on how to understand the railroad problem, addressed to one who, like the amateur art critic, did not know much about railroading but knew what he liked, Eastman concluded on a characteristic note. He asked Anderson whether he was acquainted with another individual of the same surname in St. Louis and asked for an appraisal of him in connection with an appointment that Eastman was trying to fill.

V. PATTERNS OF COORDINATION

"While the railroads do in many respects operate jointly as one system of transportation, the immediate duty of the individual management is to promote the welfare of its own particular railroad. Since railroads compete with each other at the more important points and for the more important traffic of the country, their individual interests are often adverse, or at least appear on the surface so to be. The executive officers have grown up in the business, and this idea of conflicting interests is ingrained and predominant. Their habit of mind is intensely individualistic and suspicious of collective action. When such action is proposed, notwithstanding that it may be for the good of the industry as a whole, the normal executive will at once seek to determine how it may affect his railroad in comparison with others. It is easy for him to fear that it may have an adverse effect from that point of view, and if he does, he is against the proposition. He is particularly wary of any collective proposal which has a Nation-wide aspect for he sees in it what he regards as a tendency toward "nationalization" of the railroads, and at all events a decrease in the importance of the local managements."

Third Report of the Federal Coordinator, p. 7

This chapter will discuss patterns of coordination which the federal coordinator considered and rejected. The following chapters will deal with the politics of his attempt to "coordinate" within the framework of the statute he was entrusted to execute. For these pages, we may suppose that coordination is the effort to align independent structures of power in such a way as to permit unified action for common purpose, each of the structures of power being permitted to retain its autonomy and independent existence. This is a political definition, as distinguished from an engineering, an economic, or a sociological definition.

Coordination can be achieved by many methods, from the least coercive to the most. First, simple liaison is, perhaps, the least coercive form of coordination, since it involves only the maintenance of an uncomplicated system of intercommunication. Each structure of power simply tries to take into account the course its partner pursues in the achievement of the common purpose. The divisions of two separate military units in the field may wish to keep in touch in this fashion, with no common point at which decisions binding both units are made. Where liaison is used, the assumption is that cooperative and unified action will be achieved by the exchange of information and reports.

Second, committees are a familiar device for achieving a unified approach to common objectives without impairment of the individuality of the component groups. They may be used either for the exchange of reports and information or they may be used for the formulation of common decisions, each of the component members of the committee feeling free to accept or reject the common decision as to desirable courses.

Third, a more formal form of coordination occurs under a common director from whom each of the component groups agrees to accept directions insofar as they bear upon the common purposes to be achieved and no other. Decisive power in such arrangements is almost always in the plurality of the groups brought under common direction, for the director of coordination is without a power base of his own. He may, however, be given authority to command, in which case we have a fourth form of coordination.

The Emergency Railroad Transportation Act contemplated a combination of two, three, and four. Regional committees of the carriers were given the initiative in proposing unified actions to eliminate waste and preventable expense, with the coordinator empowered to direct benignly where he thought it desirable, but with an authority to command where necessary.

A coordinated relation, then, is one in which procedure exists for making decisions about unified action to achieve a common purpose; and an uncoordinated relation is one where this procedure is absent. Control of the procedure may be inside the structures to be coordinated, as in the devices of liaison and committee membership. This may be called internal coordination, as distinguished from coordination procedures external to these structures, as in coordination by command. In coordination by command, the power to decide is removed from one or more of the constituents and is lodged elsewhere. Coordination therefore involves that most central of the problems of politics, the distribution of power among a collectivity of groups, and problems of coordination are most realistically understood as struggles for power.

Eastman was well aware that many efforts at coordination in the railroad industry had failed. As he said in his *First Report,*

The numerous committees of the American Railway Association or other railroad organizations, often do excellent work and recommend the adoption of certain standards or practices which they believe would be of general advantage. The fact is, however, that these recommendations frequently fail of general adoptions, because of the high degree of individualism among railroad managements. Carrier officers may resist because of pride of opinion or even for fear that adoption of the recommendation would in some way threaten their individual importance . . . Similar difficulties have been experienced by the Association of Railway Executives.[1]

How risky therefore was any attempt to secure coordination, even for limited purposes, by devices that moved the center of decision from the individual carriers to some agency outside their immediate influence and possibly outside their control. Carrier managements, being chieftains within their own principalities, were habitually unable to bow to superchieftains, for few or none wanted decision to be moved from his hands and lodged in those of another.

Public Ownership of the Railroads

Many patterns of coordination — internal and external — have been designed for the railroad industry from time to time, some put to practice and some never closer than talk. From the viewpoint of owners and managers, the most sweeping and universal of the forms of external coordination is public ownership of the railroads. It is the most sweeping because the power to decide all questions of management is transferred from the carriers to a public authority. The former corporate boundaries of the carriers no longer define the jurisdictions of a *multiplicity* of power centers. Decisions no longer proceed by the slow and awkward conciliation of the prejudices and jealousies of a thousand holders of small units of power, any one of whom may withhold his consent. This does not necessarily mean that the central decisions will be either arbitrary or ignorant, or even swift, for the larger such a collectivity becomes, the more careful it needs to be guaranteed that all decisions heed the requirements of a tremendous diversity of local variations. But the capacity to withhold consent by veto no longer lies in any locality. The power to decide is transferred to the public agent or agency.

Various arguments have been advanced to support public ownership based on conceptions of the proper relation between government and business and considerations of economics and social ethics. In political terms, the case for public ownership would be as follows. If the carriers represent a single transportation net, it is wasteful of energy, money, time, goods, and human resources to permit the net to remain Balkanized, divided up into quarreling struggling principalities, the executive heads of which spend much of their time in intrigue to fashion combinations and coalitions of influence within the transportation net for the purpose of enlarging their own spheres of control. The concentration of power in the public authority and the application of this power to situations requiring action are a more efficient use of it than division and separation in small units which only with difficulty can be spliced, linked together, and combined to produce sufficient quanta of power to achieve the same result. In fact, the whole history of the railroad industry exhibits a persistent attempt on the part of the carriers to produce by private combination, within and without the antitrust laws, the same concentration of power and smoothness of flow that public ownership and operation would produce easily and quickly.

Eastman was an early advocate of public ownership of the railroads. In 1927, for example, the National Association of Railroad and Public Utilities Commissioners, of which he was a member, published a *Report of the Committee on Public Ownership and Operation*. The committee had been created in 1916 and had issued ten previous reports on the subject of public ownership and operation. Its eleventh report was a rather tired and dispirited rehash of previous arguments, in the course of which the committee said, "Your Committee on Public Ownership and Operations is so old and the subject has been covered so thoroughly by previous Committee reports that we do not feel that we can add anything new to what has been stated before." [2] The majority of the committee then in five pages said what previous committees had said, that public ownership and operation was not in the public interest, and that it generally provided inferior service. Eastman wrote a ten-page dissent to the five-page report.

He did not put the case for public ownership on the political basis described above. Nor was the question of public ownership one of theory respecting the proper relation of government to business. It was, in his opinion, a question of expediency, merely, since the railroads were not private business to begin with but public utilities. "They perform functions of the State," [3] he held, and quoted language from a Supreme Court decision that said, "That railroads, though constructed by private corporations and owned by them, are public highways, has been the doctrine of nearly all the courts ever since such conveniences for passage and transportation have had any existence." This (and other references) was decisive for him. Government was entitled by the law, if it chose to do so, to operate and control railroads. But, although the authority of the government might be crystal clear to Eastman, he recognized that the question of public ownership of utilities was one of the most contentious and controversial issues of public policy. Indeed, he observed, "The question is peculiarly one in which prejudice is likely to play a part, prejudice which may be and usually is quite unconscious. Aside from religion, there is perhaps nothing that so excites prejudices as the fear of being separated from the opportunity for profit." That public ownership of railroads or indeed of any utility would reduce the opportunity for private profit was self-evident.

Under public ownership and operation of railroads and other public utilities, the field for profit on the part of bankers would unquestionably be curtailed very materially. The officers of the private companies fear that they would be displaced or their salaries reduced. Certain of the directors may fear the loss of the lucrative opportunities which grow out of advance knowledge of coming corporate events. Those who furnish the private companies with supplies or services, often under the generous guardianship of holding companies, fear interference with existing profitable relationships. Those who perform functions which are not strictly public but may be affected with a public interest, such as insurance, fear that more direct public interference with their affairs may be encouraged. Even we ourselves, as part of the present system of private operation under public regulation, may possibly fear interference with our jobs.

All these fears and many others were sources of prejudice, conscious or unconscious, "against which those who wish to think soundly must be on their guard." He might have added that the advocates of public ownership had a formidable array of group interests to overcome when the resistant combination included bankers, company officers, directors, suppliers, holding companies, insurance companies, and public officials in danger of losing their jobs.

Eastman made a distinction between public ownership and public operation, each of which could exist apart from the other. The advantages of public ownership for *new* enterprises were several. It reduced the cost of procuring capital and made it unnecessary to earn a profit over such cost. It made reduction and retirement of the debt feasible. It freed the public of the vexation, expense, and dangers of the valuation doctrine. The advantages of public operation were also considerable. It would make unnecessary the present system of duplicated and duplicating managements. It would substitute for private managements, which tended to become self-perpetuating institutions, managements responsible directly to the whole people. Answering the suggestion of opponents of public operation, that political corruption would be a major problem, Eastman said that "business and political morality tend to rise or sink to a common level." [4] Public operation would lessen the danger that managements would be directly or indirectly dominated by banks and other interests that have dealings with utilities. And public operation would improve the relations between the roads and their employees and the general public by changing the emphasis of the management from private profit to the public good.

But although a good case could be made for the public ownership and operation of new enterprises, practical considerations counselled against making such a move too hastily in dealing with existing properties. Proper preparations, supported by public opinion, would have to be made. The valuation problem would possibly mean dangerous overpayment by government for property and stocks. Eastman concluded,

Without further elaborating such considerations, I am persuaded that the policy of public ownership and operation must await gradual development under the slow processes of evolution. It can and should be adopted for the future, and from time to time, circumstances will arise in the case of particular existing properties which will make possible the adoption of the new doctrine under comparatively favorable conditions. In the meantime, we as public officials entrusted with the duty of regulating private operation, ought to do everything in our power to make the present system work as successfully as possible.[5]

Although these views seem to be mild enough — public ownership and operation of the railroads might be a good thing some time but not now — they appeared to some members of the railroad industry to be dangerously radical. Indeed, Eastman himself said, "A belief or disbelief in public ownership and operation has in fact become a shibboleth by which the conservative test political and economic sanity." When Eastman was appointed federal coordinator of transportation in 1933, *Railway Age* said, "The economic philosophy and policies of Commissioner Eastman, who has become federal coordinator, repeatedly have been discussed and criticized in these columns. He has been an advocate of government ownership, and the *Railway Age* has questioned whether an advocate of government ownership was qualified to participate fairly and constructively in the administration of the Transportation Act, which was passed to restore and contribute toward the success of private management." [6] *Railway Age* said that it respected Eastman's ability and allowed that he was a natural, if not inevitable, choice for federal coordinator. He thus just managed to pass the 1933 equivalent of a loyalty test, and almost immediately he exhibited the same lack of reverence for the sacred cow of the railroad industry that he had shown in 1927. It will be recalled that, in his correspondence with many at the time the Emergency Railroad Transportation Act was being formulated, he had expressed himself privately in favor of government ownership several times.[7] He was to do the same in public.

Some six months after his appointment as federal coordinator, Eastman made a report to Congress on his progress to date. In answering the question, "Is there need for a radical or major change in the organization, conduct, and regulation of the railroad industry which can be accomplished by Federal legislation?" he addressed himself to the question of public ownership and operation. Some of it seemed to be a restatement of the 1927 report. Public ownership and operation were not inconsistent with the American theory of government. The Supreme Court has recognized that the railroads are a public industry. The question is not one of right but of expediency, and so on. But the discussion in 1933 was much more sophisticated and elaborate.

Eastman met two arguments against government operation of the railroads that were then current, based upon federal operation of the roads during World War I and the example of the Canadian National Railway. He refuted anonymous critics by citing and quoting the testimony of Walker D. Hines, former director-general of railroads, who concluded,

The effect of Federal control was to provide, as to the country's war needs, and as to the interests of railroad security holders, a protection which had become impracticable on the part of private control in view of the emergencies and limitations with which it was confronted. Any fairly balanced study of the situation as a whole must lead to the conclusion that in periods of extraordinary difficulty the Government's temporary operation of the railroads accomplished with credit the objects which made resort to its imperative.[8]

As to the Canadian National system, ownership was forced upon the Canadian government in 1917 by the inability of private capital to maintain the lines. Said Eastman, "It is conceded that these lines have been operated more efficiently and have given better service since than before public acquisition." Recommendations of the Royal Commission in 1917 for divorcement from political control were not followed, however, and so the system became a political issue. It was run by a Liberal government until 1930, when the Conservatives came into power and appointed a Royal Commission to look into the operation of the railroad system under its political opponents. Eastman implied that political considerations may have tended to produce the critical report which emerged from this inquiry, although he did not specifically say so. In any event, although a Conservative government investigated the activities of its adversary, the resulting report was not entirely adverse to the Liberals. In fact, from the political point of view (that is, as a problem of the most efficient concentration of the collective power of individual managers to make decisions) the report said that "the railway has been energetically administered, and has deservedly won approval by its success in welding together the various working forces of the separate companies in the consolidated system." And, further, that it was an "efficient transport system affording a service of high standard and with a loyal and enthusiastic staff of officers and employees." [9]

Eastman acknowledged the hypothetical validity of some of the objections to public ownership but thought they could be surmounted and overcome. Political party interference could be averted by creating an independent corporation to run the railroads. Or, following the example of the London Passenger Transportation Board, the trustees of the railroad could be appointed by a nonpolitical board. The possibility of interference with labor relations, including wages and working conditions, was, he thought, real, but "the present situation would probably not be changed materially." Referring to the fact that he had been unable to persuade the Congress to enact the Emergency Railroad Transportation Act in the form in which it had been submitted to Congress by the administration,[10] he said, "At the last session of Congress, it was evident that the employees of the privately owned railroads had more influence than the employees of the Government." [11] Indeed, at the time, the railroad employees were not advocates of public ownership, and Eastman hazarded the opinion that they might be influenced in this belief by the thought that their principal weapon, the strike, would be of less avail against the government than against private employers.

Interference with rate adjustments, particularly to help certain groups or localities, was a major risk under public ownership because "every Member of Congress is naturally anxious to secure benefits for his district." Another danger in public ownership was possible interference with construction programs, particularly to promote large expenditures for the benefit of certain localities, "or as a means of social relief." Although these were major dangers, Eastman thought ways could be devised to guard against them.

As to the problem whether the railroads of the country could be effectively and efficiently managed as a single unit, Eastman acknowledged that this was "a most serious question." The railroads, he thought, presented difficult problems of administration, not being concentrated in one or a few places, as is a manufacturing plant, but spread over a vast expanse of territory with the employees on the move or stationed at a vast number of places. He thought that a general supervisory or administrative force might not easily be able to keep in touch with either the employees or the patrons. But this objection, like all other objections to public ownership and operation, he thought could be worked out in time with the right people in charge. The elimination of competition which public ownership and operation would entail was not perhaps so real a problem as some critics would suppose, since the roads would have competition from rival forms of transportation, various forms of intermanagement competition could be fashioned within a system publicly owned and operated, and initiative and enterprise were not necessarily related to competition anyway, as the experience of the telephone and electric industries shows.

No domination of the public enterprise by labor groups could be expected, or at least no more than already existed in the railroad industry as privately owned. All the economies in operation that could be obtained by private consolidation or coordination could be achieved under public ownership, even though they were labor-saving economies. In fact, the possibilities were greater. Asked Eastman, "Would the opposition of labor to such economies be more effective under public ownership and operation than under private? In view of the experience with the Emergency Act, it is probable that there would be no great difference in the two situations."

As a realist in some respects, Eastman was aware that "there is no aggressive sentiment in favor of public ownership and operation." The financial world was less hostile to the idea of public ownership than it had been in the past, because some institutional bondholders such as the insurance companies presumably thought that it might improve their situation, and because of doubt as to whether the railroads would be a "source of large profits in the future." As he observed, somewhat dryly, "Fundamental objections to the operation of an industry by the Government tend to disappear in direct ratio with profits." Had he been a more philosophical man, Eastman might have tried to generalize this sharp insight into a "law of reversible opinions," capably of mathematical demonstration, with the rate of profit serving as the independent variable. The mythical "man in the street" was indifferent rather than hostile. Labor was lukewarm. The greatest hostility to the idea was from railroad managements, supply houses, and the larger shippers. After measuring the prospect with an admittedly nonmathematical eye, Eastman concluded, "On the whole, there is now little effective support in public opinion for public ownership and operation."

The strongest of all of the objections to public ownership at the time, however, was the probable cost of acquisition if the government were to force the sale of railroad properties. Eastman had little confidence that the government or the courts would be able to withstand the pressure of aggressive railroad lawyers. "When governments acquire property, they normally pay more than it is worth, just as they normally sell for less. This has been the universal experience with railroads." The reasons he thought were obvious. The sympathies of tribunals are with the individuals who are forced to part with their property. "Doubts are resolved in their favor, and their lawyers are apt to be more aggressive than Government counsel."

With his wonted thoroughness, Eastman appended a tentative plan for public ownership and operation of the railroad systems of the United States.[12] Under this plan, railroad properties would be owned by a federal corporation chartered by Congress, the stock of which would be owned by the United States. These railroad properties would be acquired in exchange for bonds in the federal corporation — United States Railways — and managed by a board of trustees appointed by the President with the consent of the Senate for staggered terms of ten years. The trustees were to be removable only for cause and were to receive the same salaries as justices of the Supreme Court. The authority to run the railroads was to be vested in the trustees, who were to conduct affairs after the manner of a private corporation and upon a self-sustaining basis so far as possible. There would be an advisory council representing the principal interest groups in the railroad industry. Provision was made for the payment of federal and state taxes, for the issuance of bonds, and for the exemption of United States Railways from regulation by the ICC except in the matter of rates, accounting, and construction. United States Railways was to be empowered to acquire other agencies of transportation, subject to approval by the Interstate Commerce Commission.

As might have been expected, the reaction of the carriers and their spokesmen to these suggestions about public ownership of railroad properties was not entirely joyous. But Eastman did not let the idea go. In a letter to the vice president of the Delaware and Hudson Railroad shortly after his proposals were made public, he said, "One thing that ought not to be overlooked in any discussion of government ownership is that it is not a sufficient answer to say that it will not work perfectly or will lead to certain evils, for this can be said of everything that is of human origin." [13] As a practical matter he did not believe, he said, "that we shall come to public ownership and operation unless and until the railroads cease to be an attractive field for the investment of private capital," a prediction which the "law of reversible opinions" would seem to justify. He also wrote to his friend Felix Frankfurter, at the time in England, saying that he found "a tendency among the intelligentsia to be a little critical" because he did "not attempt to rush the country either into public ownership and operation or into a great compulsory consolidation plan." [14] He had been told that his "bump of caution" was perhaps too large but he was afraid that nationalization might become "an unloading process for the benefit of security holders, and that is one of the reasons why I am holding back as I endeavored to indicate in my report."

To an English correspondent who criticized the proposals for public ownership, he said,

My own leaning towards public ownership and operation has grown out of close observation during the past thirty years of privately owned railroads and other public utilities. I have seen them exploited in various ways. I have seen them affected by and also affecting politics, and I have also seen them suffer in many instances from lack of initiative and other forms of dry rot. A high degree of public regulation seems inevitable in this country, but it results in a divided responsibility and a slowing down of management which have unfortunate effects.[15]

And to an American correspondent who sent him a clipping containing unhappy comments on public ownership by a vice president for the Chesapeake and Ohio Railroad, he said, "I appreciate your remarks in regard to these vice-presidential outpourings. I had not supposed that there was much sentiment in the country in

favor of public ownership, but the activity of railroad officers com-
batting the idea leads me to believe that I may be wrong in regard
to the state of public sentiment on this matter." [16] Perhaps it was
this new appraisal of public sentiment that led Eastman the same
day to write to a Boston friend, "I am hoping that plans for pooling can be perfected which will accomplish the desired results without putting all the railroads under a single management or a very
few managements, but it may be that this expedient will prove impracticable. If actual corporate unification should be necessary, I
see no escape from government ownership." [17]

In his *Third Report,* made in January, 1935, Eastman was back
on the familiar theme, this time in somewhat stronger language.
After reviewing the pros and cons of public ownership, he was still
uncertain whether the time had come to push for government
ownership but, "It is universally conceded," he said, "that this particular industry performs a public function and that the ultimate
responsibility for proper performance rests with the Government.
The only question of importance is the practical one of the way to
get the best results." [18] He did not seem to be quite so worried that
security holders would unload on the government as he had been a
year earlier, and he based his conclusion that public ownership was
not feasible in 1935 only on the ground that public opinion did
not yet seem ready to support such a proposal.[19] He and a friend in
Congress were to test the truth of this conclusion, and to verify it.

On April 14, 1935, Senator Burton K. Wheeler of Montana,
chairman of the Senate Committee on Interstate Commerce, introduced a bill to establish a federal corporation, to be called
United States Railways, to take over the railroads of the country
on January 1, 1936. The roads were to be acquired either by consolidation of the existing companies with the federal corporation,
with an exchange of their respective securities, or by eminent
domain with payment for the properties in debentures of the
United States Railways. Eastman had helped Wheeler prepare the
measure, which followed Eastman's recommendations very closely,
even to the title of the corporation. In a letter to his friend George
W. Anderson, Eastman explained his participation as follows:

So far as Senator Wheeler is concerned, I am trying to help him in the
preparation of a measure for public ownership and operation. In other

words, it seemed to me that if he was going to present such a bill it ought to be as workmanlike as possible, and I am endeavoring to help him along those lines, although the task is not at all an easy one . . . It will not be greatly liked by the holders of railroad securities, because they will feel that it is not sufficiently liberal to the owners of the properties. That may perhaps be a just criticism, although of course the courts will protect them in just compensation in any event. However, I felt that it would be better to err on the side of making a good trade for the Government, so far as the original bill is concerned, rather than to err in proposing too liberal a trade from the point of view of the security holders.[20]

When he introduced his bill, Wheeler said, "The bill contains many of the recommendations he (Eastman) had heretofore made. It is fair, however, to say that the Coordinator has not suggested the bill, nor does he recommend the immediate government ownership of the railroads." [21] Wheeler had given indications earlier that he was interested in stirring up some talk about government ownership, perhaps for the purpose of generating enough force to obtain a thorough investigation of railroad financing and management.[22] When his bill was actually introduced, it was believed by *Railway Age* to have been intended more to provoke discussion than to get enactment in the sitting session of Congress.[23]

Discussion was indeed stirred. At a dinner of the Hartford (Connecticut) Chamber of Commerce, Eastman was asked by a dinner guest a question which Eastman recalled as "something like this: 'Do you believe that the Government can conduct a business as well as a private individual?' " [24] In a typically long answer, with four enclosures, Eastman wrote, "I believe it to be quite possible for the Federal Government to attain as high a level of average efficiency as private individuals attain, but this does not mean either that I would favor the conduct of business generally by the Government, or that the Government could always be counted upon to do a good job." He thought that public ownership and operation could be made to take such a "form that as good and as enterprising management can be had as under private ownership and operation, in fact better than has characterized private ownership and operation, on the average, in the past." Evidence of this was the experience of the Boston Elevated Railway Company, the Eastern Massachusetts Railway Company, the Canadian National

Railway, and the Central Electricity Board and the London Passenger Transportation Board in Britain.

The president of the New York Central was not to be taken in by any reasoned argument supported by evidence. Public ownership would add too much to the national debt and would also lead to the nationalization of other industries supplying the railroads. But the crusher in the argument against public ownership was the inevitable substitution of the principle of patronage for the principle of merit which was said to characterize the selection of personnel in the railroad industry, including presidents. Said the president of the New York Central: "Politics lives on jobs, as you all know. It is obvious that under a government which is based on the political party system, the railroads under a system of government ownership would be administered primarily for the need of that system. Under government ownership the job of every one of a million railroad employees sooner or later would become a political prize, with merit and experience taking a back seat." [25] But, although railroad presidents might want to protect the merit system of the American railroads, some of the owners, responding to the "law of reversible opinions," were supporting the agitation for public ownership. Congressman Sam Rayburn, chairman of the House Committee on Interstate and Foreign Commerce, said that holders of junior railroad bonds were playing an important part in the agitation.[26] The Railway Labor Executives Association eventually got into the public debate started by Senator Wheeler and, after passing a resolution favoring government ownership as the only positive method of improving services and abolishing private financing, appointed a committee to direct a nationwide campaign for federal ownership.[27]

Railway Age was quite tart about the entry of the Labor Railway Executives Association into the public discussion, imputing to the unions motives of which the carriers were assumed to be free. The unions were acting "apparently on the theory that the American public in the role of taxpayer would prove a more generous employer than it is in the capacity of shippers and passengers"; the unions were also assumed to believe that "Uncle Sam, operating with public money, would be less interested in earning interest charges than private investors." [28] The unions were just interested in money and jobs. The president of the New York Central was interested in the merit system.

The RLEA committee established an office in Washington for the purpose of conducting a campaign in the second session of the Seventy-fourth Congress in support of the Wheeler Bill.[29] On the other hand, the executive vice-president of the Transportation Association of America announced plans for a nation wide drive to crystallize opposition to public ownership of the railroads. He said, "If government ownership comes the last line in the trenches against state socialism will be gone";[30] and he called for a million members to subscribe a dollar each, in addition to contributions from large and small businesses, presumably to keep the trenches manned with fighting public relations men.

This rapidly developing storm of windy propaganda blew itself out fairly quickly. Neither Wheeler nor the Railway Labor Executives Association seemed to be seriously interested in anything more than building up a head of pressure that they could direct towards the accomplishment of more modest goals that they thought they could get and really wanted; for example, railroad pensions, protection against dismissals, and other forms of security enacted into legislation. For a while, however, they talked hard talk. On December 18, 1935, the RLEA committee sent a missive to every member of Congress attacking the "present absentee control by great banking institutions." They suggested that "the only way out of the morass in which the roads have been placed by bankers is over the road that leads to government ownership and democratic control of the main arteries of commere — the railroads." [31] Congressman Lundeen of Minnesota threw another bill on the fire to keep it burning brightly, a bill to provide for government ownership of the railroads like the Wheeler and Maverick bills.[32] But the big play was not for government ownership. Labor unions wanted most of all a guarantee that their members would not be fired. Section 7(b) of the Emergency Railroad Transportation Act took care of the unions for three years. They moved to establish the same protection in separate legislation — the Wheeler-Crosser Bill,[33] providing thereby against the time — which was to be soon — when the Emergency Railroad Transportation Act would expire and the federal coordinator with it. Early in 1936, the feint towards public ownership was abandoned, energies were concentrated to get the Wheeler-Crosser Bill through Congress, and the price for this nuisance legislation was the Washington Agreement of 1936, in which the carriers and the unions came to terms on dismissals and agreed to scuttle the Emergency Railroad Transportation Act and the federal coordinator. Wheeler announced that he was not going to bring up the public ownership bill at the current session of Congress, and the Railway Labor Executives Association Committee struck its tent and silently stole away to St. Louis.[34] No hearings were held on the bill.[35]

In his last report as coordinator, Eastman said that in the previous year's report, "The conclusion was reached that conditions are not clearly propitious for public ownership or for the enforced unification of the companies into a few great systems." [36] The propitious season never seemed to come while he was coordinator but one of his letters exhibited real doubt whether he should not have pushed hard for government ownership. In corresponding with a recent doctor of philosophy who had written a dissertation on Eastman's work, he noted that his biographer had been perplexed by some of Eastman's apparent inconsistencies during his career as a public servant "and by a certain hesitation in action." [37] Eastman said, "On hesitation of action in issuing orders as Coordinator, I . . . am confident of my ground. There have been excellent reasons for not issuing them." And then he said,

My one feeling of doubt is on the subject of Government acquisition of the railroads. I have not recommended such acquisition since I have been Coordinator, although prior expressions of belief indicated such a recommendation. Conditions have been such, however, that I have shrunk from advocating present acquisition. I think this was sound judgment, but it may have been weakness. All that I am sure of is that I have followed the best light I had.

And it may in fact have been weakness and the loss of opportunity. The quickness with which the carriers organized a propaganda campaign to combat the propaganda campaign of the RLEA indicates that the carriers were certainly not in a mood passively to have the centers of carrier decision moved from the constituent corporations in the railroad industry to Washington. It is quite likely, therefore, that even if Eastman had come out strongly in favor of the public ownership of the railroads, he would have en-

countered a first class combat. But if he were to wait until there
was no prospect of vigorous opposition, he might have waited
forever.

As Eastman himself said in his letter to Professor Cover, his
vacillation may have been weakness. By 1936 he was certainly not
as fearful that the government would be buying a dead horse as
he was in 1933. He might have wholeheartedly entered into the
plans of Wheeler and others to promote the idea of public ownership if he could have been sure that Wheeler was not just maneuvering. His previous feeling that the unions were hostile seemed to
have some support in the event. The unions organized and paid
money to thump the tubs for public ownership. Had he really
moved closer to the unions in 1935 and 1936, he might have
achieved one of his goals, if not public ownership, perhaps, then,
the establishment of a permanent federal coordinator. He did none
of these things. He seemed to be on dead center, moving neither
towards the carriers nor the unions. It is conceivable that a bold
stand on public ownership in 1935 and 1936, which he believed
was the logical solution to the railroad confusion, would have cost
Eastman little more than the precarious goodwill of people who
were to whisk him out of office as federal coordinator anyway.

Grand Consolidations

Public ownership totally displaces private decision and concen-
trates all ultimate decisional authority in a central place. What
Eastman called "grand consolidation" would have reduced the
then existing 700 centers of decision to a small number, 21 say, as
in the ICC plan of 1929, or 7, as provided in the Prince plan of
1933. In a sense, most of the principal Class I railroads today are
"consolidations." The Burlington, for example, was put together
by the absorption of some 200 smaller railroad lines. The National
Resources Planning Board said in 1942, "There have been at one
time or another some 6,000 independent railroad concerns in the
United States," [38] but the trend towards concentration eliminated
more than 80 per cent of them as independent centers of decision
and policy. A committee of the Association of American Railroads
has pointed to this trend as evidence that the railroads, by themselves, move towards consolidation, and that therefore government
action to force this result is mischievous. The talismanic phrase is

"consolidation along natural and evolutionary lines," the implication of which is that there is a wholesome social force that, if left alone, will shape the pattern of railroad organizations to conform to an optimum relationship among the constituent parts of the industry.[39] The AAR has asserted that "If left to themselves, no doubt the railroads gradually would have evolved a number of consolidated systems, created along natural lines in ordinary course of business. They were not permitted to do so, the obstacle, so far as the federal government is concerned, being interposed almost accidentally." [40] The obstacle was the application of the antitrust laws to the railroads in the case of *United States* v. *Trans-Missouri Freight Association*.[41]

The story of the attempt of the Department of Justice to curb the Darwinian rivalry of the Hills, the Harrimans, and their like, and to mitigate the development of consolidations "along natural and evolutionary lines" need not be recounted here. It is enough to recognize that after 1890, the official policy of the United States, as expressed in the Sherman Antitrust Act and later in the Clayton Act, was the enforcement of competition, not only in industry and manufacturing and retailing, but in the railroad industry also. But the policy was not constant outside the railroad industry, and, within it, it was changed officially by the Transportation Act of 1920. That statute required the Interstate Commerce Commission to develop a plan for the ultimate consolidation of all the railroads into a limited number of systems, the procedure being the preparation of a preliminary plan, the conduct of hearings on the preliminary plan, and the promulgation of a final and complete plan after such hearings. The Commission issued a preliminary plan in 1921, asked Congress repeatedly, beginning in 1925, to be relieved of the responsibility for preparing a final plan (the pleas were unheeded), issued a "final" plan in 1929 for the consolidation of the roads into 21 systems, granted a number of exceptions, and was ultimately relieved of the obligation of preparing any such plan by the Transportation Act of 1940.[42]

The Congress in 1920 did not propose consolidations merely to achieve savings and economies in operation. The consolidation scheme was linked to another and new concept in the regulation of the railroads. It was recognized that under equal rates some railroads would earn more than other railroads. The law provided, therefore, that one-half the earnings in excess of 6 per cent of the value of a railroad's property should be paid into a contingent fund administered by the ICC for the benefit of the weaker roads. The consolidated systems were to be designed in such a way that each would provide roughly the same level of earnings under uniform rates. The recapture provision thereupon would become unnecessary. Moreover, the Commission was charged with the duty, so far as possible, of maintaining competition, and of leaving existing routes intact. These were formidable limitations. The outcries from carriers, shippers, and other interest groups over the tentative plan proposed by the Commission in 1921 were loud; and it was never able to do much more than barely comply with the precise requirement of the act of 1920.

It is within this curve of legislative policy and administrative tendency from 1920 to 1940 that the small sector occupied by the federal coordinator of transportation must be considered. As will be recalled, some of the reforms enacted in the Emergency Railroad Transportation Act of 1933 dealt with the Transportation Act of 1920. One of these was the repeal of the recapture provisions of the 1920 statute. With this repeal, one of the purposes of the consolidations provided for in the 1920 act was vitiated. A case still could be made for consolidations; but not the case that was made thirteen years before. Reliance was placed throughout, of course, on the initiative of the carriers to effect consolidations under the supervision of the Commission, and the authority of the Commission to supervise consolidations was increased in certain respects. Paragraph 5 of the 1920 Act was revised so as to bring all mergers, consolidations, leases, purchases, and other methods of acquiring control under a single heading;[43] the Commission was empowered to grant authority to carriers to consolidate when it was satisfied, first, that the consolidation was in the public interest. The earlier requirement that the securities of the new company should not exceed the value of the consolidated properties was removed.

In February, 1933, the National Transportation Committee, nominally headed for a time by Calvin Coolidge and representing the interests of institutional investors in railroad properties, urged that consolidations be pushed along and, where necessary, forced upon the carriers. As if to show that this notion knew no party, Alfred E. Smith in a separate report also urged compulsory consolidations. And, has been indicated earlier, F. H. Prince, the Boston banker and former president of the Pere Marquette Railroad, proposed a scheme of consolidations that he estimated would save the sum of $743,489,000 in annual operating costs.[44] A committee of the Association of American Railroads was later to classify all consolidation plans into two groups, the practical and the academic.[45] The practical method is "that of negotiating and effecting the various unifications which have resulted in the present large systems." The academic method (although sometimes employed by very practical men, according to the AAR) "deals with comprehensive plans for allocating all the important railroads into a number of systems." Since practical men using practical methods had succeeded in producing the worst economic disaster in the history of the country, it is of some interest that practical men thought better of academic methods in 1933 than the AAR did in 1934 or thereafter.

The possibility of making what he called "grand consolidations" was explored at length by the federal coordinator. Before 1929, there was no Commission plan, it will be recalled, and railroad managers, without Commission approval (because none was needed) and largely through the device of the holding company, scrambled "for properties thought to be of strategic importance . . '. The whole tendency was unhealthy, because it resulted in speculative rises in stock prices, the investment of capital on improvident terms, and preoccupation of railroad executives in empire planning." [46] It is undoubted that this form of consolidation "along natural and evolutionary lines" quickened the interests of Eastman in "academic" methods of achieving consolidation, as it had Coolidge, Smith, and Prince.[47]

Eastman therefore turned over the Prince plan to William B. Poland, a man of considerable railroad experience as an engineer and as an administrator in the United States and abroad, for analysis and recommendation; and he employed Leslie Craven, a member of the faculty at the law school of Duke University, to study, among other things, the legal aspects of grand consolidation plans. The Prince plan proposed the consolidation of the railroads of the country into seven systems, one in the Eastern Region and three each in the Western and Southern Regions. The estimated savings in operating expenses were based upon 1932 traffic figures.

As such, the savings would have accounted for about 30 per cent of the operating expenses in that year; and, instead of deficits, it was estimated that the roads would have had earnings on their capital stock of amounts ranging from 1.8 to 13.9 per cent.[48] Poland's figures did not bear out this rosy promise. His estimate, based upon the high 1929 traffic volume plus 20 per cent (an extreme estimate), however, was $218,000,000. Both Poland and Eastman said the estimate erred in being too conservative; that is, too low. It was less than one-third the original estimate, but, "Nevertheless it is a large amount of money, which would improve railroad net earnings materially." The Poland report gathered force and strength from the fact that the study was made in cooperation with advisory committees in each of the three railroad regions appointed by the carriers and representing all of the principal carrier interests. On the general desirability of the plan the members of the committees had a variety of opinions, but "A majority are inclined to favor the consolidation of the railroads into a comparatively few systems, and those who have this view are mostly favorable to a scheme somewhat like that of the 'Prince Plan.' " [49] Private testimony somewhat later by John W. Barriger, the original author of the Prince plan and one of those who worked with the coordinator while the survey was being made, explained both the conservatism of the Poland estimate and the attitude of the committees towards consolidation. After explaining some of the differences of assumption originally made by the Prince plan and the Poland report, Mr. Barriger said, "The Poland Committee disregarded many of these (opportunities for saving through unified operation) in the interest of maximum conservatism. It so happened that the Poland Committee included several members who were much opposed to large-scale consolidation in any form and I think that the majority members whittled down the figure to one which the dissenters would accept in order that the report would have the signature of all of the committee members." [50] It is entirely possible, therefore, that the savings in operating expenses to be achieved through some form of sweeping consolidation such as the Prince plan were more than the Poland estimate. Whatever the sum, as Eastman indeed said truly, it was probably a "large amount of money."

In the opinion of Leslie Craven, there was ample constitutional authority in Congress to require compulsory consolidations of a kind to save between a quarter and a half billion dollars a year in operating expenses. He favored compulsory consolidation because "thirteen years of experience under the Transportation Act have demonstrated that if there are to be consolidations, they must be compulsory," and he mentioned the "egotism and individuality of the separate managements, together with the inherent difficulties of their consolidating the properties themselves" as tending to make it unlikely that consolidations could come to pass very soon. He proposed legislation to require consolidation within and before the end of a relatively short period, suggesting four years, and succeeding such coordinating activities as might be accomplished under the Emergency Railroad Transportation Act through the office of the federal coordinator of transportation. Corporations chartered by the federal government were to be created to "hold the consolidated systems," such corporations to be private enterprises but upon the boards of which there would be public representatives, who would be members of the staff of a permanent federal coordinator. Thus, as early as 1933, the establishment of a permanent federal coordinator was proposed, a recommendation to which Eastman would return. In Craven's plan, the permanent coordinator was a central figure. On the basis of legislation which Congress would have to enact, the coordinator would promulgate the consolidation plans, prescribing the groups and the constituent lines, and indicate which of the several alternative methods of consolidation should be followed. The statute was to permit him to require compulsory consolidation in a proceeding somewhat like the reorganization proceedings prescribed for bankruptcies. Consolidation was to be effected by an exchange of securities without cash; and overcapitalized companies in consolidation proceedings were to be reorganized. There was to be an "amalgamation board," established as a special administrative tribunal, with power to approve or modify the proposed plans. Its findings of fact were to be final unless arbitrary or based on errors of law.

But, although the pressures from certain quarters to effect grand consolidations was strong, Eastman did not recommend this course. He said,

Any attempt to make such a plan effective speedily would require new legislation. It would precipitate a controversy in which many railroads, many communities, and labor would join with equal vigor and from which it would be difficult to emerge. Disregarding this practical difficulty, I am convinced that such a consolidation would have to be compelled and that it would not be wise, even if it be legally possible, to force so radical and far-reaching a change upon the country under present conditions. Nor am I persuaded of the merits of any plan of consolidating the railroads into a very few systems which would follow and emphasize regional lines, and retain, but at the same time vitally disrupt, competitive conditions.[51]

His comment that grand consolidation was "so radical and far-reaching a change" might seem hard to understand when it is remembered that such consolidation had theoretically been the law of the land since 1920, and the Interstate Commerce Commission had promulgated a grand consolidation scheme in 1929, which could be changed but to which presumably all subordinate proposals for merger or consolidation were expected to conform. But the Craven plan called for *compulsory* consolidations. The radical part of the Coolidge, Smith, Prince proposals was that somebody make the carriers do what Congress said thirteen years before they ought to do. We have seen that the Commission wished to be relieved of the task of making and putting consolidation plans into effect; and so it was, eventually. Eastman was not ready to take it on because of the resistance to it that could be forecast, resistance by carriers, communities, labor, and others.

Although Eastman did not feel that he was in a position in 1933 to recommend grand consolidations, he did not abandon the possibility entirely. He said in 1935 that many felt that the large economies and improvements in service "which are possible through collective action and coordination by the railroads can only be secured through large-scale consolidation or other forms of actual unification." [52] He again went over the disadvantages and the advantages of consolidations, repeating from his *First Report* that the one defect of the Prince plan was that it sought to abate competitive waste but retained railroad competition in considerable measure. But he could not bring himself to recommend such consolidations because he felt that they were neither desirable nor feasible. In 1935, he was still hopeful (on what evidence it is difficult to see) that important savings could be made by wooing the carriers to do voluntarily what they had indicated they were not going to do at all. In 1936, he was prepared to recommend — not grand consolidations to be sure — but specific encouragement to amalgamation, merger, and unification in certain specific local situations. But the superior method of eliminating waste and duplication was "greater cooperation and coordination of operations," which would produce "much less uneven and unbalanced change in the competitive situation than would be brought about by concentration of the companies into a few great systems." [53]

Ralph Budd, president of the Chicago, Burlington, and Quincy Railroad, was more decisive than Eastman. While Eastman weighed the advantages and disadvantages of compulsory grand consolidations, which he hesitated to endorse, and argued for various small consolidations and pooling arrangements which the carriers showed little promise of accepting, Budd was saying that extensive consolidation appealed to him as the method holding most promise of "really substantial economies and operating advantages, as well as opportunity to improve the service." [54] Budd said that a reduction of the number of railways from 866 operating companies to about 20 "would eliminate a tremendous amount of overhead organization, would enable the traffic to be concentrated on the most favorable routes, using the best parts of the several lines as they now exist, and would automatically bring about the most desirable type of coordination of terminals, coordination under a few strong ownerships." Both the advantages of private operation and of competition would be preserved and maintained. Indeed the desirable features of competition would be enhanced "because the lesser number of strong roads, able as well as willing to give good service, would insure a higher quality of competition than can be obtained from too many lines competing with each other, and weakening each other by excessive competition." The rights of employees and of stockholders in such consolidations would be scrupulously preserved, and Budd, for the former, suggested that forms of dismissal compensation could and should be worked out to protect workers.

The talk about planned consolidations, voluntary or otherwise, turned out to be just that — talk — in the period of the federal coordinator. It was also to be talk later, for, although there was a strong move to secure such consolidations in 1938 and thereafter, the movement came to nothing. Indeed, the Transportation Act of

1940, as has been said, relieved the Interstate Commerce Commission of the duty of prescribing a consolidation plan, and the concept of planned consolidations was to be abandoned as the policy of the United States. At one point in 1937, even the conservative *Traffic World* said, "We have always opposed compulsory consolidation, but our opposition has been largely on the ground that the railroads ought to have their chance to bring about voluntary consolidation in a natural way. Well, they have had that chance; they have profited nothing by it; perhaps the time has come to advocate compulsory consolidation." [55] But the carriers resisted, and the carriers were joined by labor unions and many community interests and pressures, some of them doubtless stimulated by the carriers. A presidential committee of three Interstate Commerce Commissioners, known inevitably as the committee of three, recommended in 1938 that a federal transportation authority be established for two years to plan and promote carrier action to eliminate waste and to aid coordination and consolidation.[56] There were other recommendations also in an effort to improve the chronic diseases of the railroad industry. Congress made no move on these recommendations and President Roosevelt appointed a group of three railroad executives and three union representatives, known just as inevitably as the committee of six, to make recommendations to improve the regulation of transportation. The committee of three gave consolidation a high place; the committee of six gave consolidation a minor place and recommended that the Commission be relieved of responsibility for making a general plan of consolidation, which eventually was done.[57]

The record of the federal coordinator on consolidations is one of hesitation and confusion. At no point did the coordinator seem to be clear-cut in his thought about consolidations. He showed an invincible preference throughout for exhortation and encouragement to the carriers. Although he sometimes referred to the possibility that consolidations would have to be coerced, because the carriers would be neither exhorted nor encouraged, nothing of this sort was attempted. He was always impressed by the power of the railroads to make things difficult if they were to be crossed, and he showed a persistent desire to avoid such difficulty. His attitude on consolidations was therefore very much like his attitude on public ownership, tentative, approving, doubtful, hesitant, and elaborately cautious. In a time that may have called for bold strokes, he preferred to wield a small brush to execute miniatures of policy. But his approach to this and other aspects of transportation regulation should be viewed in relation to the administration of which he was a part, even though he expressed doubt as to whether he belonged to it. There was no clear-cut policy there, either, and numerous agents and agencies were pulling this way and that in the restless struggle of competing views, programs, and program makers. Although it was a time of bold action in some degree, it was also a time of contradictory efforts, in which economy was vying with deficit spending as a government policy; efforts were directed towards increasing the real wages of workers while increasing the cost of food by enhancing the prices received by farmers; and competition was contradicted by the program for the cartelization of industry through the National Industrial Recovery Administration. The conciliation of these competing aims took place at the political level, understandably, but, while the conciliation was going forward, the coordinator had no very clear line to pursue.

Railroads and the NRA

One illustration of the difficulty encountered by Eastman is supplied by the policy of the administration towards the National Industry Recovery Administration and the collateral question of the relation between the NRA and the railroads. The codes were a device for permitting the dominant members of an industry to write the rules by which an industry should be governed. These rules, although adopted by private decision, nevertheless were given the character of officiality by the National Industrial Recovery Act and condign punishments were prescribed for violation. In political terms, grand consolidation and code-making under the NRA were both examples of external coordination, the principal characteristic of which is the transfer to a single member or to an outside agency of the autonomous power to decide matters of policy of the separated elements of a collectivity. The external agent under the NRA was the code authority. The procedure of code-making conceivably might have become available to the railroads as a method of coordinating their activities so as to eliminate waste and other preventable expense, but this was not done. The

Emergency Railroad Transportation Act of 1933 was the special arrangement provided for the railroad industry, the coordinating committees took the place of the code authority, and the coordinator took the place of the administrator of the NRA.

But the substitution of the coordinating committees for a code authority does not imply any close correspondence either between the Emergency Railroad Transportation Act and the National Industrial Recovery Act or between the purposes for which the coordinating committees and the code authorities were established. These acts were different in content and purpose. All that is suggested is that the code technique presumably could have become the technique for achieving the general purposes of the Emergency Railroad Transportation Act, had the carriers wanted it that way. In political terms — as a problem in the distribution of private power — a code authority might have served as the agency of external coordination, the result *politically* being the subordination of the power to make decisions to an agent external to the hegemony of the railroad carriers. Even politically, the resemblance, perhaps, stops with this — for the degree of control that the roads could have wielded over the external agent to which they were supposedly subordinate would have been greater under the codes than under the coordinator. On the other hand, the degree of freedom of individual local action under the coordinator was undoubtedly greater than it would have been under the codes, for the coordinator was virtually helpless to enforce his orders and the code authority, for a time at least, might have been more successful.

The possibility that the railroads might become part of the National Industrial Recovery Administration was not ever really serious, although it did not entirely disappear until the Supreme Court nullified the National Industrial Recovery Act in 1935. Early in 1933, Eastman gave President Roosevelt a memorandum on the question of the application of the National Industrial Recovery Act to the railroads, the chief point of which was that the railroads were already under special regulation in the Emergency Railroad Transportation Act. Somewhat later, General Hugh S. Johnson, the administrator of the NRA, wrote to Eastman to ask him about the Pullman Company, and Eastman replied that to put the Pullman Company under a code would be as incongruous as to put the railroads under a code.[58] The chief reason was that the company (in its sleeping and parlor car business) had a "complete monopoly and is subject to public regulation." Even if it were subject to the NIRA, it would be bordering on the ridiculous to subject this monopoly to a code of fair competition. It needed no new regulation since it was already under the jurisdiction of the ICC. And as to its labor relations, all of the sleeping car employees were party to the railroad wage agreements that Eastman had negotiated for the President in 1933 and all railroad employees were exempt from the NIRA and the codes. Said Eastman, it "is a little difficult to see how a code could well be applied to the sleeping car conductors, who are in the same boat with the railroad employees. It seems to be a case where the tail should go with the hide."

Although he had had a firm understanding with Roosevelt about the railroads and the NIRA, and although this understanding was renewed in letters such as the one to General Johnson on the Pullman Company, the question was not so absolutely settled as Eastman had thought in the summer of 1933. In February, 1934, Johnson wrote to the Association of Railway Executives, "By direction of the President I am calling your attention to the fact that there has been filed with the National Recovery Administration no Code of Fair Competition covering the Railroad Transportation Industry, nor do I believe that any of the separate railroad systems have signed the President's Reemployment Agreement." Johnson invited the ARE to present a code, and hinted that he had authority to impose one if none were forthcoming. The ARE sent the Johnson letter to Eastman, who wrote to the President about the matter.

Eastman said that the matter between Johnson and the ARE was outside his (Eastman's province) but that he felt he had to remind the President of the events of the previous August "in order that apparent inconsistency in positions may be avoided." And then he reminded the President in some detail of the position on the relation between the NRA and the railroads to which the President had previously committed himself. The reminder was enough to turn the trick and the railroads were not required to formulate a code or to accept an imposed code.

Eastman thought that the code technique was a valueless approach to the coordination of different transportation interests with each other — the coordination of water, rail, highway, pipe-line, and plane interests — because the primary dependence in the code process upon industrial self-regulation and self-regulation was an unreliable guardian of the public interests when these interests were in jeopardy or conflict.[59] The code technique was used for the regulation of motor buses and trucks, and water lines, and there was talk for a while that the codes would contain schedules of minimum rates. Eastman thought that this would be unfortunate, if it came to pass, because the "railroads will take advantage of the publication of such rates to cut under them and slaughter the water or motor lines." [60]

But, although the roads were codeless, they were affected by some of the other codes, and Eastman generally bespoke the interests of the carriers where these interests were jeopardized by the NRA.

He went to bat for the carriers over the price of coal as fixed in the Bituminous Coal Code. His argument was not that the prices should be at a lower level, although he thought they should have been, but rather that the railroads had been given no voice in the fixing of the price. "Under the Code," he said, "competition as the word is generally understood, has been eliminated. There is no competition in price, quality, or service. The only redress for aggrieved consumers therefore is to be found in appeal to the Code authorities," [61] where the coal producers dominated. Eastman suggested that the government carry out the mandate of the statute and appoint a National Bituminous Coal Industrial Board with disinterested persons in its membership. His particular interest as coordinator was in the increasing cost to the carriers of coal at a time when he was trying to find methods of reducing the cost of railroad operation.

He encouraged the railroads to take a bold attitude in dealing with the NRA. In a long letter to R. V. Fletcher in March, 1934, Eastman remarked that he found it difficult to think the subject through because of lack of knowledge of what the NRA was trying to do with respect to bituminous coal. Apparently (to him) the policy was to fix a uniform price in a given district without regard to the cost of producing it at the individual mines, and without regard to any differentiation among the consumers, regardless of the volume or steadiness of their demands or the character of the coal they required.[62] Said Eastman, "If the Government is to intervene in business and interfere with the free play of the laws of business, the buyer has an equal interest in this matter with the seller, and is equally entitled to be heard and to be consulted." His best advice was that the railroads "demand a show-down from the N.R.A."

These and other experiences with the NRA confirmed his growing feeling that the code experiment, at least for the regulation of transportation agencies, was highly undesirable. And he was to have a fairly dramatic way of expressing his distaste. General Johnson sent two men around to Eastman in May 1934 to suggest to him that he might take charge of the administration of the codes dealing with land transportation. In a letter to the General, Eastman declined on several grounds, one of which was, "I am not in sympathy with the code method of regulating industries engaged in public transportation." [63] He believed that a "centralized and permanent means of control by the Government of all forms of transportation" was essential but that it should not "be based on the principle of industrial self-control."

From the beginning of Roosevelt's first term, Eastman's conception of the task of regulating the transportation industry pushed action on several levels at once. Early in 1933, he concentrated upon getting Congress to enact a bill to permit the carriers to make coordinations in the interest of eliminating waste and preventable expense. At the same time, he was aware that a program of coordination to cut expenses, although useful, would not meet the requirements for the regulation of a highly competitive transportation industry, of which the railroads were only one part, although a principal part. Many of the ills of the railroad industry were the result of the unregulated competition of rival transportation agencies. Other patterns of regulation had to be considered. Public ownership, grand consolidations, and codes of fair competition — although all had their peculiar advantages and disadvantages — did not promise to meet the needs of the transportation industry. Research was early begun on the need for new forms of regulation, especially of transportation services competitive with the railroads. Ahead lay a possible program for the comprehensive regulation of all forms of transportation in their relations with each other under the control and supervision of a single agency of the federal government. But while the development of such plans had to proceed slowly, and with the help of Congress, the coordinator gave supervised self-coordination within the railroad industry a full trial.

VI. COORDINATION: CONCEPT AND ORGANIZATION

"The coordinator can order, but he must leave administration to the railroads." *Fourth Report of the Federal Coordinator*, p. 40

The previous chapter discussed the more comprehensive forms of coordination of railroad properties and operations that attracted the attention of the federal coordinator during his tenure of three years under the Emergency Railroad Transportation Act of 1933. All of these — public ownership and operation of the railroads, grand consolidation, and coordination by code — were rejected. Certainly the first two of these had a superficial simplicity about them that was attractive. Most of the economic and political ills of the railroad industry, begotten or worsened by the depression, were made harder to solve by the structure of the industry, a congeries of competing and struggling groups, prey to the competition of rival forms of transportation, but unable to abate the competitive tensions among themselves. The creation of one center of major decisions, or of a few, in place of the existing melange of managements, seemed to have some attraction for the coordinator, however inopportune the time to establish it, but the Emergency Railroad Transportation Act required him to bring about coordination of existing carrier activity for the purpose of eliminating waste and preventable expense, and he turned his hand to this difficult task.[1]

The Dominant Concepts: Conciliation, Consultation and Compromise

The whole work of the coordinator was inevitably shaped by his concepts of role and address, by his role as coordinator and by his address or approach to the groups with which he would have to deal. The principal concepts were conciliation, consultation, and compromise; and both the coordinator's organization and program were strongly shaped by the basic outlook these ideas represent.

This chapter considers concept and organization, in that order. Many of the coordinator's conceptions will be drawn from his practice, as well as his statements.

Something of the coordinator's conception of himself and his role may be gathered, of course, from his letter to Paul Y. Anderson at the time of the enactment of the 1933 legislation, when he made it clear that he was no "czar" appointed by the President under the statute to force the railroads to follow courses of his choosing; not even a baby czar, clever as this characterization may have sounded to the author of the phrase. It was also clear that he did not consider his office to be one requiring either a large staff or what the management experts call a "straight line responsibility." Not that such straight line arrangements weren't suitable in their place. Carriers, Eastman thought, could use "a staff and line form of organization, under which general policies and planning will be laid down by the staff and the execution will be left to local officers with a large measure of autonomy and jurisdiction over comparatively small units or areas." [2] But what might be suitable for the operation of a carrier was not necessarily suitable in the operation of a coordinator of the carriers.

Committee and Consultation

Eastman's lifetime occupational habit was to administer by consultation; the Emergency Railroad Transportation Act wrote this procedure into the law. As we have seen, the statute itself required the establishment of regional coordinating committees which were expected to make recommendations to the coordinator for projects of coordination to be undertaken and to work on such other agenda as he might suggest. The center of administrative gravity, in short, was supposed by the statute to rest in the regional coordinating committees but Eastman was given the authority by direct order to prescribe the necessary courses.

His reliance upon these and other committees went beyond matters that involved coordination in the narrow technical sense. Thus, in the completion of his study of the Prince plan, he asked the railroads to supply auxiliary committees to the regional coordinating committees to help in the study.[3] At his request also, Dr. Karl A. Compton, chairman of the Science Advisory Board, which had been established by President Roosevelt by executive order of July 31, 1933, appointed a subcommittee of his board to cooperate with a similar special committee of railroad carriers "in an effort to ensure to the railroads the maximum benefits from the utilization of modern science and engineering." [4] Although the coordinator had no jurisdiction to compel action by transportation facilities other than the railroads, he got the railroads to take the lead in appointing committees representing the carriers to confer with similar committees appointed by certain water carriers and bus lines, to consider the matter of competitive-rate adjustments for the purpose of increasing rate stability and "avoiding purely destructive competition." [5]

Extensive use of committees (and there were many more) strongly reflects the concept that the coordinator had of his job. Although committees take time, talk too much, decide relatively little, and produce more frustration per hour spent in chairs than possibly any other form of administrative activity, they have an important role and function. Their importance, however, is political, not administrative. They are not really devices for getting business done fast. They are devices for getting incompatible and even sometimes hostile groups to work with each other. The experience of doing so frequently has helpful byproducts completely unrelated to the immediate agenda of the committee. In some critical areas of regulation, the only way to formulate a rule is to consult all of the parties in interest as to the form that the rule should take. The committee, then, in small, represents the principal group structure of the larger universe in one portion of which common or collective action is required. As a political device the committee often operates on the principle of equal representation, but this is not absolutely necessary. The joint committees of carriers and, to a limited extent, of agencies established no hierarchy of precedence among the major groups. The committee, in short, was used by Eastman as federal coordinator of transportation as a useful political technique to secure and hold, if possible, the consent to coordinated *policies and actions,* of major interests which the structure of the committees symbolized in their composition and membership.

Conciliation and Compromise

One reliable witness to Eastman's conception of the job of the coordinator was Eastman himself when he recommended that the Congress establish the federal coordinator on a permanent basis.

Such an office [he said] should not assume the form of a bureaucratic establishment. It should be carried on with a comparatively small and flexible staff. It should be regarded as a means of Government aid to, rather than domination of, the transportation industry. The officer in charge should not have the aspect of a director general or administrator of industry. So long as the railroads are privately owned and operated, the emphasis should be on the private management. It should be aided in the development of initiative and enterprise, rather than restrained. The officer of the Government should lend his aid to the promotion of leadership in the industry, to organization for common ends, and to the initiation of general studies of various phases of operation, service, charges, and management, where such studies are needed. He should have full power to procure information and require studies, and should also be authorized to utilize the services of men loaned by the industry for specific purposes, but not to require such services. To secure such help, he should depend upon his ability to convince the industry of its value. He should in short be primarily a means of concentrating and bringing to focus the best thought of the industry rather than a means of supplying or imposing thought from without.[6]

After three years of experience in trying to deal with willful men who were not very responsive to what he thought was reasoned argument, Eastman still thought well enough of the experiment to want to enact it permanently into federal legislation. He was clearly aware of the political strength of the groups with which he had to deal but believed that the hortatory rather than the coercive approach would succeed oftener. As he said, in another place, "The Coordinator can order but he must leave administration to the railroads. Good administration requires, above everything else, belief in a plan and zeal to make it succeed. A project to which the carriers were generally opposed could not receive such administration. That is why voluntary action by the carriers is to be preferred, if it can in any way be induced." [7]

Often, however, it could not be induced. Indeed, there were many sharp criticisms and strong attacks from the start. Late in his

tenure Eastman said that to "a considerable extent the first reactions of the railroad world to [his] reports were somewhat hostile
or at least antagonistic." [8] This is a mild observation, for, despite
his belief in persuasion and voluntary action by the carriers,
Eastman and his staff were often under heavy fire. *Railway Age*,
in an editorial in August, 1934, referred reproachfully to what it
said was the habit of Eastman and his staff "to broadcast through
the press caustic criticism of committees of railway executives and
other railway officers whose views do not agree with theirs." [9]
Although conciliation and compromise were strong Eastman characteristics, the first president of the Association of American Railroads, J. J. Pelley, was to say that the roads "objected to the idea
of a coordinator with power to exercise authority without responsibility in the domain of management";[10] and he urged that the
coordinator was no longer needed in 1935 "since the railroads
have established an authoritative organization to manage their
own affairs within the industry," the AAR.[11]

Although personal admiration for Eastman was expressed by
Robert V. Fletcher, counsel for the AAR, he was reported to have
said at one point, following the line stated by Pelley, "No individual should be clothed with the authority to make peremptory
orders determining how many trains should be run and how many
men should be dismissed from the service. It is too much power
to give to anybody." [12] The remarks of Pelley and Fletcher were
made at a time when the continuation of the office of the coordinator for another year was being considered, and the AAR
was prepared to take over the coordinator's functions in the railroad field. In a letter to the sponsor of the resolution to continue
the life of the coordinator, Senator Burton K. Wheeler, Pelley
said, "Without in any way reflecting upon the present federal
coordinator, nothing of substantial value in the way of coordination has been accomplished." [13] But before the Association of
Commerce a few days later, he did "reflect upon the present federal coordinator" by remarking that Eastman had interpreted the
Emergency Railroad Transportation Act more strictly than was
needed, with the result that the act had prevented the achievement of unofficial as well as official actions looking towards economy. This was doubtless a reference to the refusal of Eastman to

permit the carriers to sabotage the spirit of the act and the plain intention of its language to protect workers.[14]

The eventual reward of conciliation was defeat for the coordinator. When the life of his agency was extended for one more year in 1935, the opposition to Eastman voiced by Pelley and Fletcher increased. *Railway Age* rebuked Eastman for saying in a speech to the Motor Truck Club in Boston that in the history of the railroads practically every safety device such as the air brake and automatic coupler required by governmental authority had been bitterly resisted in the beginning, and had ultimately been of benefit and advantage to the railroads.[15] It was indicated that this statement was a departure from Eastman's customary commentary, which had "usually" been "intelligent" and "fair." M. J. Gormley, Pelley's executive assistant, made a speech in November 1935 before the Transportation Association of America in which he accused Eastman of moving to support proposals to unify terminal facilities only after the railroads had taken the lead.[16] Mr. Harry G. Taylor, chairman of the western division of the Railway Executives, told a meeting of the New York Traffic Club that Eastman "has been going about the country with a spyglass letting the public peer into the affairs of the railroads." [17] *Railway Age* was still punching even after it was clear that the federal coordinator was done and that his office was going to be allowed to expire.[18]

The Power to Order

Since the AAR made much of the coordinator's "power to exercise authority without responsibility in the domain of management" and of the authority to "make peremptory orders," attention may be turned to this phase of the coordinator's powers, because his failure to exercise these authorities in any substantial degree is clearly connected with his conception of his job and his estimate of the limitations of an order. As his work came to a close and the coordinator summed up what he had been able to do and what he had not been able to do, he said that, with one minor exception, he had made no orders because of the strong probability that the railroads would not accept them. If he had had to apply his slim resources of people and money and time to fighting the railroads and labor unions in prolonged litigation, it would have been at the expense of existing projects, the studies, for example.[19] Furthermore, the time he felt was not ripe for orders. His approach was gradualistic, after careful study of the facts and consultation with all interested parties, and it takes time to work in this fashion. Orders that were premature would do more harm than good. He implied strongly that the time was, however, fast ripening. After two years of study of situations where orders might be useful, he said, "it now appears that a number of such situations may soon develop." [20]

Actually, the coordinator misspoke in the *Fourth Report,* for at that time he had actually issued three orders and was preparing to issue another. The first was General Order Number 1, issued on July 1, 1933, which requested the railroads to supply certain basic data on railroad employment.[21] This was made necessary and important by the labor provisions of the Emergency Railroad Transportation Act of 1933, which forbade the reduction of the labor force through economies for which the act was responsible, below the May, 1933 levels.[22] This order was not rescinded by the coordinator but remained in effect for three years. It was finally rescinded by the Interstate Commerce Commission in July, 1936. The Commission had no particular use for these data since they were relevant only to the enforcement of the labor proviso of Section 7b of the Emergency Railroad Transportation Act, which had expired.

The second order was Special Order Number 1, and it was issued also in July, 1933. On July 1, 1933, the Boston and Maine and Maine Central Railroads made an agreement for consolidating their accounting work. Payroll and timekeeping work for the two roads was to be handled in Portland, and all other accounting work was to be done in Boston. As a result of this consolidation, some 115 employees were transferred from Boston to Portland, 118 or so from Portland to Boston, and 70 were dropped. Since the reduction in force produced by this consolidation was not "by reason of any action taken pursuant to the authority" of the Emergency Railroad Transportation Act, none of the 70 workers had any right to reinstatement or to compensation under Section 7b.[23] Section 7d was given a broader construction than 7b by the coordinator, however, and it was decided that the transferred workers probably had compensation owed them under the act.[24] The order of the coordinator appointed an examiner of the Interstate Commerce Commission to hold hearings on the expenses and other property losses of the transferred employees. No official action was necessary, however, because the railroads and their employees settled the matter between themselves, and Special Order Number 1 was canceled by Special Order Number 2.[25]

The fourth order was of more consequence than the other three, and it was eventually litigated. Two southern railroads, the Louisville and Nashville and a subsidiary, the Nashville, Chattanooga & St. Louis, operated the southern portion of a Chicago-to-Florida passenger service, the Dixie Route, that went through Evansville, Indiana. It had been their practice to interchange through passenger cars with the Chicago and Eastern Illinois at Evansville. The two southern roads proposed to transfer their interchange at that point from the Chicago and Eastern to the New York Central, and the Chicago and Eastern complained to the coordinator against all three. An informal hearing was given to the complaining and defending railroads by a joint committee of the regional coordinating committees, in which the presidents of two of the defending railroads participated and counseled with the committee in executive session after the complaining railroad had gone home.[26] It is perhaps not astonishing that the recommendation of the joint committee was that nothing be done and that the interchange from the Chicago and Eastern to the New York Central be permitted to take place. Although Eastman held no hearing of his own, his staff had made a separate investigation. The coordinator found as "true" the facts asserted by the complaining railroad and felt justified in proceeding to issue the order requested by the Chicago and Eastern, restraining the two southern railroads from switching to the New York Central at Evansville.[27] Eastman in his order invited the defending railroads to appeal to the Interstate Commerce Commission, as they were permitted to do under the Emergency Railroad Transportation Act of 1933, but they preferred to go directly into the federal district court for the northern district of Illinois, where the prayer for an injunction to restrain the enforcement of Eastman's negative order was dismissed.[28] Although there was talk for a while that the case might be appealed to the Supreme Court, this step was not taken and no appeal was taken to the Interstate Commerce Commission either, which was the proper procedure in the first place, as the federal district court told the lawyers for the Louisville and Nashville.

These, then, were the only orders actually issued by the federal coordinator. The power to issue such orders was always present, of course, and on one or two occasions the authority was brandished somewhat, although no orders actually developed. For example, the *New York Times* carried a story in which Eastman was reported to be wondering whether he should issue an order lowering the salary of General Atterbury, the president of the Pennsylvania Railroad, to $60,000 in conformity with the action of all other railroad executives who had reduced their salaries to this level at Eastman's request.[29] Eastman had called the railroad executives together in July, 1933, and suggested to them that they cut their salaries voluntarily to $60,000, although he personally favored a ceiling of $50,000.[30] All of the railroad executives complied except Atterbury of the Pennsylvania. Two days after the report about a possible order directed against Atterbury, the *New York Times* reported that the Pennsylvania Railroad had fallen into line. It was characteristic of Eastman that his suggestion for a voluntary cut should be accompanied by a homily on psychic income. He strongly suggested in a press release of August 25, 1933, that "money is by no means the only compensation" of a railroad executive; he also receives compensation in the "joy of creative work well done." [31]

There were other occasions when the authority to issue orders was mentioned, as when the National Industrial Recovery Administration ruled that storage services voluntarily furnished by transportation agencies, including marine terminals, came under the merchandising warehouse code. On May 7, 1934, Eastman addressed a letter to the three regional coordinating committees calling their attention to this ruling and suggesting to them that steps be taken to adjust charges for these services in accordance with the rule of the NRA. He asked the committees to report to him by June 15 as to whether his recommendation had been followed in order that, if necessary, he might "consider the entry of an appropriate order." [32]

The problem was that the railroads gave the use of their terminals to ocean steamship lines free of charge. This practice often resulted in a deficit for publicly-owned piers. The committees did not take the requested steps. In a speech before the American Association of Port Authorities in New York, in September, 1934, Eastman was still threatening to issue an order. At this time, however, he was using the threat to try to persuade port authorities to come to some agreement with the railroads on the problem. The railroads were willing to make charges for the use of their terminals if all of the other pier operators undertook to do the same thing.[33] Over a year later Eastman was still threatening to issue an order. In a speech to the American Association of Port Authorities in Houston he said of the possible charges that the railroads should make for the service they had been providing free, "If they do not, I shall have to determine whether I shall undertake to compel such charges with a view to a just and needed increase in railroad revenue, against the opposition of not only the shippers and the water lines but also of the railroads themselves." [34] Eastman eventually came to the conclusion that the only way adequately to regulate the matter of charges at maritime terminals was by statute, and he later drafted legislation for the purpose.

Eastman not only issued the orders indicated and threatened to use orders as has been described,[35] but he also refused to issue certain orders which were suggested to him. Adamson, a New York lawyer, filed a petition with the coordinator in 1933 to require the Pennsylvania Railroad to absorb the Long Island Railroad. After inquiring into the matter and after correspondence with Adamson and with Atterbury of the Pennsylvania, Eastman refused even to refer the matter to the eastern coordinating committee.[36] It was evident, however, that the reason was not that economies would not result, but doubt about his powers under the Emergency Railroad Transportation Act of 1933. In a letter to Atterbury, Eastman said, "If the two companies concerned were not part of the same system, it would be clear to me that I lack power to require a merger or consolidation. Here, however, the Pennsylvania is practically the sole stockholder of the Long Island, so that the maintenance of the latter as a separate corporation or its union with the parent company would seem to be wholly within the control of the Pennsylvania Railway Company and a matter of management policy." [37] Atterbury wrote a reply saying that the matter was not one for the coordinator to concern himself with. A year later Atterbury said friendly things about consolidations but thought that the matter needed more study.[38]

Eastman summed up his conception of the job he was appointed to do and the limitations inherent in the use of the most coercive authority at his disposal in a speech in Pittsburgh before the National Association of Credit Men on June 20, 1935. After commenting upon the difficulties he had encountered in working with the railroad carriers in coordination and cooperation, he said,

It is questionable whether these cooperative plans, or some of them should be enforced by fiat, either the fiat of a central railroad organization or the fiat of the Government. They must be administered by railroad officers, and no one can administer well a plan in which he does not believe. Beliefs cannot be instilled by order. The power to order which the Emergency Act gives to the Coordinator can be used to advantage where a few companies are out of line with the prevailing opinion, or where it is necessary in the public interest to bar the operation of the anti-trust laws or State prohibitory statutes, and no doubt in various other situations. I doubt whether it should be used to compel comprehensive and important changes in methods of railroad operation or management which are dependent for their success upon keen administration and to which railroad opinion is generally hostile. To accomplish results in such cases, it would be necessary to change men as well as methods.[39]

By deliberate choice and long conviction, Eastman preferred to employ the arts of persuasion, address, and exhortation on the basis of established factual situations. He conceived of his job as the federal coordinator in the same terms. If he had attempted to exercise authority more often, as in the case of the dock charges, or undertaken by order to get terminal unifications, it is entirely likely, as he said himself in his *Fourth Report,* that he would have been involved in litigation. The quickness of the railroad carriers to take him into court in the Dixie Route case and the speeches of Pelley and Fletcher on the matter of the coordinator's authorities were clear signs that his estimate of the situation was probably correct. He would doubtless have spent much time and the energies of his meager legal staff in fighting crucial battles in the courts. It is possible to wonder, however, whether that was not the place to choose to go. Throughout his entire three years, in which he did not know from one year to the next whether his authorities would be renewed, he was constantly being frustrated by the carriers whose cooperation he was trying to woo. In the end, his patience did not save the agency. Moreover, his careful effort to be reasonable at all times, to avoid coercion, to elicit such small impulse towards cooperation under his leadership that the carriers might possess, did not persuade them to support the maintenance of a permanent coordinator.

The Coordinator's Organization

The organization of the office of the federal coordinator was shaped both by the statute he was appointed to administer and by his conception of what he was supposed to do. The stated purposes of Title I of the Emergency Railroad Transportation Act of 1933 were (1) to encourage and promote or require action by the carriers and their subsidiaries to eliminate waste and preventable expense; (2) to promote the financial reorganization of the carriers; and (3) to provide for the study of other means of improving conditions surrounding transportation in all its forms, and the "preparation of plans therefor." The second of these three stated purposes laid no duties upon the coordinator but was addressed rather to the Interstate Commerce Commission. Section 15 of the act required the Commission to withhold approval of Reconstruction Finance Corporation loans to the carriers when it should be of the opinion that the carrier was in need of financial reorganization in the public interest.

The Regional Coordinating Committees   The first purpose, as Eastman pointed out in his *First Report*, was a duty laid upon the coordinator and the carriers together. The act accordingly provided for the establishment of a system of railroad coordinating committees, which were to exercise initiative. Matters on which they could not agree were to be referred to the coordinator. But the administrative road between committee and coordinator was not a one-way street, for the coordinator was expected to bring to the attention of the regional committees from time to time matters appropriate to their competence and jurisdiction. The coordinator was instructed by the act to confer freely with these committees and, as the *First Report* said,

If in any instance they are unable for any reason, legal or otherwise, to carry out the first stated purpose of the act, it is their duty to recommend to the Coordinator that he give appropriate directions to the carriers by order, and he is authorized "to issue and enforce such orders if he finds them to be consistent with the public interest, and in furtherance of the purposes of this title." If, also, "a committee has not acted with respect to any matter which the Coordinator has brought to its attention and upon which he is of the opinion that it should have acted," he may issue an appropriate order.[40]

This arrangement between the regional coordinating committees and the coordinator, a device which some have called "co-optation," [41] divided and shared the power to make the public policy, the division constituting a recognition of the strength of the groups with which the coordinator was expected to deal. The coordinator had paramount authority, since he could legally review proposed orders and issue them or not as he chose, or act by himself if the committees should not act in any matter which he should bring to their attention. But authority and power are different and the whole history of the coordinator and of his relations with the regional coordinating committees indicates clearly that the balance of power rested with the committees. Far from being a czar over the carriers, Eastman at best was more like a lame duck President trying to deal with a recalcitrant Congress.

Superior leverage rested with the carriers because the regional coordinating committees institutionalized power patterns already existing among the carriers. There were three such regional committees and they represented and were dominated by the principal carriers within each of the regions.[42] The eastern regional coordinating committee, for example, was appointed by the eastern presidents' conference, a step sanctioned by the Association of Railway Executives, which urged that the regional committees be chosen by the existing regional organizations in the railroad industry.[43] *Railway Age* reported that the eastern presidents' conference had met on June 29, 1933, to make the appointments to the regional coordinating committee for the eastern region.[44] The eastern regional coordinating committee was made up of the presidents of the Pennsylvania, the Baltimore and Ohio, the New York Central, New York, New Haven, and Hartford, and the Chesapeake and Ohio, the dominant lines in the East and the dominant railroads in the eastern presidents' conference. The New York address for the coordinating committee (143 Liberty Street) was the same as that of the eastern railroad presidents' conference. The western regional coordinating committee was created by the western association of railway executives and was made up of the presidents of the Santa Fe, Burlington, Milwaukee, Union Pacific, and Southern Pacific roads, five leading roads in the western conference. The chairman of the western association became executive secretary of the western regional coordinating committee.[45] The southern regional coordinating committee was made up of the presidents of the Louisville and Nashville (which was to come under the coordinator's order-making authority), Illinois Central, Atlantic Coast Line, and the Southern, and the receiver for the Seaboard Air Line.[46]

The regional coordinating committees gave officiality to the private distribution of power within the railroad industry. They were also the nuclei of power that come to dominate the Association of American Railroads, for, after the AAR was formed, nine of the fifteen railroad executives on the regional coordinating committees were also on its board of directors.

It will be recalled that the electric railways and the short line roads had wanted representation on the regional coordinating committees at the time the Emergency Railroad Transportation Act of 1933 was being considered. Having the right to determine how the small roads and electric lines should be represented, the coordinator approved a plan of the American Short Line Railroad Association to permit it to nominate one member for each of the three regional coordinating committees and four members to constitute an advisory board to work with the special member of the coordinating committee.[47] All short lines, whether members of the association or not, were to vote either for the nominees of the association or any other person, and each short line was given one vote regardless of mileage. The result of the balloting constituted the association's recommendation to the coordinator for selection as the special members of the regional coordinating committees. Representation was also accorded the electric railway lines.

The regional coordinating committees were encouraged to establish working committees and subcommittees since it was unlikely that busy railroad executives would have the time to devote to the daily affairs of the regional coordinating committees. This the regional committees did do, in some cases continuing the committees of the preexisting regional organizations, such as the traffic committee of the eastern presidents' conference.[48] The eastern regional coordinating committee also established a law committee that maintained a strong interest in further relief of the railroads from the operation of the antitrust laws. The law committee was made up of general counsel for the New York Central, Pennsylvania, and Baltimore and Ohio Railroads, and the chairman of the board of the New York, New Haven, and Hartford, who was also the president of the Railroad Credit Corporation.[49]

But while they were organizing committees presumably to carry out certain provisions of the Emergency Railroad Transportation Act, the carriers and their regional associations (not the regional coordinating committees) were quietly organizing other committees to defeat the purposes of the act. Section 7b of the act, it will be recalled, forbade the reduction of workers below the levels of May, 1933, by any action authorized under the act. Presumably this meant that any action of a carrier independent of the act, and not pursuant to it, that also reduced its count of workers below the May 1933 level was lawful and outside the purview of either the act or the office of the federal coordinator of transportation. At the time of the appointment of the eastern regional coordinating committee, the eastern presidents' conference also appointed a committee to work with the coordinating committee in eliminating preventable waste.[50] This "waste committee," known as the "general committee," was thought not to be under the act; and therefore outside the jurisdiction of the coordinator. It was expected to do what the regional coordinating committees could not legally do without violation of Section 7b.[51]

Eastman strongly criticized these general committees and forced the carriers to abolish them. He called them an "ostensibly independent set of general committees" that "had the earmarks of a device to avoid the provisions of Section 7b of the Act."[52] He addressed a communication to the three regional coordinating committees suggesting that, in order to keep "entire good faith" with the President and the Congress, "projects for economy which are found to require consideration by committees of carriers of any region collectively should be handled as the act contemplated";

that is, through the regional coordinating committees.[53] In his *First Report,* Eastman suggested that he had perhaps provided the clue which led to the formation of the forbidden committees by his interpretation of Section 7b. His ruling on Section 7b had been that the restriction of the act did not apply "to any lawful action taken by individual carriers or by carriers jointly which does not result from any authority conferred by the act or involve the use of any agency or mechanism which it creates." [54] And then he said, "Subsequently, it developed that in each region the carriers had created a general committee, separate and distinct from the regional coordinating committee, but with much the same duties." But if his ruling suggested to the susceptible a way to avoid the provisions of the Emergency Railroad Transportation Act, he certainly did not encourage them to persist in their avoidance.

In the message which the coordinator sent to the regional coordinating committees informing them of his opinion that the "general committees" were in violation of the spirit, at least, of the act, the coordinator asked for reports on a number of matters which, if properly investigated by the regional coordinating committees in good faith, might produce the kind of economies of operation which they presumably were seeking through the general committees, but without violation of the letter or the spirit of Section 7b. He asked them to report on the prospects for the unification of facilities, including terminals and shops, unification of service, including consolidation of traffic or train, freight or passenger service, other forms of service, and discontinuance of circuitous or uneconomical routes.[55] He explained that the object of this request was that "the regional coordinating committees shall assume the leadership and responsibility which the act intended that they should assume, and take charge of the general committees." [56] But, as the carriers had designed it, the general committees were to wield the real power by operating behind the façade of the regional coordinating committees, which were to be in the nature of a front organization. The general committees, however, were disbanded "and the regional coordinating committees assumed direct charge of the organization and prosecution of the investigation of economy projects." [57] Whereupon the regional coordinating committees cooled noticeably towards economy by consolidation, cooperation, and coordination. The carriers then turned towards the organization of the Association of American Railroads as a device for governing the industry.

The Coordinator's Regional Staff At the time the carriers were organizing regional coordinating committees, the coordinator was organizing his own office, setting up a regional staff, a central staff, and a research staff. The coordinator's regional staff was exactly what its name suggests; it was a staff service, not a line responsibility. It was not supposed to coordinate; it was not supposed to decide which carriers should make what concessions in order to achieve a single harmonious approach to some problem of coordination, such as the unification of terminal facilities in Chicago. In fact, the coordinator's regional staff was not even supposed to provide the impulse for making studies leading to such coordination. Except as the coordinator furnished it, this impulse was supposed to be spontaneous in the regional coordinating committees, and the function of the coordinator's regional staff was that of aid and support, research and technical advice and suggestion.

The coordinator established regional staffs in each of the three regions, and placed each under a regional director reporting directly to him. Each regional director had a traffic assistant who reported to him and who was responsible for maintaining relations with the shippers in the region. It was the function of the regional director to maintain relations with the regional coordinating committees and to work with the carrier organizations through those committees. To help both of these two functionaries, there were a small number of technical assistants and the usual office staff. More specifically, the regional directors had to do with operating and management economies local to the region, such as the unification of terminals, joint use of shops and other facilities, pooling of service or traffic, elimination of wasteful routing, and the like. The traffic assistants were expected to follow this work also, since the shippers, who of course were not represented on the regional coordinating committees, were vitally interested in service changes.

The original conception of the role of the coordinator's regional staff was quickly dispelled. In each of the regions, they found the regional coordinating committees in a posture of obstructive inertia after they were told by the coordinator that they were not established to serve as a respectable screen behind which the general committees could methodically go about the business of defeating the intent and purpose of Section 7b. As the coordinator himself said in his *First Report,* "More difficulty has been encountered in the work of the regional staff than in any other branch of the coordinator's work." [58] The reason, he explained, was his interpretation of the requirements of Section 7b. "The carriers," he said, "felt that the Coordinator had gone unnecessarily far in his endeavor to keep good faith with Congress with respect to these restrictions. There was a decided tendency, if not to abandon the search [for economies] entirely, at least to prosecute it in an indifferent and half-hearted way. The Coordinator was insistent that the search for possibilities of economy through such coordination should go on, and his regional directors have worked hard and faithfully toward that end. As a result, much of the original vigor of the carriers' organizations which are looking into these matters has been restored; but it took time to do this, and the ground had not been so fully or so well covered as it otherwise would have been." [59] This was a highly optimistic statement to make, since the *First Report* covered only the first six months of the coordinator's operation. By the time he wrote the *Fourth Report,* he described the aftermath of his action against the general committees somewhat differently. He said, "The result was a general disposition on the part of the railroads to regard Section 7b as a bar to any effective action and to lapse into inactivity, so far as the purposes of the Act were concerned. The Coordinator found it necessary to take the initiative to an extent which had not been anticipated, and under a broad interpretation of his duties." [60]

An example of the way in which the initiative passed from the regional coordinating committees to the coordinator is supplied in the western region.[61] After the collapse of the general committee, it was found necessary for the coordinator to go to the regional coordinating committee's headquarters in Chicago. A tremendous opportunity to effect economies existed in this region. The coordinator reported that "the lines involved were reluctant to make investigation and report, in view of the many and complicated interests involved, and the traffic relationships of each line." [62] So, at the suggestion of the coordinator and in agreement with the coordinating committee, Eastman's regional director assumed the task of making a report on terminals in Chicago, St. Louis, Kansas City, Omaha, the Twin Cities, and the Twin Ports. Because the regional coordinator had so little staff at his disposal for so large a study, it was necessary to utilize the staff of the carriers, as the act originally intended. Of this, Eastman said,

almost without exception, in undertaking to conduct the studies with railway employees, the director encountered a desire to protect individual railroad interests. This was quite natural. However, to get anything like a reasonable approach to the possibilities, this attitude had to be changed. To do so required time, patience, and diplomacy. It has been necessary to educate not only subordinate officers making the survey, executives making the reports, the executive secretary, but in general the coordinating committee. The undertaking is a complete innovation and all the planning, organization, reorganization and invigoration of the undertaking have been done by the Coordinator's staff.[63]

The coordinator reported that he thought that the change of attitude on the part of the carriers, their officials, and the regional coordinating committee was under way.[64]

The story of regional difficulty was repeated with variations in the eastern and the southern regions. Of the eastern region the coordinator said in his *First Report,* "The same general difficulty has been experienced in this region, as in the other regions, in securing vigorous prosecution of studies where no opportunity for early accomplishment is in sight." [65] Of the southern region the coordinator said, "Even more difficulty has been experienced in the Southern region than in the other regions in inducing a vigorous and thorough study by the carriers of the opportunities for economy through coordination.[66]

In view of the difficulties encountered in getting the regional coordinating committees to cooperate actively in the search for economies through coordination, it may be wondered why the coordinator did not change his form of organization and develop a large and independent research staff of his own in the field to undertake the work that the carriers seemed little disposed to do. There were difficulties. The original design of the coordinator's office, one that seemed to be required by the act, supposed that the burden of the action in the field would be assumed by the regional coordinating committees. They existed not only as political reproductions of the major pattern of carrier interests — as a device for wooing and winning their consent to the purposes of the act and the programs of the coordinator — but they were regarded as administrative structures through which the major work of the coordinator would be fulfilled and accomplished in the field. They lost their second function because they never seriously tried to exercise it. But the coordinator could not replace it. He had developed a small staff to work with active regional coordinating committees in the field. He could not have developed a large staff to replace the reluctant regional coordinating committees as the principal administrative agencies in the field, even had this been possible under the act. It was probably impossible, for the existence of the regional coordinating committees was provided for and guaranteed by the act.

In any event, a large and presumably competing administrative staff under the direction and control of the coordinator would have found itself nullified and stultified. The information which such a staff would have needed was in the possession of the carriers and without their consent, willing or forced, there would have been little that the regional administrative staff of the coordinator could have done effectively. The coordinator was, therefore, limited in the development of a field organization by the original conception of the act, his role and obligation under the act, the place provided for the carriers as the active units of organization in the field, and their reluctant attitude toward compliance with either his idea of what they should do or the purpose that the act intended they should fulfill.

The Coordinator's Central Organization   The regional staff of the coordinator, although reporting directly to him through the regional directors, maintained a working relationship with the other units in the Washington office of the coordinator. This office was divided into two kinds of staff, central staff and research staff, and all were under the immediate jurisdiction of the coordinator. The central staff was divided into sections as follows: transportation service; car pooling; purchases; labor relations; and cost-finding.

The section of transportation service concerned itself with the problem of the modernization of railroad service to meet new competitive conditions, and the merchandising of such service. Right after it was organized, it launched four major surveys in the fields of transportation service, merchandise traffic, passenger-traffic, carload-traffic, and a marketing survey.

The section of car pooling concerned itself with the investigation of the uses and conditions of equipment and of car pooling plans or other methods of reducing empty-car mileage. The advantages of car pooling had been urged upon the railroad industry after the period of federal control during World War I. Some had suggested that considerable economy would result if all cars or certain classes of cars were held in joint ownership by the carriers, such as refrigerator cars, which were partly pooled through ownership by car companies which operated over several systems. A plan for pooling was "vigorously pressed upon the railroads by the National Association of Owners of Railroad Securities through its president, S. Davies Warfield; but it was rejected by the American Railway Association." [67] The controversy over this issue was waged with passionate feeling, one result of which was to fix the attitudes of the partisans of both sides in an immovable resistance to reason. Eastman, however, felt that there had not been enough investigation of the possible economies to be obtained through car pooling where it was feasible, and he assigned the responsibility for examining the question further to his section of car pooling. And the difficulties were considerable. For example, one of the serious questions to be worked out was the distribution of the responsibility for "the heavy repairs" which (without pooling) are made in the home shops of the owner carrier. To aid the section on car pooling, Eastman appointed a special advisory committee on the subject. Other connected studies were also the responsibility of the section on car pooling.

The section of purchases made studies looking towards the promotion of economy in the selection and procurement of physical property, a problem that has always bothered large organizations, including the federal government. Not the least of the problems by any means is the establishment of a standard and uniform nomenclature and the simplification of specifications. Work had already been done by the Interstate Commerce Commission on the improvement of coal purchasing methods, the results of which the coordinator was able to press forward with the carriers through the regional coordinating committees.[68] They, in turn, passed them on to committees of the American Railway Association for advice, recommendation, negotiation, and action.

It was the coordinator's judgment when he started the work of the section of purchases that the carriers, collectively, had done much constructive work on standardization and simplification but, as a whole, little on the investigation of new devices and practically nothing on the improvement of purchasing methods. Although committees of the American Railway Association and the American Railway Engineering Association cooperated with each other on standardization work, and a considerable number of projects had been started, relatively few had been made effective. The reasons in the main were the ones basic to the structure of the railroad as a system of independent and competing powers, under the direction and control of executives whose interests seemed to be those of the carriers with which they were associated rather than the industry as a whole, which perhaps is understandable. Eastman listed the causes of failure to do more as (1) jealousy between roads and between individual executives, sometimes but not always resulting from competitive conditions or methods; (2) lack of authority in the American Railway Association to enforce its decisions against any individual road against its will except in the case of rules for interchangeable equipment; and (3) the committee method for developing standards for physical items, methods, and practices, where "individual opinion often influenced by background or connection" carried too much weight. Eastman said that "More than 200 committees of the various divisions of the American Railway Association hold from one to a dozen meetings each per year. While no figures are available as to the cost of these meetings, including the salaries and expenses of those who attend, plus the time they put on committee work outside of meetings, the total cost is probably out of proportion to the actual results accomplished." [69]

Section 13 of the Emergency Transportation Act directed the coordinator, in considering needs for further legislation, to investigate the "stability of railroad employment and other improvement of railroad labor conditions and relations." The section of labor relations was established by the coordinator primarily to conduct such investigations. It also had to aid in the enforcement of

Section 7b. The coordinator had no other authority to deal with railroad labor as such.[70] Despite this, there seemed to have been a "general impression among many railroad employees" that he had broad control over wages and working conditions, and he received thousands of letters with respect to such matters. Railroad employees were not the only ones who believed this, for similar thousands of letters were received from "local attorneys, civic and business organizations, State and municipal authorities, and Members of both Houses of Congress. A mass of similar correspondence (was) referred to the Coordinator by the President, the National Recovery Administration, the Secretary of Labor, and other Departments of the Government." The section of labor relations took care of most of this correspondence. In fact, there was so much of it that the work of the section in making studies and investigations of railroad employment questions was much handicapped.

Section 13 of the Emergency Act also required the coordinator to investigate "cost finding in rail transportation," a subject matter connected with the basic economic concerns of the carriers, since cost finding influences rates. The Interstate Commerce Commission had held lengthy public hearings on the subject some years previous to the enactment of the Emergency Railroad Transportation Act and, as it was with proposals for the pooling of cars, sharp differences of opinion appeared and these differences tended to become partisan positions to be defended without regard to the merits of the various proposals. One aspect of cost finding that concerned the carriers seriously was the public relations aspect. The results of cost finding, if expressed as averages, could be misunderstood. As Eastman said, "They [the carriers] fear the true significance of average cost will not be understood by the public, and that where they are below the rates charged the difference will be construed as an overcharge and this will create dissatisfaction among shippers which will be hurtful to the railroads." [71] Eastman put the cost-finding section to work on the development of a cost-finding system that would be as accurate as possible, would translate expense into cost and distribute it accurately and equitably among the objects and units that should bear them, and would reflect as closely as possible the rate-cost ratio as it actually was.

All of these sections in the central office of the coordinator were part of his apparatus for helping the carriers to "coordinate," or rather to aid him in his duty under the statute, "to encourage and promote or require" coordination by the carriers so as to eliminate waste and other preventable expense. In addition to these formal sections, there was also a group called "the research staff" that assisted the coordinator in making studies bearing on the need for further legislation in the transportation industry and other matters. In a sense, all of the formal sections were also research units but the function called "research" was separated off and characterized as indicated. In the early days of the coordinator, the research staff did what might be called "quickie" jobs. Leslie Craven worked on the legal aspects of the Prince plan and concluded that grand consolidations were lawful, however impracticable they might be at the moment. William Poland did the major work on the Prince plan, concentrating upon the questions of economic feasibility. Other parts of this staff worked on more general and longer lasting assignments. The work of the research staff was to become more important as the vision of a railroad system coordinated by the carriers under the direction of the coordinator faded from sight and attention concentrated on the framing of basic legislation designed to "coordinate" the entire transportation industry.

The coordinator's field organization was designed primarily, as indicated earlier, to aid and abet the carriers in fulfilling the responsibility for coordination that was laid upon them by the Emergency Railroad Transportation Act of 1933. The key piece in the organization, the critical unit of organization without which carrier-volunteered coordination could not occur, was the system of regional coordinating committees. Conversely, without carrier willingness to fulfill the act in good faith, the key piece was useless. The rest of the field organization was designed to support the regional coordinating committees. With the regional coordinating committees inactive, the coordinator's organization was somewhat like a well-designed automobile without an engine. He could sit in it but he could not drive. His organization could study the road but there was no assurance that it was going to travel on it.

VII. THE COORDINATOR'S OFFICE

"Eastman probably stands justly condemned as an administrator in the sense that he lacked adequate capacity for delegating to his subordinates the handling of details. In the matter of the selection of subordinates, however, the criticisms directed at him must be weighed against his capacity to win the loyalty of his subordinates and to bring out their best abilities, and against his capacity to instill in them something of his own devotion to the public service."

Carl Brent Swisher

Concept and organization are the spirit and form of administrative enterprise. People and money are the sinews. And just as the individual in his daily activities and the corporation in the conduct of its business are not discrete and disconnected from the social universe of which they are a part, so the administrative agency is part of an administrative galaxy, the elements of which move in a weave of intersecting orbits with the White House at the center. The office of the coordinator, however, was closer to the Congress and the carriers than to the White House, although Eastman himself performed important services for the President as a trusted expert of broad experience and national distinction.

The first half of this chapter will deal with the staffing and financing of the coordinator's office and with his official relations with other agencies of the government. The second half will deal with the coordinator's relations with the President.

Staffing the Office

Two years after the expiration of the office of the federal coordinator, one observer said of Eastman's staff selections

From the very start it was apparent that the total of available funds would be small and that in consequence, the burden of the work would have to fall elsewhere, either on the railroads or on the Commission. The Coordinator selected for his staff only experts of the highest standards. Many were high railroad officials, the great majority of the others were closely connected with the transportation industry. The shortness of the term to be served and the high appeal of the call to service in the moment of national emergency undoubtedly made possible the Coordinator's securing of exceedingly able men from the entire country . . . In sum, the Coordinator, favored by circumstances, secured within a remarkably short time, an expert, well-organized staff well able to deal with the major task of research which was its major assignment, reinforced by continuous free access to the technical resources of both the railroads and the Commission.[1]

That not all of his success in choosing a staff was due to the high appeal of the call to service in the moment of national emergency is evident in the judgment of another commentator,[2] who remarked after Eastman's death in 1944,

He was tolerant of interruptions and tolerant and considerate in the face of opposition. He gave a great deal of time to the solution of the personal problems of the members of his staff. Some of his friends say that he was not a good judge of men. They illustrate by accounts of the patience which he displayed with incompetent or offending members of his staff whom other officials would have dismissed in short order. They admit however that his faith in individuals often proved justified in the long run and that he succeeded in bringing out good qualities in men which others would not have brought to the surface. He was criticized by railroad executives for his choice of subordinates as Federal Coordinator of Transportation and later as Director of the Office of Defense Transportation. They did not contend that he surrounded himself with "yes men," for they knew he welcomed opposition, but they argued that he did insist on an atmosphere of such compatibility in relationships with his employees that he was prevented from taking as employees men who had the best qualifications for particular jobs. This criticism was based on the assumptions however that compatibility in a major organization is not highly important and that a government executive has the same power as a private executive to whip into line able but not necessarily too well disposed subordinates. Eastman probably stands justly condemned as an administrator in the sense that he lacked adequate capacity for delegating to his subordinates the handling of details. In the matter of the selection of subordinates, however, the criticisms directed at him must be weighed against his capacity to win the loyalty of his subordinates and to bring out their best abilities, and against his capacity to instill in them something of his own devotion to the public service.[3]

Perhaps clearer than anything said by these observers is the evidence of Eastman's relation to his staff which certain letters of his provide. He was required to get the approval of the President for his appointments, and this gave him some trouble, as a letter of June 20, 1933, to Marvin McIntyre, the President's secretary, indicates.[4] He wrote to McIntyre to move along two Executive Orders to permit the development of his office, one dealing with Eastman's duties with the Interstate Commerce Commission and the other with his power to appoint without the approval of the President. He was relieved of his duties as a commissioner but was required to submit his nominations to the President. The office of the coordinator was not under the Civil Service Commission and not required, therefore, to follow the Classification Act of 1923 in the setting of salaries for positions under the coordinator. Eastman wanted to create four positions paying the incumbents a salary of $15,000 yearly, and he wrote to the President in support of his desire after a conference in which he had stated the case for his proposal. He wanted men capable of dealing with the highly technical aspects of railroad operation and he said,

In selecting these men I have found that it will be necessary, in order to get those whom I want and need, to pay as much as $15,000 in four instances, all of them key men in my organization. In this connection, I call your attention to the following considerations:

1. The Emergency Railroad Transportation Act, 1933, contains no maximum limitation on the salaries which I may pay. An amendment to that effect was offered in the House but was defeated by a decisive vote.

2. I am not seeking the services of railroad executives with great salaries able to accept heavy sacrifices in pay because of past accumulations. I am seeking younger men with moderate compensation, but nevertheless men of standing and large experience who will be able to deal with the executives on equal terms.

3. The work will be temporary, and may last for only one year. These men will have to establish their headquarters at points other than where they now live; but due to the temporary nature of the work, they are reluctant to transfer their homes. This means considerable added living expense.[5]

He pointed out that the railroads were paying the expenses of the office of the federal coordinator (discussed more fully below) and he concluded his plea with the observation, "Judged by railroad standards it is a very moderate salary, in view of the importance of the position. When the Government operated the railroads during the World War, it paid salaries as high as $50,000 per year, and many which were in excess of $15,000." He was successful in getting approval for the four $15,000 salaries, which thereby established four people in his organization who were getting paid considerably more than he was.[6]

Eastman acted fast in hiring his key personnel and by July 10, 1933, was able to announce the composition of the skeleton structure.[7] The composition of the coordinator's staff changed, of course, over the period of three years that the Emergency Railroad Transportation Act was in force, but many of the original key men stayed on, and some were given increased responsibilities. Boatner, for example, the original western regional director, in 1934 was given general supervision of all of the work carried on by the regional directors under the coordinator and, in a further shakeup of staff in 1935, Boatner was given the responsibility for attempting to promote terminal unification, the last "big thing" that the coordinator sought to achieve before his office expired. It was of Boatner that Eastman said in a letter in 1936, "I have the highest regard for his character and ability." [8] Of R. L. Lockwood, in the same letter, Eastman said, "Of all my staff he was, I think, best liked by railroad men." Of one other, N. D. Ballantine, director of the section of car pooling, Eastman said, "Many railroad men, apparently, dislike or depreciate Ballantine. I think they are wrong . . . After considerable study of his reports and the replies which the railroads have made to them, I am convinced that he really knows more about the car handling matter than most of his critics."

One indication of the value of the people Eastman picked to be with him is their subsequent success. John L. Rogers became a member of the Interstate Commerce Commission. Robert E. Freer became a member of the Federal Trade Commission. James W. Carmalt and Otto S. Beyer became members of the National Mediation Board. Murray Latimer, who did research for Eastman on labor problems in 1933–34, became a member of the National Railroad Adjustment Board. Jack Scott, one of his legal counsels, became undersecretary of the Department of Commerce in charge of transportation. As one writer in 1946 put it, "Outside of strictly political circles, it has long been deemed a distinction to be, or to have been, 'An Eastman Man.' " [9]

At no time did the coordinator have more than 117 members on his staff, in all grades and classifications. But for this small number of positions to fill, he received more than 800 letters from various sources recommending people to his attention. Of this number he received 252 letters from members of Congress, 58 from members of the administration, and two from the Democratic National Committee. More than 500 letters were received from private sources. The railroads recommended some people, and the labor organizations recommended a few, but most of the letters were sent to the coordinator by private individuals interested in employment with the federal coordinator for themselves or for others.

In making placements, Eastman was not unaware of the political considerations that certain kinds of appointment might entail — in his relations with the carriers, for example, and in his relations with the Roosevelt administration and the Democratic Party. In a letter to the president of the Boston and Maine Railroad before his selection as the coordinator was official, Eastman said,

It is possible that I shall have a job as so-called Coordinator of the Railroads. Of course this remains to be seen, and it may not eventuate, but the possibility is sufficiently great so that I have felt it desirable to give some consideration to men available for my staff, if I should be Coordinator. I would want, among others, men in each region as assistant coordinators who would be absolutely trustworthy and loyal, of good judgment, with operating experience, and possessed of initiative and ideas. Moreover, I could not well take these men from the larger roads, in view of their intense rivalry and jealousy.[10]

The deliberate policy of not taking men from the larger carriers did not deprive Eastman of access to good people, however, for many good men were out of work at the time; and even in better times the irresistible attraction of large rich enterprises for the able men is often a fiction nourished by large rich enterprises. It is of interest, however, that Eastman's point in his letter to French was not that there were good men everywhere, but rather that he might encounter political difficulties if he should hire from the large carriers. As a compassionate administrator, Eastman also kept in mind the interests of staff of the Interstate Commerce Commission, members of which he tried to place when they were victims of reductions in force.[11]

Eastman and several of the more importunate members of Congress did not always see eye to eye on the importance of having what the Congressmen liked to think of virtuously as "geographical distribution." In fact, the coordinator's enterprise was so small and the work was so technical that it was impossible to have key people from all parts of the country represented in it. In a letter to a Boston politician, Eastman answered the suggestion that New England (meaning Boston) needed representation by saying, "Between Chandler and myself, we shall be fairly well informed about the New England situation." [12] In at least one instance Eastman sent to one of his regional directors the name of a job applicant suggested by the White House, with the comment, "I do not wish to be governed by political considerations in this matter." [13] He refused the request of Millard Tydings of Maryland for a Baltimore representative,[14] informed James A. Farley that the recommendations of Democrats played little part in the selection of the coordinator's staff,[15] and discussed with Boatner the tactics of resistance to senatorial pressure to hire specific people.[16] Since there was always a certain amount of turnover, the interest of the politicians in the jobs under Eastman did not abate and in January 1934 there is a record of Eastman's compliance with the request of Senator Fred Steiwer for a geographical list of the employees in the coordinator's office.[17] Despite this polite harassment from the Hill, Eastman could nevertheless express real sympathy for Congressmen driven to "distraction" by job requests.[18]

In the main, he followed the advice he gave to President Roosevelt at the end of his second year as coordinator when he told him that good men could administer a poor law and that the President in considering appointments to the Interstate Commerce Commission should actively seek out candidates rather than rely on those who present themselves.[19] He sought out his own candidates for employment and indeed went very carefully into their backgrounds and records, sending out numerous letters to individuals who might have some knowledge of the candidate Eastman had in mind. Indeed, one of Eastman's key men had a previous record of weakness for drink which had contributed to loss of positions of trust and responsibility, but Eastman hired him after a thorough check into all of the circumstances which led him to discount the man's reputation. In making his appointments, Eastman seems, on the whole, to have been more heedful of the expected reactions of the railroad people than of the Administration, the Congress, or the politicians. At the beginning of his last year as coordinator, Eastman said, "In selecting men for my staff, I have generally tried, among other things, to get the railroad viewpoint from what I believe to be reliable sources"; and one of the tests of availability was whether the candidate had and would be able to keep the confidence of experienced railroad men.[20]

Within the official family of which he was a part, however, Eastman sometimes tended to resist the application to him and his office of the rules that were to govern other agencies in hiring people. Frank C. Walker, later postmaster-general but in 1933 in the Treasury Department, sent a memorandum to Eastman asking him to appoint some official of his "department," preferably the personnel officer, to serve with the acting director of the Bureau of the Budget to work out plans for the standardization of personnel and wages.[21] This Eastman did not want to do. He had no personnel officer since he was his own hiring officer and the paper work in connection with personnel transactions could be given over to an executive assistant, which it was. But he had four hard-won positions at $15,000 each to protect, positions that were entirely out of line with anything that the government was paying for comparable employments at the time. His letter to Walker was a long recital of all of the reasons why he should not be required to do what other agencies were required to do. His organization was small. It had only $400,000 to spend. This money came not from the Treasury but from the railroads. The work required specialized expert assistance. "My small army must consist mostly of officers, with very few privates, since what I need is expert counsel and advice, largely on technical matters, leaving the detailed work for the railroads to do." [22] The recital of differences between Eastman's organization and the rest of the government went on for four tightly written pages, at the end of which he said, "I do not believe that either of us [that is, the executive assistant] could be of much help to the Acting Director of the Budget, and we have no time to spare. However, if after reading this letter, you think that I should designate a representative to advise with the Acting Director, I shall conform to your wishes." There is no evidence that Walker insisted on having his way.

Financing the Office

Mention has been made several times of the principal source of money available to the coordinator — the sums accruing to him in each of the three years that the Emergency Railroad Transportation Act was operative from an assessment made upon the railroads by the statute. The assessment was figured at the rate of $1.50 a mile the first year and at $2 a mile during the second and third years. Although this seems a somewhat strange way of obtaining revenue for the support and maintenance of a government agency endowed with the authority to require possibly unwelcome and distasteful actions by the carriers against their desire, it perhaps should be remembered that the principal authors of the statute were the carriers themselves, and that they regarded the statute as a form of self-regulation, the levies being embodied in the statute as a self-assessment. The carriers did not stint or draw back in providing the funds required by the statute at the rate established, and indeed were themselves in favor of the increase from $1.50 in the first year to $2 in the second and third years.[23] The coordinator had available to him from railroad sources in fiscal 1934, $402,767.30; in fiscal 1935, $526,146.30; and in fiscal 1936, $522,399.56.[24]

These, however, were not the only funds available to the coordinator. In November, 1934, President Roosevelt by Executive Order made available $140,000 for the completion of studies of railroad pensions and retirement insurance which had originally been launched with an allotment of $384,000. In order to do this, it was necessary for the President to treat the coordinator's office as an agency under the National Industrial Recovery Administration, and in fact the original labor study made in connection with enforcing Section 7b was carried on as a Federal Civil Works project because of its connection with employment. Another small sum was made available from the NIRA in the last year of the coordinator's official life.

When it became evident in 1936 that the Congress was not going to extend the Emergency Railroad Transportation Act, friends of the coordinator in Congress proposed a Joint Resolution to authorize the coordinator to continue for a period of 90 days to complete studies with such funds as were then in hand. But the carriers and the Railway Labor Executives Association both opposed this resolution and it did not carry. On June 16, 1936, the Coordinator had on hand about $29,000 of which $10,000 was already obligated for printing. On June 26, the board of directors of the AAR adopted unanimously a resolution to allow the coordinator to use the money remaining for the purpose of completing studies and the members waived their right to the return of unexpended balances. The American Short Line Association also waived its claim to any balances. But, although the AAR could block the extension of the act with the help of its labor friends, it could not rewrite the sense of the existing act, which required that the unexpended funds be returned to the donors in proportion to their assessment. Eastman asked for a ruling of the comptroller-general to permit him to take advantage of the AAR resolution of June 26 but the comptroller-general said that he had no authority to waive the plain requirements of a clear statute. Ultimately, Eastman made an arrangement with the AAR and the American Short Line Association under which they gave him in advance their best estimate of the amounts which they would receive from the Treasury when the unexpended moneys were returned to them by the Treasury.

In addition to these funds, the coordinator had the services of personnel of the Commission who were carried on the Commission's pay roll. No estimate has been found of the total salaries of employees loaned by the Commission but the total must have been a considerable amount.

Just as he wished to be exempt from the jurisdiction of the National Emergency Council and the Bureau of the Budget in the matter of personnel classification, so Eastman wished to be free of supervision by and responsibility towards these agencies with respect to money matters. His budgets appeared in the President's Budget as it was submitted to the Congress, and the office of the federal coordinator was formally under the jurisdiction of the Budget. But, as has been said, much of the work for Eastman was done by staff of the Interstate Commerce Commission, and, although he was not an active member of the Commission while he was coordinator, he nevertheless concerned himself with some of the relations between that agency, his agency, and the Bureau of the Budget. Thus he frequently protested by letter to the Bureau of the Budget against cuts in fact or in prospect that touched work of the Commission,[25] in some cases carrying his protest to the President of the United States and to important Senate committees. As to the coordinator's own office, however, Eastman really had no quarrel with the Bureau of the Budget except over the matter of his responsibility for reporting to it or to the President before reporting to Congress, which is discussed at a later point.

Relations with Other Agencies

Enough has been said so far to indicate one predominating characteristic of the coordinator's relations with the other official groups within the administration and with Congress. Within the federal establishment, Eastman regarded himself as independent, if not indeed autonomous, not only with respect to the partisan political relations that normally exist between top agency heads and the President, but even without the minimum administrative integration that Presidents try to achieve, and sometimes do. Eastman thought of his agency as an "independent" agency; that is, one that did not normally report to the President at all, except out of politeness, but to Congress instead. This issue was fully aired in correspondence over a considerable period of time.

As late as December 19, 1935, the status of the coordinator in the federal establishment was still being discussed, and the outcome, as is often the case in these matters, was a compromise. The National Emergency Council was an effort to organize the top civilian staff services of the President in some integrated and responsible relation to each other. It experimented with many devices for the improvement of the President's staff services, one of which was the requirement that the agencies of the federal establishment deal with Congress primarily through the President, since he was their administrative and political superior.[26]

The National Emergency Council wanted all of the federal agencies, certainly all of those outside the quasi-judicial category, to integrate their activities under the direction of the President.

Whatever may have been the case against such a proposition so far as the Interstate Commerce Commission was concerned, it does not seem that the federal coordinator was exercising any "quasi-judicial" function in trying to get coordination of terminal and other facilities and services in the railroad industry. Indeed, if anything, this was rather more like a straight business operation than that of most Federal agencies. But the Emergency Railroad Transportation Act provided for appeals to the Commission from coordination orders and required Eastman to report to Congress through the Commission. The coordinator was pleased with these arrangements, even though the Commission, as we shall see later, found some of his suggestions unacceptable, especially those dealing with the reorganization of the Commission.

In December, 1935, Eastman wrote to President Roosevelt about his controversy with the National Emergency Council and the Bureau of the Budget over whether he bore a subordinate relationship to the President.[27] The council had repeatedly requested him to go through the Bureau of the Budget or the President in reporting to Congress. He could not obey this suggestion, he said, because, as the head of an independent agency, he had to speak for himself. In the last six months of his "independence," Eastman worked out a final arrangement which left his position intact. He agreed to send recommendations and messages intended for Congress to the National Emergency Council as soon as possible after sending them to Congress.

It is entirely possible that this "independence," however it might have been applauded by the interest groups that were even then preparing to scuttle the federal coordinator of transportation, cost him the achievement of some of the goals he sought in his last year. He wanted to establish the office of the coordinator on a permanent basis but, after the passage of the Emergency Railroad Transportation Act, he was never strongly supported by the administration in his relations with Congress. It was surely not because the administration was not in a mood for substantial reform in transportation and in the relation between the government and that industry.

The declarations of independence which Eastman made to second echelon bureaucrats in the Roosevelt administration were repeated by Eastman to Roosevelt himself. In a continuation of his letter of December 19, 1935, Eastman shortly afterwards told the President in writing that "there are few things more important than to keep these independent establishments absolutely free from political influence." [28] He declined to attend a Jackson Day Dinner in 1936 because of his independence of the President, although he said, "I am in sympathy with the President and most of his views and have no doubt that I shall favor his reelection." [29] Five years after his experience as federal coordinator, Eastman summed up his official relation with the President in the words, "I kept him well informed, I think, in regard to what I was doing, but there was nothing in the way of dictation or control of my activities on the part of the President." [30] From time to time in the course of his administration as federal coordinator, Eastman felt impelled to dispel rumors that put him closer to the mind and feeling of the President than he actually was. He told a well-known reporter that he was not close to the administration in drawing up the 1933 transportation legislation;[31] he told another individual, who had reported an item asserting that Eastman stood 27th in a list of 49 advisers to Roosevelt, that he doubted that his standing was that high;[32] and he said to still another, "I do not know whether I am entitled to be classed as 'a member of the Administration.' " [33]

Eastman and Roosevelt

In the period between January 1933 and December 1936 there were 98 communications from Eastman to Roosevelt and his White House staff, McIntyre, Howe, and Early. Some 48 of these were in response to communications from the White House. Twenty-eight of these were drafts of letters or speeches for Roosevelt's use; 10 were comments on transportation matters; 5 were recommendations for appointments and 5 dealt with technical information of one sort or another. The other 50 communications were initiated by Eastman, of which 32 were suggestions for action to be taken by Roosevelt; 14 were recommendations for appointments; and 4 were stands taken in opposition to certain matters of policy or program. These were generally concerned in some way with the maintenance of the independence of the coordinator. Roosevelt, Mrs. Roosevelt, the NRA, Departments of Commerce, State, and Treasury, the Reconstruction Finance Corporation, and

James Farley were all sources of recommendations to the coordinator of people who had written to them for employment under the Emergency Railroad Transportation Act of 1933. There is no evidence uncovered that any member of the administration pressured Eastman to take anyone he did not want. Besides four recommendations for appointment which Eastman received from Mrs. Roosevelt, she was interested in having him try to settle three cases involving alleged discriminations against railroad workers, asked him for a list of the members of the coordinator's staff, and asked how many women he employed in executive positions.

Eastman's relations with the rest of Roosevelt's official family were, in the main, formal and not close or personal. In his voluminous mail, the only people outside his own office whom he called by first names were James Farley, Jesse Jones, Marvin H. McIntyre, and Donald Richberg. And even with these he was sometimes formal, and sometimes not. He said to one correspondent, "I do not feel that I may, with propriety, interfere with the operation of another department of the Government." [34]

On the other hand, he did not want other departments of the government encroaching upon his jurisdiction. He wrote to the Secretary of Commerce that he felt that Roosevelt's request that Roper organize a transportation study committee might conflict with what he was doing under the Emergency Railroad Transportation Act.[35] He objected to having the Central Statistical Board review a questionnaire he wished to send to respondents under the act, because to do so would cause delay and anyway he doubted whether the board had the technical competence to judge the adequacy of the questionnaire.[36] He turned aside proffered help by the National Emergency Council in the field administration of the coordinator's office on the ground that the field service of the NEC could not very well aid in the prosecution of all federal activities in their areas. And he showed resentment when the NEC asked for clarification of some matters in one of his reports to that agency.[37]

In his relations with Capitol Hill, Eastman found it necessary to write about 1000 letters to members of Congress between January 1, 1933 and June 16, 1936. Some 400 were concerned with railroad labor matters, answering the queries put to Congressmen by railroad unions or answering questions raised by members of Congress in connection with the actions of the coordinator. (Besides these 400 letters, another 180 were direct answers to union members or representatives.) Whereas the administration made 58 suggestions to Eastman about employment in the coordinator's office, Congressmen made 252 suggestions. Of the 1000 day to day communications with Congress, 179 concerned issues of railroad policy and 37 concerned questions of policy involving other forms of transportation. Although Eastman considered himself to be an agent of Congress rather than of the President, he did not seem to have a very close relation with many members of Congress.[38] He communicated more with Congressman Samuel Rayburn of Texas and Senator Burt Wheeler of Montana than with any others, because they were the chairmen of the House Committee on Interstate and Foreign Commerce and the Senate Committee on Interstate Commerce, respectively, Wheeler having succeeded Dill.

His formal political affiliations and activities with respect to the Democratic Party were even more tenuous than his relations with the administration and the Congress. Mention has already been made of his passing on to one of his staff the name of a job applicant suggested by Roosevelt's staff, with the remark, "I do not wish to be governed by political considerations in this matter." [39] He did pass on to Henry Morgenthau, then in the Farm Credit Administration, the request of the chairman of the Democratic Central Committee of the District of Columbia, to see whether the wife of the latter could be given more demanding work in the Farm Credit Administration.[40] And in another connection he asked for political clearance for an Amherst classmate in whose behalf he said that although he was a Republican "it means little or nothing except that he was brought up that way." [41] To the suggestion that his many speeches might be given publicity through the Democratic National Committee, Eastman said that it would be hardly appropriate to do so since they were wholly nonpolitical.[42] And he asked Farley to be relieved of the responsibility for compiling a list of applicants endorsed by Democratic Congressmen because of lack of time and because such endorsements had played little part in the selection of his staff.[43] He declined appointment to a committee to nominate Roosevelt for a second term on the ground that he had been an Independent since 1919,[44] although, when Roosevelt won again, Eastman wrote to a friend, "Personally, I think that it would have reflected a little healthier condition if it had been closer, but except for that of course I am well pleased." [45]

He had no close relations with union representatives, and Donald Richberg seems to have been the only one whom he called by his first name. From others he received a small number of gifts, mostly at Christmas time. Railway executives sent him pears, cherries, celery, walnuts, cigars, maple sugar, and several Zippo lighters, for which he had a preference. Chambers of Commerce rather often suggested that they might pay expenses on trips around the country but he rarely accepted because he had free transportation as federal coordinator. He was skeptical of publicity and propaganda campaigns as a method of securing acceptance and support, whether for the carriers[46] or for himself, when in 1935 there was a question whether his authorities would be renewed for a year.[47]

Among the organs of public opinion, he had strong preferences. To one correspondent he wrote, "The *Chicago Tribune* and the *Journal of Commerce* are both degenerate. Their influence is definitely bad." [48] He had a generalized grievance against the press of which he said, "The trouble with press accounts is that they seldom indicate with any adequacy what was actually said." [49] Of the trade papers, he remarked at the beginning of his term as coordinator that he had never been "in very close step with the editorial policy" of *Traffic World;*[50] and close to the end of his term he said, "anything which could overcome the acid condition resulting from a reading of editorials in the *Traffic World* is worth a good trial. My present remedy . . . is to avoid it by neglecting to read the editorials." [51] But he told editors of the *Nation* and the *New Republic* at different times that he read both "religiously." [52]

Although Eastman never really counted himself as a member of the administration (if he had, he would have had no doubt about it), he was used by Roosevelt as an adviser in a number of useful and important ways.

Although handling labor relations was no part of the coordinator's general responsibility (he was merely to make studies in this area) and no part of Eastman's responsibilities as a member of the Interstate Commerce Commission, Roosevelt employed his counsel in a variety of labor issues that occurred during Eastman's tenure as federal coordinator. While he was trying to establish his new organization, Eastman was asked by Roosevelt to comment on a report made by an emergency fact-finding board appointed under the Railway Labor Act of 1926 to investigate a strike involving the Kansas City Southern Railway Company and the big four railroad brotherhoods. This Eastman did in a seven-page letter that reviewed three courses of action which the President might follow, with the arguments for and against each, and a recommendation that one of the three be followed, with the reasons for adopting this as against the others.[53] He prepared draft letters for Roosevelt to send to the president of the Brotherhood of Locomotive Firemen and Enginemen, explaining why the railroads were not under the National Industrial Recovery Administration, although he said that his "ideas as to why the railroads should not be included in that program may not be your ideas or those of General Johnson." [54]

The unions had direct access to the President, so that Eastman sometimes found himself given the responsibility for framing replies for the President's signature to questions raised by union presidents in a private conference with the President, to which Eastman had not been privy. For example, he wrote separate letters for the President on the railroads and company unions, alleged carrier evasions of the labor restrictions of the Emergency Railroad Transportation Act, the Boston and Maine consolidation of accounting work, and the matter of bringing the railroads under the NRA.[55] In his draft on the railroads and company unions, Eastman referred to the already considerable correspondence that the unions had had with him about alleged company unionism on several railroads, with requests that he issue orders and take action, and so on. As to the violations of the labor restrictions of the Emergency Railroad Transportation Act, Eastman pointed out his own action against the "waste" or "general" committees and demonstrated that most of the other union complaints were about actions by individual carriers in their private capacity and not under color of the authority of the act. The difficulty with this arm's length correspondence was that Eastman could never be sure that the letters that Roosevelt sent were the ones that Eastman had drafted, as the President frequently did not indicate to Eastman what action he had decided to take. Throughout his first year as coordinator, Eastman found himself drafting correspondence several times explaining to labor leaders why the carriers were not under the NRA. The burden of these answers was that the carriers and the unions were not being overlooked, and that the coordinator was making special study into the grievances of the unions and their proposals for the stabilization of employment in the railroad industry.[56]

The Rail Wage Controversy   One of the most difficult matters that Eastman handled for Roosevelt in his term as coordinator, but quite outside the statutory requirements of that office, was a rail wage controversy that developed like a serial story. In 1932, the carriers and the unions agreed that the unions should take a 10 per cent cut in wages. The cut was to be operative until October 31, 1933. Before this date, and in accordance with the procedure prescribed by the Railway Labor Act of 1926, the carriers gave notice on June 15, 1933 that they intended to seek a total reduction of 22½ per cent in basic rates of pay. Roosevelt asked Eastman to enter the controversy and get the parties, if possible, to call off the impending dispute on the proposed cut. This Eastman did, appealing to both carriers and unions to withhold any unsettling action for a determinate period of time so as not to embarrass the President and the programs for relief and recovery then just getting under way. Both carriers and unions agreed to continue the previously agreed 10 per cent reduction from October 31, 1933 to June 30, 1934. The date at which either party could give notice of a desire to change the wage agreement was changed from June 15, 1933 to February 15, 1934.

Long before February 15, 1934, rolled around, it was evident that the carriers were again going to file notice of a desire to reduce wages below the agreed 10 per cent, and Roosevelt again asked Eastman to intervene in an effort to get the 10 per cent reduction extended for another six months before notice was filed under the February 15 deadline for such filing. In a masterful letter on the strategy, Eastman told Roosevelt that to "play the role of good samaritan again" was not easy.[57] In the previous year, it had been possible to get an extension of time without discussing the merits of the controversy at all. But many things had happened since then. "The country," Eastman said, "is now committed to a depreciated dollar, for the specific purpose of increasing prices.

The NRA already has increased prices." There was strong talk in Congress about restoring the cut in federal salaries and strong feeling existed in the NRA about increasing wages and shortening hours. Eastman did not think that the merits of railroad wages could be overlooked, and that a settlement of the controversy might have to depend upon the findings of a fact-finding board on the issues. He suggested that the union leaders might be persuaded to get along with the status quo for another six months if Roosevelt could give them assurance that the administration would support their proposals for the amendment of the Railway Labor Act of 1926, which proposals Eastman approved. The day before the deadline, Eastman drafted a letter for Roosevelt to send to the conference committee of managers and the railway labor executive association, asking for a postponement of any action on wages for another six months, on the ground that such a dispute would upset the recovery program.[58] This letter was sent but the carriers filed notice anyway and made the letter public after doing so.[59]

During the late winter and spring of 1934, Eastman was extremely busy doing freehand mediation work for the President.[60] For bargaining purposes the carriers had proposed a 15 per cent reduction in basic wage rates and the unions asked for a 20 per cent wage increase. Eastman was formally asked by Roosevelt to try to bring the parties together.[61] Eastman first proposed that the existing 10 per cent reduction be continued for another six months, with the carriers raising the wages of certain classes of low paid employees, both sides to abide by the decision of a fact-finding board to be appointed by the President. The carriers accepted this suggestion and the unions rejected it, going directly to Roosevelt on the dispute, despite the fact that Eastman was supposed to be mediating it for Roosevelt.[62] In the conference with Roosevelt the unions said they might forego the 10 per cent increase over basic rates (20 per cent over prevailing wages) but that they would not agree to continue the 10 per cent reduction under the original agreement of 1932.[63] Eastman conducted further fruitless negotiations and then issued a statement on March 30, saying:

In my negotiations, I have not undertaken to form an opinion on the merits of the basic wage rates. This would require long study and separate consideration of each class of railway employees. What I have tried to do is to bring about a temporary settlement of the controversy along the lines indicated in the President's letters . . . While I would not say that the present differences of opinion are irreconcilable, it is clear to me that I cannot compose them as long as there is possibility of appeal to higher authority. While I shall not abandon the role of mediator, it is probable that a settlement of the controversy will have to await the return of the President.[64]

President Roosevelt was off on a fishing trip when the statement was issued.[65]

President Roosevelt came back from his fishing trip and met with a small committee of the carriers and Eastman, and a small committee of the unions. At the meeting with the unions, Roosevelt read them a letter he had sent to Eastman telling him to continue to negotiate along the lines previously indicated; that is, to work for an extension of the prevailing wage for another six months, immediate relief for the lower paid workers, and the appointment of a fact-finding board to look into the whole wage rate problem and report.[66] The President's action was in response to Eastman's suggestion, contained in a memorandum to the President dated April 20, that he should take such a stand and make public his intention to do so. Eastman said that he had been "given an intimation, which I believe to be well founded," that such an action by the President "will probably turn the trick with the men." [67] After the President's statement, following Eastman's advice, Eastman immediately went into conference with the parties in interest and urged them to try to come to an agreement on the basis of the President's proposals of April 20. The union representatives told him that they were unwilling to agree to a settlement along the lines laid down in the President's letter and the carriers said that they were unwilling to agree to any proposal more favorable to the unions than that contained in the President's letter.[68] Eastman resigned as mediator, for the second and last time.[69]

In a letter of explanation to the President, Eastman said that he thought the result of his withdrawal might be good because it would bring the parties "up against the stark necessities of the situation," and he felt that ultimately there would be an agreement.[70] After Eastman's withdrawal, Whitney of the Trainmen's Union made a public statement in which he said that Eastman was "unavoidably biassed," and that, "Instead of acting as mediator in this controversy, the coordinator has adopted the position of an advocate seeking acceptance of the President's suggestions. He has gone 100% with the railroad managers, while at the same time refusing to see our side." [71] But the denouement came fast. Six days after Eastman's departure as mediator, the carriers and the unions agreed that the workers would get 2½ per cent of their 10 per cent reduction restored by July 1, 1934; another 2½ per cent restored by January 1, 1935; and the remaining 5 per cent restored by April 1, 1935.[72]

The net of this action was that the carriers succeeded in discrediting Eastman with the unions by granting considerably more to the unions than they had evidently led Eastman to believe they were prepared to yield. It is hard to escape the conclusion that the carriers were using Eastman as a front man for their side; and curiosity again provokes wonder as to where Eastman got the "intimation" that a strong word from the President would "probably turn the trick with the men." Eastman's failure as a mediator cannot be laid at the door of the President, who did as Eastman advised him, or at the door of the unions, whose position in a time of talk about increasing prices and wages had been mentioned sympathetically by Eastman in his letter of February 6, 1934. Although the unions did by-pass Eastman and go directly to the President, there is no evidence that the President gave them what they wanted, and indeed the evidence is to the contrary. The final agreement was made by the carriers with the unions after the carriers had told Eastman that they were not prepared to grant the unions any terms more favorable than those outlined in the President's statement of April 20, when he was acting on Eastman's advice.[73]

Railroad Pensions   Although Eastman's attempted mediation of the 10 per cent wage controversy was unsuccessful, the President continued to look to him for advice in other labor matters. Before Roosevelt extended the life of the coordinator by one year in 1934, as he was empowered to do under the statute, Eastman, who wrote the Executive Order by which his tenure was prolonged, asked Roosevelt not to announce the extension until he (Eastman) could confer with the labor unions about an amendment of Section 7b of the act.[74] Somehow Roosevelt informed the unions that he was going to extend the office of the coordinator and Eastman lost what he thought was a chance to persuade the unions to accept a less stringent version of Section 7b. It is perhaps doubtful whether he could have done this in view of the suspicion with which the unions regarded him after the wage controversy.

Shortly after the wage controversy, Eastman tried to persuade Roosevelt not to support three bills introduced in Congress at the request of the railroad unions to establish a pension system, to provide a six-hour day on the railroads, and to limit the length of trains.[75] The principal ground for objection was that, at the suggestion of the unions, the Emergency Railroad Transportation Act had empowered the coordinator to look into pensions and other problems connected with the stabilization of railroad employment and that the coordinator was working up legislation in the whole general area.[76] When the pension bill was passed despite Eastman's opposition to it in his correspondence with the President and in his appearances before the Senate and House committees, Eastman advised the President to sign it because, although crude, "it is in line with sound social policy." [77] Furthermore, "it would not be easy to prepare a strong and persuasive veto message." He thought that there was a need for appointing the best possible board to administer the act, a suggestion in line with his often stated notion that good men could administer a bad law, but that bad men could wreck the administration of a good law. When the Supreme Court declared the pension unconstitutional because pension schemes had nothing to do with interstate commerce, Eastman wrote a long letter to the President asserting that the basis of the decision was really the question of *fact,* not of law, and urged that the facts could be presented in such a way as to prove that pensions have a great deal to do with the efficiency of operating the railroads.[78] He was still lecturing the President on the subject in an eight-page letter in August, 1935.[79]

Steel Rail Prices Eastman also acted for President Roosevelt in matters other than labor controversies. Perhaps the most spectacular of Eastman's extracurricular activities outside the labor field was in the matter of the steel rail prices.[80] Eastman is credited with the idea of having the railroads purchase more steel rails as part of a plan to stimulate heavy industry.[81] It was recognized that the current price of $40 a ton was a bar to such purchases, but there did not seem to be much prospect that the price would rapidly go lower. During the eleven years from 1922 to 1932 the price of steel rails had stayed at $43 a ton while the price of most other steel products had been declining. Roosevelt asked Eastman to find out from the railroad carriers how much they would order if the price were lower, and Eastman collected the necessary information, reporting that the railroads were prepared to order 844,525 tons of rails if the price were below $40.[82] The government was prepared to advance the money to the railroads to make the purchases.[83] The chairman of U.S. Steel and the presidents of Bethlehem Steel Company and Inland Steel Company were called into a White House conference with the President, Eastman, and Donald Richberg, the former RLEA lawyer, now counsel to the NRA.[84] The steel representatives let it be known that they might offer some reduction under the prevailing price of $40 a ton, but Eastman told them that the "bargain prices" had to be less than $35 a ton. He added that if the steel companies could not go this low for railroad commitments totaling 844,525 tons, they had better let government accountants inspect their books to find out why not.[85] The formal invitation to bid was sent out by Eastman to U.S. Steel, Bethlehem, Inland, and Colorado Fuel and Iron Company, upon receipt of which he would allocate the orders from 47 railroads to the lowest bidder.[86] There is a certain irony in the spectacle of the United States government asking the great steel companies to be competitive in this transaction with the government and the railroads. The steel companies did not disappoint the sardonic spectator. All four companies sent letters to Eastman dated the same day and naming the identical price, $37.75 for first quality rail.[87]

Eastman wrote to Roosevelt the next day with the observation, "It is, of course, impossible that such an identity of prices could have been arrived at without consultation or collusion." [88] Eventually, a compromise price was reached. Morning and afternoon conferences were held with the steel operators and the final price was exactly halfway between the $35 that Eastman proposed and the $37.75 that the steel companies proposed. It was said that President Roosevelt had taken out a pencil and decided upon a compromise cost by exactly splitting the difference. The final price was $36.375 a ton.[89] The trade magazine, *Steel,* reported that "Mr. Eastman was beaten." [90]

Other Matters   Eastman was able to give Roosevelt good advice in dealing with some of the many highly organized interests in the transportation industry, for it was a milieu with which he was in close contact. He not only knew the names and numbers of all the players but he understood very well the object of the game and could keep score. The President received a letter asking him to express himself favorably towards the thirteen shippers advisory boards and to endorse their suggestion that they, the shippers advisory boards, act as a "non-political form of contact" between the President, the "Coordinator," the members of Congress, and the "shippers." Roosevelt turned this letter over to Eastman to draft a suitable reply. Eastman said, "I should advise the President to ignore this request." [91]

In the course of his answer Eastman described the shippers advisory boards as follows:

These Regional Advisory Boards were originally organized in 1923 and are an offspring of the Car Service Division of the American Railway Association. While the railroads have no membership in the Boards, I understand that at the meetings of the latter there are quite as many railroad representatives as shipper representatives, that the railroads take an active part in the deliberations, and that they meet all of the expenses. I think it fair to say that the Boards are regarded as in the nature of semi-railroad institutions. On the other hand the National Industrial Traffic League is an organization of shippers' traffic men which is wholly independent of the railroads and very active in considering proposed transportation legislation and similar matters. The U.S. Chamber of Commerce is another organization which considers such questions extensively.

The draft reply that Eastman prepared for Roosevelt was a noncommittal note of thanks for advice and information.

Conclusion   The political portrait of Eastman that emerges from the foregoing is that of a solo performer, not really a member of the orchestra, although capable of blending his notes with those of the generality like the virtuoso in a concerto performance. A great man for stating the facts and assuming that all men of right reason would be moved thereby, he added to his natural penchant for standing alone a seeming unwillingness to cultivate the support that he needed if his desire to perpetuate the office of coordinator were to be fulfilled. He was in doubt whether he was a member of the administration, and yet the execution of the Emergency Railroad Transportation Act was an important part of the early New Deal program. But Eastman seems to have stood aloof and at the edges of events and outside the places where the decisions were made that were to affect his strong desire and to frustrate it.

The nature of his commitments tended to produce the collapse of the coordinator although they did not make this collapse inevitable. His conception of his job was to help the carriers reduce waste and preventable expense by coordination. He was still operating on that conception long after it was evident that the carriers not only were not going to coordinate, but indeed were going to eliminate the coordinator. In 1936 he was still talking about the need for a permanent coordinator to help the carriers to coordinate themselves. His organization was largely designed to fulfill this conception, and his staff was selected in large part for this purpose. His aloofness from the other branches of the government, except for the purpose of protecting his jurisdictional interests, was also based upon the dominating conception that he was there to help the carriers. He insisted to the Bureau of the Budget and the National Emergency Council that he was not like other agencies, argued with the comptroller-general that he was unique, and told Roosevelt that he was "independent." His entire political posture was governed by his dominating conception, and reinforced, incidentally, by his behavior as a commissioner over a long period of time. For even in the Interstate Commerce Commission, Eastman was the "great dissenter"; he stood alone. Although standing alone is sometimes a virtue (when it is not a compulsion), it can be costly to the stander. In 1936, Eastman was indeed standing all alone.

VIII. THE MORE PERFECT UNION

Today it is recognized that the railroads of the country together form a single transportation system. Joint operations are on the whole of more importance than local operations. Trains or cars move freely from one railroad to another, and through routes and joint rates exist in multitudinous quantity. However, the single system is still made up of a large number of parts which are separately owned and managed, and there is no effective centralization of authority over many matters of common interest. The situation is in some respects like that of the States prior to the adoption of the Constitution. These separate sovereignties in fact constituted a single nation, and they were linked together by the Articles of Confederation, but the bonds of union were loose and ineffective. It was necessary to "form a more perfect union," and hence the Constitution.

First Report of the Federal Coordinators, p. 8

The Association of American Railroads (AAR) has been mentioned more than once. It is necessary to defer discussion of the accomplishments of the coordinator to allow explanation of the AAR, its origin, and its role in the life of the coordinator; for, after his office was established, the railroads were soon convinced that they preferred to coordinate themselves and so set about to do so. The AAR was established in 1934 for the purpose, among others, of wielding the powers of the coordinator when the carriers and the unions should succeed in forcing them to lapse; and it served as a focus of the discontent of the carriers with the coordinator until the termination of his authorities was achieved.

Twenty years after the organization of the AAR, its birthday was noted in an editorial in *Traffic World* which stated the circumstance of its establishment with candor. In speaking of the year 1934, the editorial said, "Talk of government ownership and operation was rising again. There had just been created by statute the office of the federal coordinator of transportation. The man appointed as coordinator, however justly he may have deserved the encomiums heaped on him after his untimely death, was, at

the time of his service as federal coordinator, quite openly a be-
liever in a socialistic approach to the question of transportation
ownership and operation. We do not mean to imply that the creation of the Association of American Railroads was the result of
panic. The facts show it was quite the reverse — it came into
being after calm consideration and full discussion." [1] Mixed motives serve multiple ends and the AAR had several ends to serve.
It quickly became what it was intended to be, an agency to develop
new forms of communication among the railroads and to organize
more efficiently and effectively the power of these groups in their
dealings with governmental and other authorities. But, although
a strong case could be made for cooperative actions by the useful
works and common services of the railroads, it is nevertheless true
that the AAR was early bent upon displacing the public coordinator with a private coordinator.

It was quite in the spirit of the early days of the New Deal that
the AAR was organized. The whole theory of the National Industrial Recovery Act had been that industry was to be encouraged
to regulate itself and to establish self-government. It has also been
seen that the Emergency Railroad Transportation Act of 1933 intended to extend to the railroad carriers the same opportunity,
though with a different type of objective. The establishment of
more effective instrumentalities of self-government in the railroad
field was deliberately encouraged by Eastman, although he was
eventually to be the loser by this advice. In January, 1934, he said,

The states prior to the adoption of the Federal Constitution formed
one nation in fact but they were very loosely tied together by the
Articles of Confederation, and it was necessary for them to form a more
perfect union for the purpose of handling matters of common concern.
Now, that is the situation with respect to the railroads at the present
time. They really form a single national system, but they are separately
owned, and the bonds of union between them which enable them to
deal with matters of common concern are rather loose and ineffective,
and the question is whether they can't form a more perfect union, as
the States did through the adoption of the Constitution.[2]

After the AAR was formed in October, 1934, *Railway Age* carried the analogy to the establishment of the federal union further
when it observed that the railroads had not only wanted to "form
a more perfect union" but that they had "desired as well to 'estab-

lish justice, insure domestic tranquility, provide for the common defense, promote the general welfare, and secure the blessings of "liberty" to themselves and to their posterity.' " [3] The comments of both Eastman and the *Railway Age* were more than figures of speech. The vocabulary of the public government fits the activities of private government so aptly because the phenomena of power in both are of the same genus.

Early Steps Toward Private Coordination

The movement towards a more perfect union of the railroad carriers had its roots in the past. Indeed, the carriers showed an early tendency to organize to promote a community of similar interests, as in the area of standardization. The nature of railroad operations emphasizes the need for interchangeability of cars. This unique need led to early steps to facilitate interchange. The first railroad organization was the Master Car Builders' Association, which was set up in 1867 to enable the carriers to reach an agreement on a standard gauge of track.[4] The American Railway Association, which was to become the most important railroad organization before the AAR, was organized in 1891. Through the years, and especially between 1919 and 1921, the ARA was very successful in absorbing organizations which had previously been independent and in creating new suborganizations for specific purposes. The development of an intercarrier bureaucracy followed the same general pattern as the merger movement in private industry. The ARA, however, concerned itself primarily with operating railroad problems. The area of general railroad policy and, specifically, the industry attitude towards governmental agencies was not organized effectively until the establishment of the Association of Railway Executives in 1914.

As is usually the case, informal organization in the development of unified railroad policy antedated the establishment of a formal bureaucracy for this purpose. Before 1914, railroad executives were not unaccustomed to meet more or less informally to settle their attitudes, but the formalization of this group interest in the ARE created an instrumentality which was to become the main point of contact between the carriers as a whole and the government. By 1934, the ARE consisted of about 150 of the 170 Class I railroads in the country.[5] Three regional associations were in existence in 1934: The Eastern Presidents' Conference, The Western Association of Railway Executives, and the Southeastern Presidents' Conference. There also were (and are) state associations and other subgroupings within a region.

The growth of this external bureaucracy was a trend towards unified representation of common railroad affairs. Internally within the railroad industry a similar trend towards reducing the number of systems was in motion. By 1933, the railroad industry had changed from a large number of independent lines to a lesser number of systems.[6] These systems (indeed Class I roads generally) worked together in providing joint services, some of which were organized in separate associations.[7]

Too much can be read into these parallel movements for combined operations, one within the industry in operating matters and one external to industry in the relations between the carriers and the government. For, although there was partial and piecemeal organization for specific matters such as engineering, research, accounting, and finance, there was no strong centralization of the industry. Despite these experiments in institutionalized cooperation, underlying impulses to preserve and defend status positions, for organizations and individuals alike, were strong. The universality of this behavior is expressed in a remark by R. V. Fletcher, who played an important role in the formation of the unified railroad association which the AAR became. He said that the problem was "somewhat like that of welding the Protestant churches into a unified church."[8]

The similarity between the creation of the federal union and the growth of railroad organization was strikingly close during the depression. Economic necessity was influential if not decisive in both movements toward union; but the impulse in the railroad industry to unite was not entirely internal. Long before Eastman spoke out in 1934, several agencies of the federal government had called for greater railroad cooperation. The Interstate Commerce Commission began doing so in its decisions and reports as early as 1931.[9] In the famous Salt Lake City address on the railroads, Franklin D. Roosevelt criticized the competitive waste in the railroad industry and called for greater intercarrier cooperation. In the fall of 1933, Eastman said, "our national railroad system suffers from much waste motion and unapplied or misapplied effort, due to its ownership by many separate companies and the consequent fact that it is operated by a small army of independent feudal chieftains who fight a good deal among themselves and band together for the common good with considerable difficulty." [10] At still one other point, Eastman lent his influence to the impulse to unify the segmented parts of the railroad industry. In his *First Report,* he said,

The numerous committees of the American Railway Association, or other railroad organizations, often do excellent work and recommend the adoption of certain standards and practices which they believe would be of general advantage. The fact is, however, that these recommendations frequently fail in general adoptions, because of the high degree of individualism among the railroad managements. Carrier officers may resist because of pride of opinion or even for fear that adoption of the recommendation would in some way threaten their individual importance . . . Similar difficulties have been experienced by the Association of Railway Executives in its activities . . . The general situation, in brief, is one in which the numerous separate owners and managers of individual parts of the single railroad system are in need of a "more perfect union," just as the States were prior to the Constitution. The time is propitious for such a movement, because the competition which the railroads now have from other transportation agencies makes intense competition within their own ranks a much less sacred thing than it once was from the public point of view.

The Framing of the Constitution

The specific movement that led to the formation of the Association of American Railroads was started by a group of security holders. Milton W. Harrison, the president of the Security Owners' Association, which was devoted to "organizing the security holders of the country for concerted action to protect railroad investments," [11] arranged a meeting of 81 directors of railroads and representatives of institutional investors in railroad securities at the Metropolitan Club in New York City on November 14, 1933. One of the speakers at this conference strongly urged the members to organize.

I remember going over on the boat years ago [he said] and talking to quite a philosopher who asked me what the three modern wonders of the world were. I suggested a number of things. He said, "Not at all. It is a matter of organization." He said, "The three modern wonders of the world are the German Army, the Catholic Church and the Standard Oil Company."

"If anything counts in Washington, it is organization. I think this meeting is very helpful. The fact that we have gotten a man like Mr. du Pont to take his time, after his splendid work in connection with the repeal of prohibition, which shows what organizations can do, is very hopeful and helpful. It ought to be a fighting force, first, and a force to cooperate with what is being done, and if they are going to do anything that is unwise, then a force to try and put over with the politician the fear of God, and that the investor and the shipper and everyone who uses the railroad, who has anything at stake in the country is going to be heard from in a way that the politicians will not forget and which he is ready to listen to.[12]

This meeting led to the formation of the Directors-Investors Committee, which was to play an active role in improving the situation of the railroads. On January 29, 1934, shortly after the coordinator's report to Congress, one member of this committee wrote to another member that he felt that their group was better able to take action on Eastman's suggestion to unify than any other groups because "in spite of the treatment he has received, the investor holds the whip hand in that he must be satisfied with the new conditions before he can be brought back into the picture." [13] By May 1, 1934, H. W. DeForest, chairman of the Directors-Investors Committee, outlined a plan which was presented to the ARE with the caution that the plan, if approved by the ARE, "should be presented as the plan of the railroad executives and not as in any way emanating from our committee." [14] This plan, about whose source the investors group was so cautious, urged the carriers to accept all of the recommendations made by Eastman in his *First Report* as coordinator and to establish a small committee of railroad executives, representing the carrier point of view, to serve as a continuing advisory group to Eastman. So far as can be ascertained, this was the extent to which the investors actively undertook to organize the central kind of carrier organization which developed into the Association of American Railroads. A subsequent charge that the investors had played the dominant role in the formation of the AAR seems not to be supported by the record.[15]

Certainly the advisory committee of the Association of Railway

Executives, which met several times during the spring and early summer of 1934, showed no great enthusiasm for the specific proposal of the Directors-Investors Committee. Members felt that it would tend to commit them to a permanent coordinator. It was also felt that it would be difficult to find able railroad executives who would be willing to leave their companies to sit in Washington as full-time members of such an advisory and planning committee.[16] Instead of acting directly upon the recommendation of the Directors-Investors Committee, the advisory committee of the ARE instructed its chairman, R. H. Aishton, to appoint a drafting committee of six rail executives (three from the East, two from the West, and one from the South) to make recommendations that would lead to a reorganization of the carrier associations.[17] The presidential drafting committee started its work with a draft of a plan of organization submitted by Mr. Fletcher to the committee chairman, Mr. Atterbury, on June 23.[18] Much of the summer was spent in revising this draft and numerous subsequent ones.

Universal problems of politics appear in the range of considerations which this committee had to take into account. Should the new organization include all of the separate and "sovereign" railroad associations? This is one of the dilemmas of federalism, the basic issue of which is the degree to which the autonomy of the constituent units is to be trimmed, limited, suppressed, or submerged under the authority of the central group. Inside the federated railroad structure, the problem of representation was to be acute, as it is in public governmental federations. Should each member line have a single vote or should some system of representation weighted by revenue or mileage be worked out? How much representation on the central board should the various regions of the country have; that is, to what extent should geography, apart from size of carrier, be given weight? Such issues — the division of authority between central body and components, the relative status of the constituents, and the need for taking geographical factors into account — were all questions that vigorously exercised the members of the federal convention in 1787 and the San Francisco conference of 1945 that established the United Nations. And, as was the case in both 1787 and 1945, the resulting plan was a compromise among the many conflicting points of view.

Some of the members hoped to bring about an amalgamation of

most of the existing national and regional railroad organizations, as can be seen from the list of 80 such organizations, described somewhat ungrammatically as "associations to be brought under," which was made an exhibit in a subsequent hearing.[19] In the final plan, however, the principal organizations that were merged were the ARA, which had handled most of the technical and operating problems, and the ARE, which had handled problems of governmental relations. Both associations had included most of the Class I railroads among their members.

Just as the members of the constitutional convention of 1787 drew upon the traditions of their state governments, so the framing committee drew upon the traditions of these older railroad associations in framing the plan for a new organization. Many of the officers of the ARE and the ARA were appointed to positions in the new Association of American Railroads. Eventually a cluster of smaller organizations joined the AAR,[20] but many preferred to keep their independence and separateness. Among the holdouts was the American Railway Engineering Association, which had resisted affiliation with the ARA in 1919. It did, however, agree to perform the work of the construction and maintenance sections of both the ARA and the AAR.[21]

As to the franchise within the new organization, it was especially difficult to agree on voting arrangements because the individual roads differed so in size and in resources. The authors of the AAR plan faced the problem of keeping the large roads from refusing to cooperate because they felt that on the basis of one vote for each member the small lines would have a say in the association's affairs which was out of proportion to their importance; and of keeping the small roads from feeling that, with voting rights linked to size of carrier, they would have no effective voice at all because of domination by the large lines. The eventual compromise was a plurality of voting methods. It was agreed that on most matters voting power should be in proportion to the operating revenues of the voting lines.[22] For the establishment of standards, rules, or regulations affecting physical property, however, voting power was made "proportionate to the ownership of equipment or miles of track, whichever may be applicable." [23] Partly in response to the criticism of the small carriers that "miles makes right," [24] the plan of organization was later (1940) changed to give each member line one vote on questions of amending the plan.[25] Thus, three different voting schemes came to exist side by side: size as measured by revenue, size as measured by ownership of physical property, and ordinary suffrage. If this seems to be curious, one might recall that the concept of majority rule in the federal Constitution is expressed in different forms, also. A simple head count will enact legislation in Congress. But the majority must be two-thirds to override a veto. A simple majority will elect a President when an election is thrown into the House of Representatives, but it is a majority of states, not a majority of heads. The majority of states necessary to ratify an amendment is not a simple majority but a three-fourths majority. But the majority of Congressmen necessary to submit such an amendment to the states is a two-thirds majority of voting heads.

Geography bothered the presidential drafting committee as it did the framers of the Constitution. Apart from size, as measured by equipment, trackage, or revenue, the railroads had clear differential interests based upon geographical sections. The railroad executives in the North, South, and West had, and continued to have, their own separate regional organizations.

The basis of this sectional differentiation was not only the varying economic interests served in the various sections of the country but the rate structure, which tended to maintain and rigidify the economic advantages of one section of the country as against another and one class of goods against another. The original committee proposal for the representation of geographical interests in the new association provided for a board of directors comprising five eastern, four western, and three southern railroad officials. The western roads were apparently in a position to improve their representation, for they were granted one additional member "in the interest of harmony" [26] at a meeting of the advisory committee of the ARE and another at a joint meeting of that committee and the board of directors of the ARA. At the time the plan was accepted, therefore, the West had six members on the board of directors, the East five, and the South three.[27] The directors have been nominated annually by the three regional presidents' associations and, although provision is made for nominations from the floor at the annual meetings, such deference is shown to the nominations of the regional associations that they are not opposed.[28] The members of the board from the East rarely change, those from the South change occasionally, and those from the West change every year.[29]

Vexatious as were all of these matters of organization, membership, and representation, the most troublesome question confronted by the members of the framing committee was none of these. It was the amount of authority that should be given to the new organization to bind its members to follow the decisions of the officials and board of directors of the Association of American Railroads. Should the AAR be a strong federation or a loose confederation? Like Hamilton in the federal convention, there were some members of the railroad industry who felt that a strong central private government should be established. R. V. Fletcher said, "It was the hope of those who conceived this plan of organization and government that the industry would demonstrate its capacity for self-regulation and, therefore, make it unnecessary for government authority to intervene in railroad affairs." [30] J. J. Pelley, of the New York, New Haven, and Hartford Railroad, wanted a clear statement that the decisions of the board of directors would be binding upon the members and he advocated compulsory arbitration "so that no one can ask, where are the 'teeth.' " [31] Other members of the framing committee, however, took a more moderate stand. Some felt that the penalty provisions that a system of compulsory arbitration would involve might expose the plan to attack under the antitrust laws.[32] Others felt that such a penalty as expulsion from the organization was too drastic since such action might exclude roads from necessary continued participation in such matters as car service and repairs, which would be taken over from ARA by the new association.[33] It was finally decided that penalties were unnecessary, for the committee felt that "it should proceed on the theory that the railroads, if they agree to a plan, will carry it out in good faith." [34]

In spite of the fact that penalties for failing to heed board orders were not provided, several provisions gave the central organization considerable authority. The Preamble provided:

In order to promote trade and commerce in the public interest, further improve railroad service and maintain the integrity and credit of the industry, the Railroad Companies of the United States do hereby establish an authoritative national organization which shall be adequately qualified and empowered in every lawful way to accomplish said ends where concert of action and policy are required. For the purpose of facilitating the realization of this constructive object, the Members do hereby declare that their announced policies shall be authoritative and will be supported.

Article 4 further provided,

(d) . . . On a controversial question a three-fourths vote of the Board shall be necessary to a decision. Any member of the Board may declare a question controversial. No decision shall be reached nor any order made against any railroad company with respect to any controversial question without notice and opportunity to be heard.

(f) If any road or group of roads, members of the Association, shall object to any decision of the Board of Directors, the road or group of roads so objecting shall have the right to submit the question or questions at issue to arbitration as hereinafter provided in Article 19.

Article 19 provided for arbitration, according to which a member disagreeing with the board appoints one member of a special board of arbitration, the president of the AAR appoints another, and these two meet to choose a third. If they should fail to agree on a third member, a federal circuit court judge is asked to choose a man. The majority decision of the three-man board of arbitration is binding.

Lloyd K. Garrison, special examiner in the *Georgia* case, interpreted these provisions as follows:

The most reasonable interpretation of the preamble therefore in the light of the remainder of the Articles is that the subscribing members declared in general terms their intention to recognize and support the Association as an authoritative body without, however, committing themselves in advance to abide by every action it might take. They were willing to give such commitment only in special cases declared to be 'controversial' and decided by a three-fourths vote; even then the commitment was qualified by the right of an aggrieved member to disregard the decision and try his luck with an outside arbitrator, whose award would be final.[35]

That the association was expected to bind its members is evident in the fact that the executive committee did not approve of the 1934 applications for memberships made by the Bangor and Aroostook and the Wheeling and Lake Erie railway companies, both of which sought to reserve the right to resist association decisions affecting their roads.[36]

Sanctions are central in power control systems, whether they be steel or cement combintions disciplining customers through manipulation of a private price control or public governments and their police. The United States courts have held invalid attempts by trade associations to force recalcitrant members to comply with trade practice conference edicts to which they had previously agreed. The Association of American Railroads, however much some of its members may have desired to establish a coercive control over individual railroads, was careful, as the preamble shows, merely to suggest as strongly as possible the wish to employ sanctions without actually writing them into the fundamental agreement of the association. But actually the AAR never has exercised such power to coerce its members as was entrusted to it in the original plan of organization. Only one matter has been declared controversial by the board of directors,[37] and the arbitration provisions never have been used, although the possibility of using them was discussed on two occasions.[38] In 1946, after two antitrust suits had been commenced against the railroads, the strong wording of the preamble, the provisions concerning controversial questions and arbitration, and all references to "decisions" by the board were omitted from the plan of organization in order that it might "reflect more correctly the purposes and activities of the Association as they have been worked out in actual practice, after some ten years of experience with the original plan." [39] Furthermore, a guarantee of right of independent action was added to the plan: "Article 24. Nothing in this plan shall in any way restrain or prohibit any member road from acting individually and independently of the Association or any and all other member roads with respect to any of the matters covered hereby, and the right of individual and independent action is expressly reserved to each member of the road."

The AAR then did not come to exercise the control over member railroads that many hoped it would. In an appearance before the Kilgore committee in 1944, R. V. Fletcher pointed out that the AAR was not a strong central government but a confederation of member units, each of which reserved the right of independent action and each of which has been bound by AAR decisions only when it has expressly agreed to be. As he said, then,

The Association of American Railroads, like the Federal Government, is an organization of strictly limited and expressly delegated powers. I hope I properly characterized the Federal Government there. That is the way I was taught a long time ago. Inherently, it has no power whatsoever. Such authority as it exerts, in the matter of car interchange, for example, is by reason of an express grant of power, binding only on those roads that assent. It cannot make a rate; it cannot make an order; it cannot prevent a railroad from adopting and following any operating practice which it may prefer. The association is in the nature of a general staff. It can advise and it can carry out the orders of its constituent members. It furnishes a convenient and, indeed, indispensable medium for orderly and cooperative consideration of railroad problems of national significance. It depends in large degree for its usefulness upon the confidence which the members have in the intelligence, zeal, and honesty of its officers. In a small way, it is like an association of nations, where each participant reserves the right of individual and independent action, but where many conclusions are reached unanimously after careful consideration and discussion. It is something more than a trade association, but it is in no sense a super-government, with dictatorial authority. It has none of the qualities of fascism.[40]

The plan drawn up by the presidential drafting committee was submitted to the advisory committee of the ARE on August 23. It was discussed at a joint meeting of this advisory committee and the board of directors of the ARA on September 20 and at a meeting of the member roads of both organizations on the following day.[41] Few changes were made in the committee draft at any of these sessions. A resolution was adopted by the member roads on September 21, announcing the consolidation of the two organizations as soon as the railroads representing three-fourths of the mileage of the lines which belonged to these organizations assented to the merger.[42]

It was announced that J. J. Pelley of the New York, New Haven, and Hartford would be named president of the new organization at a salary of $60,000 a year.[43] The tentative name of the association was the American Railroad Institute but this was changed to the Association of American Railroads when President Roosevelt, in a talk with Mr. Pelley, expressed a dislike for the original name because it had been used by so many industrial organizations engaged in price fixing.[44]

Reaction to the formation of the new organization was mixed. President Roosevelt commended the railroads for their action, saying that it would simplify the problem of self-rule.[45] Before the public announcement of the formation of the new organization was made, President Roosevelt was asked to assert that it had been organized at his suggestion. Eastman advised Roosevelt against making any such announcement. He said,[46] "I believe that you should give your hearty commendation to the new organization, but that it would be a great mistake for you to assume any sponsorship of it." In his letter to the President and in a speech made before the American Life Convention,[47] Eastman showed some fear that the organization had been established primarily in the hope that additional governmental regulation might be avoided and that existing regulations might be undercut. Jesse H. Jones, head of the Reconstruction Finance Corporation, suggested that representatives of the public and the government should be included as members of the board of the proposed AAR, but railroad officials were unanimous in their opposition and nothing came of the proposal.[48]

When railroads representing 248,512.54 miles of track (this being over three-fourths of the 296,869.03 miles of the members of the original organizations) had signed the agreement, the ARE and the ARA were officially declared to be merged into the Association of American Railroads at 10:00 A.M. on October 12, 1934.[49]

Development of the AAR

In considering the AAR as one of the complex of power structures in the group universe of the federal coordinator of transportation, it may serve to delineate the character of the AAR if it is viewed not only as it was in its inception, but as it became. The incline of the tree may illustrate how the twig was bent. Not forgetting that the AAR performed and performs many technical services for the member roads, interest in the politics of coordination places the policy-making activities of the AAR close to the center of attention. For the coordination of fixed physical facilities is one thing and the coordination of organizations with a lively feeling about the policies they wish to promote is quite another.

The basic statement of AAR transportation policy was made by that organization itself at its inception. These were said to be: "Restoration of Confidence in Railroad Securities; Equal Opportunity as Among All Agencies of Transportation; and the adoption of Methods which will permit Efficiency and Economy." [50] In order to restore "confidence in railroad securities," the association early asked that the ICC recognize the revenue needs of the railroads, assure the continuance of private operation and ownership, and allow Reconstruction Finance Corporation loans to solvent carriers. To bring about equal opportunity among all agencies of transportation, it requested that the railroads be relieved of excessive regulation, that competing forms be brought under government regulation, and that government cease all subsidies to other forms of transportation.[51] For competitive reasons in some instances and to encourage efficient and economical rail operation in others, the AAR asked that the antitrust laws be relaxed so that "natural" consolidation could take place, that the long- and short-haul clause be repealed, and that the roads be allowed to own competing forms of transportation.

The public representation of the policies of the AAR carries special interest. The association is reluctant to have the term "lobbying" used in connection with any of its activities, because of the word's frequently sinister connotations. When the AAR filed its first report on its legislative activities under the Regulation of Lobbying Act of 1946, legal counsel advised that it was not required by the law to file, because such a minor portion of its whole budget was devoted to legislative activities.[52] But during the Senate commerce committee investigation of railroads a definition of the term "lobbying" was used which the representatives of the AAR agreed applied to the association's legislative work. It was called "assembling and promulgating information relative to legislation affecting railroads, and with the further duty of organizing the States for offense and defense on all matters of legislation, State and Federal, affecting the railroads." [53] Mr. Fletcher added that he felt the definition should also include the presentation of an industry's point of view to the people of the country.[54]

To carry out its legislative program, the AAR and its predecessor, the ARE, have made use of a complicated network of local railroad and nonrailroad organizations which have cooperated with the central association in various ways. In 1932, when rival interest groups, particularly the truckers, were securing from state legislatures what the railroads thought were undue advantages, the ARE took steps to organize state associations to disseminate information favorable to the railroads and to supplement the activities of the national organization on federal legislative matters. These state associations were to be entirely supported by the railroads within each state and were to have autonomy in local matters.[55] In 1934, the system of state associations was tightened up when specific railroads were assigned the task of supervising the work of each state association.[56] After the merger of the ARE and the ARA, the system was carried on by the AAR. Mr. Fletcher testified in 1938 that the state associations "were in constant contact with the national Association, and what was happening in Washington they were kept informed about, and if they could be helpful they were asked to do it." [57]

The railroads from time to time have also called upon various railroad employees, other than executives, attorneys, and publicity directors, to play a part in the formulation of public transportation policy. For example, the assistant general manager of the Wabash Railway Company wrote the secretary-treasurer of the Ohio Railroad Association that he had addressed "all Supervisory Officers of the Wabash System, asking them to handle the matter through their various departments in an endeavor to get more members of the public to express to their Senators and Congressmen the view that the Office of the Federal Coordinator should be discontinued and the Association of American Railroads be permitted to handle railroad affairs." [58]

In addition to the state railroad associations and the operating employees of the carriers, the national association has also made use of nonrailroad organizations in order to get a broader backing for its programs. Local chambers of commerce, for example, have been called upon to sponsor bills which were drawn up by the railroads, as can be seen by the following excerpt from a letter by R. V. Fletcher: "Mr. Russell stated to me recently . . . that [a bill for the regulation of buses and trucks] was being championed by the Chamber of Commerce of the State of New Jersey and for that reason Mr. Russell thinks it inadvisable to let it be known, even among our own people, that this bill was prepared by railroad counsel or is in any way sponsored by any committee of the Association." [59] They have also been called upon to send witnesses to Congressional hearings: "I have discussed this matter with Mr. Karl S. Dixon, Assistant Secretary of the Ohio Chamber of Commerce, who would be available to go to Washington on what you might consider the most important of those bills. He would, however, require coaching by you or some other experienced railroader." [60]

In 1935 the AAR empowered the regional shippers advisory boards (which the railroads had originally organized in 1923 to deal with the problem of car shortages) to form legislative committees. One letter stated that the purpose of these organizations was to help prove to the "political gentlemen" that the railroads are not alone but are "backed by sound public opinion." The author went on to describe one of the meetings of a legislative committee, stating that "the antagonism shown was from a small minority of Barge Line advocates and enthusiasts, which we use as 'scenery' occasionally, and they performed nobly in this case, although they do not know it." [61] On another occasion, a list of 958 government, carrier, shipper, farm, and business organizations which supported the Reed-Bulwinkle bill was presented to Congress in 1947.[62] Senator Tobey of New Hampshire sensed the "fine Italian handwork" of the AAR.[63] It would be hard to believe that such a remarkable example of nonrailroad support for a railroad measure organized itself.

This complicated and intermeshed network of cooperating nonrailroad groups, railroad employees, and state railway associations has been used in the presentation of the railroad viewpoint to the members of Congress. Attention has been paid to congressional elections, the choice of members of committees which perform work which affects the railroads, appearances at committee hearings, and the influencing of important Congressmen.

A letter written from the AAR to the chairman of the Missouri Railroad Association gives some insight into the method used to get railroad minded people elected to Congress.

I have noted with great interest the replies which prospective members of Congress have made to the questionnaire sent out by the Missouri Railroad Employees and Taxpayers Association. It is gratifying to know that a few of these Congressmen are really quite specific in their replies. However, some of them do no more than give the stereotyped response, which is that the matter will be given consideration. I think persons who make a reply of this character should be interviewed further and that it should be made very clear to them that we are in earnest and that if they expect support and assistance from us they will have to pledge themselves in a more definite way.[64]

The AAR, as did its predecessor, the ARE, showed an interest in seeing that members of congressional committees which handle transportation legislation were disposed to be favorable to the railroad interests. Particular interest has been shown in the membership of the rivers and harbors committees and the commerce committees. For example, in 1933 the ARE followed a railroad suggestion that state legislative committees gather information on Congressmen who might be made members of the Rivers and Harbors Committee. A railroad executive wrote to R. V. Fletcher, "As soon as we have the reports on these men we can then take the next step and ascertain whether they would be willing to serve on this committee. Then we can go a step further and try to get them on the Committee." [65]

The AAR has felt that its own personnel should largely confine their activities to appearances before congressional committees, but at the same time the association tends to feel that much work needs to be done beyond these appearances. With respect to one of the predecessor organizations, a railroad general counsel summed up this feeling by saying that "hearings before Committees are largely matters of scenery to satisfy the public and . . . the effective work cannot be accomplished in the appearances of members of [the ARE's] staff before Committees . . . the effective work in opposition to bills harmful to the railroads can only be done through personal interviews with Congressmen conducted by men personally acquainted with the Congressmen they interview and for whom the interviewed Congressmen would have a feeling of respect and confidence." [66] The association has made a conscious effort to see that railroad men and other prominent citizens contact Congressmen on specific legislative matters and that letters were sent to them which favored the railroad's position.

The AAR and Federal Agencies

The relations between the AAR and the administrative branch of the federal government are less spectacular and (excepting formal appearances in general rate-level cases) less well documented, but they are certainly as important as the association's relations with Congress. The association feels that attempting to mold a public opinion which is favorable to the railroads is vitally important in helping bring about desired administrative action, but it also has other methods for influencing federal functionaries.

The AAR is naturally interested in the transportation policies of the President and the various department officials of the federal government. Important association officers spend time presenting their point of view to these people. In the early days, for example, one of the first acts of the AAR's executive committee was to pay "courtesy calls" on President Roosevelt, Federal Coordinator Eastman, Interstate Commerce Commission Chairman William E. Lee, Secretary of Commerce Roper, RFC Chairman Jesse H. Jones, and W. A. Harriman, the head of the administrative division of the National Recovery Administration.[67] The first president of the association, John J. Pelley, was chosen in part because of his friendship with President Roosevelt,[68] and he had other close White House and congressional contacts also. He was not only a "permanent poker partner" of Jesse H. Jones and Steve Early but he was also close to Fred Vinson and James Byrnes.[69] Such contacts presumably provide useful access to influence when the President has a bill to sign or an appointment to make which will affect the railroads, or when some departmental transportation policy is under consideration.

There have been instances when the network of railroad organizations has been mobilized to propagandize members of the administration. Soon after he became coordinator of transportation, Eastman issued a questionnaire concerning further transportation legislation, asking for answers from any interested parties. As can be seen from the following excerpt from a letter written by the general solicitor of the Seaboard Airline Railway, the railroads sought wide cooperation in answering this series of questions.

It is, of course, of vital importance to the railroads of this country that the replies of the various chambers of commerce, etc., be, as far as possible, favorable to the contentions we have frequently urged.

With this in view, Judge Fletcher, General Counsel of the American Railway Association, has prepared a series of answers to the questionnaire referred to, which is intended to present the views of the railroads as well as to be fair and in the interest of industry, two copies of which are enclosed.

Please take up with the Chamber of Commerce or any other civic organization which you think can be prevailed on to act favorably and urge them to return the questionnaire to the Federal Coordinator of Transportation with replies which will represent as far as possible our views (which are contained in Judge Fletcher's answers to the questionnaire) on this troublesome question.[70]

The program was evidently not as effective as it was hoped, for Eastman wrote the following note to Mr. Fletcher: "It is quite evident from the answers which have come in in great volume, that many of them have been the result of a campaign of solicitation and propaganda on the part of railroad officers and agents . . . Such activities on the part of the railroads defeat their own purpose. The nature of the answers obtained in this way is evident on their face. They are not entitled to much consideration and do not receive it. The main thing that they accomplish is to burden the mails of the recipients." [71]

Pressure on the independent regulatory commissions as well as on executive officers of the federal government has been habitual, as the comments of the Interstate Commerce Commission in the Five Per Cent case of 1914 attest:

The Commission from the beginning of this proceeding has been subjected to an apparently concerted effort to secure through propaganda an early approval of the proposed increase in rates . . . There appears to have been a set purpose to convince us that the people were of one mind respecting the very important questions involved in the case, and that, in order to satisfy every public requirement, there remained nothing for the Commission to do but to register this consensus of opinion by immediately entering an order permitting the carriers to make their proposed charges effective. The letters and telegrams received disclosed an unmistakable purpose to hurry the Commission to a conclusion before the record had been closed and before there had been an opportunity to hear, much less consider, the testimony that the protestants and others desired to offer in protection of what they conceived their interests as shippers. Respectable journals joined in demanding the immediate approval of the proposed rates. Cartoons appeared in the public press depicting the Commission as an obstruction to progress and prosperity . . . One traffic association offered to deluge the Commission's offices with thousands of telegrams; other organizations started chains of letters, some of which, in identical language, are still reaching the offices of the Commission from widely separated parts of the country; others took the trouble to send to members of the Commission clippings from newspapers and magazines containing editorials and news items relating to the cases and denouncing our delay in disposing of it.

Most of these communications were doubtless well intended, but they have not been helpful. Those that have been examined disclose that the writers were without any real understanding either of the many intricate questions involved in the investigation or in the facts disclosed upon the record; and they show little appreciation of the statutory standards by which we must be controlled when considering the rates and practices of the carriers.[72]

Similar pressures occasionally have been brought to bear on the ICC since 1914,[73] but it may be said that the railroads and the AAR have shown greater respect for the Commission and have brought less direct pressure to bear on it in recent years. Professor E. Pendleton Herring wrote in 1933, "The carriers are well aware of the dangers of partisan interference, and find the threat of congressional participation particularly distasteful. Theirs has been a losing fight against governmental regulation, but its arrival despite their efforts does not alter the fact that they vastly prefer regulation by an expert board rather than by a political assembly swayed by the winds of expediency." [74]

There is a surprisingly large amount of day-to-day technical contact between the AAR and the Interstate Commerce Commission which tends to go unnoticed. Herring has pointed out the necessity for this kind of close relationship between the governing body and those who are being governed. He has said, "the greater the degree of detailed and technical control the government seeks to exert over industrial and commercial groups, the greater must be their degree of consent and active participation in the very process of regulation, if regulation is to be effective or successful." [75] The ICC, for example, does not have the time, the finances, or the technical knowledge to carry out its huge regulatory task without calling for assistance from the railroads and other carriers.

Interstate Commerce Commissioner McManamy, in an address before the American Railway Association in 1930, made this statement:

One of the first duties of the Association was to provide . . . rules from which have grown our present rules of interchange and other rules established by this body, which, if just and reasonable, as required by the Interstate Commerce Commission, are the law. Paragraphs 10 and 11 of section 1 of the act make it the duty of each carrier to establish, observe and enforce just and reasonable rules, regulations and practices with respect to car service. This organization, having undertaken the task of establishing such rules for all carriers, is therefore a law-making body, and it is but fair to say that there have been but few instances in which the Commission has found it necessary to modify or change the rules of interchange which you have established.[76]

Both the framers of the Interstate Commerce Act and the commissioners themselves have made provision for constant contact between the Commission and the railroads. The ICC, for example, came to rely heavily on the technical competence of the AAR (as it did on its predecessor, the ARA) in connection with car service, safety measures, locomotive inspection, and transportation of explosives. The car service division of the AAR serves as the collective voice of the railroads and it supplements the Commission's work of directing transportation in an efficient fashion.[77] The safety work of the Commission calls for testing the various safety devices in practical railroad experiments. This testing is carried on largely by the individual lines with the cooperation of the AAR's safety section.[78]

The statute that gave the Commission supervision of transportation of explosives authorized that body to make use of the services of the railroads' bureau of explosives.[79]

Appraisals of the AAR

The position of the Association of American Railroads as one of the principal combinations of groups in the environment of the federal coordinator may be appraised by reference to judgments made about it. Four principal comments have been made both inside and outside the railroad industry. First, it has been said that it has been run in an undemocratic fashion and that the large lines tend to dominate its activities. Second, its lobbying techniques have been made the subject of adverse comment. Third, it has accomplished so much intercarrier cooperation that it has become involved in the antitrust laws. Fourth, it has been said that it has failed to accomplish the purposes for which it was established. These judgments will be considered in order.

The complaint that the smaller lines have little to say about the formulation of AAR policy has been a persistent one. For example, Patrick H. Joyce, then cotrustee of the Chicago Great Western, made the following remarks at a meeting of the Western Association of Railway Executives in 1937:

Another thing I would like to inject into the AAR, and I am not particularly criticizing them. We small railroads don't have anything to say. We had a meeting here early last spring when the pension question was taken up . . . A lot of time was spent on the pension question, and it was well done. A man from the D.T.&I. Railroad got up and said what are we going to do about the labor situation. Mr. Clement had made a motion to adjourn, and Mr. Pelley was gone from the platform before anybody knew what was going on. I had it on the tip of my tongue to ask the same question before the D.T.&I. man spoke and going along the lobby and around the rotunda after the meeting a dozen or more men mentioned the same question. When you have a town hall meeting of the AAR why not have a town hall meeting and let everybody talk and invite the press and let them hear your discussion? There are brains on small railroads as well as large railroads.[80]

Much later, Robert R. Young, chairman of the board of the Chesapeake and Ohio, withdrew his line and its two subsidiaries, the Pere Marquette and the Nickel Plate, from participation in the public relations activities of the AAR, though not from the operating aspects of the association's work. He announced in 1947 the formation of a public relations organization to be known as the Federation for Railway Progress, which would include railroad stockholders, employees, shippers, and travelers as well as operating railroad people. Although the C&O is not a small line, one of Young's criticisms, like that of the small railroads, was that the AAR was dominated by certain large lines. He said in a press conference, "Everybody knows that the New York Central and the Pennsylvania control the Association." [81]

In any organization made up of units of such varying size it is doubtless difficult to give everyone a feeling of having a fair say in the formulation of policy. Furthermore, under any plan of organization, the larger members tend to become the informal leaders, even if not given formal authority. However, it may be in the AAR there is evidence that works against Mr. Young's thesis that the New York Central and the Pennsylvania, the lines named by Mr. Young, have dominated all the AAR's activities. They evidently did not control the presidential drafting committee,[82] for example. In fact, Senators Wheeler and Truman suspected domination by the Union Pacific when they wrote their report on *Investigation of Railroads,* because the AAR had supported the Pettengill bill which tended to favor the western over the eastern lines.[83]

The second general criticism of the AAR is that some of its lobbying techniques have been unethical. Senators Wheeler and Truman closed their report on the *Investigation of Railroads* with the following paragraph:

The railroad industry as a public utility serving the public interest has a responsibility to inform the public of its activities, to promote legislation for the general good, and to contribute to the solution of the industry's problems. But this report indicated that the railroads and railroad associations have often resorted to indirection in offering information to the public; that railroads and railroad associations have not always been open, frank, and aboveboard in presenting legislation to Congress; and that railroads and railroad associations have often been more concerned with the selfish interests of a few rather than the needs of industry as a whole.[84]

In appraising these charges, made after a sweeping Congressional investigation of the railroads, two factors are relevant.

First, the intense pressure group competition in the field of transportation policy formulation influences the types of activity which the railroads choose to pursue. As every day's newspaper shows, pressure groups, with great imagination and inventiveness, exploit a wide range of methods to influence public policy. When one group puts new and effective methods into practice, an opposing group, if it is interested in success, thinks it must devise equal or better methods to counteract the effect of the offensive. Almost no holds are barred, short of bribery. The following quote from R. V. Fletcher's testimony during the Senate Commerce Committee's investigation of the railroads sharpens this point: "You see, we cannot live in a vacuum and we cannot live under ideal conditions. I wish we could, because I am a firm idealist in my fundamentals of philosophy. But we live in a practical world.

We are confronted in the various States by a very strong pressure brought to bear upon State legislatures to constantly liberalize truck laws. I am not criticizing them. I suppose that is their business. But it is our business to try to hold down the operation of trucks to what we considered to be their legitimate function, the short-haul field." [85]

An interchange between Chairman Burton K. Wheeler and Mr. Fletcher at another point in the hearings is enlightening. In the group competition that characterizes the transportation industry each group tends to assume that the other sides of any particular issue will be adequately and fully presented by the opposing groups, and that its function is to be partisan, not impartial. The assumption is also widespread that pressure groups might be willing to modify the nature of their competition but only if all competing groups can be brought to limit themselves in a similar manner. These conceptions of group competition appear in the following colloquy:

THE CHAIRMAN. Well, the average fellow at the crossroads does not have the opportunity to know all the facts; he hears only one side, and therefore does not know whether the proposed legislation would be beneficial or not. Nevertheless you go ahead and get him to write a letter, and perhaps it may have some influence on some Congressman or some Senator, I don't know.

MR. FLETCHER. The theory is, and I think that there is much to back it up, that efforts will be made on other sides of the question, and we think an explanation should be made of our side of the situation. We happen to know of people doing the same thing who are on the other side of the question.

THE CHAIRMAN. Perhaps that is true. But whether it comes from your side or the other side it is not a very healthy or intelligent way to legislate. You ought to be able to present your views to Senators and Congressmen in Washington, and the question of the propriety of enacting legislation which is proposed ought to be decided on the facts as presented to Congressional committees.

MR. FLETCHER. I think so.

THE CHAIRMAN. Instead of influence attempted to be brought to bear, by either, by way of propaganda which represents one side or the other, and, generally speaking, not very intelligent propaganda at that.

MR. FLETCHER. If we could get some kind of understanding throughout the country, to the end that all groups would accept your theory, we will certainly go along.[86]

Second, the railroads have had a "bad name" in liberal and progressive circles, some of it earned and some of it not. It is not true to say that the Roosevelt administrations of the 1930's were fundamentally hostile to management, for the National Industrial Recovery Act was a program for the improvement of business enterprise, and the trade associations were strong supporters of the idea. Furthermore, as has been shown, the drafting of the Emergency Railroad Transportation Act of 1933 was in large part a matter of friendly cooperation between government and management, with the unions excluded from strong participation or decisive influence. But when so much is said, it remains true that the government in the 1930's in Congress and the White House was more responsive to the appeals of farmers and workers, organized and unorganized, than had been the case in the past, and there was official hostility to much that the railroads proposed. As a result, the railroads in their separate and individual activities and through the AAR tended to stay in the background and to get other organizations to push their programs for them. As Joseph H. Hays, counsel for the Western Association of Railway Executives, said, "Many times railroads have a legitimate interest in a perfectly fair proposition, but when such proposition is made to a legislature or legislative body there is, of course, a great deal of opposition. Very frequently a perfectly meritorious proposition is dubbed a railroad measure and therefore a purely selfish measure when, in fact, other groups are equally interested . . . from the standpoint of political experience, even though we have an interest in the matter, we stay in the background as much as possible." [87]

The third general criticism — that the railroads under the AAR have gone so far in the direction of intercarrier cooperation that they have violated the antitrust laws — was eventually litigated. In 1943, Georgia's Governor Ellis Arnall,[88] Vice President Henry Wallace,[89] and Assistant Attorney General Wendell Berge[90] charged that the railroads and the AAR had conspired to fix freight rates which had put the South and the West at an economic disadvantage; to delay the introduction of technical railroad improvements; and to keep motor, water, and air transportation in a subordinate position. On August 23, 1944, in the District Court of Lincoln, Nebraska, the Department of Justice filed suit against the AAR, the Western Association of Railway Executives, and various western lines, claiming that they had "acted collusively to maintain non-competitive rates for transportation and to prevent and retard improvements in the services and facilities of the railroads for the Western part of the United States." [91] They asked that the AAR and the Western Association of Railway Executives be dissolved and that various practices be enjoined. On September 15, 1944, the state of Georgia initiated an antitrust suit, charging a railroad conspiracy in rate fixing which discriminated against the South and injured the economy of Georgia.[92] The litigation eventually failed.

These attacks caused the railroads to turn to Congress for relief in the form of the Reed-Bulwinkle bill,[93] which was designed to stay the application of the antitrust laws to any intercarrier rate agreements which have the sanction of the ICC. At the time when the AAR was pressing for the passage of the Bulwinkle bill, Robert Young formed his Federation for Railway Progress, which waxed critical of railroad cooperation on rate matters. Mr. Young stated at a 1946 press conference: "Bluntly we think the quarter of a million dollars a year we have been paying for the AAR dues can be better spent by ourselves . . . For the past three years the AAR has been lobbying to exempt the railroads from the antitrust laws when its money and energies might better have gone to improve equipment and service, to fight for the billions in rail securities which are being unjustifiably squeezed out in reorganizations, and to preserve a fair balance between wages and rates . . . At least 90 per cent of the Association's members feel the same way we do but haven't dared do anything about it." [94] One critic of the railroads concluded that the pressures of informal solicitation and public and private propaganda to get the Reed-Bulwinkle bill through Congress were as comprehensive and ingenious as the *Investigation of Railroads* had found them to be in other respects.[95]

The fourth general criticism, that the AAR has failed to accomplish the purposes for which it was set up, has been made by people both inside and outside the industry. Fred W. Sargent, then president of the Chicago and North Western, complained at Senator Wheeler's investigation that the AAR had been unable to settle such problems as the division of rates for through freight and the charges to be made for privately owned cars.[96] Senators Wheeler and Truman, in *Investigation of Railroads,* criticized the carriers in the following manner:

However, the railroads have failed to achieve stated objectives of the Association which they set up for this purpose. The plan to absorb over a hundred railroad organizations into one all-powerful association finally resulted in amalgamating only 8. The coordination of railroad facilities which was expected to save the carriers millions of dollars annually was completed in only 24 cases out of more than 500 during a period of 3 years, and these projects were so small that there was little resultant saving to the railroads. Machinery for self-regulation has proved of little avail in the vital fields of freight-rate divisions, private car rates, and Pullman Co. contracts. Railroad executives testified before this subcommittee that not only has nothing been achieved, but that it is futile to expect any results from this railroad association because it is dominated by a few powerful roads which are only working for their own interests and not for the interests of the railroads as a whole.[97]

The third criticism, that there has been too much interrailroad cooperation, is in some respects inconsistent with the fourth, that there has been too little cooperation. The fact that both accusations are frequently heard reflects both an organizational weakness on the part of the AAR and a basic inconsistency in American transportation policy.

The AAR has been able to unite the railroads behind a program of common action only when there has been a will on the part of most of the railroads to cooperate with each other through the means of their control organization. The control which has been given to the AAR's car service division by the member railroads, for example, shows that the organization has real power in certain aspects of its work, even without the authority-giving provisions of the original plan of organization.

On the other hand, the AAR, even before 1947, when it had considerable "constitutional" authority, has been incapable of eliciting railroad cooperation when action meant loss of financial or competitive advantage to individual lines. It has been unable, for example, to deal effectively with one of the most persistent railroad problems, the equitable division of freight rates among the various lines in the country. Mr. Fletcher thought that the AAR could solve this problem, and he wrote in August, 1934, "I would suppose that the railroads might agree to be bound at least by a gentleman's agreement that when they disagree about divisions they will submit the matter to arbitration and not go to the Commission with the controversy." [98] Yet it was recognized in the Wheeler railroad hearings, some years later, that the machinery of the AAR could not settle the division problem. Mr. Fred Sargent said:

You see, as the Association of American Railroads is organized, it is composed of directors who themselves are presidents of railroads. Naturally it would be difficult for the president of a given railroad to lay aside his own interest, the interest of his own individual property, in the common good, we will say, to help balance railroad earnings of the territories that were undersustained. He would thereby be taking revenues from his own property in order to help support other territories. And the difficulty is not with the men, and they are very fine men, able directors, and it is an able organization, but the difficulty is that the thing cannot set up. And, naturally, as I see it, the Association of American Railroads, is not in a position to take part in these sectional controversies which involve individual railroads within the organization. I do not think we can hope to get any relief through the Association of American Railroads.[99]

AAR president Pelley agreed at the same hearings that his organization's "concern is more with matters that save money for the industry. And this thing you are talking about is not that; it just takes money from one railroad and gives it to another." [100] He admitted that the problem of divisions is "probably a matter that would ultimately have to be settled by the Commission." [101]

This sketch of the carrier organizations and of the Association of American Railroads which represents them in important areas of public policy and political contact is a picture of an active combination of groups bent, in a competitive environment, upon presenting the interests of the constituent members in the most favorable light and in the most insistent way. It is also a picture of an organization that had roads of access to and points of support in places of influence immediately surrounding the federal coordinator, beyond him to the White House and the Congress, among other federal agencies, throughout the states and localities, and among a host of collateral interests and associations. The organization was strongly impelled towards a centralized internal political structure, but was and has been inhibited from making this centralization tight and complete by the antitrust laws and by the strong individualism of purposeful men and the powerful roads they command.

Coordination is a simple stereotype of the textbooks of public administration but the coordination of the railroads was a problem of the utmost complexity because of the structure of the industry and the development of the Association of American Railroads as an agent for marshaling the consensus of the carriers both for and against the federal coordinator. In addition, the development of a single consistent national transportation policy was complicated by the fact that the official agencies of the government were neither singular nor consistent in their approach to national transportation policy. Some agencies of the federal government in the 1930's (and before and after that time) were bent upon enforcing railroad competition, while other agencies were equally bent upon eliminating competition. In this dilemma not only the Interstate Commerce Commission and the federal coordinator of transportation but the Association of American Railroads was perplexed. For the association, in its way, was trying to "coordinate" the railroad industry by nongovernmental action. The dilemma that contrary federal policies presented to the AAR was well expressed in an editorial in the *Railway Age* shortly after the initiation of the antitrust suits in 1944. Said this journal of carrier opinion: "What kind of government have we developed, when one branch of it attacks citizens in the courts, alleging wholesale violation of the law, because they have done what two other branches of the government [federal coordinator of transportation and Interstate Commerce Commission] and the President himself only a few years ago encouraged them to do in the supposed interest of the nation." [102] This complaint is somewhat disingenuous, since the time of the federal coordinator had long since gone, and the federal government, in 1944, was not enforcing inconsistent policies. But the complaint was basically justified, for the policy of the federal government over the period from 1933 up to the end of World War II changed both emphasis and direction more than once.

IX. REPORTS AND REPERCUSSIONS

"Based on its research work, the staff of the coordinator has made many recommendations for changes in present practices covering a very wide field. Most of these recommendations, requiring agreement among the railroads on a plan for concerted action, have not been accepted by the railroads, although some of the ideas advanced have been put into effect, and Mr. Eastman considers that 'the leaven is working.'"   *Railway Age,* January 4, 1936

The first of the two principal functions of the coordinator — the reduction of waste and other preventable expense by coordination — was largely frustrated by the carriers in 1933 and thereafter,[1] but the second of his principal functions — the making of studies for the improvement of railroad operation and management and for the development by the Congress of necessary new regulations — proceeded with efficient skill from the outset.

The recommendations for self-improvement were, in the main, received by the railroads with critical hostility, although some of the ideas proposed by the coordinator's staff were tried and put into effect. With the organization of the Association of American Railroads, the carriers had created a spokesman through which this resistance to self-improvement could be expressed with one voice, and through the activities of which the office of the coordinator could be brought to an end. This conclusion awaited only the cooperation of the labor unions, which cooperation the carriers bought in 1936, as will be described.

The varied and often voluminous reports prepared by the staff of the coordinator covered a wide range of subjects but were pointed to specific trouble spots. They can be classified approximately as follows: (a) reports intended primarily to increase and improve the economy and efficiency of rail service (for example, the merchandise traffic report); (b) reports intended to effect economies in the use of railroad facilities and to improve railroad practices (for example, reports on purchasing practices and car pooling); (c) studies of means of deriving added revenues for services or facilities provided (grain elevator reports and the work on wharfingers); (d) labor reports, divided between those on rail labor and those on labor in other branches of transportation; (e) report on alleged subsidies to competitors of railroads; (f) reports on legislation; and (g) miscellaneous reports (report on short line railroads). The reports on labor in other forms of transportation, on public aid, and on certain aspects of legislation dealt with matters which AAR referred to as important.[2]

This account of the politics of railroad coordination is not directly concerned with the technical sufficiency of the recommendations made by the coordinator for the self-improvement of the railroad industry. Even the experts may disagree about the merits of engineering and management proposals which were thoughtfully produced after earnest investigation by the coordinator's staff, and just as earnestly if not quite as thoughtfully rejected by the experts speaking for the carriers. A study of the politics of administration is concerned, however, with the environment of clientele groups that an administrator inhabits, the extent to which he is able to win the consent or woo the acquiescence of this clientele to his purposes, the intensity of the resistance with which they confront his proposals, and the development of institutions by them for working administrative authority around to their desire or supplanting and replacing it when this maneuver is not possible. The administrator lives in a state of tension with the groups with which he is expected to deal; and evidence of the tension between the coordinator and the carriers is the reception accorded to almost all of the recommendations for self-improvement that his staff made.

The following pages will consider some of the reports made by the coordinator for the self-improvement of the railroads and the reception accorded them; and the next two chapters will deal with his recommendations for new legislation and the denouement of his experiment in persuasion.

The Traffic Reports

One of the most interesting of the traffic reports[3] was the one on merchandise traffic, submitted to the regional coordinating committees on March 22, 1934. The report with recommendations had been prepared by the coordinator's section of transportation service under the direction of John R. Turney, one of the staff not infrequently attacked by the carriers and their spokesmen as a man of undoubted talent, but criticized for his "theoretical" proposals, and resented because of his sometimes caustic candor. Three advisory committees had worked with the section of transportation service, including a rail committee that included the president of the Railway Express Agency, three railroad vice presidents, and the three regional traffic assistants in the coordinator's field organization. The bureau of accounts and the bureau of statistics of the Interstate Commerce Commission also lent aid.

The report, an impressive 422 pages of text, tables, and exhibits, said that the rail carriers had lost the bulk of the available merchandise traffic which they had formerly handled. They had lost this traffic because delivery was too slow, incomplete, inconvenient, and unsafe, because of complex classifications and rate schedules, rigorous packing requirements, cartage and multiple rates, and because of a rate level that was in some cases too high. To the members of an industry which habitually complained about the competition of the truckers, upon whom they blamed much of their economic distress, traced in part to alleged government subsidies to their competitors, the merchandise traffic report said, "As now conducted, highway transportation of merchandise is relatively more economical than rail transportation for all distances." It did suggest that "realization of the potential improvements in rail service and methods" would make rail transportation more economical for distances over 150 miles, although highway transportation for distances less than this would continue to be more economical than rail transportation.

With considerable imagination and undoubted boldness, the section of transportation service proposed coordinated national action to pool all rail merchandise services into two competing merchandise agencies, somewhat like Railway Express, each to operate throughout the United States and to represent roughly comparable traffic and financial strength. These national merchandise agencies were to be owned by the railroads to which they provided service, were to be operated by an independent management in which the public was to have representation, under contracts encouraging direct and economical routing, with protection for the revenues of each participating carrier. The section also recommended direct collections of merchandise at the patron's door and its transportation in shockproof equipment at overall speeds in excess of twenty miles an hour. There were other recommendations to simplify classifications, to liberalize packaging requirements, and to revise the system of charges.

The report was transmitted to the regional coordinating committees by Eastman with a certain amount of trepidation. He said, "It would be most unfortunate if the railroads should regard the report, or any part of it, as an indictment of railroad management, and direct their thoughts to the preparation of a brief in defense."

The merchandise traffic report was examined by a national committee of railroad officers, which produced a report of comment and criticism. The carriers objected to the national pooling of merchandise traffic, criticized the estimates of savings, thought that the proposal for special shockproof cars for the transportation of merchandise was too expensive, concluded that the speeds recommended by the coordinator's staff were unnecessary, thought that the criticism of the packing requirements was correct to only a limited extent, and in general showed that reserve about self-improvement that was to put them into a position of objection to the most of the coordinator's suggestions. The chief counter-recommendation of the carriers was that they be permitted to establish merchandise pools themselves, individually or in groups, regionally or otherwise, with the pooling accomplished either by the Railway Express Agency or by the organization of an l.c.l. freight traffic agency. After the submission of the railroad committee comment and criticism, efforts were made to harmonize the two reports. These efforts were successful at the level of general principle but unsuccessful in procedure and detail.

The merchandise traffic report was made public by Eastman in March 1934. Previous experience doubtless warned him of expected reaction. Some had not received his *First Report* very cheerfully,[4] complaining about the size and number of the questionnaires his staff sent out and the "radical" nature of some of the recommendations. In October 1933, Eastman had told the Associated Traffic Clubs of America that many questionnaires and some "radical" proposals could be expected.[5] Most of the accounts in the trade press about the merchandise traffic report pointed out its principal novelty, the two national competing traffic pools,[6] and the reaction in general was that the plan was impractical.[7] The rejection of the scheme by the railroads was perhaps not unexpected since self-improvement is difficult, like a psychoanalysis, unless the patient is convinced that he needs the treatment. But not quite as expected, or as predictable, was the sharp hostility of the truckers, speaking through the American Trucking Associations, Inc. It was their position that, while the report definitely pointed out the advantages of truck transportation over rail service, it showed the way to the eventual absorption and domination of trucking facilities by the railroads.

Against a background of complaints from Eastman that the railroads were more zealous to prove his staff wrong than to improve their service and that they did not readily respond to recommendations that entailed any important surrender of authority of the individual managements, a meeting was held on March 15, 1935, between Eastman and Pelley, of the Association of American Railroads. It was agreed, in the interest of "saving time and circumlocution," that the AAR instead of the regional coordinating committees would study and comment upon certain of the Eastman reports, including the merchandise traffic report.[8] The reasons suggested for the transfer of this responsibility from the regional coordinating committees to the AAR was that the previous procedure was "roundabout." [9] It was, of course, since generally the same people who comprised the regional coordinating committees ran the eastern, western, and southern railroad presidents' associations, and in turn were the founding fathers of the Association of American Railroads. Pelley was shortly afterwards to say that railroad problems were not complex and that these problems would be alleviated if burdensome laws were repealed in their application to railroads and equal laws were applied to their competitors.[10]

In the summer of 1935, Eastman held a long conference with the board of directors of the AAR and committee members to discuss the reports, among other things. It was said of this conference, "The board was holding its monthly meeting in Washington and Mr. Eastman expressed a desire to take advantage of the opportunity to confer with the committees in a joint meeting, as most of the directors of the association are also members of the committees." [11] At this time the principal report discussed was the merchandise traffic report, and Eastman was reported to be pleased with the attitude of the executives towards cooperation. He was less pleased when the AAR held its annual meeting in Chicago early in November. In addressing the association he expressed disappointment at the slow progress being made. The action of the AAR on the merchandise traffic report was to recommend the installation of new systems for the collection and delivery of merchandise freight on railroads locally, jointly, and between different freight territories, these installations to be accomplished as quickly as possible. Although an important step, this was far from the bold plan that the coordinator's staff had recommended in the merchandise traffic report and seemed to justify Eastman's assertion, often made, that the railroads were evidently incapable of national action in the national interest when it seemed to collide with local management ambitions serving a local management interest.

Eastman was still trying to placate the implacable ones as they moved him out of his position by abolishing the office of the federal coordinator of transportation. On May 29, 1936, Eastman issued a report of his own on the merchandise traffic report. After reviewing the findings of his section of transportation service and of the various committees that looked over these findings, Eastman said that the two principal fears entertained by the railroad men were "nationalization" and the jeopardy to the interests of individual railroads, both of which he thought were groundless. Of the first, he said,

I am unable to follow the reasoning which ends in the fear of "nationalization." An important part of the merchandise traffic of the many individual railroads has long since been pooled, or "nationalized." That is the express traffic, which is handled for the railroads by the express agencies in much the fashion now proposed for handling of all merchandise traffic. The pool of the Railway Express Agency, Inc. is virtually nation-wide. If the working of this express pool has offered grounds for criticism, it has not been a ground that a dangerous precedent in "nationalization" has thus been set.[12]

There was more substance to the fear that the interests of individual railroads might be jeopardized, resulting from a redistribution of the merchandise traffic. But, though the possibility might be admitted, there was no real reason why the possibility should become an actuality since properly drawn pooling contracts would avert such a danger.

The carriers' alternative proposal was that they be permitted to develop such pools by their own action, regionally and locally. Always ready to see reason even in proposals offered to defeat his own, Eastman in his conclusion said that such independent action by the carriers might have been a step towards the development of larger pools, and eventually of the national pools he thought necessary for efficient management of merchandise freight traffic. It was with this thought in mind that he had "been acquiescent in the expressed desire of the railroad committees to try out their own plan of procedure." But the thought was not father to the deed. As Eastman put it, "Unfortunately, this policy has not borne much fruit. It is now approaching two years since agreement was reached on the necessity for action, but the action was left to the initiative of the individual railroads. This seems enough time at least for a start to have been made, yet the merchandise problem today is largely exactly what it was two years ago." Regulation of the interstate operation of motor carriers had become a fact, store-door collection and delivery had been widely introduced, and individual railroads had purchased truck lines and arranged some coordination of rail and highway transportation, but "of joint railroad action to get at the root of the merchandise problem, which is the multiplicity of services, facilities, and routes, there has been nothing." Indeed, as to the store-door collection and delivery, "it had been independently established, without the other changes in operation, service, and rates which should have gone with it, so that the net effect has apparently been to make railroad merchandise operations more expensive, in opposition to the essential need."

Freight Traffic Report

Work on the freight traffic report was begun by the section of transportation service under John R. Turney as soon as the office of the federal coordinator was organized but it was not until 1935 that the three-volume study was produced.[13] The coordinator's studies ran into a snag at the start when on September 28, 1933, Eastman made public certain plans with the Pennsylvania Railroad to experiment with store receipt and delivery of less-than-carload freight. W. W. Atterbury, president of the Pennsylvania, had written to the coordinator to ask whether Eastman would object to the filing by the Pennsylvania of tariffs providing for store-door receipt and delivery of less-than-carload freight, to which the coordinator replied that he would welcome such an experiment.[14] Some time thereafter, according to the account in *Railway Age*, E. E. Williamson, president of the New York Central, wrote to Eastman to say that he thought the coordinator should forbid the experiment by the Pennsylvania, at least until the coordinator had completed his own study of the handling of less-than-carload freight by all transportation agencies. The argument against the experiment was that the service proposed by the Pennsylvania would impair the net earnings of all the carriers in the eastern region and would also violate certain provisions of the Interstate Commerce Act. To this, "The Coordinator replied . . . that he would not be justified in forbidding the experiment without evidence pointing unmistakably to the conclusion that it will result in waste; that the experience already had with such store-door service, both in this country and abroad, does not point that way; that there is no better way to add to knowledge on this subject than by actual tests; and that if the experiment results in infractions of the Interstate Commerce Act, there is a remedy before the Commission." [15]

In these exchanges between the presidents of the Pennsylvania and the New York Central and the coordinator, it was clear that the New York Central was apprehensive about the competition it expected from the Pennsylvania in its own territory. Williamson called the Pennsylvania proposal "one of the most powerful weapons by which one carrier can penetrate another's territory," to which Eastman replied that the New York Central was "hardly in a position to complain of competitors' doing directly by tariff what it is doing indirectly and without tariff." [16] This statement had reference to the fact that the Pennsylvania plan was practically identical with the practice followed for years by the Universal Carloading and Distributing Company, which was controlled by the New York Central through a so-called loan and option agreement.

Despite this off-stage scuffle between the New York Central and the Pennsylvania, Eastman in the autumn of 1933 was full of enthusiasm for the study of freight traffic that Turney's section of transportation service was to undertake. In a speech in Baltimore the coordinator said in October,

The study of carload traffic . . . has within it greater possibilities for good than any other which the Section of Transportation Service will undertake . . . The Section will endeavor to measure the volume, origin and destination of available carload traffic grouped by principal commodities, and the distribution of this traffic among the several transportation agencies which are to handle it. It will investigate the needs of shippers with respect to the kind of equipment, size, dimensions and design, facilities for loading protection of lading, the speed and completeness of the service, and within a limited field the charges which each class of traffic will bear. It will appraise the extra transportation expenses incurred by shippers in furnishing and maintaining sidings, platforms, docks, etc., and in packing, crating, and draying their freight to and from the rail head. It will examine the possibility of securing better and more economical transportation service through the adoption of lighter equipment and a number of other proposed changes in equipment design.[17]

In addition, the study was going to include a survey of costs in the handling of carload traffic from the beginning to the end of the movement, separated between line and terminal, between the different types of terminal service, and by different types of trains on main lines and branches.

The report that emerged in 1935 was described as calling for "a comprehensive and radical revision of present methods of handling carload freight traffic,"[18] and Eastman himself felt that it was the most important report of his section of transportation service.[19] One of the most striking features of the report was the suggestion that the existing freight traffic sales unit — the carload — was obsolete for nonbulk commodities, with the corollary recommendation that containers were the solution. The purpose in advocating the wider use of containers was to reduce packing costs and provide door-to-door service. It was also recommended that rates be simplified and consolidated, that motor vehicles be used extensively in terminal service, that intermediate yard switchings be eliminated, and that short and fast trains be developed and put into service.

The procedure followed in the handling of the merchandise

traffic report was followed in the submission of the freight traffic report to the carriers. It was received by the AAR and turned over to a committee for analysis and recommendations. This committee submitted a report to Pelley under date of March 3, 1937, and said that no reply had been made to the coordinator when the report was originally submitted "on account of the approaching termination of that office." [20] The committee "reached the definite and final conclusion that there is nothing of value in the suggestions and recommendations contained in the report either to the individual railroads or the industry as a whole." As for the suggestion that the carload freight movement of the country use containers as the unit of loading, the committee said,

We cannot believe that the American railroads are much interested in providing a vehicle primarily intended to make readily and economically interchange of traffic with trucks and water lines or in a coordination of such instrumentalities of transportation when the effect of which will be a curtailment of the rail service and a substitution for a large portion of the rail service movements in part through competing agencies such as the trucks and the waterways. We believe that the interests of the railroads demand that they shall provide that kind of a vehicle for transportation which best meets the requirements of the shipping public and the railroads themselves without any regard to whether another kind of a vehicle would more readily adapt itself to a coordination of service as between the rail carriers on the one hand and their competitors on the other.[21]

There were also specific criticisms of other portions of the freight traffic report but they were perhaps contained in the observation, already noted, that there was "nothing of value in the suggestions and recommendations contained in the report either to the individual railroads or the industry as a whole." [22] *Railway Age,* however, thought that the report constituted a contribution of great value, and urged that it be given careful and sympathetic study "in order that no meritorious suggestions may be ignored." [23] It also said, "It is unfortunate that these reports are written in dogmatic, pedantic style with the more or less plain implication that railway executives know little about their own business." [24]

Passenger Traffic Report

The survey of passenger traffic by the section of transportation service was begun in October, 1933.[25] Two questionnaires and personal letters from the coordinator were sent to more than 100 of the larger railroads to elicit information about the volume and nature of traffic, the agencies for moving it, fares, costs, service requirements of passengers, and other related matters. A "passenger ballot" was distributed by the coordinator to 200,000 representative travelers in all parts of the United States. It took the form of a novel 24-page booklet asking for "votes" on various phases of transportation service.[26]

The passenger traffic report was submitted by Eastman to the regional coordinating committees on January 17, 1935, with the comment that a letter to him from a member of the informal advisory committee had said that some of the conclusions "reflect the feeling of a writer who is more inclined to be interested in things as they should be, rather than in things as it is practical to make them." [27] To Eastman this characteristic was "one of the merits of the report, for it is astonishing how often the impractical can be converted into the practical, given the will to do it." The "writer who is more inclined to be interested in things as they should be" was, of course, John R. Turney, the head of the section of transportation service, who in his letter transmitting the report to the coordinator said of it, "In a study — the primary objective of which is constructive criticism — it is difficult to avoid becoming hypercritical. The report is not intended as an indictment of carriers or of their management. In a small field I have done many of the very things which the report criticizes. The situation is not peculiar to this industry." [28] A unanimous opinion of the committee of three vice presidents of the Association of American Railroads which appraised the report was that "there is nothing in the passenger report of value to the carriers for general application nationally." [29]

Despite the exhibition of the customary skepticism from the Association of American Railroads, Eastman was later to express satisfaction with the way in which the railroad industry came to think about problems of passenger traffic. In stating his own conclusions about the passenger traffic report and the comments

made on it by the railroad enterprisers, he thought that the latter
had been somewhat more concerned with detail and less with principle than he "would have liked." But he thought that the consequences of the passenger traffic report were praiseworthy. He had
observed that there was a lack of progress in dealing with the
merchandise problem, but "similar comment on the passenger
traffic situation would be untrue." [30] He was glad to recognize and
to congratulate the railroads on the fundamentally important steps
they had taken and were taking towards a profitable passenger
service. Said Eastman,

The whole railroad attitude toward the passenger service seems to have
changed, and this was necessary. The fundamentals of the problem are
being attacked. By air conditioning and modernization of cars, railroad travel is being made comfortable. By the speeding up of trains,
railroad travel is being made more convenient. By reductions in basic
fares, railroad travel is being made economical. At the same time, attention is being given to reducing operating costs as well as to increasing
traffic volume. Furthermore, these forward steps have been taken, not
here and there, but quite generally over the country.[31]

Perhaps the reason for the contrast between the carriers' skepticism about what could be done and Eastman's optimism about
what the carriers were able to do is to be found in the nature of
the recommendations made by the section of transportation service
for the improvement of passenger traffic administration. The report discussed travel requirements desired by the respondents to
the passenger ballot with a certainty about prevailing opinion
that the carriers could not easily contradict. Among these were
safety, accessibility of railroad service, hospitality, convenience,
and comfort. Painstaking care was taken in the report to discuss
the particular demands of three classes of travelers: suburban or
commuter travel, local travel of less than a day's journey, and distance travel. The particular demands of each of these classes (and
subclasses) were analyzed with respect to four elements that vary
with different types of transportation service: schedules, frequency,
speed, and accommodations. There was one matter in particular
in which the section of transportation service took the carriers to
task, the practice of "tipping." The passenger traffic report said on
this point,

It is difficult to harmonize the attitude of railways toward "tipping" in passenger service, with that toward the same practice in freight service, where instant dismissal is the penalty for accepting gratuities. Tipping is more than a petty annoyance — it creates unnecessary and wasteful expense on the part of the traveler and substitutes the incentive of personal gain for a desire to render real service, resulting in extravagant treatment of one passenger and discourteous treatment of another. A trip on the railways reveals open palms extended at every step.[32]

Although Eastman was able to congratulate the carriers on the improvements they were able to make in the conduct of passenger traffic services, tipping was one area in which the practice of today still follows the precedent of two decades ago and more.

Purchasing and Standardization

Other sections of the office of the federal coordinator besides the section of transportation service were concerned with the elimination of waste and other preventable expense and the improvement of railroad methods. Among these was the section of purchases.

In a speech to the Railway Business Association in Chicago on November 11, 1933, Eastman pointed out that people could disagree on the causes of the depression but there was no room for disagreement on the need to revive the capital goods industries,[33] for the products of which the railroads were important customers. "If the railroads could begin buying again in some volume," he said, "it would reduce unemployment where it is most acute and have a healthful effect on the entire situation." Of course, the ability of the railroads to buy in volume depended in the main upon other factors than careful housekeeping practices among the carriers, but the improvement of the purchasing methods of the railroads was not unconnected with their reestablishment as important customers for hard goods. Eastman pointed out that he had established a section of purchases to promote economy in railroad purchasing, which he hoped to achieve through standardization and simplification of physical items and practices.

In 1934, in line with the coordinator's policy, the Association of American Railroads approved a system of regional boards to make periodic reviews of purchases by individual railroads and to promote observance of standards of equipment, for the purpose of conserving carrier revenues. It was Eastman's hope that this kind of public attention would do much towards eliminating the prevailing reciprocity between railways and equipment manufacturing companies under which railroads had tended to give emphasis to purchases of equipment from companies routing their traffic over the purchasing road.[34] At the same time Eastman persuaded the American Railway Association to appoint a special committee to study purchasing methods.[35] R. L. Lockwood, the head of the coordinator's section of purchases, spread the word in public speeches.[36] This activity went forward when the purchases and stores division of the American Railway Association completed arrangements with six Chicago railroads to furnish copies of all orders issued after May 1, 1934.[37]

This work of investigation and exhortation yielded the usual crop of reports. One matter of concern to the section of purchases was the sale and handling of scrap.[38] The sale of scrap represented a substantial amount of money. Even on the basis of the low volume of 1933 transactions, it was estimated by the coordinator that an increase of 15 per cent in net realization would amount to more than $4,000,000 annually. The difficulty in the sale and handling of scrap was symptomatic of a chronic ailment of the railroad industry — the administration of these transactions in small units under the separate managements of the individual railroads.

In an effort to overcome this specific aspect of a chronic weakness in the structure and organization of the railroad industry, a constant theme in many of the coordinator's recommendations, the section of purchases proposed [39] that the individual roads cooperate with each other for the purpose of making a joint study of the data in the report, that the possibility of establishing group marketing agencies be studied, and that the roads study methods by which the dismantling and scrap handling operations of groups of railroads could be centralized. Other more specific and technical recommendations proposed that scrap be prepared to the highest quality grades, that the roads themselves dismantle equipment to be scrapped rather than sell it on wheels, that scrap-sorting operations be consolidated with dismantling operations on individual railroads, and that uniform accounting systems be established. The recommendations to cooperate in making a joint study of the report, to establish uniform accounting systems, and to consolidate sorting and dismantling operations on individual railroads would, as the report pointed out, have no relevancy if it were possible immediately to concentrate all scrap handling in a few central plants. But since this change was unlikely, it was felt that there were things that specific railroads could be doing as they moved, if at all, towards the desirable degree of cooperation and centralized activity.

In still one other field — scientific research — the coordinator tried to persuade the railroad industry to centralize its facilities. In 1933, he persuaded the scientific advisory board of the National Research Council to appoint a committee to study the matter of scientific research for the railroads in cooperation with the railroads themselves and with the coordinator's office. He then requested the regional coordinating committees to appoint a committee to collaborate with the scientists and engineers.[40] If it seemed expedient to do so, the committee was to formulate a plan for carrying on such research, to aid in the initiation of the plan, and to advise in its subsequent operation. The appointment of this group was regarded by *Railway Age* as a challenge to the scientists by the railroads.[41] It was said that if the survey of the committee found useful application for centralized scientific research to be conducted by the railroads, all interested in the continued improvement of steam transportation would be indebted to it. And if it found that the centralized conduct of scientific research by the railroads on a large scale would be useless duplication of the effort then being put out from hundreds of sources, both railroad and industrial, all contributing to the continued development of steam railway transportation, "then a troublesome ghost will have been laid." The implication seems to have been that it would be desirable to lay the "troublesome ghost."

The committee held its first meeting in December 1933 and agreed that a survey should be made of the facilities and procedures used by the railroad industry in work of this nature and, further, that they should be compared with those of industrial organizations in which the results of research have been outstanding.[42] The work of the committee was finished in less than a year and its report was made public by Eastman on October 16, 1934.[43] It recommended that the railroads establish a centralized scientific research department to serve the interests of all of the railroads, and went into detail about the way in which it should be inaugurated, the qualifications to be considered in the selection of a director, and some of the issues of organization and budgeting. Eight months later, in an address before the Society of Automotive Engineers, Eastman said of his committee and its labors, "In a well-considered report, they reached, I am happy to say, the unanimous conclusion that the railroads ought to establish a centralized bureau for scientific research, and in the organization plan of the new Association of American Railroads there is provision for such a Department of Planning and Research, although it has not yet been established." [44] But his pleasure at having a unanimous report on a controversial ghost did not blind the coordinator to the kind of argument that would be adduced against it. In the same speech at White Sulphur Springs, he also remarked,

Some railroad officers, I am told, fear that such concentration of effort along these lines may stifle or discourage general initiative in the industry. They suggest that any program which is to bring into being new ideas, new methods, new instrumentalities of service needs all the initiative it can command. Apparently they feel that the more officers of individual companies labor on these matters, the more chance there will be for initiative or genius to emerge. The trouble with this theory is that most of these men will not have adequate facilities for research, and their efforts will be uncoordinated and often misdirected. The result is bound to be unnecessary and uneconomic diversity in practice and types of equipment, and inability to grasp some of the major opportunities.[45]

Sixteen months after the "well-considered report" with its "unanimous conclusion" that the railroads ought to establish a centralized bureau for scientific research, Eastman was still preaching the gospel of centralization to his anarchic congregration. He had appointed a mechanical advisory committee in June 1934 to assist his staff with respect to mechanical problems affecting the railroads. In the letter transmitting the report of the mechanical advisory committee to the regional coordinating committees, he said of it,

To my mind the report emphasizes the need for the creation by the Association of American Railroads of a central department for scientific, engineering, and economic research, well equipped and manned by men independent of any individual railroad or equipment company

. . . As you know, I have continually urged the creation of such a department, and in this I have the unanimous support of the committee appointed at my request to investigate this subject, jointly by the Regional Coordinating Committees and the Science Advisory Board of the National Research Council. Why, in view of the conclusions reached by the distinguished committee, such a department has not yet been created, I am at a loss to understand.[46]

The reasons surely were not hard to find, however. Among these were human inertia, the cost of establishing central research facilities, the continued interest in and use of the steam locomotive, and the lack of training of most railroad heads in ways that would cause them to look upon research as productive. Moreover, from its inception in 1934, the Association of American Railroads was seemingly more bent upon abolishing the office of the coordinator than in cooperating with it in the fulfillment of its responsibilities. And the persistent separatism of the carrier principalities was a divisive influence that was more glandular than rational.

Car Pooling

The established pattern of resistance to proposals for centralization worked against other reports. For example, on October 23, 1934, Eastman submitted to the regional coordinating committees a proposed plan for a freightcar pool, suggesting that a beginning be made with boxcars.[47] Ten pages were given over to answers to railroad objections to the operation of a freightcar pool. With Eastman's consent, the subject was turned over to the Association of American Railroads by the regional coordinating committees, whose membership so closely corresponded to that of the directors of the AAR. The association rejected the coordinator's proposal. As a substitute, the association on May 1, 1935, put into effect what was called the "average per diem plan for car hire settlement" for the use of boxcars, a plan designed to reduce empty boxcar mileage and roadhaul and terminal expense, while preserving the "principle of individual ownership." [48] On November 7, 1935, the car division of the association made a report to its members on the operation of the plan in which, although admitting that the data were insufficient, substantial success was already claimed in reaching the goals of the plan. Eastman had this report analyzed by his staff, which was critical, and tendered the criticism to the presidents of the Class I railroads in January, 1936, because he believed it "worthy of your careful consideration."

Fiscal Work

To take another example, on March 30, 1934, Eastman sent to the regional coordinating committees a copy of a massive report in two volumes suggesting the establishment of a central transportation clearing house for the settlement of interline accounts. The report was by N. B. Haley, a member of the staff of the Interstate Commerce Commission used by the coordinator as a consultant. The British railways had utilized such a central transportation clearing house for nearly a century, and a large number of motor bus companies had recently established such a clearing house in Chicago for the settlement of their interline accounts. A joint committee of railroad accounting and treasury officers, however, made an unfavorable report on Eastman's proposal and it was then transferred to the Association of American Railroads for further study. Somewhat along the same general line, the coordinator brought to the attention of the regional coordinating committees the recommendations prepared by his staff under the general supervision of N. B. Haley, for the establishment in New York City of a transportation fiscal corporation and a transportation trust company, both to be owned by and to work for the railroads collectively. The New York Stock Exchange required that companies whose securities are listed on the Exchange maintain transfer offices below Chamber Street. Most of the railway fiscal offices and agencies in New York City were in the financial district where the rent is highest. It was the feeling of the coordinator's staff that the item of rent would be one of the important savings were the railroads to handle their fiscal work through a consolidated office. There is no record of action on the recommendations to save money in the handling of bond registrations, interest payments, dividend payments, stock transfers and the like, and the railroads continued to maintain separate offices for these fiscal transactions or employed individual banks and other agencies to do it for them.

Grain Elevators

A third, although not final, example of the difficulty if not the futility of administration by study and report is the investigation of the rentals received by railroads for the storage of grain in elevators owned and operated by the roads. The reports, prepared by Research Assistant J. A. Little, were released to the public on August 30, 1934 with the observation that they had been sent to the regional coordinating committees.[49] The reports found that, in many cases, the rentals received by the roads under lease of their properties to private parties were inadequate and that, at certain of the large grain markets, the administration of these elevators resulted in much cross-hauling of traffic and unnecessary switching. It was recommended by Mr. Little that much better financial results could be secured if the ownership and operation of the railroad owned elevators in the large markets were pooled. The recommendations were rejected by the regional coordinating committees and by an association of the then present lessees of the railroad-owned elevators, who made a counter study of the position of their lessors and reached opposite conclusions from those of the coordinator's staff.

With that monumental patience and respect for the facts that characterized much of the coordinator's work, he had a resurvey made of the grain elevator situation in the light of the criticisms of the Little report by the grain elevator lessees and the regional coordinating committees. Many of the criticisms dealt with the accounting and valuation data used in the Little report, and all of these were reviewed and in some respects revised. On May 29, 1936, just about as he was leaving office, Eastman sent the revised report to the regional coordinating committees with the observation that the conclusions, which he endorsed, remained unchanged.[50] His final observations in this late report in the dying days of his administration seemed to be somewhat tart. He said,

This grain elevator situation is a typical product of railroad competition, when left to its own devices. It is a survival of the old rebating days. The elevators have been leased on inadequate terms to large concerns with a view to attracting or holding grain traffic to the lines of the owning railroads. If this practice were confined to a single railroad, or to a few out of many, it might be of competitive benefit; but when it becomes a general practice, it also becomes a general burden, without benefit to any railroad. Moreover, the privileges thus granted to the lessee operators of the elevators create an unwholesome situation in the grain markets which works to the disadvantage of the grain producers, as Mr. Little clearly shows in his reports. Rebates and like special railroad privileges always benefit the strong at the expense of the weak.

If the railroads concerned are able to cooperate with each other in a sound collective undertaking, they have an opportunity here to clean up a situation which is now burdensome to them, in a manner which will cut their expenses and add to their revenues and at the same time correct unwholesome and unhealthy grain-market conditions to the material advantage of the grain producers.

He also observed that it was "uncertain" whether he would be able to follow the matter up in his capacity as federal coordinator of transportation, but he indicated that he would bring to the attention of the Interstate Commerce Commission some of the practices uncovered by Mr. Little that were violations of the Interstate Commerce Act and the Elkins Act.

The Railroad Labor Reports

Much work was done by Eastman and his research staff in the preparation of studies and reports which led to legislation affecting both the carriers and their competitors, and the workers, organized and unorganized. These will be discussed in the next chapter. But, in addition, Eastman and his staff, and especially Otto S. Beyer, director of the coordinator's section of labor relations, were indefatigable in their search for facts about railroad employment and workers. Soon after the establishment of the coordinator's office, the section of labor relations organized an advisory committee of distinguished prestige in the field of labor relations and labor market administration. It included J. Douglas Brown, then director of the industrial relations section of the Department of Economics and Social Institutions at Princeton; Meredith Givens of the Social Science Research Council; Walton Hamilton of the Yale Law School; Alvin H. Hansen, then professor of economics at the University of Minnesota and later at Harvard University; William Leiserson, who became a member and then chairman of the National Mediation Board; Isador Lubin, who became commissioner of labor statistics of the Department of Labor and later an official of the United Nations; Isaiah L. Sharfman, chairman of the Department of Economics at the University of Michigan and the author of the definitive work on the first five decades of the Interstate Commerce Commission; Sumner H. Slichter of the Harvard Business School; and William H. Stead, then associate director of the employment service in the Department of Labor. This group canvassed the entire railroad labor situation and made certain recommendations for study to the coordinator, especially in connection with coordination projects and other labor-saving improvements. These he listed as "merging of seniority rosters, reimbursement of transfer expense, specialized placement service, unemployment benefits, dismissal compensation, retirement annuities, hours readjustments, limitations on hours and mileage." [51]

As did all of the staff of the federal coordinator, the section of labor relations worked prodigiously and produced numerous reports.[52] A year before the expiration of his office, the coordinator reported that benefits to the railroads from the activities of his office were largely "benefits to come, which will accrue gradually." [53] Although he thought that it was possible even then to identify direct financial benefits from certain of his activities, he felt that research takes time and that it is impossible immediately to digest and assimilate the results. This was true of the many technical management and operating studies made by the coordinator's staff, and it was true of the studies of workers and wages. Acting under Section 13 of the Emergency Railroad Transportation Act, the coordinator, mainly through his section of research, prepared a series of studies on wages, hours, and working conditions in forms of transportation competitive with railroads.[54] These reports did not provoke controversy but were viewed as important contributions to an understanding of transportation conditions in general, and in particular those conditions affecting interagency competition.

The Public Aids Report

Railroads were not only concerned with inequalities of regulation[55] and with labor conditions in competitive fields of transportation, but also with subsidies that they ascribed to their competitors. The coordinator gave the subject of public aids exhaustive study in a four-volume printed report, *Public Aids to Transportation*, which was released in 1940, four years after the expiration of his office. All forms of transportation were covered but the greatest controversy centered on the question whether commercial users of the highways were paying their fair share of the cost of providing highway facilities. The railroads were not happy about the findings of the report on this subject, and made efforts to refute them.[56] The disagreement still persists. The public aids report had a great measure of influence and is the only Eastman study that still receives fairly common notice in current discussion. The report played a part in the planning of the work being done to find ways and means of assessing proper charges against motor vehicle users and other beneficiaries of the gigantic road program which Congress initiated in 1956.

Although not on public aids, one other report of the coordinator has had a subsequent history of importance, the *Report on Cost Finding in Railway Freight Service for Regulatory Purposes.* This report, issued in June, 1936, was a pioneering and influential work which led the way to the development of the Commission's cost work, now very much a going concern.

X. COORDINATING THE COMPETITION

"Much of the demand for regulation and restriction of the other transportation agencies has come from the railroads, for their own protection. Equally selfish interests are uppermost in the opposition. The controversy has been largely between private interests, but it is the public interest which must be paramount and controlling."
Second Report of the Federal Coordinator, p. 5

It was said earlier that coordination is really a problem in the exercise of power. The literal term means to be in equal rank or order, with the suggestion that harmony will emerge and conflict will vanish when this conjuncture occurs. As between two organizations, it means an alignment of their jurisdictions so that they do not clash. Every organization is a center of power, in weak or strong concentration, with a mechanism for making the decisions that direct the group, under leaders who operate the mechanism. A realignment of jurisdictions may reduce the number of such centers of power, and the leaders who operate the decision mechanism may object to realignment because it eliminates them or contracts their authority. The elimination of conflict at the points where organizations and groups impinge upon each other is certainly a matter of the public interest, since those not immediately privy to the conflict may be adversely affected, and the way in which all may protect themselves is through the instrumentality of the government. Government is superior power brought to bear upon the operators of private groups to eliminate marginal conflicts between such private groups that threaten the totality.

But the power of government is fractured, diffused, and split. It is divided up into small units of force administered through administrative conduits. The office of the federal coordinator of transportation carried power of too small voltage to force the carriers to realign their jurisdictions in such a way as to achieve the purposes of the Emergency Railroad Transportation Act of

1933; and auxiliary power, like that of the White House, or of influential unofficial group constituencies, was not available.

The railroads thought much better of coordination as a principle when the proposal was to eliminate some of the force of the competition of agencies and facilities outside the railroad industry — the motor buses and trucks, the waterways and pipe lines, and even the embryo air transport industry. Although the carriers and the coordinator may have started from different premises and expected somewhat different results, they were both agreed on the need for "coordinating" the principal rivals to the railroads.

From the point of view of the railroads, federal regulation of the rival forms of transportation was justified on the ground that it would help them. Eastman's view was broader. Under the title, "Coordination," in his *Second Report,* he said,

The presence and use of these differing forms of transportation raises the question whether destructive competition should be lessened and constructive coordination be increased. Stated more concretely, the question is whether it is sound public policy to encourage duplication of facilities and warfare all along the line, or to find the work which each form of transportation can do best and endeavor accordingly to build up a national transportation system in which the various agencies will function with more regard to correlation and less to competition and with a minimum of waste.[1]

In moving towards the coordination of other forms of transportation with the railroads, Eastman was to be more successful than he had been in persuading the railroads to take the internal coordination medicine he prescribed. In political terms, the reason was simple. The power of Congress itself was brought to bear, and the Congress, the Interstate Commerce Commission, the carriers, the coordinator, and the White House were able to accomplish an advance in the motor bus and trucking industries that the coordinator alone found impossible in his dealings with the railroads.[2]

Eastman's General Transportation Policy

The coordinator early set out the framework within which his thought about the coordination of all transportation was to fit. In a speech before the Interstate Bus and Truck Conference at Harrisburg in October, 1933, he said, "A predominant idea behind the creation of this office was that our national railroad system suffers from much waste motion and unapplied or misapplied effort due to its ownership by many separate companies and the consequent fact that it is operated by a small army of independent feudal chieftains who fight a good deal among themselves and band together for the common good with considerable difficulty." [3] Although this speech was before the bus and truck people and not the carriers, this conception of the railroad industry was one that Eastman was to convey to the railroaders themselves in spoken and written statements. Of his general ideas, Eastman said, "The second thought, and a very important one, was that the railroad system is only a part of the transportation system of the country, and that the latter is in need of attention in its entirety." With these premises, it was clear to Eastman that the relief of the railroads would have to be achieved not by relaxing the regulation of the railroads but by extending regulation to the other forms of transportation.[4] And to complete the master scheme for the coordination of all transportation, Eastman suggested that federal controls should be administered by a single agency of the federal government, the Interstate Commerce Commission.[5] He was to repeat all of these themes in many speeches in 1934 and 1935, while consideration was being given in Congress to the enactment of specific proposals for the regulation of the entire transportation net under the jurisdiction of the Interstate Commerce Commission.[6]

The National Transportation Conference

Outside the Congress, numerous groups interested in the railroad industry organized to formulate a general transportation program that would help the railroads by regulating their competitors. The first meeting of what came to be called the National Transportation Conference of 1933 was held in Chicago in July to discuss the making of a united front on new transportation legislation. At this meeting of some 32 representatives of transportation, business, and financial associations, leadership was supplied by Harry A. Wheeler, president of the Railway Business Association, an organization of suppliers in the railroad industry.[7] Wheeler had been head of the United States Chamber of Commerce in 1919 and had organized a similar combination of railroad interests to prepare a united front on transportation legislation at that time, successfully enough to have some influence on the Transportation Act of 1920.[8] As one of the reporters of the conference put it, Mr. Wheeler in discussing the need for the 1933 conference said,

The experience of the last session of Congress and of other sessions also, had shown the committee hearings were frequently worse than useless, due to the divergent and conflicting testimony presented. In effect the committees found it necessary to write their own bills. By bringing the major interests together in meetings extending over a number of months and letting them "fight it out," common ground would be reached on many matters before Congressional hearings began. The major engagements of the battle would be over, the smoke cleared away, and helpful assistance would be possible.[9]

There is irony in the solicitude expressed by Mr. Wheeler that Congressmen might have to write the laws that Congressmen enact. But, irony apart, the experience of the Transportation Conference usefully illustrates the interest structure of the railroad industry and the collateral groups serving it and served by it. A national transportation policy was to be developed by the cross pull of pressures inside this congeries — "letting them 'fight it out' " — and it was then to be presented to Congress for ratification. In this instance, groups that were to "fight it out" were strongly oriented towards the railroads.[10]

As a starter, the two subjects to occupy the conference were the desirability of private ownership of the railroads and equality of regulation. There was no concealment of the intention to develop an industry view on these and other matters so that a united presentation could be made "before Congressional committees at hearings on the permanent transportation legislation Roosevelt has indicated will be presented at the next session of Congress and Coordinator Eastman has been instructed to get in shape." [11] But the University of Chicago professor of transportation, Lewis C. Sorrell, who was made secretary of the conference, was reported to have said that the representatives were meeting with "open mind." [12] At a meeting of the conference in September, the members managed to make up their minds, and came out sturdily for private ownership and operation of the railroads,[13] although they were less clear about regulation of transportation by highways and waterways. But this time the Conference was on a permanent basis, with Harry Wheeler in as permanent chairman,[14] and it proceeded to set up certain research committees to prepare reports on rates charged for transport by railroad, highway, and waterway and the ratio of facilities provided by each agency to the amount of traffic offered.[15] At exactly the same time, Eastman announced his desire to get from shippers, trade associations, organizations of transportation agencies, boards of trade, chambers of commerce, and so on, facts and comment on a wide range of matters having to do with federal legislation, and especially the regulation of competing forms of transportation.[16]

The Transportation Conference was ready to report after some nine months had passed and it came out with proposals that could have been predicted.[17] It repeated its opposition to government ownership and operation of the railroads, recommended that Interstate Commerce Commission control of the railroads be lessened, and recommended that federal regulation be extended to include the highways and waterways. At about the time of this report, Eastman was saying to an audience of bankers,

In one of my reports, I have discussed the possibility of public ownership and operation of the railroads frankly and in no unfriendly spirit. I have no desire to assume the role of propagandist for public ownership and operation, or to have such a policy adopted until the people of the United States either want it or believe it to be necessary, and in that event it is highly desirable that the country should be prepared to undertake it in the best possible way and with all possible safeguards. Personally, I have been a rather close observer of private operation under public regulation for nearly 30 years, and I started with a definite disbelief in public ownership and operation. I am not of that mind now, for reasons which I have undertaken to give on other occasions.[18]

Instead of a lessening of the regulation of the railroad industry, Eastman had committed himself to a policy of extending regulation to competing forms of transportation,[19] not for the purpose merely of "equalizing" the burden of regulation on the railroads but for the far more legitimate purpose of developing the transportation net of the country as a unity. As to the extension of federal regulation to the highways and waterways, Eastman had already submitted specific proposals for such regulation to the Congress with the full approval of the Interstate Commerce Commission.

The Legislative Program of the Unions

Before considering Eastman's specific recommendations for new legislation, attention must be given to the legislative program of the railroad unions during the period of the coordinator, if only to underline and point up the multiplicity of interests concerned with the writing of rules for the regulation of the railroad industry and its competitors. Although the unions had no grand scheme for the coordination of the transportation system, such as those considered by Eastman, and tended to concentrate on the hours, wages, and working conditions of railroad employees, their positions on these specific matters and their support of other specific bills had some place in the evolution of Eastman's general transportation policy.

Like the Transportation Conference, the Railway Labor Executives Association met in the months after the establishment of the office of the federal coordinator to prepare a program of legislation to be submitted to him in connection with his forthcoming recommendations for legislation, and to the Congress. One of the immediate decisions was to oppose the Prince plan for the consolidation of the railroads.[20] The leaders of the RLEA met with Eastman[21] and with President Roosevelt in pre-Congress sessions to enlist support for a program that included revision of the Railway Labor Act of 1926, a six-hour day, a train-limit bill, a full-crew bill, amendment of the hours-of-service law, and amendment of the employers liability act.[22]

With the cooperation of Senator Burton K. Wheeler of Montana and Representative Robert Crosser of Ohio, legislation was immediately introduced in Congress to regulate the size of train crews and the length of trains, to establish the six-hour day, to bring sleeping car and express companies under the Emergency Railroad Transportation Act, and to amend the Railway Labor Act of 1926.[23] In a letter to the subcommittee of the Senate Committee on Interstate Commerce, Eastman said that he had no objection to the inclusion of sleeping car and express companies under the Emergency Railroad Transportation Act, provided the amendment was properly worded.[24] Hearings were held on all these measures, and certain others besides, and a special committee of the Railway Labor Executives Association headed by George Harrison, president of the Brotherhood of Railway Clerks, stayed on guard in Washington to procure the enactment of the legislation if possible.

The Senate Committee on Interstate Commerce in May reported a railroad retirement pension bill in spite of Eastman's testimony that "the information now at hand does not permit of wise and well-considered legislation on the subject of pensions." [25] He intervened in the proposal to amend the Railway Labor Act of 1926 and proposed the establishment of a national board of adjustment as a substitute for the bill proposed by the RLEA. The Senate committee followed Eastman's recommendation in this matter. Eastman's advice on the bill to establish a six-hour day for railroad employees was not asked, and the House Committee on Interstate and Foreign Commerce bottled up the bill until it was forced to report it by a discharge petition.

Although the pension act was passed, later to be declared unconstitutional by the Supreme Court,[26] most of the legislative program by the Railway Labor Executives Association in the Seventy-third Congress failed of enactment and it was necessary to reintroduce it.[27] The program for the Seventy-fourth Congress included measures to establish the six-hour day on the railroads, to require full crews on the trains, to amend the Federal Employers Liability Act and the Hours-of-Service Law, and to provide for more rigorous inspection of tracks, bridges, and signals.[28] These proposals, as were those that constituted the trade union program for the Seventy-third Congress, were addressed less to the rehabilitation of the industry than to the protection of the immediate interests of the workers. This fact was clearly evident in the proposal made by George Harrison, chairman of the Railway Labor Executives Association, that the unions would attempt to include in any new railroad legislation a section similar to that in the Emergency Railroad Transportation Act of 1933, controlling and limiting dismissals arising from the enforcement of the provisions of the act.[29]

Eastman's general transportation program and that of the trade unions were far apart, and the distance between them was nowhere more clearly apparent than in Eastman's speech before 1500 representatives of 21 railroad brotherhoods in Chicago in January 1935.[30] After speaking about the historical and economic causes for the distressed condition of the railroad industry, and after underscoring the difficulty railroads faced in competing with rivals not under the same degree of regulation, Eastman said,

Now I may be right in all this and I may be wrong, but in either event what ought railway labor to do: It seems perfectly clear to me that this is no time to add to railroad expense, and that labor will suffer if this is done. Take the 6-hour day . . . The 6-hour day, unless it is put in at the expense of labor, will add at least $400,000,000 to railroad expenses. The railroads cannot possibly stand that without harm, unless an equivalent burden is put at the same time upon their competitors; and I doubt whether they can stand it without harm even then, unless a like burden is put upon all industry . . . The shortened workday, if it is anything, is a general issue. It cannot be applied to the railroads alone without disaster.[31]

Of the full-crew bill and the train-length bill, Eastman was equally critical. He said, "Perhaps they can be sustained on the ground of safety, although I think you will agree that this is, at least, debatable. But as mere 'make-work' measures, what will they do to the railroads in their competition with the trucks and boats and all the other competitive agencies? Has railway labor anything to gain by putting such a handicap on their own form of transportation?" [32] Eastman said that he was fully aware of and deeply sympathized with the economic pinch felt by railroad workers and hoped and trusted that some of the activities of the federal coordinator would ease it. He told his audience that he was in favor of pensions and dismissal compensation, the latter to be available to workers laid off as a result of consolidation or coordination projects enforced under the Emergency Railroad Transportation Act of 1933.[33]

Eastman's words fell on unresponsive ears. As Harrison of the Railway Clerks told the press, "The statement made today by the Federal Coordinator of Transportation, Hon. Joseph B. Eastman, before the railway employees, will have no effect whatsoever on the legislative program of the railway labor organizations. Their program has been introduced in Congress and every possible effort will be directed toward securing its enactment." [34] And Congress eventually enacted a bill that seemed to bear out Eastman's statement that more study was needed before a reasonable pension system could be developed.[35]

The experience that Eastman had in developing the outlines of a general transportation policy, which the Emergency Railroad Transportation Act of 1933 entrusted to him, was not unique. Indeed, his experience was typical. The making of railroad policy was not centered in the Congress. The power to make such policy was diffused, scattered, and distributed among the many parties in interest, in fact, if not in law. The carriers were interested in promoting specific schemes for the rationalization of the industry that would serve the carriers. The unions had no comprehensive plans for the rationalization of the industry, but they did have programs to protect the position of the existing workers, whether broad schemes for the regulation of the industry were adopted or not. General transportation policy emerged residually from the efforts of the carriers, the coordinator, the unions, shippers, and many others to establish rules that would govern their relations with others. What emerged from this legislative struggle was the minimum consensus to which all of the interested parties would agree.[36]

Regulating the Motor Carriers

Eastman's proposals for the regulation of motor carriers, water carriers and other forms of transportation under the Interstate Commerce Commission were contained in his *Second Report* and repeated, with some changes, in his *Third Report,* issued in March 1934 and January 1935 respectively. These reports were studiously documented and thoroughly considered. They were not, however, the first suggestions for the regulation of the motor carriers[37] nor indeed the only suggestions during the period of the coordinator.[38] In fact, there had been a total of some 34 bills presented to Congress from 1925 to 1935 for the regulation of motor carriers, some of which proposed the regulation of carriers of persons and of freight and some of only the carriers of persons. Despite expected opposition from organized shippers and truck operaters, Eastman, after a characteristically thorough survey of opinion, came to the conclusion that "there is a rather general demand for Federal regulation of motor carriers, although views differ as to how far control of truck rates should go and as to numerous details of regulation." [39]

The case for regulation of motor carriers, in Eastman's opinion, was very strong, because of the anarchic nature of the competition. Intercity trucking, he found, was disorganized, and much of it was in an economically unsound condition because of the small scale of operations, the existence of three distinctive but highly competitive kinds of operators, and the ease of entering the business. The three kinds of operators were common carriers, contract carriers, and private operators, and the small scale of operations made it possible for poorly trained, inadequately financed, irresponsible fly-by-nights to demoralize rates out of desperation or ignorance. The depression had increased the difficulties of the industry because it had drawn many unemployed into the business, made thousands of second-hand trucks available at low prices, and by low labor, fuel, and tire costs had invited their purchase. But the motor carrier operators were not alone to blame for the disorderly state of the industry. Shippers and truck manufacturers or their sales representatives had done much to disorganize the rate structure and encourage incompetent operators to enter the business. [40]

Coordination was the cure for this disorderly competition, and in this aspect of his work of three years, Eastman seems to have been clearer about what coordination entailed than he was in promoting it in the internal affairs of the railroads. After describing the competitive phase of the motor carrier industry, Eastman said, "Coordination is the obverse side," and he proceeded to define it with the help of one of the earlier ICC investigations into the motor carrier industry. [41] Coordination, as previously defined by the ICC, was the "combining [of] two or more forms of transportation in the interest of better service or economy." [42] Such coordination could be achieved through a single transportation agency or through the cooperative efforts of several transportation agencies. Eastman added, "Coordination may also mean a division of the field of transportation, each agency concentrating on the work it can do best with a minimum of overlapping." [43]

There was little coordination in the motor carrier industry in this last sense. Many short or branch railroad lines were abandoned and more would be abandoned to independent motor transport or to motor transport under railroad auspices. But, he thought, there was more coordination of the first kind than was commonly supposed, some unplanned and some resting on more formal arrangements. Federal regulation would promote coordination throughout the motor carrier industry to the end that each of the two great systems in the national transportation net would concentrate on the work that it could do best, with a minimum of overlapping. This is the classic realignment of jurisdictions which is central to certain forms of coordination.

There were objections to federal regulation but Eastman thought that there was no objection that could not be overcome. The chief difficulties would be "in securing adherence to published rates, particularly by contract carriers; in preventing private carriers from engaging in for-hire operations without proper authorization; in securing accurate accounting and records; in the granting of certificates and permits; and in prescribing minimum rates, where that proves necessary." [44]

The choice of means was of greatest importance if the goal of coordination was to be realized. The codes were inadequate for this purpose because code regulation, being primarily industrial self-regulation, was ill-suited to the conciliation of group conflicts with other elements of the entire transportation industry. As Eastman said, "Proper coordination of all transportation agencies is of fundamental importance, and it is therefore necessary that their regulation be coordinated." [45] He felt that the need for coordinating all forms of transportation was strong, and, as he said, "it is difficult to see how this can be done without also coordinating regulation." [46]

The most viable device for coordinating the regulation of a coordinated transportation system was the Interstate Commerce Commission. To this suggestion Eastman anticipated certain objections that he thought he could meet. First, to the suggestion that the Commission was overloaded and could not perform additional duties efficiently, he said that the duties of the Commission were lighter in 1935 than they had heretofore been. Second, to the suggestion that the Commission was "railroad-minded" and hence incapable of dealing wisely and effectively with the problems of other forms of transportation, he had two answers. The first was that the railroad carriers had never thought that the Commission was unduly favorable to the railroads; and, second, expertness in motor carrier operations could be developed by the creation of a bureau within the Commission staffed with men having the required background.

Eastman did not feel that the Commission would make the railroad rate structure the inevitable base for determining the charges to be made by other forms of transportation but thought that the normal basic rate would be determined by the form of transportation showing the lowest cost. This was in accord with the principle of coordination he accepted; namely, the division of the field of transportation in such a way that each transportation agency would concentrate upon the work that it could do best — adequate service at reasonable prices. He was not unaware that the Commission's procedures were thought by some to be too bureaucratic, rigid, and cumbersome for the effective regulation of 1935 transportation, but this objection was not fatal to his proposal to lodge regulatory authority over motor carriers in the Commission. Every effort would be made to improve these procedures.[47]

With these facts, warnings, qualifications, caveats, and cautions, Eastman then proposed a scheme for the regulation of the motor carrier industry under the jurdisdiction of the Interstate Commerce Commission. His measure was based largely on the Rayburn bill, to which the Commission had already given its approval, but differed from it in a number of respects.[48] Like the Rayburn bill, Eastman's proposal aimed at comprehensive regulation of the motor common carriers, less comprehensive regulation of the contract carriers, and no regulation of the private carriers.[49] The chief supporters of the legislation at this time were the railroads, the state utilities commissioners, the Interstate Commerce Commission, the motor common carriers, and the big truckers. Those opposed included the smaller truckers and the motor truck manufacturers.[50] The principal labor organization, the International Teamsters, was somewhat inert,[51] although it did not remain so, coming to favor regulation strongly.

While the truckers were split for a time in their attitude towards federal regulation of the trucking industry,[52] the representatives and spokesmen of the buses were constant in their support.[53] That the motor bus operators were interested in supporting federal regulation of their own industry may seem unusual, but without such regulation the interstate operators were exposed to disorderly competition and were prey to "chiseling" under the code rates by the railroads which were not under codes. Eastman understood the plight of the motor bus operators sympathetically and demonstrated this fact both before and after his proposals for statutory regulation in speeches before members of the industry.[54] When the truckers, after the demise of the codes, also turned towards support of the motor carrier bill, he found value in their experience under the codes because it helped to show them that, when competition flourishes, the "little fellow" is bound to suffer, and that therefore the "guiding hand of the Government is needed." [55]

As had been noted, the shippers were charged by Eastman with some of the responsibility for the state of the motor transport industry, and the shippers, through their strongest organization, the National Industrial Traffic League, opposed "any Federal regulation that goes beyond the keeping of records, the filing of reports, and joint arrangements for complete service between railroads and trucks." [56] As one of the trade journals put it, "Shippers — meaning the manufacturers and dealers of the country — as represented by their traffic men, do not, for obvious reasons, want equality of regulation; they prefer to keep the immediate advantages that result to them from unhampered competition by trucks and water transport." [57] This definition of shippers was too narrow, for the shippers of unprocessed farm products — to wit, the farmers — were also beneficiaries of "unhampered competition," and had an even more direct stake in motor vehicle regulation since they owned and used their own trucks on the highways. Farm organizations, such as the National Grange, opposed various aspects of the Eastman proposal and showed fear that a "railroad-minded ICC" might pull up both common carrier and contract truck rates to the level of rail rates by taking complaints from competing carriers.[58]

The array of group forces in favor of enactment of the motor carrier bill made passage of such a measure more likely than at any time in the previous eight years to which the Interstate Commerce Commission had given it its intermittent attention. The Rayburn bill, which anticipated the report and recommendations of the federal coordinator, was introduced in the House of Representatives on January 12, 1934, and hearings were begun on January 17.[59] It was not clear at the outset, however, whether the President would strongly press for the enactment of bus and truck legislation at this session of Congress,[60] and the hearings were limited to two weeks. Formal committee action on the measure was postponed by Rayburn, the chairman of the House Committee on Interstate and Foreign Commerce, until Eastman's report and recommendations and the reaction of the President to both.[61] The ICC supported the Rayburn bill with minor changes. Eastman's report and recommendations appeared in March 1934, and his proposed bill was introduced as S.3171, but no action was taken on this bill or on the Rayburn bill in the last session of the Seventy-third Congress.

New hearings before the Senate Committee on Interstate Commerce and a subcommittee of the House Committee on Interstate and Foreign Commerce were held in February and March 1935.[62] Eastman, McManamy, chairman of the legislative committee of the ICC, and officials of the NARUC supported the measure in the House subcommittee.[63] Most of the questioning was conducted by skeptical Congressmen who showed concern as to whether regulation might not increase truck rates and stifle the development of the industry. Eastman did not believe that truck rates would be increased substantially but thought that there would be increases in some rates that were uneconomically low.

In the Senate committee, apprehension was expressed as to whether individuals who operated their own trucks might not be put at an unacceptable disadvantage. Senator Wheeler of Montana said that there was some feeling among the members of Congress that there should be no regulation of motor vehicle transportation on the ground that it was a new industry. The American Trucking Associations, Inc., argued that the code provisions for the trucking industry should be given a full trial. Events were to show that this trial was not to last longer than some two or three months more. A representative of the National Industrial Traffic League said that his organization favored by a slight majority "reasonable and logical regulation" of highway transportation but felt the Eastman measure did not insure fair treatment for shippers. This view was echoed by other shippers' organizations, such as the American National Livestock Association and the National Wool Growers Association, both of which said that they supported reasonable regulation but objected to most of the detail of the Eastman bill. Complete and utter objection was voiced by spokesmen for the National Grange and other farmers' organizations.[64] As the hearings came to a close, it was reported that Eastman would sit with the members of the congressional committees when the bills were to be considered in executive session.[65]

On April 8, the Senate Committee on Interstate Commerce voted in favor of the Eastman bill with many amendments in detail that had been suggested by Eastman, the ICC, and interested groups. Important among these was an amendment recommended by the ICC giving it the power to fix the qualifications and hours of service of employees in motor vehicle transportation, including the employees of private carriers. The Senate Committee decided against giving the ICC the power to compel the establishment of through rates and joint rates for motor carriers and railroads, although provision was made for the permissive establishment of such rates.[66] On April 16, the Senate passed the bill without a record vote and the measure was sent to the House.[67]

The anxieties expressed by some of the House members over the effect of regulation on truckers, especially the self-employed operators, influenced the action of the House subcommittee on the Eastman bill. Representative Huddleston of Alabama, in fact, reported a brand new bill to the full House committee which provided for regulation of the motor bus industry only and made no provision for the regulation of truckers.[68] The full House committee voted 11–8 against the bill reported to it by Huddleston, appointed a new subcommittee from which Mr. Huddleston was omitted, and referred the Senate bill to it.[69] Reporters asked President Roosevelt whether the motor carrier bill was a "must" bill, and although he said that he objected to the notion that he had given Congress any list of "must" bills, he nevertheless said that it should be included among those it would be desirable for the Congress to pass. The House committee made a favorable report on the bill in its Senate version on July 23 and proposed only a few changes from the form in which the measure had passed the Senate. Among these changes was an exemption of all intrastate rates from federal regulation, in distinction from the rule on railroad rates laid down in the Shreveport doctrine.[70] This change was meant to please the state commissioners under whose jurisdiction intrastate rates normally would come unless they discriminated against or otherwise burdened interstate commerce. Agricultural shippers were heeded when the House committee exempted from the operation of the bill the hauling of livestock and unprocessed agricultural products; and the American Newspaper Publishers' Association, which had been critical of both the Rayburn and the Eastman bills, was pacified when trucks engaged exclusively in the hauling of newspapers were exempted from the operation of the bill.[71]

The Senate accepted the House amendments and so, after "years of controversy and ten years after the introduction of the first bill on the subject," the bill became law.[72] In its final form, the measure was called the Motor Carrier Act, 1935, and the legislation was made a part of the Interstate Commerce Act. Jurisdiction over interstate motor common carriers was vested in the Interstate Commerce Commission. It was authorized to pass on applications for certificates of public convenience and necessity. A "grandfather clause" entitled those who were in bona fide operation on June 1, 1935, to such certificates without further proof that the public convenience would be served. The Commission was empowered to fix the maximum, minimum, or going rates for common carriers, to fix the requirements for reasonable service, and to establish and enforce standards for accounting, records, and the qualifications and maximum hours for the personnel of common carriers. Other provisions empowered the Commission to regulate security issues, consolidations, mergers, acquisitions of control, the organization of motor carriers, and the management of their business.

Contract carriers could get permits on a showing of consistency with the public interest. They were subject to the same regulations as to minimum rates, accounting, hours of service, and safety regulations as applied to common carriers. Private carriers were subject only to the latter provisions.

After the enactment of the new statute, opinion of the business and other communities interested in the legislation was generally approving. *Business Week*[73] had found it possible to be in the affirmative and the negative, although not at the same time. In March this journal had said that "nobody likes the Eastman bill, not even the railroads." But in August the railroads had "been sitting tight — hoping, praying for some bus regulation — but not too loud." [74] *Railway Age* said that it had been active throughout in the move to get the statute on the books.[75] F. E. Williamson, president of the New York Central, was reported as saying, "While the law was urged by the railroads in their own interest, I believe it will prove equally beneficial to the operators of highway vehicles who conduct their businesses according to sound business principles and safety considerations." [76] In October, Eastman told state administrators that he thought that the dissimilarities between motor vehicle and railroad regulation predominated over the similarities, and promised that he and the Commission would enter their new duties with a full sense of their importance and complexity.[77] Two days later, he said before another group that the Motor Carrier Act, 1935, had "laid on the shoulders of the Interstate Commerce Commission one of the biggest and most difficult jobs which has ever come its way." [78] To the American Trucking Associations, Inc. (which eventually came to support the legislation after playing a somewhat ambivalent role), Eastman said, "If it had not been for the support of the Associations, I do not believe it [that is, the statute] would now be law." [79]

The effective date of the Motor Carrier Act, 1935, was October 1, 1935, and events moved inside Congress and in the Commission to get the new system of regulation under way, with more difficulty in the former than the latter quarter. Money above the regular appropriation for the ICC was provided by the Congress in a bill that got caught in a filibuster conducted by Senator Huey Long of Louisiana.[80] Congress eventually enacted the appropriation but delays in other respects required postponement for several months of the date of effectiveness of many of the provisions of the act.[81]

In the meantime, the ICC had made some internal reorganization to prepare itself for the administration of the new powers. An additional division of the Commission (consisting of three commissioners) was created to carry out the new motor vehicle responsibilities, with Eastman as the chairman. A new bureau, the bureau of motor carriers, was also formed inside the Commission, with John L. Rogers, Coordinator Eastman's executive assistant, as the director.[82] When the new bureau was set up, the Civil Service Commission rated the positions lower in the pay scale than Eastman had. He was moved to address a fervent argument to the Commission to up-grade the classifications.[83]

One immediate result of the move to coordinate the competition of the railroads by legislation bringing the motor vehicle carriers under the Interstate Commerce Commission was a closer union of the motor carriers and the railroads, although the two sets of carriers have been at each others' throats ever since. One of the first moves was a statement by the National Association of Motor Bus Operators that they would cooperate with the ICC in every way possible.[84] It was then reported that the truckers and shippers, pushing forward for cooperation under the new act, had invited the railroads to sit down with them and consider desirable means of improving "strained relations and coordinating transportation service by rail and highway." [85] As its contribution to the warm glow of good feeling that temporarily, (at least) seemed to be stealing over formerly bitter partisans, *Railway Age* said that the act meant that the highway common carrier was now a public utility[86] and suggested, "Some sort of coordination should be made between the rail and the highway pricing agencies." A "harmony conference" of representatives of the motor and rail carriers met in Washington on December 30, to Eastman's expressed gratification, and steps were taken to set up a permanent organization to bespeak the new-found community of interest.[87] The National Industrial Traffic League, the American Trucking Associations, Inc., and the Association of American Railroads sent ambassadors to this treaty conference, each of these organizations being the bureaucratic arm of a powerful empire of economic interest.[88] It was said that this was "the first time that representatives of the land transportation agencies and their shipper customers ever came together to discuss their problems from a national standpoint around a conference table." [89]

The impulse that moved these adversary groups into combination was not altruism, of course. The formal invitation to confer came from the truckers but the suggestion, according to report, was initiated by the shippers.[90] Although the railroads had their grievances against the truckers, both had a grievance against the shippers, since they were responsible largely for rate reductions by playing carriers off against each other. But both truckers and shippers were aware that the railroads were formidable adversaries in a competitive struggle, and the roads were not sure that they wanted to "cooperate" with the competition they had just succeeded in helping to "coordinate."

The Water Carriers

In his *Second Report,* Eastman devoted much less attention to the water carrier industry than to the motor carrier industry but he nevertheless came out with the same conclusions and made the same recommendation that the industry should come under closer federal regulation.[91] The ICC already had some jurisdiction over the water carriers and the shipping board bureau of the Department of Commerce also had some.[92] Indirectly, the ICC had had a considerable effect upon the water carriers, under the famous Section 4 of the Interstate Commerce Act — the long-and-short-haul clause — which forbade railroads to charge more for a short haul than a long haul in the same direction. This provision, included in the original act of 1887 and strengthened in 1910 and 1920, had originated in the competition of the railroads with the water carriers. Through the ruthless manipulation of long-and-short-haul rates, the railroads "practically destroyed the earlier competition on many of the inland waterways, and also impaired some coastwise competition and such intercoastal competition as existed prior to the construction of the Panama Canal."[93] Although the remedial effects of the strengthened Section 4 had been very beneficial to the water carriers, and a combination of other factors had done much to restore water transportation to a place of considerable importance in the national transportation system, the industry suffered from "too much and uncontrolled competition." "Within the industry itself," said Eastman, "competition has been particularly severe."[94] He thought that self-regulation through conference agreements had been beneficial in many respects but that they were not a solution. Conferences had been unable to bring into the fold all of the operators on the same routes. Pooling arrangements and fines had not succeeded in keeping competitors in line.[95] In addition, the water carriers had suffered, as had the railroads, from the competition of the unregulated motor carriers. All of these influences and the competition of the railroads had produced demoralization of the water transport industry.

There was another, although related, reason for bringing the industry under closer regulation. This was the fact that the ab-

sence of regulation "stands in the way of the coordination between all forms of transportation which it is so desirable to bring
about." [96] It will be recalled that, although the railroads were interested in bringing the motor carriers under control for the
greater security of the railroads, Eastman's conception was broader.
He thought of a national transportation system, with each of the
transportation agencies concentrating upon that kind of traffic it
could handle most efficiently, each of the elements of this national
system working under federal regulation in a coordinated pattern.
The water carriers were to be brought within this design for universal coordination.

Eastman had not been without experience in attempts to bring
the rail and water carriers closer together in plans for the coordination of their rates. Eastman and Major General T. Q. Ashburn,
president of the Inland Waterways Corporation, a federally operated water carrier, brought executives of rail and water services
together late in 1933 to consider cooperative and coordinated rate
actions.[97] General Ashburn, in a speech to the National Rivers and
Harbors Congress in October, advocated the coordination of all
forms of rail, highway, and water transportation into a national
cooperative system under the jurisdiction of a reconstituted ICC,
a speech that could have been written by Eastman himself.[98] The
General no doubt would have been happy to have Congress provide for such a coordinated system, inasmuch as the Inland Waterways Corporation earlier in the year had come under attack from
railroads and other transportation and warehousing interests as
an instrumentality through which the War Department competed
with private transportation systems.[99]

In his *Second Report,* Eastman recommended that the Interstate
Commerce Commission be given jurisdiction over the water carriers. Common carriers were to be put under the duty of charging
just and reasonable rates, to be filed with the Commission. Thus,
one of the shortcomings of the industry, from its competitors' point
of view, inability to know what rates the water common carriers
were charging, would be removed. The Commission would be
given authority to fix maximum and minimum rates whenever it
should be of the opinion that the existing rates were unjust or
unreasonable, unjustly discriminatory, unduly preferential, or
prejudicial. Its authority was to apply to the division of joint rates.

It also could fix the minimum rates charged by contract carriers. Pooling and other operating arrangements would be brought under the jurisdiction of the Commission.

Common carriers in water transportation were to be required to get certificates of public convenience and necessity, except that those which had been in business in 1933 were to be given such certificates upon proof of this fact and a showing of ability to perform the service required. Contract carriers were to be required to secure a permit to operate, with the proviso that those operating in 1933 could continue to do so for 90 days after the effective date of the act without getting such a permit and thereafter until the Commission should order otherwise. Private carriers were to be required to register with the Commission. A water carrier would have been permitted to hold a certificate, a permit, or a registration, but not more than one kind of any such authorization. Other provisions would have brought within the jurisdiction of the Commission consolidations, mergers, acquisitions of control, the issuance of securities, accounts, records, reports, and other aspects of the management of transportation by water carrier. The proposed act transferred to the Interstate Commerce Commission the jurisdiction of the shipping board bureau over water carriers engaged in domestic commerce.

This act was not accepted by the Congress. In fact, Eastman's conception of a coordinated transportation system with jurisdiction over all forms of transportation lodged in the ICC was not to be realized during his term as coordinator. In the Transportation Act of 1940, four years after the end of the office of the federal coordinator of transportation, Congress indeed vested jurisdiction over the water carriers in the ICC, but the original Eastman proposal in 1934 was frustrated during his term as coordinator. The way in which it was frustrated is a part of the account of the office of the federal coordinator, however, and exhibits the same scattering of powers in a somewhat disorderly industry with which he had to struggle.

When he made his recommendation for water carrier legislation in 1934, Eastman was more optimistic of success in public statements than the event was to justify. In a speech in April he said that transportation was rapidly becoming demoralized and added, "The Federal Government must take the driver's seat and bring about some degree of order and coordination. It must get on top of this problem and not out of its way. From the evidence which my staff has gathered I feel sure that this opinion is growing all over the country, and I believe it is now the dominant opinion. . . . If a census were taken today of water carriers, I am confident that it would be found that a very substantial majority of those engaged in common carrier operations hold to this view." [100]

As in the case of the motor carrier bill, no action was taken by the Congress on Eastman's water carrier bill in 1934. While he waited for action, Eastman concluded that the latter might be amended in certain respects.[101]

The proposed legislation got a hearing in 1935. Among the groups opposed to the legislation were certain inland waterways associations and farmers' organizations. Among the latter were the American Farm Bureau Federation, the National Grange, the Farmers National Grain Corporation, and the Northwest Farmers Union Legislative Committee. These of course were agricultural shippers who had an economic interest in cheap transportation and in a competitive situation in which they could play off one transportation agency against another for small advantages in rates, even though possibly at the cost of injuring the transportation system as a whole. Many of these interests had, of course, appeared in opposition to motor carrier legislation. Some of them protested to President Roosevelt against giving the ICC powers over the water carriers.[102] A not unusual objection to Eastman's proposal was that the ICC was too railroad-minded, and it was feared that the water carriers would find themselves regulated by the economic necessities of the railroads.[103]

The Eastman bill was introduced in both the House and the Senate. It encountered a different experience in each. The Senate Committee on Interstate Commerce held hearings on the measure and reported it favorably to the Senate, with the recommendation that it be passed in amended form. The bill was not referred to the House Committee on Interstate and Foreign Commerce, which might have been expected to deal with it as its opposite number in the Senate did. Instead, the bill was referred to the House Committee on Merchant Marine and Fisheries, which failed to bring the hearings to a conclusion.[104] The strongest group support for the bill came from the railroads and the common carrier water operators on the Mississippi River system and in the inter-coastal trade.[105]

Railroad support for the bill served to persuade some that the purpose of the legislation was merely to protect the railroads against water competition and that it would result in raising water rates to the level of railroad rates, or at least in establishing a relation between the two which would be governed primarily by rail conditions in disregard of the inherent advantages of water transportation. This was considered by Eastman in a speech in Philadelphia at the height of the discussion of his measure.[106] This was one of the persistent themes against the motor carrier regulation also and Eastman thought it important enough to deal with at some length. He asserted that water rates most certainly should be regulated on the basis of water and not rail conditions. As he had said in discussing the effect of regulation on motor carrier rates, he thought that the effect of regulation on water carrier rates would be to raise some water rates or charges, but only "to prevent the kind of piratical rate cutting or rate wars which in the end are harmful to all concerned." He disagreed thoroughly with the counter-suggestion to his, that the regulation of water carriers ought to be administered by a separate body and not by the Interstate Commerce Commission. The only way to secure unity and consistency of action in a national transportation system was to put the regulation of the transportation agencies under one federal administrative authority. No one need fear that the Commission had any bias in favor of the railroads as against the water lines or highway vehicles or any other kind of carrier. He thought that most of the opposition to his bill, so far as the carriers were concerned, was coming from the contract carriers and those that were controlled by industries. The contract carriers were chiefly bulk cargo carriers serving the big shippers.

Although they were not included in the original plan for regulation, Eastman came to believe that regulation should be extended over the operators of port terminal facilities and over the operations in these facilities. Some of these operators were steamship companies, some railroads, some states and municipalities, some independent private concerns. He called them, collectively, "wharfingers," a word, he said, "which we discovered in the dictionary after some research." [107] He had found that many of the practices in these facilities could not well be justified economically. Steamships using European wharves had always had to pay a charge, but the general rule in the United States had been to furnish the service free. The principal objectors to his suggestion to bring these practices under federal control were the states and the municipalities, but he thought that the whole custom of giving something for nothing was "for the assumed advantage of the local real estate owners and commercial interests at the ports, and the burden ought not to be loaded on the backs of the public which uses the railroads or on the taxpayers generally." [108]

But when the Senate came to consider the bill reported favorably to it, the authority of the Commission over the "wharfingers" was eliminated; the authority over the contract carriers was much restricted in favor of bulk carriers not actually and substantially competitive with transportation by interstate common carriers in the same trade or route; and the authority over the private carriers was eliminated entirely.

In his last report on the office of the federal coordinator, Eastman was still arguing the need for comprehensive regulation of water carriers in the interest of a coordinated national transportation system. He considered some seven pages of objections to the water carrier bill and with much citation and argument sought to deal with each.[109] He denied that the Commission had been wholly occupied with rail regulation; that it had steadily refused to recognize some of the powers given to it for the protection of the water carriers; that the Commission by law and practice was schooled to give paramount consideration to the needs of the railroads; and that in the regulation of going rail-water rates it had narrowed the differential from 20 per cent to 15 per cent and then in most cases to 10 per cent of the all-rail costs. He was particularly concerned at the elimination of the provisions for regulating port terminal facilities and promised a separate bill for Congress to consider. But it was too late to rescue the water carrier bill during his tenure as coordinator, and his recommendations were not acted upon.

Coordinating the Commission

In all of this labor of study and recommendation for the development of a coordinated national transportation system, Eastman did not overlook the need for what he often referred to as a "radical reorganization" of the Interstate Commerce Commission itself, to make it a serviceable instrumentality for the performance of its new duties.[110] The proposed reorganization of the Commission was "contingent upon the enactment of the legislation . . . for the Federal regulation of water carriers and motor carriers. It would have no point in the absence of such legislation." [111]

The proposal was fairly sweeping. He suggested a Commission of sixteen members in place of the present eleven, not more than eight of whom should be from the same political party.[112] There was to be a permanent chairman (instead of one rotating annually) appointed by the President (instead of selection by the commissioners). The person designated as chairman by the President was to serve in this capacity during his entire term of office. As chairman he was to serve as the administrative director of the Commission and as the chairman of its control board. The agency was to be divided into four divisions with commissioners at the head of each: railroad division (five members); water and pipe line division (three members); motor and air division (three members); finance division (three members). The control board was to consist of the chairman and the chairmen of each of the divisions, and it was to decide general transportation policies for the guidance of the divisions, to determine when investigations should be conducted, and to decide all legislative matters. In each of the divisions, the members were to choose their own chairman. Besides these fifteen functionaries there was also to be a permanent coordinator of transportation, whose job it would be to handle planning, prevention, and coordination functions.

Under the Emergency Railroad Transportation Act of 1933, Eastman as coordinator made his reports to the members of the Commission, the chairman of which then transmitted them to the Congress with such comments as the Commission thought appropriate. When the *Third Report* was transmitted to Congress, the chairman of the commission, Hugh M. Tate, said of the proposed bill to reorganize the Commission, "We cannot recommend its adoption." [113]

It was said that the scheme was premature and undesirable; that the increase in the size of the Commission was unnecessary for efficiency; that organization details should be left to the Commission rather than made rigid by statute; and that every change proposed (except the increase in size) could be accomplished by a slight amendment to the Interstate Commerce Act. Although some of these objections had merit, criticism was doubtless reinforced by the anxiety of the Commissioners about their status. It was said that Commissioners not members of the control board would be little more than examiners. Satisfaction was expressed with the system of annual rotation of the chairmanship adopted by the Commission in 1910 after rejecting the prevailing practice of selecting a chairman for his full term of office. It did not seem as though the Commission wanted any of its members to establish irrecoverable precedence in this small but classless society.

Of particular interest in view of the precarious tenure of the federal coordinator was the attitude of the Commission towards making the office a permanent one inside the ICC. The Association of American Railroads had organized itself to render the cordinator unnecessary, as has been pointed out at several places. The Commission tended to support the AAR against the coordinator. It said of the Eastman suggestion to make the coordinator a permanent functionary in the Commission, "It is at least arguable that research and planning should be left primarily to the transportation industries . . . The railroads of the country have entered upon this task by a reorganization and consolidation of their cooperative organizations. They should at least be permitted to attempt to demonstrate the efficiency of the organization which they have created." [114] Apart from the fact that this was a position that gave aid and comfort to the well organized interest group with which the Commission then did most of its business, it showed an extremely narrow conception of the compass of the Emergency Railroad Transportation Act of 1933. The act gave the coordinator authority to issue orders to compel coordination. The office of the coordinator was not merely a research bureau for the railroads, as the Commission seemed to suggest.

Business Week took a crack at the Commission for what seemed to many to be an unnecessarily reductive view of the coordinator and his proposals.[115] Said the journal, "Evidently the commissioners share the resentment of numerous rail officials against the Coordinator's rise to power and publicity. It suggests that vesting the direction of railroad planning and research in a single individual outside the industry might result in a cooling of the carriers' interest in self-help, argues that the Association of American Railroads should be given a chance to show what it can do, that, if government participation or supervision is needed, this should be centered in one of the commission's own bureaus." Eastman himself was moved to comment upon the attitude of the Commission in his speech to the Propellor Club in Philadelphia in April.[116] He suggested that successful regulation would depend upon sympathetic understanding of the peculiar problems of each form of transportation, and he expressed doubt as to whether "the Commission yet appreciates how great it may be." He thought it important that the work of regulation be done promptly and well and without the long delays and cumbersome procedures that often characterized public regulation. And then he said,

As I see it, it will be necessary to reorganize the Commission radically, if these results are to be accomplished. I have proposed a form of reorganization designed to secure all the advantages of separate commissions without their disadvantages, to insure specialized attention to the problems of each form of transportation without conflict or inconsistency in policies, and to improve administration and procedure.

The Commission says that I am all wrong about this. With the utmost respect for the view of my colleagues, I am of the same opinion still. It may be that we are all a little pig-headed.[117]

The Congress failed to act on Eastman's recommendation for a radical reorganization of the Interstate Commerce Commission in 1935. In 1936, he went over the same ground as before. In his *Fourth Report* he argued the need for reorganization on the basis of the increased work that the Commission was going to have in administering the Motor Carrier Act, 1935, and perhaps others; and he answered each of the objections to his recommended reorganization that had been voiced by Commissioner Tate the year before.[118]

Part of his case for reorganization was to disappear when the Congress refused to bring the water carriers under the jurisdiction of the ICC.[119] But he was prepared to alter the case he had made. As he said, "Experience is not unlikely also to show such a reorganization is desirable even if no further duties are imposed." [120]

XI. END OF THE LINE

"It is essential that the Coordinator have authority to issue orders, if he is to have the necessary influence with the carriers."
Fourth Report of the Federal Coordinator, p. 43.

Eastman wanted to make the office of the federal coordinator permanent, but the Congress in 1936 declined even to extend its life on a temporary basis for a year; and so the office was allowed to lapse. There were many judgments as to its effectiveness. The following pages will review the steps that led to the demise of the coordinator, and then appraise some of these judgments.

Termination and the Terminals

In February 1936, the coordinator announced that he would issue an order regarding coordination of certain terminal facilities, and he thus put in train the events that were to lead to the demise of his office. The previous summer, V. V. Boatner, of the coordinator's staff, had estimated that the railroads could save more than $56,000,000 a year through consolidation of freight or passenger terminal facilities.[1] Eastman urged the railroads to unify their terminals, and at an executive joint meeting of the regional committees and the directors of the Association of American Railroads, he urged adoption of the terminal unification plans.[2] The carriers failed to follow, or even to make an appearance of an attempt to do so, whereupon Eastman said to a meeting of the AAR, "I had hoped that the railroads would carry out these terminal consolidations voluntarily but they have not done so. If this is not done I may have to take the matter in hand and issue some orders." [3] To the usual argument that Section 7b made any realistic coordination impossible because of restrictions placed upon the discharge of workers made unnecessary by the coordination, Eastman suggested that men so released be placed elsewhere, that the carriers get together with the men and get them to go along with the plan, or take the Section 7b to the courts to see what they might be willing to do about it.

After another interval of time, this one shorter, Eastman then announced on February 1, 1936 that he would order terminal unification shortly in eleven cities.[4] At the same time he said that he had tried to persuade the carriers voluntarily to act on terminal unification and that he was prepared to take other steps of increasing magnitude.[5] If Eastman's order requiring terminal unification had been promulgated, it would have been his first exercise of power in an important case.[6] But the order was never issued. The railroad unions, perhaps for bargaining purposes with the carriers, undertook to write a bill to forestall layoffs by forbidding any reduction in railroad employment, regardless of the future course of business, unless express authority to do so had been secured from the Interstate Commerce Commission in each case.[7] This legislation was introduced in the Congress by Senator Wheeler of Montana and Congressman Crosser of Ohio and was known, of course, as the Wheeler-Crosser bill, although it had been written by the Railway Labor Executives Association and introduced at the request of this organization.[8] The thought that the legislation was introduced for bargaining purposes is supported by the report that the bill would be withdrawn if labor and management should be able to reach an agreement on dismissal compensation within a short period of time.[9]

Spokesmen for the railroads expressed outrage.[10] But the labor unions had not only the ear of the Congress but that of the President as well. In the meantime, the unions were busy on another front, the terminal unification order (or threatened order) itself. Regional committees representing the union organizations met with Eastman and asked him to withhold his order until March 31, at the least, because they wished for more time in which to prepare protests.[11] Eastman, in a speech before the Chicago Traffic Club in March, took notice of the furor that had been created.[12] In his opening remarks he said that his topic was supposed to have been "transportation regulation" but that another matter was uppermost in his mind at the moment and he wanted to say something about it. He said, "If I were to give it a name, it might be called 'The Troubles of a Coordinator.' The discussion may be a little dolorous, like the editorials of the 'Traffic World,' not to mention the 'Railway Age.' It has some aspects of comic relief, but I am sure you can discover those for yourselves without my pointing them out." He then went on to talk about the possibilities of savings through coordination, and the specific gains that might be achieved through terminal unifications, which he thought particularly promising. But what were the obstacles?

The first was "a railroad labor obstacle" which had assumed large proportions. Since proposing to issue orders requiring certain terminal unifications, he said,

I have been bombarded with protests coming, directly or indirectly, from the railroad employees. The burden of these protests is this: The country has been passing through a severe depression. Millions have been, and still are, unemployed. We have been trying to correct that situation and put men back to work. There are signs that the country is on the way out of the depression, and employment is on the increase. At such a time it is the height of unwisdom and contrary to sound public policy to force projects which will deprive railroad employees, who as a class have suffered acutely in the depression, of work and add to the number of unemployed. This argument is offered, not only by the employees themselves, but by many men holding public office, and in some cases by commercial organizations in the towns affected.[13]

The other obstacle was the negative attitude of the railroad managements themselves.[14] Eastman said that he asked only that the carriers give "more than mere lip-service" to the idea of coordination and "get down to work." *Railway Age* counseled its clients to proceed with coordinations wherever they promised economies but at the same time to carry to the Supreme Court the question of the constitutionality of the Emergency Railroad Transportation Act, and especially Section 7b.[15]

It seems to be reasonably clear that both the carriers and the unions regarded the threat to issue orders requiring terminal unification as a showdown on the coordinator's powers. The carriers were not willing peacefully to exchange "cooperation" for command, although it was generally recognized that the coordinator did have the statutory authority to require compliance with his orders. They just did not want him to wield command, and up until 1936 he had done little. He had relied, as the preceding pages have shown at length, on the gentle compulsions of sweet reason, leaving the carriers the choice as to which of these compulsions they would sweetly surrender to. As for the unions, the coordinator's interpretation of Section 7b had adequately taken care of what they regarded as the immediate threat presented to them by the Emergency Railroad Transportation Act. So long as this interpretation prevailed, and so long as the carriers disregarded the coordinator's suggestions for coordination, their position was not seriously challenged. When he proposed to go ahead with terminal unifications, the program became "socialism" for the carriers and "heartless big business" for the unions.[16]

With the coordinator proposing coordination by order, the carriers considering taking the coordinator to the courts, and the unions planning to build a statutory sanctuary for railroad workers displaced by coordination projects, Eastman suggested to Roosevelt that he intervene in the impasse.[17] Roosevelt then sent a letter to Pelley, the head of the Association of American Railroads, and to J. A. Phillips, vice chairman of the Railway Labor Executives Association, recommending that both sides settle their dispute by negotiation and not by litigation. Although *Railway Age* had suggested a trip to the courts and Eastman himself had told the carriers to get his powers construed in the courts if they thought his interpretation of the Emergency Railroad Transportation Act was incorrect, the Roosevelt letter to the carriers and the unions recommended that the parties in conflict settle their controversy over dismissals by negotiation. This it will be recalled was what Eastman in the *Fourth Report* had recommended after doubt had been cast on the constitutionality of his bill to deal with the railroad retirement issue. Said the Roosevelt letter,

It is a matter which is capable of being settled to better advantage by negotiation than by legislation. Given sufficient time, the managements and the men ought to be able to agree, in their common interests, upon a reasonable plan of protection. If they do not agree and legislation is sought as the only solution, I fear harm to the railroad industry. Both sides will take extreme positions. The effect of such legislation may be to discourage and prevent progress. Litigation will ensue. The courts may strike down what is attempted, so that the battleground may again shift to Congress. The relations between the managements and the men will be embittered with unfortunate results in many ways.[18]

Roosevelt added that negotiations should not be permitted to fail without a personal conference with him, and then said that Eastman had agreed to a postponement of his terminal unification orders at the request of the President, although Eastman felt that he was proceeding under a direct mandate from Congress.

The Washington Agreement

The negotiations to which Roosevelt referred had already been in progress a month.[19] Representatives of the carriers, headed by H. A. Enochs, personnel chief of the Pennsylvania Railroad, and of 21 unions, headed by George Harrison of the Railway and Steamship Clerks, began meetings in New York in February to discuss the protection of workers displaced in unification. It was reported that management believed that it was acting to lessen the usefulness of Eastman as federal coordinator, since it was doing directly and voluntarily what Eastman could not compel it to do, namely, settle the problem of the displaced railroad workers. It was also suggested that this move was part of a management compaign already under way to insure that the office of the coordinator would not be extended.[20] On the union side, the aims of the negotiation were said by Harrison to be as follows: "We are willing to negotiate for an agreement which would continue the protection to employees afforded by the law. Lacking such an agreement we would favor an extension of the present law when it expires in June. If we were compelled to ask for new legislation, we would seek to have protective measures based, not on the employment level in May 1933 but on present levels." [21]

The conference immediately struck a snag when the unions asked for an agreement to protect employees displaced by economy moves by individual railroads as well as by unification.[22] The coordinator's interpretation of Section 7b had protected workers from displacement by acts authorized by the legislation but had not protected them from displacement by acts of individual roads not specifically taken pursuant to the Emergency Railroad Transportation Act of 1933.

Besides the threat that the unions would favor extension of the 1933 act if agreement were not forthcoming, the Railway Labor Executives Association had the Wheeler-Crosser bill as further leverage against the carriers. The RLEA was reported to be willing to withhold the Wheeler-Crosser bill if the railroads would agree not to put into effect any merger until twelve months after the expiration of the Emergency Railroad Transportation Act, so as to give time to work out the displacement problems.[23] The advantage that the unions thought they had in the Congress, an advantage strong enough to encourage them to use two acts of legislation as instruments of bargaining with the carriers, was one that they were not likely to forego easily. So it was, then, that they expressed resentment of Roosevelt's suggestion that they try to work out an arrangement with the carriers without resort to Congress. Phillips, the acting chairman of the Railway Labor Executives Association, said, "From my viewpoint it would seem that the President went out of his way to suggest that railroad workers should not appeal to Congress for needed reforms. We heard no one indulging in such admonitions when the railroads had control of Congress." [24] Phillips was not specific as to the time when the "railroads had control of Congress" nor was it entirely clear whether he was implying that the unions had control of Congress now, but the executive committee of the RLEA decided to tell the President of its willingness to continue negotiations, although Phillips could not forbear another thrust at the White House. He said, "Railroad workers have not forgotten that the President took a definite position against the restoration of the 10% reduction in the pay at the beginning of the negotiations in 1934, but the 21 standard organizations were able to overcome that handicap and made a satisfactory settlement. The political and economic strength of these organizations should be just as effective in 1936 as in 1934." [25]

With "punitive" legislation temporarily laid aside as a weapon of influence in the struggle with the carriers, the unions then built up the tension across the bargaining table so as to force the development of the carrier position and the early recovery of their legislative advantage. Shortly after promising the President to continue negotiations, the unions let it be reported that they believed a break with the management was imminent. Phillips wrote to Roosevelt on March 16, "We believe that already a reasonable length of time has been devoted to the task and that we cannot be expected to continue negotiations to the point of jeopardizing the rights and interests of those we represent. However, we are meet-

ing with the carriers' committee again today and, should negotiations fail, we will, in compliance with your request, arrange to
confer with you." [26] It was then reported that the conference had
all but broken down and that there was an impasse; and it was
said that the unions were ready to call upon the President, but
management felt that the "negotiations to iron out points have
hardly begun." [27] The maneuver to press into the White House
and then to recover the legislative weapon that had been temporarily laid aside looked for a while as though it would be frustrated by Roosevelt's desire to go off on a fishing trip.[28] But the
superior influence of the unions prevailed, Roosevelt postponed
his scheduled fishing trip, requested both sides to continue negotiations, and lifted his injunction against pressing for legislation.[29]
The unions were thus able to restore their bargaining position to
what it had been before Roosevelt's intervention.

With recapture by the unions of their full maneuverability,
both sides entered upon the specific struggle about terms. Management's offer was either to give the displaced employee six months'
pay, in which case he would sever connections with the railroad, or
half salary for three years (for those with five years of service),
in which case he was subject to recall. Dismissals would be made
according to seniority so far as possible, with the carriers providing
for moving expenses and property loss up to a maximum of
$1000.[30] The union counterproposal was a sliding scale of com-
pensation based upon the length of service of the displaced worker.
Those with three or more years of employment status were to
receive an allowance of two-thirds wages for a maximum unemployment period of ten years. Those with less than three years employment status were to receive two-thirds wages for a maximum
unemployment period of five years. The less-than-three-year men
were also given an option to accept a lump sum payment of one
full year's allowance and surrender of seniority rights.[31]

With these positions stated, the adversaries then locked in the
final struggle to force their wills upon each other by concentrating
and using the influence outside the bargaining room that they were
able to command. The Association of American Railroads started
a drive to kill the Wheeler-Crosser bill,[32] and the unions undertook to make good their assertion of influence with Congress by
agitating the Wheeler-Crosser bill as desirable legislation.[33] At the

bargaining table the parties came to no immediate agreement. The railroads offered to grade dismissal payments according to length of service as the unions had suggested but otherwise the carriers made few changes in their original proposals.[34]

At one point in April the negotiations collapsed, and the unions intensified their pressure to get the Wheeler-Crosser bill through the Senate. It moved from a subcommittee of the Senate Interstate Commerce Committee to the parent committee itself. The pressure was intensified when the unions also decided to support a bill proposed by Eastman to set up a system of unemployment compensation for railroad workers who were not going to be covered into the Social Security Act of 1935.[35] This bill was thought by carrier managements to represent an "alliance" between the unions and Eastman, an alliance that they thought could have been avoided had the negotiations proved successful.[36] The lesson was obvious. The way open to the carriers to avoid an extension of the Emergency Railroad Transportation Act, the Wheeler-Crosser bill, and other unwanted legislation was to make an agreement with the unions. The negotiations which had been broken off in April were resumed, and it was then predicted that a solution could be expected soon.[37]

The prediction was fulfilled. At the end of the first week of May, the details of a possible agreement were reported. They were essentially the same as those on which agreement was concluded two weeks hence.[38] Even when the displacement plan was finally drafted and the unions were ready to sign, management deferred the final step until it had explored once more the situation with respect to the Emergency Railroad Transportation Act of 1933. The unions promptly announced that they would continue to push the Wheeler-Crosser bill.[39]

Agreement was finally announced on May 21 and it constituted a compromise between the first positions asserted by the carriers and by the unions.[40] The agreement was to last five years from June 18, 1936, and men displaced by unification projects were given two alternatives. They could have a dismissal wage of 60 per cent of their average monthly wage earned during their last twelve months of employment, if they had worked a year. These monthly payments were available for a period of six months after dismissal. The period of payment was extended for employees with longer terms of service up to fifteen years and over, the period of eligibility in these cases being sixty months. The alternative was a separation allowance ranging from three months' pay for those employed fifteen years and over. Employees demoted by a consolidation were to receive their previous pay for a period of five years; and the carriers agreed to pay moving and traveling expenses for workers compelled to move as a result of consolidations.

According to *Railway Age,* the last minute hitch before the signing occurred when the railroads proposed that the agreement should not be binding in the event Congress should enact any legislation covering the subject matter.[41] This would have included not only the Wheeler-Crosser bill, on which hearings had been suspended to allow the parties to come to an agreement, but also legislation to extend the office of the federal coordinator. The unions and Wheeler were so much in the saddle, however, that Wheeler announced that he not only would resume the hearings on the Wheeler-Crosser bill, but that he proposed to introduce legislation to extend the coordinator's office for two more years. A time was set for the resumption of the hearing but Wheeler was the only member of the committee present. At the suggestion of R. V. Fletcher, of the AAR, Wheeler agreed to postpone the hearing a day. Fletcher told him that it seemed futile to go ahead with the hearing because of the probability of an agreement; that is, because of the probability that the carriers would yield their point. Wheeler kept the screws turned tight with the assertion that he had no objection to the request but that the committee of which he was chairman had been waiting and hoping for an agreement and he did not want the time to run along and have neither an agreement nor a law.[42]

The agreement did not cover all of the railroads, but the carriers who signed it promised that its terms would cover consolidations entered into with railroads not under the agreement. The pact covered only dismissals arising from consolidations and specifically provided that it did not apply to "rises and falls and changes in volume or character of employment brought about solely by other causes." [43] It was hoped by the unions that, during the five-year period, practically all of the displaced employees would be able to get back into railroading through the exercise of seniority rights, since the annual attrition from retirements because of old age, disability, and other causes was about 5 per cent.[44] Although he had not participated in the making of the agreement, as he had in previous wage controversies (as Roosevelt's representative), Eastman praised the outcome of the negotiations. He thought that it was "far better for all concerned than an attempt to provide such protection by legislation." [45] He thought that the opportunity was now open for many improvements in railroad operation "in line with the government's program of coordination reflected in the Emergency Railroad Transportation Act of 1933."

End of the Line

Although the unions seemed to have been taking the part of the federal coordinator of transportation when they refused the suggestion of the carriers that they write the demise of the coordinator's office into the Washington agreement of May 21, 1936, they had not been, as will be seen. After the agreement, the last act took place in the drama of an administrator squeezed out in the power struggle among the groups he was supposed to regulate. On May 19, just before the heads of group empires signed the treaty of May 21, Roosevelt was asked at a press conference whether he would urge congressional action to extend the administrative life of the federal coordinator, and he said that he would welcome such a step. He also said that he had talked with the chairmen of the House and Senate commerce committees about the matter, pointing out to them that the work assigned to the federal coordinator had not been completed. He said also that he would like to see the work of the coordinator completed, but that the question was really and finally up to Congress.[46] The chairman of the Senate committee, Burton K. Wheeler of Montana, six days later introduced Senate Joint Resolution 271 to extend the Emergency Railroad Transportation Act for three years, the only change to be the deletion of Section 7b, which had been made unnecessary by the Washington agreement.[47]

Eastman encouraged the interest in extending the office of the coordinator but with characteristic and costly independence he did nothing affirmative or effective to produce the result. He told Roosevelt that coordination under a coordinator should be pressed forward "now that the chief obstacle which has stood in the way of progress along these lines since 1933 has been removed." [48] In accord with the suggestion in his *Fourth Report* that the coordinator should continue to function even though the Association of American Railroads was prepared to replace him, Eastman told Roosevelt that "in the three years' experience under the Emergency Act, they have not shown an ability to make the necessary progress towards coordination if they are left to themselves. There are too many conflicts of interests in the railroad world to permit of successful cooperation and collective action without government aid. Some governmental stimulus, such as is provided by the Emergency Act, is necessary." [49]

Roosevelt responded to this plea and in a note to the federal coordinator said, "Thank you for yours of May 25th. I wholly agree that the work of coordination should go forward and that there should be a continuance of the Emergency Act. I have made this very clear both to Senator Wheeler and to Sam Rayburn. To let the whole of this work die this year would be a grave mistake." [50] Grave mistake or not, Roosevelt had indicated that the question of the extension of the Emergency Act was for Congress to decide, which in effect meant that Congress was to kill the proposal, not the White House. Wheeler apparently realized that there was no chance for his resolution to pass without more aggressive help from the administration, for he cancelled an executive session of the Senate Commerce Committee which was scheduled to take up his resolution on May 29. Both unions and management opposed the resolution, the committee had no plans for a hearing, Congress was eager to close so as to get to the real work of the year, the Republican and Democratic national conventions, and there was therefore no one particularly interested in pushing the cause of the coordinator. A House resolution similar to Wheeler's was introduced by Congressman Russell of Massachusetts but it was not even considered by the House committee. Paradoxically, the chances of an extension of the Emergency Act were lessened when the early adjournment of Congress was postponed. The speaker of the House died, and the Congress went into recess from June 8 to June 15, leaving only two days in which to act on the extension of the Emergency Act, instead of the week to two weeks that would otherwise have been available.

On June 4, Eastman told Roosevelt that he had been approached by Harrison and Jewell of the Railway Labor Executives Association.[51] They told him (what has already been related) that the negotiations with the AAR over the labor protection agreement at one point had reached an impasse because of the insistence of the carriers that the agreement should contain a provision for its termination if legislation such as the Emergency Railroad Transportation Act were enacted affecting the subject under negotiations. The unions were said to have countered with the suggestion that the agreement would be ended if legislation provided them with comparable protection, but the carriers of course would not accept this suggestion. They were not primarily interested in protecting the unions or the workers they represented. They were interested in preventing the extension of the Emergency Railroad Transportation Act and the renewal of the authorities of the federal coordinator.

Thereafter, said Eastman to Roosevelt, "Messrs. Harrison and Pelley both visited the White House, and there gained the impression that while you were in favor of the continuance of the Coordinator, the matter would not be pressed. In view of what they knew of the situation at the Capitol, this was regarded as sufficient assurance that the Coordinator would not be continued. However, the impression was conveyed to me that to make assurance doubly sure, the employees gave the managements to understand that if the Resolution [that is, to extend the tenure of the Coordinator] should be pressed, the employees would join the managements in opposition. Thereupon the agreement was signed."

Thus it appears that, while Wheeler was holding the pressure on the carriers with his on-again, off-again hearings on the Wheeler-Crosser bill, and, while he publicly refused the carriers' suggestion that the rejection of the Emergency Railroad Transportation Act and the coordinator be written into the Washington Agreement, the unions were agreeing with the carriers under the table to scuttle Eastman. And it is a matter of public record that, although the unions talked of extending the Emergency Railroad Transportation Act for two years before making the Washington agreement, they and the carriers both opposed Wheeler's resolution after the agreement was made. The smell of the double-deal executed by unions and carriers was piquant enough to catch the nostrils of the trade press. It was stated that there were reports that the union leaders and the carriers had made a deal, with one version linking the President as a party to the "understanding." [52] That there was some basis for this version of the "deal" is evident in Eastman's statement to Roosevelt.

Wheeler, as an administration representative in the Congress, continued to try to compromise an issue presumably already settled. He worked up a second version of his resolution to extend the office of the coordinator. To harmonize the statement of Roosevelt that extension would be a good thing with the understanding that the carriers, unions, and Roosevelt had that extension would be a bad thing and should not be pushed, Wheeler proposed that the coordinator's powers to issue orders be taken away for one year.

Railway Age said, "It is understood, however, that this would also be opposed by both the railroads and the labor organizations." [53] In fact, it was, although not without a certain amount of make believe by the unions. Eastman told Roosevelt in his letter of June 4 that he had been asked (presumably by the union representatives) whether he would be willing to serve as coordinator if the act were extended without the power to issue orders. "I replied," he said, "that I would be unwilling, because in my judgment such action would be equivalent to a repudiation of the policy of coordination as reflected in the Act upon your recommendation in 1933." A day or two later, Eastman was visited by Tom Corcoran, of the White House inner circle, and Max Lowenthal, who told him that in all of the circumstances "it was impossible to accomplish anything in Congress on this matter without the help of railroad labor." They urged him to continue on as coordinator, saying that Roosevelt wanted him to do so, even if the power to issue orders were removed from the act, and Eastman reluctantly consented.

When Lowenthal and Corcoran took the proposition to Harrison, however, they found that Harrison was not content merely to eliminate the coordinator's power to issue orders. Harrison wanted to strike out of the Emergency Act of 1933 all reference to the avoidance of unnecessary duplication of services and facilities. Eastman said that the idea was absurd, and that to eliminate all reference to the avoidance of unnecessary duplication was an express repudiation of the whole idea of coordination. Mr. Harrison said that the union leaders would not support extension unless all such references were eliminated, and at this point Eastman lost whatever interest he had in an extension of the act of 1933.

Wheeler, however, framed a compromise resolution, although by this time there was very little to compromise indeed. He worked up a travesty of the original act in which the statute was extended for one year, the coordinator was deprived of all power to issue orders, and the references in Section 4 of the original act to unnecessary duplication of facilities and services were eliminated. This version was upheld by the Senate Committee by a vote of 9–7 but there was little support for the proposal from any quarter, Congress was in a hurry to finish up its work and go home, and the resolution was never introduced.[54]

The insistence by Harrison that all reference to unnecessary duplication of facilities and services be eliminated made the final result inevitable. Or rather it was inevitable from the time the union men and the carriers made their deal, and Harrison's intransigence seems simply to have been a familiar tactic to make sure that no compromise agreement of any kind could be made. Eastman told Roosevelt in his June 4 letter that Harrison seems to have insisted upon language that would "enable the employees to say that the whole idea of coordination had been scuttled by Congress and the President." Eastman then said, "To my mind, if the ship were to be scuttled, the captain ought to go down with it, so I continued to withhold consent."

On the last day of the session, Wheeler introduced a third resolution. It would have continued the coordinator's office for three months to permit him to finish up the studies that were nearing completion. This also failed and the federal coordinator went out of office on June 16, 1936, although some funds were later provided by the carriers to complete studies that were then under way.

None to Mourn

Although Eastman thought that the office of the coordinator had proved its value, there were none to mourn its passing, and indeed few to mark it. As it was put in one place,[55] Eastman lost his office because "there was nobody in the White House or in the

Interstate Commerce Commission, no railroad men or shippers, to press legislation to extend his term." In view of the personal popularity of Eastman this lack of interest may seem to be somewhat strange. Why was it that there were none in high places to carry on the fight for him in Congress to make the office of the coordinator a permanent one? It had not been without benefit. Eastman, in fact, was able to point out certain specific benefits from the experience with the office of the coordinator, among which he listed the reduction in the salaries of railroad executives, the reduction in the price of steel rails, the promotion of voluntary cooperation between transportation agencies, improved purchasing methods, which he thought had resulted in savings of $2,000,-000, and new traffic arrangements with savings of $500,000.[56]

There were other benefits but the root difficulty was in the structure and attitude of the principal industry with which he had to deal. As the railroads with candor said at one point, "So long as there are separate corporate entities a definite responsibility rests upon the management of each one to protect and promote the welfare of its individual interests." [57] In the opinion of one observer, the railroads, despite the fierce competition against each other, felt so secure "against Mr. Eastman's thrusts" that they felt free to accept those recommendations of Eastman's "which they liked, and to ignore the remainder if adopting the remainder happened to impair their individual strategic positions." [58] Another observer a year after the end of the office of the coordinator said that the underlying impediment to coordination "was the disinclination of the individual carrier to surrender an advantage, real or imaginary, in strategic location and to share that advantage with a competing carrier under unified operation." [59]

Eastman earlier had recommended that the carriers establish a more perfect union, and they had responded by organizing the Association of American Railroads.[60] As Mr. Pelley, the president of the association, had more than once indicated, the AAR was prepared to take over and perform the functions of the federal coordinator of transportation. The railroads, therefore, both by experience and organization, were not likely to support the extension of the coordinator's office nor to advocate making that office a permanent one.

Nor were the unions any more likely than the carriers to perpetuate the work of the coordinator.[61] As an observer whose work has already been cited put it,

The proposal for a fourth year had general public support but it was opposed by organized labor, because Mr. Eastman had spoken frankly about the unwisdom of certain proposals advocated by their leaders and because of alarm about unemployment, and by the railroad executives, who resented some of Mr. Eastman's criticisms and objected to many of the measures he advocated. Politically, the objections of the railroad executives probably had little weight. It is more likely that the opposition of labor was responsible for the Administration's decision to take no further action.[62]

There does not seem to be much evidence that the unions had any interest in the coordinator other than job protection. Their interest in coordination was limited to the concern that produced Section 7b of the Emergency Railroad Transportation Act of 1933, limiting discharges from employment that might result from coordination projects.

But it could be reasonably argued that the labor restrictions, in the nature of things, were temporary. It could be expected that they would grow less restrictive every year after 1933. As Eastman himself said, the importance of the labor provisions was exaggerated to divert attention from other reasons for the failure of the railroads to do much in the way of coordination under the direction of the coordinator. The unions were eventually able to get agreement with the carriers on the matter of dismissal compensation,[63] and when this agreement was achieved, the unions had no more interest in the coordinator.

Railroad Labor

Just as railroad management pursued its own conception of self-interest and did not hesitate to reject the suggestions of the coordinator when those suggestions seemed to be in conflict with the conception (which seemed to be almost all of the time), so did the unions jockey and maneuver for special advantage without evidence of any special desire to support the coordinator in his works or to make his office a success. They did not hesitate to use this office in the endless criss-cross, thrust, and pull of organized pressure, counterpressure, and influence when such actions seemed useful. But the unions were in no sense a constituency of the coordinator on which he could count for support in Congress, the White House, or with the carriers. And of course the carriers were not a constituency in this sense either, certainly not after the co-ordinator refused to permit the carriers to do by subterfuge what the Emergency Railroad Transportation Act of 1933 refused to let them do directly. Although the carriers, as early as 1934, made overt moves to abolish the office of the coordinator, they were unable to do so until 1936 because the unions resisted this move, not because they wished especially to continue the coordinator in office, but because they wished to obtain concessions from manage-ment in the form of dismissal compensation. When management agreed to pay the price in 1936, the unions joined with them in scuttling the coordinator.

But the unions should have been more grateful to the coordi-nator. It is true that he said that Section 7b did not protect work-ers absolutely from dismissals or furloughs after the effective date of the Emergency Railroad Transportation Act of 1933 because such protection was limited to dismissals occurring "by reason of any action" taken pursuant to the authority conferred by the statute. The limitation did not bind individual railroads singly or jointly if the reductions in force did not rest upon any authority conferred by the act or involve the use of any agency or mecha-nisms created under it. Members of the Railway Labor Executives Association called on Mr. Eastman on July 28, 1933, to protest this interpretation but the act was clear on the point. At the same time, Eastman also held that the benefits of economies achieved under the act should not be enjoyed by carriers without compen-sating employees for special expenses imposed upon them in bringing these economies to pass.[64] And he strongly rebuked the carriers for trying to circumvent the limitation of the act, even though he had lent color to their position.[65] Although he had originally opposed the limiting labor amendment, he came to feel that it had been wise.[66] He did not fail to express his sympathetic understanding of the special position of the workers in the rail-road industry, as in his remarks before the New York Bond Club in June 1934 when he said to the assembled bankers, "It is easy for us who are safely removed from the field of operation, to give little thought to the acute suffering and hardship which such a program [for greater economy in operation] may bring to individuals and even entire communities, but you may be sure that these results are not overlooked by those who have to endure them." [67] He was also no less unflinching in his advice to the union leaders whom he addressed as "a recognized and powerful force in the railroad industry" that reductions in costs could lead to increased employment, not less.[68] But he actively intervened with the Baltimore and Ohio Railroad, when it obtained ICC permission to reroute its service, and obtained agreement that the B&O would pay dismissal compensation to about 50 employees who would lose their jobs.[69]

Eastman did much to protect the workers and their independent unions from the company unionism that certain of the carriers were promoting in violation of the law. Section 7e of the Emergency Railroad Transportation Act of 1933 reaffirmed the protections of the Railway Labor Act of 1926 and extended to the carriers under the Emergency Act certain provisions of the Bankruptcy Act of 1933. All of these provisions were designed to give railroad workers absolute and uncoerced freedom of choice in joining any labor organization, and they forbade railroad management from using railroad funds to maintain any labor organization. In September, 1933, Eastman received complaints that led him to believe that Section 7e "has been overlooked or misunderstood." He sent to all railroads subject to the Emergency Act a comprehensive schedule of 53 questions for the purpose of eliciting the facts of the matter.[70] As he waited for the returns, Eastman had the Pere Marquette issue a statement disavowing company unionism after the Brotherhood of Railway and Steamship Clerks and the railway employees department of the American Federation of Labor had complained to the coordinator that company influence had been used in the formation of the Pere Marquette General Office Employees Association and the Pere Marquette Shop Crafts Association.[71] On December 7, 1933, the coordinator, on the basis of the returns to the questionnaire,[72] sent to the regional coordinating committees a communication listing seven suggestions for their consideration in bringing company practice into line with the law and expressing the hope that, "whatever views they might entertain as to their strict duties under the law," they would take leadership in complying because they were in the best position to take such leadership. He threatened prosecution for continued noncompliance with the law, under Section 12 of the Emergency Railroad Transportation Act of 1933, which allowed him to institute actions under the direction of the Attorney-General.[73] The eastern regional coordinating committee — W. W. Atterbury, J. J. Bernet, J. J. Pelley, Daniel Willard, and F. E. Williamson — consulted their lawyers and in a letter dated December 15, 1933, told Eastman that they had no jurisdiction "over questions of this character." Under date of December 19, Eastman sent a copy of the December 15 letter to all the regional coordinating committees saying that he found it "difficult to believe that anyone would seriously question the propriety and expediency" of exercising the leadership he recommended on December 7 "by raising technical legal distinctions."

The coordinator then followed up his communication of December 19 with a conference on January 4, 1934 with members of the regional coordinating committees, and it was arranged that the committees would prepare some recommendations to individual roads on compliance with the law.[74] What *Railway Age* called "employees associations that have no connection with the railroad brotherhoods or the American Federation of Labor" attempted to get together in an effort to work out a common policy of opposition to Eastman's plan "to divorce railway managements from any connection with or financial support of company unions" but this agitation failed to move the coordinator.[75] The railroads substantially complied with Eastman's policy, while some (the eastern and southern regional coordinating committees) continued to say that they believed the committees to be without jurisdiction to act.[76] Because the guarantees of Section 7e were temporary (being limited to the life of the Emergency Railroad Transportation Act), Eastman drafted certain amendments to the Railway Labor Act of 1926 which the Congress in 1934 enacted into law, making permanent the temporary protections of Section 7e,[77] although this was not done without objection from both the carriers and the unions.[78]

During his tenure as coordinator, Eastman was often spoken of by railroad union officials with some respect and a certain amount of friendship, but this was more evident at the beginning of his term than the end. *Labor,* the journal of the railroad unions, for example, noted in the spring of 1933 that Eastman might become a "rail czar" and said, "Everyone who has done business before the Interstate Commerce Commission concedes his fairness and ability. His energy is prodigious." [79] And shortly after his appointment as Coordinator, it was said of Eastman and McManamy of the ICC that they were like Justices Holmes and Brandeis because they dissented almost as often as these two judges "and in about the same direction." [80] By November 1934, the unions could still say, "Anything Joseph B. Eastman . . . may say is of interest to railroad workers, even when the workers are disposed to sharply challenge some of Mr. Eastman's views." [81] But by this time, the unions had had occasion to challenge some of these views very sharply.[82]

A measure of the change in attitude towards Eastman is supplied by the tone of the headline in *Labor* that announced the end of the coordinator's office. It read, "Rail Coordinator Fades Out of Picture. Congress Refuses Eastman Another Year. Opposed by Labor and Management. Last Report Calls for Shop Modernization That Would Strike Blow at Pay Envelope." [83] And Fletcher of the Association of American Railroads was quoted as saying of Eastman and the end of the coordinator's office, "It is inconceivable that any man or group of men, however wise or patriotic, can undertake the administration of 250,000 miles of railroad with knowledge he gained in the cloistered seclusion of a study or by a hasty and superficial examination of statistics." Upon the death of Eastman in 1944 the literary voice of the railroad unions said of him in headlines, "Started Out as Progressive, But Became Conservative; Was Aided in Early Battles by Railroad Unions." [84] And in the text of the report on his career, it said, "At one time the railroads opposed his appointment to the commission and the rail unions went to his aid. In recent times the unions were not pleased with his attitude on many matters and the carriers supported him more and more." [85]

Upon the termination of the coordinator's office, carrier spokesmen were pretty cheerful. R. V. Fletcher, vice president and general counsel for the Association of American Railroads, referred to the "dual control of railroads" which had existed for three years and was now ended. He said, "The experience of the railroads under the Coordinator has not been such as to carry conviction that the office should be continued beyond its present expiration date. There would seem to be no necessity for any regulating body other than the ICC . . . To add to this heavy burden the office of the Federal Coordinator, with powers over matters which are distinctively and purely managerial, is to increase the burden to an intolerable degree." [86] Mr. Fletcher thought that, outside of certain recommendations to Congress for new legislation, the coordinator had made "no substantially helpful contributions to solution of the railroad problem." But, it was not his fault; the whole theory of the act had proved to be unsound. It was at this point that Mr. Fletcher expressed the opinion that no group of men, "however wise and patriotic, can undertake the management and administration of 250,000 miles of railroad . . . when the knowledge of these men is gained in the cloistered seclusion of a study or by a hasty and superficial examination of statistics."

The studies of the coordinator, he said, were not received by railroad men with hostility. The suggestions were theoretically attractive; they were just unworkable. Indeed, the shoe of hostility was presumably on the other foot, for, Fletcher said, "When with care and with great respect, the defects in these plans have been pointed out, those responsible for their promulgation have received the suggestions with marked impatience and with the constantly reiterated assertion that the railroads have not been open-minded, nor progressive, nor amenable to suggestions." The "great respect" that the carriers accorded to the plans of men whose knowledge was "gained in the cloistered seclusion of a study or by a hasty and superficial examination of statistics" surely deserved a better response than the assertion that they were not open-minded, progressive, or amenable to suggestions, despite their constant failure to accept suggestions. Mr. Fletcher thought that the experience of three years abundantly demonstrated that railroad problems have to be worked out by the railroads and that "no cut and dried program . . . can be handed down by a bureau chief and applied in any way which is consistent with the rights of property and with the demand of the public for sound transportation methods."

In making these stern judgments, Mr. Fletcher was speaking the same line as his employers. Daniel Willard, president of the B&O Railroad, praised Caesar but was glad he was dead. He was reported as approving the end of the coordinator's office but said, "Mr. Eastman filled the position of Coordinator ably, and it is to be doubted that anyone could have filled it better." Mr. H. G. Taylor, chairman of the Western Association of Railway Executives, hailed the end of the Emergency Railroad Transportation Act as a sign that government regulation may be decreasing. "I think we are all agreed," said Mr. Taylor, "that it was more or less an abortive effort to make changes and progress that the industry was capable of making for itself. There seems to be an assumption that there does not exist in the railroads the capacity to solve their own problems, and they must of necessity go to some governmental agency for help." [87]

Mr. Eastman did not subscribe to the view that the transportation agencies could accomplish coordination by themselves. In a memorandum to Roosevelt on July 25, 1936, he wrote as follows:

"Much lip service is given to the principle of coordination in transportation, but who is to bring it about? If the principle is to be applied to all kinds of transportation, it cannot be left to the railroads nor to any other transportation group. Nor can it be expected that the groups will unite for this purpose without external aid. The Government is the natural and best-equipped agency to promote such coordination and probe its possibilities, and if the Government does not take on the job, it is not likely to be done. Even within any particular transportation group, such as the railroads, it may be doubted whether any effective coordination can be accomplished without Government help. And if they have done nothing else, the investigations conducted by the Coordinator have shown the great advantage which the Government has in assembling information from all quarters." [88]

This was the end, and Eastman's further relation with Roosevelt as coordinator consisted almost entirely of efforts by Eastman to get some money so that he could finish his reports.

Exeunt Omnes

The evidence of the maneuvering in the last weeks preceding the end of his office shows Eastman with many friends and no support. He had been disinclined to build a power base of his own, or even effectively to engage the use of the President's, which was considerable and was to grow stronger and larger. The two agents of the President, Corcoran and Lowenthal, were simply trying to save the face of the coordinator and the President, to enable the coordinator to keep his shop open, as Roosevelt said it should be, and yet to leave him nothing to sell, as the carriers and unions had decided when they made their deal to defeat him. Because of Eastman's long association with the carriers and the nature of the efforts he had made in their behalf, they should have been his natural ally, but strong and purposeful interest groups are dubious and unreliable friends when power is at stake. It was worth more to the carriers to dispose of the coordinator by making the deal with the unions than it was to maintain their close relationship with him. He needed them but they did not need him. And Roosevelt was able to get along without the support of either the carriers or that of Eastman who, after all, represented nothing but his own independence and conscience.

XII. A MATTER OF ADMINISTRATIVE STYLE

"Power is not a permanent but a shifting thing."

Eastman, *The Twelve Point Primer*

Pliny attributes to Zeuxis the remark that criticism comes easier than craftsmanship. This was the theme of many of the comments on Eastman as coordinator made by Fletcher and Pelley. The genealogy of this wisdom from Pliny to Pelley invests it with the authority of years, but even though Eastman was not running a railroad, the difference between — or perhaps the duality of — criticism and craftsmanship can be exaggerated. It is just possible that critics make craftsmen better and vice versa.

Administration is doubtless as much a matter of style as it is rules; but railroad detractors of the coordinator concentrated on the wrong aspects of Eastman's style when they disparaged him as the author of visionary, impracticable proposals — the kind that would not occur to claims adjusters, traffic controllers, shop foremen, and other practical people. There was another quality of Eastman's administrative style that deserved discussion, but the railroad men were so close to it and benefited so much by it — indeed, had a vested interest in it — that judgment about it, especially skeptical judgment, would have been hard to make.

The preceding pages have supplied ample evidence of Eastman's habitual style, as much a part of his administrative personality as his self-composure and his perpetual pipe. Consultation, conciliation, and compromise were elements of technique at the service of this style, but they were not the whole of it, for technique may vary according to the circumstance, but style, which is an organized attitude, is constant. Eastman's style was that of the judge, and there are many points in his experience as coordinator where his stance was judgelike. His numerous — and to the industry, provocative — essays on the case for and against public ownership of the railroads were "opinions," in some instances gratuitously offered, but in no instance really to be mistaken as blueprints for programs. Even when Wheeler introduced a bill for government ownership of the railroads in 1935, and Eastman helped him write it, Eastman was acting as an impartial officer, not as an advocate. He was saying, in effect, if judgment is to be for the government, the decree should contain the following particulars. As Wheeler said, Eastman did not suggest the bill, nor did he recommend government ownership. Much of Eastman's professional correspondence, both inside the government and out, consists of very long letters in which he discusses the arguments for and against some proposition or delivers a judgment supported by citations to statistics or other corroborative texts. Even in the beginning work on the Emergency Railroad Transportation Act, after it was clear that the central administrative piece was going to be a functionary called a "coordinator," Eastman wanted his orders to be made reviewable by the Interstate Commerce Commission, much as though he were the Commission's principal examiner whose preliminary judgments could be appealed.

Eastman's was an austere kind of leadership. It functioned with distinction in a context in which all the other elements of relationship were held stable, where the interactions of the parties were governed by rules of address and the decorum of the chamber — within the context, for example, of the hearing rooms of the Interstate Commerce Commission or of the court room. The characteristics of his administrative personality were implacable intelligence, an unwavering devotion to facts, and strong self-discipline, virtues we prize in judges. Along with these was an aloofness from the free and easy (and easily changed) identification with the political directors of the day that one associates with administrative enterprisers from the class room, business offices, and law firms. A Moley could blow hot and cold on the New Deal, but Eastman, although he had preferences, did not have political attachments, for his public attitude was objective independence, as it had been from the time of his first appointment in 1919.

Eastman himself understood his professional penchant. On December 18, 1941, Roosevelt created the office of defense transportation, the directorship of which Eastman thought should have gone to Ralph Budd of the Burlington Railroad. The unions preferred Eastman to Budd, however, and Roosevelt appointed the former to head the agency. Eastman wrote at the time: "I do not believe that I have any special qualifications for the job, which seems to me to call for administrative talents rather than judicial, and I have never considered myself particularly gifted as an administrator." The revealing thing is not that he deprecated himself as an administrator, but that he impliedly thought of himself as the possessor of judicial talents, which he had. An ingrained habit of mind, generated by temperament, perhaps, and reinforced by more than two decades of service on the Interstate Commerce Commission, admirably equipped Eastman for the things he did best — research, judgment, and recommendation. These traits, so important in the judge, were less serviceable in situations that called for improvisation, contrivance, and risky adventure, fluid situations subject to influence by personality and political tendency.

Could Eastman have succeeded in producing more coordination in the 1930's had he shed his temperament, reoriented his preferences, and altered his style? Like many effective and colorful figures of the New Deal, could he have lobbied his position, waged factional strife, solicited and bought necessary tactical support for strategic goals, marched and countermarched with allies in the committees and on the floor of Congress, in and out of the agencies and the White House? Such behavior would have violated Eastman's image of himself; it was debarred to him by the whole thrust and set of his mind and experience. One needs only recall the comparative helplessness with which Eastman watched, without influencing, the course of affairs unfolded by Corcoran, Wheeler, Lowenthal, Fletcher, Harrison, and Roosevelt after the Washington agreement.

Two occasions in the 1940's illustrate the extent to which freestyle competitive political and administrative enterprise was foreign to Eastman's thought and habit. The first occurred when he was director of the office of defense transportation, and it shows that even in a war situation Eastman was reluctant to use authority, as he had been reluctant to use his authority as federal coordinator of transportation. Eastman's biographer tells the story of the director's efforts in 1943 to cut down on unnecessary transportation so as to conserve facilities. Eastman appealed to the country to postpone conventions and other such meetings requiring unnecessary travel, and asked educational institutions in the winter of 1943 to cancel the usual Easter recess. Some did and some did not, and those who refused took the position that cancellation would disrupt school programs. As the incident is reported: "When he learned that these schools declined to help except under direct order, Joe said sadly, 'My God, I just can't force them. But if they only knew what is going on at the front, they might be more cooperative.' "[1]

The second occasion was the celebratory dinner in March 1944 to observe Eastman's silver anniversary with the Interstate Commerce Commission. On this occasion, although his strength was taxed, he made a speech setting out his credo in what he called a "twelve point primer." Among other things, he said that tribunals like the Commission should not be under the domination or influence of either the President or the Congress "or of anything else than their own independent judgment of the facts and the law." In some advice for commissioners and judges, Eastman urged that conclusions of law and policy should be made only after an inspection of all available evidence, and then objectively, and without bias. He repeated a familiar homily of his, that good men could make bad laws work but that bad men could not make even good laws work well. And what was a good man? He was one who could "grasp and comprehend facts quickly" and "consider them in their relation to the law logically and with an open mind." As for "zealots, evangelists, and crusaders," their place was before an administrative tribunal, not on it.

Eastman's statements about administrative tribunals suppose a clear and broad separation of politics and administration, a point of view advocated by Frank Goodnow at the turn of the century, and one that has dominated some thought about public administration. "Politics" is thought somehow to be outside the administrative process, something alien and different, lacking stability and predictability, threatening to the quiet continuities and contemplative perspectives of the administrative office, anarchic even, full of accident and contingency. In a solemn observation about power, Eastman said in his "primer," "Power is not a permanent but a shifting thing." And in a paraphrase of the dictum that Acton loosed upon an uncomprehending world, Eastman said, "There is nothing more important than to curb the abuse of power, wherever it may reside, and power is always subject to abuse."

As was said earlier in these pages, "The authority of a statute unsupported by the power of groups that stand to gain advantage from its enforcement against rival groups that stand to lose advantage, leaves the administrator with only the sanctions of the official agencies, including the courts." As Eastman put the same thought in his speech of June 20, 1935, before the National Association of Credit Men in Pittsburgh already referred to: "The power to order which the Emergency Act gives to the Coordinator can be used to advantage where a few companies are out of line with the prevailing opinion . . . I doubt whether it should be used to compel comprehensive and important changes . . . to which railroad opinion is generally hostile." It is extremely unlikely that Eastman could have changed his role while coordinator and gone into the political market as an enterpriser trading for the support that he needed if he were going to realize and fulfill the authority that Congress had given to him to compel those "comprehensive and important changes." Although he wanted to secure his office and to advance the programs that he thought it ought to pursue, Eastman did not abandon — perhaps could not have abandoned — his natural stance as a figure of judicious, even judicial, lineaments. His administrative style utilized facts and reason as solvents of conflict situations, fastidiously separated politics and administration, and harbored a deep distrust of power, a style befitting a judge in circumstances that called for a governor.

But, although Eastman's style prevented him from attempting more devious political efforts to make coordination in a resistant industry, it by no means follows that success would have been likely in the hands of someone bolder. Speculations about what might have happened are, of course, strictly in the realm of conjecture. As someone has said, this is history in the conditional mood. But judgments about a hypothetical past, although they may not change it, may help to clarify it. What if Roper had succeeded in building up the Department of Commerce by bringing under it much of the program and authority of the Interstate Commerce Commission and also, perhaps, the functions of the office of federal coordinator? Roper was a more political type than

Eastman, unhandicapped by the limitations of the judicial temperament, certain of his identification with the New Deal, as Eastman was not. Or General Hugh S. Johnson, who more than once showed strong interest in bringing the railroads under the code system of the National Industrial Recovery Administration? Roper was politically adaptable and Johnson was dominating and tough. Could they have succeeded where Eastman did not?

In a sense such a question supposes the answer; for if one can imagine that Roper could have succeeded in overcoming the strong resistances to the dismantling of the Commission and the transfer of its authorities, one assumes the thing to be established, to wit, that the resistances of the railroads and their friends could not check and offset the moves to control them. But these resistances were entrenched. As Eastman said in the speech before the Interstate Bus and Truck Conference in Harrisburg shortly after he became coordinator, the railroad system "is operated by a small army of independent feudal chieftains who fight a good deal among themselves and band together for the common good with considerable difficulty." With Eastman's help, however, these chieftains were able to get together on the Emergency Railroad Transportation Act in 1933 and to block more drastic controls that Roper may have had in mind. And, in 1933 and thereafter, with the help of Eastman again, the railroads were able to prevent Johnson from bringing them under the codes.

To be sure, Eastman was involved in both these frustrations of political maneuver by Roper and Johnson, but then he was the not-too-secret weapon of the railroads where issues of this kind were in play. The railroads on these and other occasions benefited by Eastman's administrative style, his organized attitude, his penchant for technical and expert solutions for railroad problems in the hands of non-political functionaries. Roper and Johnson probably could not have secured dominion over the railroads without Eastman's help and, as the argument above has urged, this was not likely in view of Eastman's antipolitical temperament. But, for the railroads, the struggle against more comprehensive political and administrative controls did not depend upon Eastman alone. He was very helpful to them but probably not indispensable, for the roots of resistance were deep in the industry, which had battled for half a century against effective regulation.

Roper and Johnson might not have been able to extend strong regulation over the industry even with Eastman's help.

The intransigeance of the railroads, immovable against an Eastman, a Roper, and a Johnson, so much a characteristic of the structure and the folkways of the industry, certainly did not vanish with the lapse of the coordinator's authorities. When the Association of American Railroads was created and the coordinator disappeared, the focus of the trouble changed but the problem did not. On its "Action Page," 21 years after the lapse of the coordinator's office, *Railway Age* found it necessary to comment upon the egotism and excessive separatism of railroad managements, as Eastman had so often, earlier. Said *Railway Age*:

A year or two ago a couple of railroad executives were discussing AAR. One of them said: "AAR's primary difficulties lie, not with its full-time staff in Washington, but with the 100-odd strong individualists who head the member railroads. If the member roads had a clearer idea of what they want AAR to do, there wouldn't be much difficulty in getting the AAR staff to carry out a consistent program." Whether this diagnosis is fully accurate or not, it is certainly true in part.[2]

This was rather reminiscent of Eastman's statement in his *Fourth Report,* when he said that "plans for greater cooperation or coordination in railroad affairs meet resistance because they are foreign to certain habits of thought which are the growth of many years."

To sum up, then, if the railroads were prepared and able to counteract the mild attempts at coordination gently urged by an Eastman, it is extremely unlikely that they would have accepted the stronger actions of a more aggressive functionary. And if one is permitted to suppose that the railroads were either too weak or unwilling to resist comprehensive and direct controls under a Roper or a Johnson, then one can suppose that Eastman might have achieved more of his program than he did. But they were not too weak, and they were unwilling, and much of Eastman's program was frustrated.

The unwillingness of the railroads to go along with the Coordinator was the decisive block, as a later experience was to verify. As we have seen, Eastman as director of the office of defense transportation was much the same man he had been ten years earlier.

But, whereas the coordinator failed to convert the reluctant, the director enjoyed success, and he enjoyed success because the railroads cooperated with him. The reasons for cooperation in the 1940's where cooperation was withheld in the 1930's are probably to be found in the different circumstances of the two periods.

Strong political leverage supported the director in 1942 and thereafter. In the war years he could count on the full force of the United States government as he could not have in the depression period. Lacking this sanction in the 1930's, Eastman would have had to build up pockets of power in the industry, in and out of the executive establishment and in Congress, to have counteracted the combination against him; and it is doubtful whether he had either the temperament or the resources to do this. In the war years, however, it was different. Although the policy of the government towards business enterprise was, on the whole, quite permissive (only men were conscripted), and the railroads were not commandeered as they had been in World War I, the alternative of government operation was not so safely distant that it could be risked by defiant withdrawal from less onerous controls.

It was not, however, only the possibility of government operation that generated a spirit of cooperation by the railroads in the 1940's. Eastman put his finger on certain other differences between his term as coordinator and his term as director when he said in 1942: "In 1933, the railroads had a great surplus of facilities, a minimum of traffic, and were drifting into bankruptcy, one by one. The problem was to find ways of saving expense and also of attracting traffic. My recommendations, which met with very little success, were directed towards those ends. At present the railroads have no surplus facilities, at least of equipment; their traffic has risen to record heights and is steadily increasing; and the problem is to move it promptly and effectively, regardless of cost." The economic situation, in short, removed the occasion for much of the aggression by the railroads which an economy of need had stimulated. There was not only enough for all but more than enough. With the economy supported by the government as the principal buyer, there was still competition among the suppliers of goods and services, including the railroads, but it was no longer a desperate struggle merely to survive. And for the first time since the early thirties, when motor competition became a serious threat, the railroads found that this competition was subject to extraordinary controls (on rubber and gasoline) from which the railroads were largely free.

This is not to say that the director had no problems of cooperation both among the railroads and the unions — especially with certain of the unions — for he had. But his style was successful in resolving them, or more successful than it had been in the 1930's. Nor is this to say that the railroads cooperated only out of motives of fear and profit. One need not discount entirely the influence of unselfish motives like patriotism in time of war, although it might be a mistake to exaggerate their appeal.

Comment on Eastman's administrative style cannot be dropped without some reference to the occupational habit it reflects; a habit based upon an outlook that has come under criticism in recent years. The outlook is not unique to Eastman but is professional among those agencies called, in the law books, the quasi-judicial agencies. Eastman's judicial style — one might almost say, his quasi-judicial style — was infused, as his words tell us, with the notion that the regulation of industry is somehow different from other forms of state policy, that it should be in the hands of neutral experts, that it should be kept free of "politics," that it is essentially an adversary proceeding between litigants of equal status. The thought for years has been that the fixing of a rate is such an invasion of economic rights as to require resolution only by the ordeal of battle between governmental agencies and regiments of fighting lawyers. This is certainly a different concept from that which applies, say, to the man who pays taxes on income derived only from wages and salaries, taxes which are taken out of income before he ever gets it.

In the last two decades the theory of the regulatory commission which Eastman argued has been attacked, most strongly by the President's committee on administrative management in 1937, which recommended that the quasi-judicial agencies be abolished as a headless fourth branch of the government. The attack failed and, instead, the whole tendency of the legislation since the early 1940's has been to judicialize the procedures of these agencies further, until they resemble lay courts. The principal move in this direction was the Administrative Procedure Act of 1946.

Eastman's conceptions have prevailed, then, but the case against them might be stated briefly without trying to resolve the contradictions. One critic has put the matter as follows:

The process of regulation is unavoidably political. So long as regulation is conditioned by the general political and social environment and remains founded on the efforts of organized groups to utilize public power to promote either private ends or the public welfare, it will remain a major aspect of political life. It is political, not in the invidious image of progressive reformers, that is, corrupt, fraudulent, dishonest, and motivated by desire for private gain. Politics refers rather to the emergence of public issues, formulation of public policies, and administration of governmental affairs.[3]

This conception of regulation is different from the conception of regulation represented by the commission movement, and supported by Eastman:

Implicit in the development of the commission movement is the notion that the political process is peculiarly susceptible to fraud and corruption and hence that regulation must repudiate and avoid involvement with politics. Escape from politics is regarded as both desirable and essential in the development of effective regulation. The goal of getting out of politics can be achieved presumably by maintaining the freedom of the regulatory commission from control by the president. Congress regards the independent commission as a government agency which exercises discretionary authority without increasing the power of the executive branch of the government.[4]

And this conception is enforced at a price that it might not be economic to pay. For by "insulating themselves from popular political forces the commissions have subjected themselves to undue influence from the regulated groups and tend to become protective spokesmen for the industries which they regulate." There is much in Eastman's experience as coordinator to verify these generalizations. He tended to think of the job of coordination as technical, not political, regarded what he called "politics" as something outside of and beyond his function, and by isolation from the political forces of his time, clearly did make himself vulnerable to the machinations of the groups he was appointed to regulate, for he virtually held his authorities by sufferance from these groups and lost them when the same groups combined to take them from him.

It would be plausible to conclude that Eastman, like Mendes-France at a later time, was a victim of "le gang," but this is not enough unless we also know that the combination that beat him was not a haphazard association of temporary and passing forces. To the contrary, for, although the combinations themselves change and the context moves from one place to another in the federal bureaucracy — and the object shifts from Eastman to Leland Olds to Ezra Benson to Commissioner Mack of the FCC — what is at work in this administrative stream is the embolism of offsetting groups. The mentality which disdains "politics" and strives for a neutral and technical perfection rejects the very solvents that would reduce the obstructions.

APPENDIX

A. Outline Histories of Legislation to Create, Amend or Extend the Emergency Railroad Transportation Act, 1933 with All Events Dated and References Noted.

Note: These histories were taken from the Index to the *Congressional Record,* 1933–36 (volumes 77–80), Section on "History of Bills." Dates of events secured from the *Congressional Record.*

73d CONGRESS, 1st SESSION, 1933

S. 1580 — To relieve the existing national emergency in relation to interstate railroad transportation, and to amend sections 5, 15a, and 19a of the Interstate Commerce Act, as amended.

Introduced in the Senate by Mr. Robinson of Arkansas, May 4, 1933, with accompanying message from President Roosevelt; referred to Senate Committee on Interstate Commerce (77 Cong. Rec. 2860)

Senate Hearings held May 9, 10, 11, and 12, 1933 (Hearings, Emergency Railroad Transportation Act, 1933)

Reported with amendments by Senate Committee (S. Rept. 87), May 22, 1933 (77 Cong. Rec. 3877)

Debated by Senate, May 26 and 27, 1933 (77 Cong. Rec. 4183; 4247–4259; 4267–4286; 4406–4441)

Amended and passed Senate, May 27, 1933 (77 Cong. Rec. 4441)

Referred to House Committee on Interstate and Foreign Commerce, May 31, 1933 (77 Cong. Rec. 4714)

Reported with Amendment by House Committee (H. Rept. 193), June 2, 1933 (77 Cong. Rec. 4884)

Made special order by House (H. Res. 169), June 2, 1933 (77 Cong. Rec. 4852)

Debated by House, June 2 and 3, 1933 (77 Cong. Rec. 4794; 4852–4881; 4934–4956; 4999)

Amended and passed House, June 5, 1933 (77 Cong. Rec. 4999)

Senate disagrees to House amendment and asks conference, June 5, 1933 (77 Cong. Rec. 5057); Mr. Dill, Mr. Smith, Mr. Wheeler, Mr. Fess and Mr. Metcalf appointed conferees

House insists upon its amendment and agrees to conference, June 7, 1933 (77 Cong. Rec. 5196); Mr. Rayburn, Mr. Huddleston, Mr. Lea of California, Mr. Parker of New York, and Mr. Cooper of Ohio are appointed conferees

Conference report submitted in House (H. Rept. 213), June 9, 1933, and agreed to (77 Cong. Rec. 5430; 5435)

Conference report submitted in Senate and agreed to, June 9, 1933 (77 Cong. Rec. 5393; 5398)

Amended bill examined and signed, June 10, 1933, in House and Senate (77 Cong. Rec. 5653; 5560)

Presented to President June 10, 1933 (77 Cong. Rec. 5622)

President requested to return bill (S. Con. Res. 5) June 12, 1933, because two words were inadvertently omitted (77 Cong. Rec. 5723; 5849)

Corrected bill examined and signed in the House and Senate. June 13, 1933 (77 Cong. Rec. 5919; 5863)

Presented to President, June 13, 1933 (77 Cong. Rec. 5966)

Approved by President June 16, 1933, Public, No. 68, 48 Stat. 211.

H. R. 5500 — To relieve the existing national emergency in relation to interstate railroad transportation, and to amend sections 5, 15a, and 19a of the Interstate Commerce Act, as amended.

Introduced in the House by Mr. Rayburn, May 4, 1933, with accompanying message from President Roosevelt; referred to House Committee on Interstate and Foreign Commerce (77 Cong. Rec. 2908; 2888)

House Hearings held May 8, 10, 11, 12, 16, 17, 18, 19, and 22, 1933 (Hearings, Emergency Railroad Transportation Act, 933)

H. Res. 169 — Providing for the consideration of S. 1580, an act to relieve the existing national emergency in relation to interstate railroad transportation, and to amend sections 5, 15a, and 19a of the Interstate Commerce Act, as amended.

Introduced by Mr. Pou, from the House Committee on Rules (H. Rept. 192), June 1, 1933 and referred to House Calendar (77 Cong. Rec. 4785; 4796)

Agreed to June 2, 1933 (77 Cong. Rec., 4852)

73d CONGRESS, 2d SESSION, 1934

S. 2411 — To amend the Emergency Railroad Transportation Act, 1933.

Introduced in the Senate by Mr. Dill and referred to the Committee on Interstate Commerce, January 19, 1934 (78 Cong. Rec. 911)

Senate Hearings held February 26 and 27, 1934 (Hearings, To Amend the Emergency Railroad Transportation Act, 1933, 1934)

Reported with amendment (S. Rept. 439) March 8, 1934 (78 Cong. Rec. 3958)

H. R. 7649 — To amend the Emergency Railroad Transportation Act, 1933.

Introduced in the House by Mr. Crosser of Ohio and referred to the Committee on Interstate and Foreign Commerce, February 5, 1934 (78 Cong. Rec., 1977)

S. 3650 — To amend the Emergency Railroad Transportation Act, 1933.

Introduced in the Senate by Mr. Dill and referred to the Committee on Interstate Commerce, May 21, 1934 (78 Cong. Rec. 9120)

Reported back (S. Rept. 1166) May 25, 1934 (78 Cong. Rec. 9554)

Indefinitely postponed (H. R. 9694 passed in lieu) June 6, 1934 (78 Cong. Rec., 10595).

H. R. 9694 — To amend the Emergency Railroad Transportation Act, 1933, approved June 16, 1933.

Introduced in the House by Mr. Rayburn and referred to the Committee on Interstate and Foreign Commerce, May 21, 1934 (78 Cong. Rec. 9206)

Reported back (H. Rept. 1764) May 24, 1934 (78 Cong. Rec. 9551)

Passed House, June 4, 1934 (78 Cong. Rec. 10440)

Placed on calendar in Senate, June 5, 1934 (78 Cong. Rec. 10476)

Passed Senate (in lieu of S. 3650) June 6, 1934 (78 Cong. Rec. 10595)

Examined and signed in Senate and House, June 8, 1934 (78 Cong. Rec. 10779; 10905)

Presented to the President, June 8, 1934 (78 Cong. Rec. 11001)

Approved by President, June 13, 1934, Public, No. 340 (78 Cong. Rec. 12209)

74th CONGRESS, 1st SESSION, 1935

S. J. Res 112 — Extending the effective period of the Emergency Railroad Transportation Act, 1933.

Introduced by Mr. Wheeler and referred to the Committee on Interstate Commerce, May 1, 1935 (79 Cong. Rec. 6669)

Reported with amendments (S. Rept. 588) May 7, 1935 (79 Cong. Rec. 7040)

Debated in Senate, May 20, 1935 (79 Cong. Rec. 7809)

Amended and passed Senate, June 10, 1935 (79 Cong. Rec. 8949)

Motion entered in Senate to reconsider, agreed to, June 10, 1935 (79 Cong. Rec. 8949)

Debated, amended and passed Senate, June 10, 1935 (79 Cong. Rec. 8951)

Passed House (in lieu of H. J. Res. 319), June 14, 1935 (79 Cong. Rec. 9329)

Examined and signed in Senate and House, June 14, 1935 (79 Cong. Rec. 9297; 9346)

Presented to the President, June 14, 1935 (79 Cong. Rec. 9414)

Approved, Public Resolution No. 27, June 14, 1935 (79 Cong. Rec. 9351)

H. J. Res. 219 — Extending the effective period of the Emergency Railroad Transportation Act, 1933.

Introduced in the House by Mr. Crosser and referred to the Committee on Interstate and Foreign Commerce, March 18, 1935 (79 Cong. Rec. 3918)

H. J. Res. 309 — Extending the effective period of the Emergency Railroad Transportation Act, 1933.

Introduced in the House by Mr. Maas and referred to the Committee on Interstate and Foreign Commerce, June 5, 1935 (79 Cong. Rec. 8743)

H. J. Res. 319 — Extending the effective period of the Emergency Railroad Transportation Act, 1933.

Introduced in the House by Mr. Crosser and referred to the Committee on Interstate and Foreign Commerce, June 10, 1935 (79 Cong. Rec. 9030)

House Hearings held, June 12, 1935 (Hearings, Extension of Emergency Railroad Transportation Act, 1933)

Reported with amendment (H. Rept. 1173), June 12, 1935 (79 Cong. Rec. 9219)

Made special order (H. Res. 258), June 14, 1935 (79 Cong. Rec. 9319)

Debated in House, June 14, 1935 (79 Cong. Rec. 9321)

Laid on the table (S. J. Res. 112 passed in lieu), June 14, 1935 (79 Cong. Rec. 9329)

74th CONGRESS, 2d SESSION, 1936

S. J. Res. 271 — Amending and repealing certain sections of the Emergency Railroad Transportation Act, 1933, and extending the effective period of such act, and for other purposes.

Introduced by Mr. Wheeler and referred to the Committee on Interstate Commerce, May 25, 1936 (80 Cong. Rec. 7835)

Reported with amendments (S. Rept. 2354), June 15, 1936 (80 Cong. Rec. 9317)

H. J. Res. 615 — Amending and repealing certain sections of the Emergency Railroad Transportation Act, 1933, and extending the effective period of such act, and for other purposes.

Introduced by Mr. Russell and referred to the Committee on Interstate and Foreign Commerce, June 1, 1936 (80 Cong. Rec. 8622)

B. Major Additions and Changes in the Emergency Railroad Transportation Act, 1933, Title I, from Original Administration Bill to Final Statute (48 Stat L211)

Section 1.

Definitions of "subsidiary," "employee," and "state commission" added.

Section 2.

Addition: Coordinator shall not sit as member of ICC when any order issued by him is being considered.

Section 3.

Change: From specification of "not more than five members" on each regional coordinating committee to "five regular members and two special members," the two special members to be representatives of railroads with revenues of less than $1,000,000 and of electric railroads, respectively. These special members to be notified when committee considers matters affecting their interest.

Section 4.

Addition: In this and some subsequent Sections "carrier" is followed by "and subsidiaries subject to the Interstate Commerce Act, as amended."

Addition: In the avoidance of waste, no existing routes to be eliminated without consent of all participating lines or upon order of coordinator.

Section 5.

No significant change or addition.

Section 6.

Addition: The Coordinator and ICC to have access to all accounts, records, and memoranda of carriers and subsidiaries.

Addition: Coordinator to have powers equal to ICC to subpoena, administer oaths, require documents, etc.

Section 7.

Addition and Change: In the original bill the Coordinator is to notify central labor committees of any contemplated orders affecting labor and is required to confer with these committees before issuing any orders. This is made more specific in part (a) of the new Section 7.

Part (b) specifies that the number of employees in service during May, 1933 may not be reduced, nor shall any employee "be deprived of employment" such as he had at that time, or "be in a worse position with respect to his compensation for such employment" by reason of "any action taken pursuant to the authority of this title" except for deaths, normal retirements or resignations not to exceed 5% per annum.

Part (c) gives Coordinator power to establish boards of adjustment to settle disputes between carriers and employees which result from action taken by Coordinator.

Part (d) requires Coordinator to see that employees receive "just compensation" for property losses and expenses incident to possible transferrals resulting from action taken by Coordinator.

Part (e) requires carriers to comply with provisions of Railway Labor Act and section 77, paragraphs (o), (p), and (q) of the Act (1933) entitled "An Act to amend an Act entitled 'An Act to establish a uniform system of bankruptcy throughout the United States,' approved July 1, 1898, and Acts amendatory thereof and supplementary thereto."

Section 8.

Addition: Any order of Coordinator must be made public, and it may become effective not less than 20 days after it is made public.

Section 9.

Change and Addition: Listing of interested parties who may protest a Coordinator order is broadened to include *groups* of carriers, shippers, or employees, and State commissions, Governors, and representatives of any State political subdivision.

Change: Interested parties may file petition protesting order *prior* to effective date of order; petitions to be governed by rules to be established by Commission.

Section 10.

Addition: A Part (b) specifying that Coordinator must notify State officials when it is his intention to relieve any carrier from operation of State laws and give State officials opportunity to present views.

Section 11.

New Section: Specifying that this title does not relieve carriers from prior contractual obligations with regard to location or maintenance of shops, offices, or roundhouses.

Section 12.

Formerly Section 11.

Addition: Proviso that no employee or officer of carrier be required to work against his will as result of any Coordinator order.

Section 13.

Formerly Section 12.

Addition: In investigating means of improving country's transportation, cost finding is to be included, as well as labor relations (formerly was only labor conditions).

Section 14.

Formerly Section 13.

Addition: Expenses of coordinating committees not to be borne by Coordinator.

Addition: Carriers to furnish free transportation to Commission employees when in Coordinator's service.

Change: From assessment on railroads of $1.00 per mile of road operated Dec. 31, 1932 to $1.50 per mile, etc.

Section 15.

Formerly Section 14.

Change: From requirement that carriers have financial structure able to weather depression in order to have loan under RFC Act approved by Commission, to stipulation that carriers be denied approval of loans by ICC when financial reorganization is considered essential in the public interest.

Addition: "Carriers" not to include receivers or trustees.

Section 16.

New Section: Final orders made by Coordinator subject to same right of relief in court as provided with regard to ICC orders. Provisions of 38 Stat L219 applicable to any such proceedings.

Section 17.

Formerly Section 15.

Addition: After termination of Title I, States may override any orders made under Title I by appropriate laws or orders.

CHAPTER II. THE SALT LAKE CITY LINE

1. The measure of the decline can be seen in the following table supplied by Dr. Charles S. Morgan, former chief carrier research analyst, bureau of transport economics and statistics, Interstate Commerce Commission. All quantities are in thousands.

Item	1929	1933	1934	1935	1936
Operating revenue	$6,373,004	$3,138,186	$3,316,861	$3,499,126	$4,108,658
Operating expenses	$4,579,162	$2,285,218	$2,479,997	$2,630,177	$2,975,366
Operating ratio	71.85%	72.82%*	74.77%	75.17%	72.37%
No. of employees	1,694	991	1.027	1.014	1.086
Compensation	$2,940,206	$1,424,392	$1,541,313	$1,666,229	$1,873,819
Dividends decl'd	$560,902	$158,790†	$211,767	$202,568	$231,733
Interest accrued on funded debt	$580,770	$590,230	$569,760	$559,187	$548,452

* Over 77 per cent in 1931 and 1932.

† $603,150 in 1930 (highest back to 1900).

Source: *Transport Statistics in the United States: Part I: Railroads, Their Lessors, and Proprietary Companies, 1956*, Table 155. Data relate to Class I and II linehaul railways except those for dividends and interest, which also include the lessors of such railways.

2. *Regulations of Railroads*, first legislative report of the federal coordinator of transportation, Sen. Doc. 119, 73 Cong., 2 sess., January 11, 1934 (hereafter cited as *First Report*), p. 4.

3. *The Railroads: Republican Mistakes and Democratic Remedies*, Governor Franklin D. Roosevelt's speech delivered at Salt Lake City, Utah, September 17, 1932, pamphlet published and distributed by the Democratic National Committee.

4. *New York Times*, September 18, 1932, p. 1, col. 8.

5. *New York Times*, September 19, 1932, p. 10, col. 6.

6. Interview with A. A. Berle, 70 Pine Street, New York City, November 15, 1950.

7. Richberg was co-author of the Railway Labor Act of 1926.

8. See Claude M. Fuess, *Joseph B. Eastman* (New York: Columbia University Press, 1952), 189. It is possible that Eastman might have been consulted by one of Roosevelt's advisors, although the President and the Commissioner had not met at this time.

9. *Ibid*.

10. Eastman to Roosevelt, "The Railroads," with covering letter, July 25, 1936.

11. Section 77 of the Bankruptcy Act provides for action, in given circumstances, by vote of more than two-thirds of the creditors or stockholders be-

fore a reorganization may become effective. Section 20b of the Interstate Commerce Act (the so-called "Mahaffie Act" that provides for voluntary adjustment of securities) calls for a 75 per cent assent.

12. Immediately after the passage of the 1920 legislation, the ICC hired W. Z. Ripley of Harvard to prepare a tentative plan of consolidation. In 1921, it put out the Ripley plan and one of its own, which resembled the Ripley plan. Nearly 12,000 pages of testimony were taken in hearings on the Commission plan. In 1925 the ICC pointed out to Congress what it felt was the impracticability of the "plan" approach but Congress did not relieve the Commission of its obligation under the 1920 act. In 1929 the Commission came out with a plan. Meanwhile, consolidations were taking place in another fashion than through Commission plan. Long-term leases, which were often accompanied by complete stock ownership, brought together a goodly number of roads. These were not actually "consolidations" but Eastman said that properties so linked were "tied together about as tightly as if they had been technically consolidated" (*First Report*, p. 22). The Commission approved a number of consolidations after 1929 which it found consistent with its plan, or which it approved after changing its plan.

13. Claude Fuess, *Joseph B. Eastman*, in his discussion of the attitude of the railroads in this period. "Even when the disastrous consequences of the depression had become inescapable, the railroad leaders did not admit the need for voluntary cooperation" (p. 185).

14. For a summary of the recommendations of the Joint Committee of Railroads and Highway Users, see *Regulation of Transportation Agencies*, Second Legislative Report of the Federal Coordinator of Transportation, Sen. Doc. 152, 73 Cong., 2 sess., March 10, 1934 (hereafter cited as *Second Report*), p. 26.

15. *New York Times*, January 30, 1933, p. 19, col. 1. The Joint Committee of Railways and Highway Users also undertook to cover the vexing question of proper taxation for the use of highways and streets. The agreement on this matter did not stand up very well or for very long.

16. See, for example, letter from Eastman to Moulton, dated January 3, 1933, in which he transmits his own analysis of the recommendations submitted to the National Transportation Committee by the Association of Railway Executives, an analysis originally made by Eastman for the Commission. In the same letter, Eastman sent Moulton a copy of a speech in which he examined in some detail the competitive conditions of the past.

17. Letter, Eastman to Moulton, January 24, 1933.

18. Letter, Eastman to Moulton, January 7, 1933.

19. See letter from Eastman to Wilfred Eldred, National Transportation Committee, February 4, 1933, transmitting various documents requested.

20. *Business Week*, February 22, 1933, pp. 6–7.

21. *New York Times*, March 19, 1933, p. 31, col. 1.

22. Letter, Eastman to Hon. George W. Anderson, February 16, 1933.

23. "Commission Organization," December 2, 1932.

24. "Plan of Organization," January 3, 1933.

25. Letter, Eastman to Couzens, February 21, 1933.

26. The analysis bore the title, "Report of National Transportation Committee on Reorganization of Commission's Work" (February 21, 1933). Its general theme was that the committee's recommendations were based upon

insufficient and occasionally inaccurate information about the organization, functions, and methods of the Interstate Commerce Commission. He believed that if the committee had had an adequate understanding of the facts, it never would have made the recommendations it did.

27. Letter, Eastman to Rayburn, February 24, 1933.

28. Letter, Eastman to Charles D. Mahaffie, January 3, 1933.

29. Claude Fuess, *Joseph B. Eastman*, 190.

30. Telegram, Eastman to Frankfurter, January 5, 1933.

31. Telegram, Eastman to Marvin H. McIntyre, January 8, 1933.

32. Here the public trustees were to be assisted by an advisory council after being appointed for a definite tenure of office by the President. They could be removed only for cause (*First Report*, p. 16).

33. *Report of the Federal Coordinator of Transportation*, 1934 H. Doc. 89, 74 Cong., 1 sess., January 30, 1935 (hereafter cited as *Third Report*).

34. Letter, Eastman to Felix Frankfurter, January 9, 1933.

35. Letter, Eastman to George Foster Peabody, January 20, 1933.

36. Letter, Eastman to Felix Frankfurter, January 24, 1933.

37. *Annals of the American Academy of Political and Social Science*, November 1931, pp. 112–119.

38. Letter, Eastman to William G. McAdoo, January 30, 1933.

39. Letter, Eastman to Felix Frankfurter, January 30, 1933.

40. It may be noted that Section 15a of the Interstate Commerce Act requires efficient and economical management and that Section 12(1), which goes back to 1887, empowers the Commission to look into the management of the business of the railroads. Section 15a requires the Commission to make findings that carriers are efficiently and economically operated before granting increases in rate levels. The evidence accepted by the Commission is "sometimes scarcely more than self-serving declarations by the applicant railroads." See Charles S. Morgan, "The Function of Research in a Regulatory Agency," *I.C.C. Practitioners' Journal*, Vol. XXIV, No. 8 (May, 1957), p. 834.

41. Letter, Eastman to George Foster Peabody, February 10, 1933.

42. Letter, Eastman to George Creel, February 10, 1933.

43. See letter from Eastman to Nathan L. Amster, February 10, 1933; letter from Eastman to Col. Henry W. Anderson, February 11, 1933. Amster was a director of the Rock Island and the Pennsylvania, and Anderson was first counsel for the receivers and then co-receiver for the Seaboard Air Line Railroad, a position he held from 1933 to 1946. Amster was also president of the Citizens National Railroads League, Inc.

44. Letter, Eastman to Daniel Willard, March 11, 1933.

45. See also letter from Eastman to F. C. Nicodemus, Jr., March 11, 1933.

46. Letter, Eastman to Hon. Clarence Dill, March 20, 1933.

47. In a letter dated March 28, 1933, Eastman's friend, Col. Henry W. Anderson, mentioned the possibility of Eastman's becoming coordinator. In a letter to Anderson dated March 31, 1933, Eastman said that he thought he might have difficulty deciding to take such an appointment if it were offered to him.

48. Eastman's views on public ownership and operation of the railroads are considered further below in Chapter V.

49. Statement made in interview, New York City, November 15, 1950.

50. In his *First Report*, Eastman, however, said, "Contrary to much popu-

lar impression the railroads are not in the aggregate overcapitalized, in the sense that the par value of outstanding securities exceeds the money invested in the properties" (p. 3).

51. Max Lowenthal, "The Railroad Reorganization Act," 47 *Harvard Law Review* 18, at 19–20 (November 1933).

52. Harold G. Moulton and associates, *The American Transportation Problem,* prepared for the National Transportation Committee (The Brookings Institution: Washington, D. C., 1933), 322–326.

53. *First Report,* p. 4.

54. Moulton, *The American Transportation Problem,* 68.

55. Letter, Eastman to Felix Frankfurter, December 16, 1932.

56. Letter, Eastman to Louis B. Wehle, December 16, 1932.

57. Letter, Eastman to Felix Frankfurter, December 20, 1932.

58. Letter, Eastman to Louis B. Wehle, December 20, 1932.

59. Letter, Eastman to James C. Bonbright, December 10, 1932.

60. Letter, Eastman to Felix Frankfurter, January 9, 1933.

61. *Ibid.*

62. Telegram, Eastman to Felix Frankfurter, January 13, 1933.

63. Letter, Eastman to Harold Palmer, January 4, 1933.

64. Letter, Eastman to Harold Palmer, January 17, 1933.

65. Letter, Eastman to Harold Palmer, January 20, 1933. Letter from Eastman to Felix Frankfurter, January 21, 1933.

66. See letter from Eastman to Felix Frankfurter, January 21, 1933, for reference to the part played by Eastman in drafting the amendments.

67. Letter, Eastman to Felix Frankfurter, January 24, 1933.

68. Memorandum of January 31, 1933. This memorandum, signed by Eastman as chairman of the Legislative Committee of the Interstate Commerce Commission, was thirty-two pages long and contained two appendices.

69. *Ibid.,* p. 4.

70. See letter from Eastman to Felix Frankfurter, January 27, 1933, where Eastman said, in part, "I agree with you in regard to the difficulties which the Commission would encounter in recommending trustees for appointment by the Court . . . In my amendments I sought to improve this situation by providing that we should recommend a list of names from which the judge should make his appointments."

71. Letter, Eastman to James C. Bonbright, February 4, 1933.

72. Letter, Eastman to Col. Henry W. Anderson, February 16, 1933.

73. Letter, Eastman to Felix Frankfurter, March 1, 1933. The Bankruptcy Act was later to be amended six times: August 27, 1935; June 26, 1936; August 11, 1939; December 20, 1950; October 24, 1951; and August 28, 1958.

CHAPTER III. THE COMPROMISE OF GROUP INTERESTS

1. *New York Times,* January 27, 1933, p. 1, col. 8.

2. The Commission, of course, was well aware of the entire range of problems in the regulation of transportation and had made important investigations into these problems itself. Its work for some years had been affected by the rise of unregulated motor transportation.

3. Of the delegation by Roosevelt to Roper of the authority to prepare draft legislation, *Railway Age* said that "Mr. Roper has had no particular

experience with or familiarity with the subject" (*Railway Age*, 94: 479–480, April 1, 1933).

4. H.R. 3754 and H.R. 3755.

5. Barriger was regarded as one who knew more about the physical plant of the railroads than any other man of the time. It was said that Barriger, upon being awakened in a sleeper, could tell the location of the train within a few miles by the sound of the rails (Interview with A. A. Berle, 70 Pine Street, New York City, November 15, 1950).

6. On the occasion of the death of Frederick H. Prince in February 1953, the *New York Times* said that after the rejection of the Prince plan, "This experience led him to propose sweeping changes in the Constitution, to make the President more independent of faction, and he criticized severely the presence of professors, whom he considered 'cowards,' in the Government" (*New York Times*, February 3, 1953). Mr. Prince had owned or controlled some 46 railroads in his lifetime and survived the depression with a fortune estimated at $250,000,000. An advocate of "rugged individualism," he was said to have been of the opinion that "every major advance in this country had resulted from free speculation and cautioned against its curtailment" (*Ibid*).

7. Interview with Raymond Moley, Newsweek Building, November 15, 1950.

8. Interview with George McGregor Harrison, Hamilton Hotel, Washington, D. C., October 10, 1950.

9. *First Report,* pp. 106–118. The analysis was prepared by William B. Poland.

10. *New York Times,* March 24, 1933, p. 27, col. 6.

11. *Business Week,* March 29, 1933, p. 18. It was predicted that Roosevelt would deal as vigorously with the railroads as he had with the banks, which he had closed all over the country right after his inauguration and permitted to reopen upon demonstration of solvency.

12. Interview with Robert Virgil Fletcher, Transportation Building, October 5, 1950.

13. Interview with A. A. Berle, Jr., 70 Pine Street, New York City, November 15, 1950.

14. In desperation, the railroads before 1887 made efforts of their own to organize the anarchy. Pools were set up but generally did not last long because of the pressure to pull away. An account of the Southern Railway and Steamship Association may be found in *Quarterly Journal of Economics,* 5: 70–94 (1891). The railroads also resorted to arbitrators, one of whom was Thomas M. Cooley, later the first chairman of the Interstate Commerce Commission.

15. Letter, Eastman to Frankfurter, March 31, 1933.

16. Letter, Eastman to Col. Henry W. Anderson, March 31, 1933.

17. Moulton, *The American Transportation Problem,* pp. lxvii–lxix.

18. Interview with Henry Bruere, Bowery Savings Bank, November 16, 1950.

19. Although this statement is true as to pooling, consolidation, and the like, there are (and were) many facilities the railroads can arrange to use in common or in substitution, one for the other, without getting Commission approval.

20. *Railway Age,* March 25, 1933, pp. 445–446.

21. At the April 1 conference with the President, four plans were brought together, as *Railway Age* later reported (*Railway Age,* 94:509–514, April 8, 1933). These were a "coordinator plan," originated by A. A. Berle and representatives of securities owners; a "modified coordinator plan," representing the work of Eastman and others; a further modification of the coordinator plan suggested by railway executives; and the Prince plan. Eastman's contribution to the discussion was an analysis of the Prince plan, which he is said to have pointed out "would involve an outlay by the government which might reach nearly $2,000,000,000 in the form of loans to make good the proposed guarantees of fixed charges for two years by the operating companies and the proposed payments to employees who would be furloughed as an incident to the curtailment of competitive service" (*Ibid.* p. 510).

22. *Railway Age,* 94:566–7, April 15, 1933.

23. The nature of some of the "opposition" that the carriers regarded with disfavor was indicated in the press report that union representatives felt that "Any program for improving the efficiency and economy of railway operations on a large scale should be accompanied or preceded by a national program for putting men to work, which would insure increases rather than decreases of employment on the railroads" (*New York Times,* April 4, 1933, p. 4, col. 2).

24. March 29, 1933, p. 18.

25. *Railway Age,* 94:509–514, April 8, 1933.

26. *Ibid.*

27. *Railway Age,* 94:566–7, April 15, 1933.

28. National Archives, Document 0–26–17.

29. Letter, Eastman to George Foster Peabody, April 18, 1933.

30. Letter, Eastman to Bernard Baruch, April 18, 1933.

31. Letter, Eastman to Samuel Untermeyer, April 18, 1933.

32. Letter, Eastman to Luther M. Walter, April 18, 1933.

33. Eastman's biographer reports that Eastman once told President Roosevelt, "Mr. President, the Secretary and I just don't speak the same language. I can't learn his and he doesn't want to understand mine" (Claude M. Fuess, *Joseph B. Eastman,* p. 199).

34. *Railway Age,* 94:601, April 22, 1933.

35. The proposals were returned to the secretary for further consideration after the ICC, through Commissioner Porter, made unfavorable representations to the President.

36. *New York Times,* April 29, 1933, p. 1, col. 4.

37. *New York Times,* p. 1, col. 5, May 5, 1933.

38. H. R. 5500 and S. 1580.

CHAPTER IV. THE CONGRESSIONAL LIMITED

1. *Railway Age,* 94:729–733, May 20, 1933.

2. *Ibid.*

3. See, for example, the representation of the interests of large steel, cement, and oil companies in the struggle over basing-point legislation after the Cement Case of 1948, where several organizations allegedly speaking for small business actually argued the case for big business. Earl Latham, "The

Politics of Basing-Point Legislation," *Law and Contemporary Problems,* vol. 50, p. 242ff. (1950).

4. 73 Cong., 1 sess., House of Representatives Committee on Interstate and Foreign Commerce, *Hearings on the Emergency Railroad Transportation Act of 1933,* p. 50.

5. *Ibid.,* p. 51.

6. *Ibid.,* pp. 13–29.

7. *Ibid.,* p. 191.

8. *Ibid.,* p. 209. Presumably, Mr. Fulbright had in mind reductions in competitive services.

9. *Ibid.,* p. 157. See Section 3 of the Emergency Railroad Transportation Act of 1933.

10. *Ibid.,* p. 131.

11. See Sections 1, 9, 10, and 17.

12. See Sections 8 and 9 of the Emergency Transportation Act of 1933.

13. The legislation of 1935 and 1940 was to be much broader and different from what the carriers were asking for in 1933.

14. *Ibid.,* p. 232. See also *Traffic World,* LI, No. 193 (May 13, 1933), pp. 934–935; LI, No. 21 (May 27, 1933), p. 1031.

15. 73 Cong., 1 sess., House of Representatives Committee on Interstate and Foreign Commerce, *Hearings on the Emergency Railroad Transportation Act of 1933,* p. 273.

16. *Ibid.,* p. 257.

17. See Section 3 of the Emergency Railroad Transportation Act of 1933.

18. 73 Cong., 1 sess., Senate Committee on Interstate Commerce, *Hearings on the Emergency Railroad Transportation Act of 1933,* p. 196.

19. 73 Cong., 1 sess., House of Representatives Committee on Interstate and Foreign Commerce, *Hearings on the Emergency Railroad Transportation Act of 1933,* p. 69.

20. *Ibid.,* p. 87–88.

21. *Ibid.,* p. 107.

22. See Sections 7 and 13.

23. House, *Hearings,* p. 291.

24. Emergency Railroad Transportation Act of 1933, Section 7b.

25. Senate Report 87, 73 Cong., 1 sess., printed in 77 Cong. Rec. 4250. This estimate is contradicted by the figures provided above, Chapter II. The evidence there is that there was a reduction of 703,000 workers from 1929 to 1933. To 1932, the reduction was 642,000.

26. *Railway Age,* 94:827, June 10, 1933.

27. *77 Congressional Record,* 4281, May 26, 1933.

28. *77 Congressional Record* 4431, May 27, 1933.

29. *Ibid.,* p. 4269.

30. *Ibid.,* p. 4417.

31. *Ibid.,* p. 4440.

32. *77 Congressional Record,* 4869, June 2, 1933.

33. *77 Congressional Record,* 4871, June 2, 1933.

34. *Ibid.,* p. 4879.

35. *Ibid.,* p. 4937, June 3, 1933.

36. See Appendix B for summary of final changes as compared with original proposal.

37. See Appendix A.

38. This is not to overlook the importance of Section 4b, which was intended to stop leaks of revenue from granting improper allowances and the like. This could have been a major basis for shipper opposition to the bill.

39. Section 15a was amended to omit mention of a fair return on fair value.

40. *Railway Age* 94:865, June 17, 1933.

41. *Ibid.,* p. 806.

42. *Traffic World,* LI, No. 21 (May 27, 1933), p. 1032.

43. Letter, Eastman to Donald Richberg, May 22, 1933.

44. Letter, Eastman to Paul Y. Anderson, May 22, 1933.

CHAPTER V. PATTERNS OF COORDINATION

1. Pp. 10–11.

2. National Association of Railroad and Public Utilities Commissioners, *Report of Committee on Public Ownership and Operation,* 1927 (n.d.), p. 1.

3. National Association of Railroad and Public Utilities Commissioners, *Report of Committee on Public Ownership and Operation,* 1927, separate statement by Joseph B. Eastman (n.d.), p. 1.

4. *Ibid.,* p. 7.

5. *Ibid.,* p. 10.

6. "Railroad Coordination and Mr. Eastman," *Railway Age,* 94:882–3, June 24, 1933.

7. See above, Chapter Two.

8. *First Report,* p. 14.

9. *First Report,* p. 15. Eastman pointed out that the report of the Royal Commission criticized expenditures upon branchline extensions and acquisitions, the construction of new hotels, and the establishment of railway and steamship services duplicating those of the Canadian Pacific; and that to a considerable extent these expenditures were prodigal and wasteful. He asserted, however, that it was necessary to consider the time in which these expenditures were made (the 1920's), and recited several examples of waste and extravagance by the private American railways in the same period.

10. He presumably had reference to the provision in Section 7b relative to the protection of jobs.

11. *First Report,* p. 17.

12. *First Report,* Appendix II, pp. 82ff.

13. Letter, Eastman to H. T. Newcomb, January 26, 1934.

14. Letter, Eastman to Felix Frankfurter, March 20, 1934.

15. Letter, Eastman to C. E. R. Sherrington, secretary, railway research service, May 28, 1934.

16. Letter, Eastman to J. C. Baer, June 26, 1934.

17. Letter, Eastman to George W. Anderson, June 26, 1934.

18. *Third Report,* p. 50.

19. *Third Report,* p. 55.

20. Letter, Eastman to George W. Anderson, February 9, 1935.

21. *New York Times,* April 15, 1935, p. 5, col. 1.

22. *Railway Age,* 98:246, February 9, 1935. Wheeler introduced a resolution on February 4, 1935, to request the Senate Commerce Committee to

investigate railroad financing and management (Sen. Res. 71, February 4, 1935). When Wheeler introduced his bill for public ownership, Representative Maury Maverick of Texas introduced a similar measure in the House, H. R. 7541.

23. "Senator Wheeler's Government Ownership Bill," *Railway Age* 98:603, April 20, 1935.

24. Letter, Eastman to Mr. Arthur K. Smith, February 15, 1935.

25. See account of address of Frederic E. Williamson, president of the New York Central Railroad, before the Utica Chamber of Commerce, *New York Times,* April 24, 1935, p. 31, col. 6.

26. *New York Times,* May 12, 1935, Section III, p. 3, col. 1. The transportation conference, 1933–1935, gathered and bound the solicited statements of numerous business associations, and the Railway Business Association printed and distributed them in a single volume in the 1936 controversy over government ownership and operation of the railroads. See *Government Ownership and Operation of Railroads, 1936.* In a recital of reasons for taking a definite stand against government ownership, the chairman of the transportation conference, 1933–1935, referred to a statement opposing such ownership and operation made by the Security Owners Association in 1933 and then observed, "at the present time spokesmen for the investing groups are not stating their stand on the question of government ownership and operation of the railroads." He then hazarded the view that, unless legislation relieved the railroads of "regulation imposed more harshly upon them than upon their competitors, these groups may consider it a duty to yield the principle of opposing government ownership to an exchange of the securities now held for those guaranteed in some satisfactory manner by the government" (p. v).

27. *New York Times,* June 21, 1935, p. 1, col. 7.

28. "Labor Leaders Favor Government Operation," *Railway Age,* 98:1017, June 29, 1935.

29. "Labor Organizations to Campaign for Government Ownership," *Railway Age,* 99:585, November 2, 1935.

30. *New York Times,* November 28, 1935, p. 51, col. 1.

31. *New York Times,* December 20, 1935, p. 38, col. 1; "Labor Begins Publicity Campaign for Government Ownership," *Railway Age,* 99:830, December 21, 1935; *Business Week,* December 28, 1935, p. 9.

32. "New Bills in Congress," *Railway Age,* 100:226, February 1, 1936.

33. 74 Cong., 2 sess., S. 4174, H.R. 11609. As the AAR saw it, "The intent of the Wheeler-Crosser bill . . . is to prevent reduction in railroad employment regardless of the future course of business, unless express authority shall be secured in each case from the ICC . . . The effect of such requirements would be to discourage improvement or enlargement of railroad service to the public, to restrict increase of railroad employment even if business should improve, and to impair the ability of railroads to compete with other forms of transportation." Quoted in "Rigor Mortis for the Railroads," *Railway Age,* 100:731, May 2, 1936.

34. "Labor's Government Ownership Headquarters Moved to St. Louis," *Railway Age,* 100:591, April 4, 1936.

35. "Wheeler Not to Press Government Ownership Bill Now," *Railway Age,* 100:485, March 14, 1936.

36. *Fourth Report of the Federal Coordinator of Transportation,* 1936

(Washington: U.S. Government Printing Office, 1936), p. 41 (hereafter cited as *Fourth Report*).

37. Letter, Eastman to Virgil D. Cover, August 19, 1935.

38. National Resources Planning Board, *Transportation and National Policy* (Washington: Government Printing Office, 1942), p. 141.

39. Association of American Railroads, Railroad Committee for the Study of Transportation, *Transportation in America* (Washington, 1947), p. 303.

40. *Ibid.*, p. 294.

41. 166 U.S. 290 (1897).

42. For an account of the time and steps taken by the Interstate Commerce Commission in fulfilling its obligations under the Transportation Act of 1920, see William N. Leonard, *Railroad Consolidation Under the Transportation Act of 1920* (New York: Columbia University Press, 1946).

43. Leonard, *Railroad Consolidation Under the Transportation Act of 1920*, p. 224.

44. *First Report*, p. 106.

45. Association of American Railroads, Railroad Committee for the Study of Transportation, *Transportation in America*, p. 297.

46. *First Report*, p. 23.

47. After the promulgation by the Commission of its consolidation plan, providing for 21 systems, the plan was modified in 1932, to provide for four systems in the eastern district instead of the five originally established. The four parties to the partition of the fifth were the New York Central, the Baltimore and Ohio, the Pennsylvania, and the Van Sweringen interests. Leonard, *Railroad Consolidations Under the Transportation Act of 1920*, pp. 199–208.

48. Leonard, *Railroad Consolidations Under the Transportation Act of 1920*, p. 226.

49. *First Report*, p. 26.

50. Leonard, *Railroad Consolidations Under the Transportation Act of 1920*, p. 227. Mr. Barriger did not have occasion to analyze the Poland report at the time it was made, but consented to furnish Dr. William N. Leonard with a brief criticism of the Poland report, of which the quoted excerpt is a part.

51. *First Report*, p. 30.

52. *Third Report*, p. 45.

53. *Fourth Report*, p. 48.

54. *Fourth Report*, p. 63, Appendix A, "Excerpt from an address before the Chamber of Commerce, Kansas City, Mo., November 13, 1935, by Ralph Budd, President of the Chicago, Burlington, and Quincy Railroad Co."

55. *Traffic World*, September 11, 1937, cited and quoted by Leonard, *Railroad Consolidations Under the Transportation Act of 1920*, p. 246.

56. The commissioners were Eastman, Mahaffie, and Splawn. The suggestion for a federal transportation authority to work for two years to promote carrier action looking towards the elimination of waste and to aid consolidation and coordination, of course bears a close family resemblance to the federal coordinator of transportation. See Leonard, *Railroad Consolidations Under the Transportation Act of 1920*, p. 249 et seq. for a discussion of the proposals of the committee of three and of the committee of six; and the steps that led to the enactment of the Transportation Act of 1940.

57. Eastman supported this proposal to repeal the consolidation features of the Transportation Act of 1920.

58. Letter, Eastman to General Hugh S. Johnson, September 25, 1933. On August 18, representatives of the RLEA met with the President and left with him a letter signed by Whitney, requesting that steps be taken by the President to impose a code upon the railroad industry. The Whitney letter was referred to Eastman who drafted a reply, and with it, a memorandum on the "Application of the National Industrial Recovery Act to the Railroads." Roosevelt signed the letter to Whitney that Eastman had written for him. The letter said in part, "you ask that I take steps to the end that a code of fair competition for the railroad industry be established under the N.R.A. I have given this matter careful consideration and am of the opinion that I cannot accede to this request. I enclose a memorandum from the Federal Coordinator of Transportation which discusses the question and with which I find myself largely in agreement." See letter from Eastman to Honorable Franklin D. Roosevelt, August 25, 1933.

59. Eastman devoted some space in his *Third Report* to the possibility of regulating the conflict of interests among rival transportation agencies and concluded that the code method would not work, for lack of adequate public supervision. He thought that it was impossible for the entire transportation net to be regulated in all its complexity except by "a permanent, independent, and nonpolitical body having a continuing and dependable policy and through definite statutory provisions which register the will of Congress." *Third Report,* p. 15; see also *Second Report,* pp. 35–38.

60. Letter, Eastman to W. H. Chandler, eastern traffic assistant, August 11, 1933.

61. Letter, Eastman to General Hugh S. Johnson, November 19, 1933.

62. Letter, Eastman to R. V. Fletcher, March 11, 1934.

63. Letter, Eastman to General Hugh S. Johnson, May 27, 1934.

CHAPTER VI. COORDINATION: CONCEPT AND ORGANIZATION

1. The first of these responsibilities was to "encourage and promote or require action" by the roads which would avoid "wastes and preventable expense." The other, stated in Section 13 of the act, was as follows: "It shall further be the duty of the coordinator . . . forthwith to investigate and consider means, not provided for in this title, of improving transportation conditions throughout the country, including cost finding in rail transportation and the ability, financial or otherwise, of the carriers to improve their properties and furnish service and charge rates which will promote the commerce and industry of the country and including, also, the stability of railroad labor employment and other improvement of railroad labor conditions and relations; and from time to time he shall submit to the Commission such recommendations calling for further legislation to these ends as he may deem necessary or desirable in the public interest. The Commission shall promptly transmit such recommendations, together with its comments thereon, to the President and to the Congress." It was characteristic of the coordinator that in the letter of transmittal of his first report, he began with a recital of the obligations laid upon him.

2. *First Report,* p. 19.

3. *First Report,* p. 25.

4. The habitual anarchy of the railroad industry was one of the first problems that the two committees thought they should deal with. It was agreed that a survey should be made to determine whether the railroad industry as then organized was adequately organized to obtain and distribute the fruits of scientific research at the lowest cost to the industry. *First Report,* p. 56–57.

5. *First Report,* p. 70.

6. *Third Report,* p. 31.

7. *Fourth Report,* p. 40.

8. *Fourth Report,* p. 37.

9. *Railway Age,* 97:193, August 18, 1934.

10. *New York Times,* March 8, 1935, p. 31, col. 8.

11. *Railway Age,* 98:366, March 9, 1935.

12. *New York Times,* March 22, 1935, p. 33, col. 1.

13. *Railway Age,* 98:810, May 25, 1935.

14. See below for discussion of this episode.

15. *Railway Age,* 99:65, July 20, 1935.

16. *New York Times,* December 1, 1935, Sect. III, p. 1, col. 3. The terminal unification order made by Eastman was one of the four orders he made in three years, one of them canceling another out.

17. *New York Times,* May 14, 1936, p. 51, col. 1.

18. For example, in an editorial titled "Mr. Eastman Puts the Cart Before the Horse," it was said, "The Interstate Commerce Commission and Mr. Eastman can think up no reasons for freeing the railroads of any of their shackles, and instead think up new ones — such as 'cost finding' — all the time to apply to them (*Railway Age,* 100:981, June 20, 1936). In recent years, however, there have been many editorials beseeching railroads to stress cost finding and use the results in ratemaking.

19. *Fourth Report,* p. 40.

20. *Ibid.*

21. For a copy of General Order No. 1, see *Traffic World,* 52:140.

22. The railroads were asked to show the figures for the labor force by occupation on a monthly basis, with comparisons between these figures and those for May, 1933.

23. See *Expenses and Property Losses Growing Out of Transfer of Employees of Boston and Maine and Maine Central Railroads Under Section 7d, Title I, Emergency Railroad Transportation Act, 1933* (mimeographed report).

24. See interpretation of Samuel Earnshaw, "The Federal Coordinator of Transportation," *Kentucky Law Journal,* 26:182, March 1938, and 26:298, May 1938 at p. 304n.

25. *Ibid.* The date of Special Order Number 2 was Oct. 9, 1933. R. V. Fletcher, later general counsel for the AAR, disagreed with Eastman's interpretation of his authority in this case. See his roundtable speech, "The Emergency Transportation Act — 1933," *Oregon Law Review,* 13:134–146, February 1934. Even at this early time (the speech was made in December, 1933) Fletcher hoped that it would be unnecessary to continue the federal coordinator for more than a year.

26. Earnshaw, "The Federal Coordinator of Transportation," p. 305–306.

27. "In the Matter of the Proposal of Louisville and Nashville Railroad Co. to Discontinue Interchange of Through Passenger Train Equipment with Chicago and Eastern Illinois Railway Co. (Charles M. Thomson, trustee) at Evansville, Indiana, and to Substitute Such Interchange with the Cleveland, Cincinnati, Chicago & St. Louis Railway Co. (the New York Central Railroad Company, lessee)" (mimeographed). This case was followed with close interest by *Railway Age:* "C.&E.I. Objects to Rerouting of Trains," *Railway Age,* 97:487–488, October 20, 1934; "Eastman Halts Change in Chicago-Florida Trains," *Railway Age,* 97:551–552, November 3, 1934; "Eastman Order in C.&E.I. Rerouting Attacked," *Railway Age,* 97:576, November 10, 1934; "Court Dismisses Complaint of Louisville and Nashville," *Railway Age,* 97:751–752, December 1, 1934; "Order as to Florida Service Again Postponed," *Railway Age,* 97:809, December 15, 1934.

28. For a full discussion of the legal aspects of the coordinator's order in this case, see Earnshaw, "The Federal Coordinator of Transportation." See also *New York Times,* October 26, 1934, p. 31, col. 3; October 27, 1934, p. 25, col. 2; November 3, 1934, p. 21, col. 8; November 14, 1934, p. 29, col. 8; November 24, 1934, p. 21, col. 3; December 27, 1934, p. 35, col. 2, for a running account of the legal moves and countermoves.

29. *New York Times,* September 20, 1933, p. 6, col. 1.

30. *New York Times,* September 22, 1933, p. 27, col. 6. For other news stories on the voluntary salary cut, see *New York Times,* July 15, 1933, p. 1, col. 7; August 26, 1933, p. 21, col. 1; Raymond Clapper, "Shall We Limit a Man's Salary?" *Review of Reviews and World's Work,* December 1933, p. 27. Clapper quoted Eastman as saying, "During the boom period, many railroad salaries were advanced to an extent which was not necessary or justified in my opinion. The effect was to engender public distrust and to lower the prestige of the positions. They were given a money-grabbing aspect which impaired their proper recognition as quasi-public positions of dignity, eminence, and service. What was done was characteristic of the times, and the railroads were neither the only nor the chief offenders. Some public utilities and insurance companies are known to have gone further than the railroads, to say nothing of certain industrial companies. When the depression came, this situation was of course greatly accentuated, and the payment of such salaries at a time when dividends were very generally being suspended, when employees were being laid off in large numbers, when many railroads were borrowing money from the Government to escape insolvency, and when some were going into receiverships, produced a very unfavorable reaction throughout the country. Salaries which had become unnecessary at any season became positively wasteful" (*Ibid.,* p. 28). Nearly all newspapers that commented on the salary slash agreed that it was a good idea. An Associated Press dispatch said, "The salaries to which Mr. Eastman referred ranged downward in 1932 from the $135,000 a year drawn by Hale Holden, Chairman of the Board of Southern Pacific Company . . . When the Southern Pacific applied to the Reconstruction Finance Corporation for a loan, it was not granted until Mr. Holden's salary was reduced to $60,000" (*Literary Digest,* July 29, 1933, p. 7).

For a detailed report on the difference of view between Atterbury and Eastman, see *Railway Age,* 95:151, July 22, 1933; 95:335–336 September 2, 1933; 94:447, September 23, 1933.

31. Quoted in Carl Brent Swisher, "Joseph B. Eastman — Public Servant," *Public Administration Review,* Winter 1945, p. 45.

32. "Voluntary Storage Service Help Subject to N.R.A.," *Railway Age,* 96:699, May 12, 1934.

33. Speech before the American Association of Port Authorities, September 13, 1933 (mimeo.) Eastman told the port authorities that they could do something about the situation because the railroads would go along with them and "if they do not agree, I have power under the Emergency Act to issue an order." This statement was reported in *New York Times,* September 14, 1934, p. 47, col. 1.

34. *New York Times,* November 12, 1935, p. 6, col. 5.

35. He also threatened in 1936 to issue orders to require terminal unifications, and this lead directly to the success of the drive to prevent the renewal of his authorities.

36. "Eastman on P.R.R.-Long Island Merger Proposal," *Railway Age,* 95:506, October 7, 1933; *New York Times,* October 3, 1933, p. 33, col. 8.

37. *New York Times,* October 3, 1933, p. 33, col. 8.

38. W. W. Atterbury, "Railroad Consolidation," *Annuals of the American Academy of Political and Social Science,* September 1934, pp. 166–171.

39. "Looking Ahead in Transportation," *Address of Joseph B. Eastman, federal coordinator of transportation, before National Association of Credit Men in Pittsburgh, Pa.,* June 20, 1935 (mimeo.), pp. 11–12.

40. *First Report,* p. 39.

41. See, for example, Philip Selznick, *TVA and the Grassroots,* University of California Publications in Culture and Society, vol. III (Berkeley: University of California, 1949), part of which is reprinted as "Co-optation: A Mechanism for Organizational Stability" in Robert K. Merton, *et al. Reader in Bureaucracy* (Glencoe, Illinois: The Free Press, 1952), pp. 135–139. Co-optation is defined as "The process of absorbing new elements into the leadership or policy-determining structure of an organization as a means of averting threats to its stability or existence" (*Ibid.,* p. 135).

42. For account of the organization of the three regional committees see *New York Times,* June 23, 1933, p. 6, col. 1 (list of all Class I railways in the eastern group and their mileages); June 30, 1933, p. 25, col. 6 (eastern regional coordinating committee chosen); July 1, 1933, p. 19, col. 2 (western regional coordinating committee chosen); July 7, 1933, p. 23, col. 2 (southern regional coordinating committee chosen). See also *First Report,* pp. 71ff.

43. *New York Times,* June 20, 1933, p. 27, col. 3.

44. *Railway Age,* 95:99, July 8, 1933.

45. *First Report,* p. 73.

46. *Railway Age,* 95:135, July 15, 1933.

47. *Railway Age,* 95:99, July 8, 1933.

48. *New York Times,* July 12, 1933, p. 25, col. 6.

49. *Railway Age,* 95:135, July 15, 1933. The Railroad Credit Corporation was a private corporation controlled by the carriers to carry out an emergency program of rate increases designed to aid needy roads, which had been devised by the ICC. See *Fifteen Per Cent Case,* 178 I.C.C. 539 (1931).

50. *New York Times,* June 30, 1933, p. 25, col. 6.

51. *New York Times,* July 12, 1933, p. 25, col. 6.

52. *New York Times,* August 10, 1933, p. 27, col. 1.

53. *Railway Age,* 95:253–254, August 12, 1933.

54. *First Report,* p. 41.

55. *Railway Age,* 95:253–254, August 12, 1933.

56. *First Report,* p. 41.

57. *Ibid.*

58. *First Report,* p. 71.

59. *First Report,* pp. 71–72.

60. *Fourth Report,* p. 35.

61. The regional staff of the coordinator in the western region originally consisted of V. V. Boatner, regional director; C. E. Hochstedler, regional traffic assistant; J. E. Hutchison, assistant regional director (San Francisco); J. P. Cowley, assistant regional director (Dallas); W. L. Bean, mechanical assistant. *First Report,* p. 72.

62. *First Report,* p. 73.

63. *Ibid.,* pp. 73–74.

64. Even as late as 1937, the president of the Atchison, Topeka, and Santa Fe was unhappy about the study of terminal unification in Chicago conducted by the coordinator's western regional director. After describing certain short-comings of the Chicago study, he said, "It is not necessary that I discuss the Chicago plan in greater detail . . . In my opinion it is sufficiently apparent that individual interests have been largely disregarded. This is not accidental, nor does it arise from deliberate desire to put any line to disadvantage or ex-pense. In great measure it is the natural consequence of the fundamental error, which underlies not only the Chicago plan but also every other termi-nal unification plan, with which I am familiar, resulting from a study con-ducted under the direction of the Coordinator. This fundamental error lies in the fact that all these studies with which I am familiar were made upon the basis of the assumption that private ownership by the several railroads of their several facilities and properties should be disregarded in framing the projects, and in estimating economies to be expected therefrom." Samuel T. Bledsoe, "Consolidation and Coordination Problems," *Proceedings of the Academy of Political and Social Science,* Vol. XVII, No. 2, January 1937, pp. 258–259. Despite the complaint of the president of the Santa Fe, there were calls for copies of the various terminal studies for many years after the expiration of the coordinator's office, and from many interests.

65. *First Report,* p. 76. The staff of the coordinator in the eastern region was: H. J. German, regional director; W. H. Chandler, regional traffic assist-ant; H. H. Temple, assistant to the director; and E. J. Bauer, assistant to the director. The staff of the coordinator in the southern region was: C. E. Weaver, regional director; M. M. Caskie, regional traffic assistant; and W. C. Kirby, assistant.

66. *First Report,* p. 80.

67. *First Report,* p. 46.

68. *First Report,* p. 52.

69. *First Report,* p. 54. Mention has been made above of the cooperation by the Science Advisory Board with the section of purchases.

70. Section 7e of the Emergency Railroad Transportation Act in fact specifically provided that the wages and working conditions of railroad em-ployees should not be changed "except in the manner prescribed in the Rail-road Labor Act, or as set forth in the memorandum of agreement entered into

in Chicago, Ill., on January 31, 1932, between the executives of 21 standard labor organizations and the committee of 9 authorized to represent class I railroads." Section 10a of the Act also provided that "nothing herein shall be construed to repeal, amend, suspend, or modify any of the requirements of the Railway Labor Act or the duties and obligations imposed thereunder or through contracts entered into in accordance with the provision of said act." These provisions were not in the original draft of the bill as it left the Administration and appeared in the Congress. They were inserted "at the instance of the labor organizations." *First Report,* p. 57.

71. *First Report,* p. 66.

CHAPTER VII. THE COORDINATOR'S OFFICE

1. Samuel Earnshaw, "The Federal Coordinator of Transportation," pp. 303–304.

2. Carl Brent Swisher, "Joseph B. Eastman — Public Servant," *Public Administration Review,* Winter 1945, pp. 34–55.

3. *Ibid.,* p. 50–51.

4. This letter said in part, "I am sending herewith copies of proposed executive orders to be signed by the President to permit me to develop my organization . . . The first proposed executive order provides (1) for my relief from all duties as Commissioner except such as I may elect to continue to fulfill, and except that I shall be required to vote in all matters before the Commission (not involving my own acts as Coordinator) where the other members are equally divided; and (2) for blanket approval of such appointments of assistants and agents as I may make as Coordinator, subject to the proviso that the blanket approval shall not extend to the appointment of any assistant or agent at a compensation in excess of $12,000 per annum. It may be that the President will be willing to give blanket approval without this proviso, and of course, that would simplify the matter."

5. Letter, Eastman to Franklin D. Roosevelt, July 6, 1933.

6. In 1933, Eastman, along with other members of the Interstate Commerce Commission, took a salary cut from $9500 to $8500. The cut was not restored to $9500 until 1934.

7. Even so, he wrote to J. W. Smith, vice president of the Boston and Maine on July 12, 1933, that "The selection of my organization was delayed because of the absence of the President on his sailing trip and the difficulty which I had in securing authority to pay salaries as high as $15,000 per year." His first organization comprised:

Director, Section of Freight Service, J. R. Turney, St. Louis, Mo. . .	$15,000
Director, Section of Car Pooling, O. C. Castle, Houston, Texas	7,500
Director, Section of Purchases, R. L. Lockwood, Washington, D.C.	7,500
Eastern Regional Director, H. J. German, Pittsburgh, Pa.	15,000
Western Regional Director, V. V. Boatner, Chicago, Ill.	15,000
Southern Regional Director, C. E. Weaver, Savannah, Georgia	15,000
Eastern Traffic Assistant, W. H. Chandler, New York, N.Y.	8,500
Western Traffic Assistant, C. E. Hochstedler, Chicago, Ill.	8,500
Southern Traffic Assistant, M. M. Caskie, Mobile, Alabama	8,500
Executive and Legal Assistant, J. W. Carmalt, Washington, D.C. . . .	7,500

Executive Assistant, J. L. Rogers, Washington, D.C.   7,500
Research Staff, Otto S. Beyer, Washington, D.C.   8,000
Research Staff, Leslie Craven, Durham, North Carolina   8,000
Research Staff, W. B. Poland, New York, N.Y.   8,000
Research Staff, F. W. Powell, Washington, D.C.   8,500

Most of these men were well established in railroading, the law, or private business and most accepted employment with the coordinator at some personal pecuniary sacrifice. C. S. Morgan, Washington, D.C., worked fulltime for Eastman for a year before he was formally transferred from the ICC staff to take the post of director of the section of research in the office of the federal coordinator at a salary of $7500, later increased to $8500.

8. Letter, Eastman to Hon. Henry C. Hall, June 25, 1936. The letter was in answer to a request for recommendations by Eastman from his staff for positions with the Association of American Railroads and the B&O Railroad.

9. C. A. Miller, "The Lives of Interstate Commerce Commissioners and the Commission's Secretaries," *I.C.C. Practitioners' Journal*, Vol. XII, June 1946 (Section Two), No. 9, p. 91.

10. Letter, Eastman to Edward S. French, May 31, 1933.

11. In a letter to William O. Talbot of Omaha, Nebraska, dated June 18, 1933, Eastman said in part "the Coordinator will have a comparatively small staff and it will be made up largely of specialists in transportation or research with staff and clerical assistance obtained largely from the Commission or from employees of the Commission who will be released on July 1 due to a reduction in the Commission's appropriation."

On November 14, 1934, Eastman notified some Railroad Retirement Board employees that they could work on projects of the coordinator so long as such work and funds for it were available. The board employees were out of employment because of the decision of the District of Columbia Supreme Court declaring the Railroad Retirement Act unconstitutional.

12. Letter, Eastman to John F. Fitzgerald, July 17, 1933. The "Chandler" mentioned was the traffic assistant in the eastern regional office of the coordinator. Although he was then in New York City, he had been Boston's traffic expert for some years.

13. Letter to C. E. Weaver, southern regional director, July 17, 1933. This action was in keeping with Eastman's practice of giving his key men considerable leeway in the selection of the people who would report to them.

14. Letter, Eastman to Millard Tydings, September 11, 1933.

15. Letter, Eastman to James A. Farley, chairman, Democratic National Committee, October 5, 1933. Eastman was answering Farley's "letter of September 27 asking me to have some one in my office compile a list of the names and legal residences of all applicants for positions in my Department who have been endorsed by Democratic Senators, Congressmen, Democratic State Chairmen, or Democratic National Committeemen."

16. Letter, Eastman to V. V. Boatner, October 13, 1933.

17. Letter, Eastman to Senator Fred Steiwer, January 19, 1934.

18. Letter, Eastman to Robert W. Mosher, April 12, 1934.

19. Letter, Eastman to President Franklin D. Roosevelt, May 13, 1935.

20. Letter, Eastman to John A. Emery, July 17, 1935.

21. Letter, Eastman to Hon. Frank C. Walker, August 3, 1933.

22. See above and compare with Eastman's conception of his job and the critical role in it that was to have been played by the regional coordinating Committees.

23. *Railway Age,* 96:789–90, May 26, 1934; 96:824, June 2, 1934; 96:848, June 9, 1934.

24. Source: United States Budget for the years indicated, tabulated respectively in 1936 (A24); 1937 (A6); and 1938 (A6).

25. Letter, Eastman to Lewis W. Douglas, April 11, 1933, protesting a Bureau of the Budget cut in funds for the Bureau of Valuation (ICC); Eastman to Douglas, April 17, 1933, expressing hope that a Budget cut of 15 per cent in funds for ICC, on top of a 16⅔ per cent reduction in 1932, does not apply to the Commissioners; Eastman to Douglas, May 12, 1933, protesting Budget action in impounding ICC funds under the Economy Act of 1933; Eastman to Douglas, September 14, 1933, objecting to Budget suggestion of a salary cutback for personnel; Eastman to Charles Follaway (Bureau of the Budget), January 26, 1934, objecting to the application to Eastman of Circular 273 of December 20, 1929 requiring him to subordinate his views either to the Bureau of the Budget or the President in reporting to Congress; Eastman to Douglas, February 2, 1934, defending the Bureau of Valuation of the ICC against further budget cuts; Eastman to Paul N. Peck (Budget), October 29, 1935, as to why the coordinator's office should be treated differently by Budget from other agencies; Eastman to President Franklin D. Roosevelt, December 23, 1935, protesting a Bureau of the Budget cut for the Bureau of Motor Carriers (ICC); Eastman to A. R. McDonald, Jan. 24, 1936, indicating that Eastman has written to the Senate Committee on Appropriations about the Bureau cut for the Bureau of Motor Carriers.

26. No business would permit its subordinate department heads to have direct access to the board of directors, or to report to the board instead of to the president and the managers of the company. Congress has shown a penchant for unintegrated government, however, despite many speeches about the need for business practice in the federal establishment. With a vested interest in what may be called administrative idiosyncracy, Congress over the years had established many agencies of the kind called "independent"; that is, agencies whose duty it was to report to the Congress before reporting to the President, if to the latter at all. The members of these agencies liked the arrangement also, for Congress was to them what King Log was to the frogs in the pool. An active president was a potential King Stork.

27. Letter, Eastman to Franklin D. Roosevelt, December 19, 1935.

28. Letter, Eastman to Franklin D. Roosevelt, December 23, 1935.

29. Letter, Eastman to W. Forbes Morgan, January 3, 1936.

30. Letter, Eastman to Erwin A. Salle, January 25, 1941.

31. Letter, Eastman to Paul Y. Anderson, May 22, 1933.

32. Letter, Eastman to Cloyd W. Miller, June 7, 1934.

33. Letter, Eastman to Benjamin Marsh, Peoples Lobby, February 18, 1934.

34. Letter, Eastman to Joseph P. Gochnaur, June 18, 1934.

35. Letter, Eastman to Daniel C. Roper, June 19, 1933.

36. Letter, Eastman to Morris A. Copeland, June 9, 1934. See also, Letter, Eastman to Eugene Leggett, National Emergency Council, October 27, 1934.

37. In a letter from Eastman to Frank C. Walker, October 17, 1935, East-

man as requested by Walker sent to him a statement of the objectives of the coordinator. In another letter, dated November 2, 1935, he expressed resentment at having to answer further questions.

38. In one letter, Eastman referred to Senator Costigan of Colorado as his friend. Letter, Eastman to Harry G. Taylor, October 22, 1935. This is the only time in the three-year period covered by this study in which Eastman makes such mention, although he did refer also to his going to Senator Tydings' wedding.

39. Letter, Eastman to C. E. Weaver, July 17, 1933.

40. Letter, Eastman to Henry Morgenthau, FCA, August 3, 1933.

41. Letter, Eastman to William G. McAdoo, July 22, 1935.

42. Letter, Eastman to Stephen Early, August 3, 1935.

43. Letter, Eastman to James A. Farley, October 5, 1933.

44. Letter, Eastman to Joseph Upchurch, June 4, 1936.

45. Letter, Eastman to Clyde M. Reed, January 5, 1937.

46. Letter, Eastman to Robert W. Bruce, August 7, 1933.

47. Letter, Eastman to M. M. Caskie, February 9, 1935. In this letter he said, "I have told the country what I think and shall be glad to repeat such thoughts on any and all occasions, but otherwise it is now up to the country to determine what it wants to do."

48. Letter, Eastman to Joseph H. Beck, June 6, 1932.

49. Letter, Eastman to J. L. Richards, June 22, 1935.

50. Letter, Eastman to Wilber La Roe, September 13, 1933.

51. Letter, Eastman to Richard T. Eddy, February 25, 1936.

52. Letter, Eastman to Ernest Gruening, August 3, 1933.

53. Letter, Eastman to Hon. Franklin D. Roosevelt, July 17, 1933.

54. Letter, Eastman to Hon. Franklin D. Roosevelt, August 1, 1933.

55. Letter, Eastman to Hon. Franklin D. Roosevelt, August 21, 1933, with drafts of the indicated letters attached.

56. See, for example, the letter from Eastman to Hon. Franklin D. Roosevelt, September 18, 1933, and draft of letter from Roosevelt to J. G. Luhrsen, president, American Train Dispatchers Association, on this subject. Eastman also dealt with many controversies that looked as though they might develop into strikes on the railroads. See, for example, the letter from Eastman to Louis McHenry Howe, secretary to the President, November 9, 1933, concerning the strategy to follow in a dispute between the Pullman Company and the Order of Sleeping Car Conductors; and see the Letter from Eastman to Hon. Franklin D. Roosevelt, December 21, 1933 on dispute involving the Mobile and Ohio Railroad Company.

57. Letter, Eastman to Hon. Franklin D. Roosevelt, February 6, 1934.

58. Letter, Eastman to Marvin H. McIntyre, secretary to the President, February 14, 1934, with draft of letter from Roosevelt to the conference and the association.

59. "Wage Agreement Extension Requested by President," *Railway Age,* 96:285–286, February 24, 1934.

60. While still involved with the controversy over the general wage reduction sought by the carriers, Eastman was also trying to settle the Kansas City, Southern wage controversy mentioned above. See *Railway Age,* 96:322, March 3, 1934.

61. *New York Times,* March 21, 1934, p. 1, col. 5; March 22, 1934, p. 2, col. 1; also *Railway Age,* 96:434–437, March 24, 1934.

62. *New York Times,* March 25, 1934, p. 1, col. 7; March 26, 1934, p. 5, col. 4; March 27, 1934, p. 5, col. 1.

63. *New York Times,* March 28, 1934, p. 4, col. 2; March 29, 1934, p. 6, col. 4.

64. *New York Times,* March 31, 1934, p. 1, col. 3.

65. For accounts of the mediation sessions and other developments, see "Railroad Labor Insists on Restoration of Pay," *Railway Age,* 96:478, March 31, 1934; *New York Times,* April 6, 1934, p. 37, col. 1; "Wage Controversy Awaits President," *Railway Age,* 96:500, April 7, 1934.

66. *New York Times,* April 19, 1934, p. 8, col. 5; April 21, 1934, p. 1, col. 1; "Wage Controversy Returns to the White House," *Railway Age,* 96:589–590, April 21, 1934.

67. Letter, Eastman to Marvin H. McIntyre, secretary to the President, April 20, 1934; Eastman did not say who had "given an intimation."

68. *Railway Age,* 96:617–618, April 28, 1934.

69. *New York Times,* April 22, 1934, p. 1, col. 3; April 23, 1934, p. 4, col. 2.

70. Letter, Eastman to Hon. Franklin D. Roosevelt, April 23, 1934. No mention was made in this letter about the "intimation" that Eastman had mentioned previously that the unions were about to concede and that a strong statement by the President would "probably turn the trick with the men."

71. *New York Times,* April 23, 1934, p. 4, col. 2.

72. *New York Times,* April 23, 1934, p. 33, col. 7; April 25, 1934, p. 8, col. 1; April 27, 1934, p. 1, col. 4.

73. Eastman wrote the statement that Roosevelt issued to the press when the wage dispute was over. See letter from Eastman to Stephen Early, assistant secretary to the President, April 26, 1934. The statement said, in part, "I congratulate both sides on the wisdom and restraint which they have exhibited. They have set a good example." See also *New York Times,* April 27, 1934.

74. See letter from Eastman to Hon. Franklin D. Roosevelt, April 27, 1934, and accompanying draft of the executive order (called a "proclamation" by Eastman) to extend the tenure of the coordinator for one year.

75. Letter, Eastman to M. H. McIntyre, assistant secretary to the President, May 18, 1934.

76. Although he resisted action on these measures, Eastman supported fully the amendments to the Railway Labor Act, most of which he had worked out himself and submitted to Congress through Senator Dill (Letter, Eastman and Frances E. Perkins to Hon. Franklin D. Roosevelt, June 14, 1934). The Secretary of Labor worked with Eastman on the amendments to the Railway Labor Act of 1926, and the letter of support for these amendments was signed both by the Secretary of Labor and the coordinator.

For an account of the development of the controversy over the amendment of the Railway Labor Act of 1926 see *New York Times,* April 1, 1934, p. 24, col. 1; "Revised Labor Act proposed by Eastman," *Railway Age,* 96:510–512, April 7, April 14, 1934; "Eastman Again Urges National Adjustment Board," *Railway Age,* 96:611–612, April 28, 1934; "Senate Committee Considers Railway Labor Bill," *Railway Age,* 96:703, May 12, 1934; "Labor Bill Reported by Senate Committee," *Railway Age,* 96:777, May 26, 1934; "Bill to Amend Labor Act Reported," *Railway Age,* 96:872, June 16, 1934; "Railway Labor Act Amendments Passed," *Railway Age,* 924, June 23, 1934; "President Signs Railway Labor Act," *Railway Age,* 96:994, June 30, 1934; "National Mediation Board Appointed," *Railway Age,* 97:150, August 4, 1934. See also following: *Traffic World,* LIII, No. 14, April 7, 1934, p. 644; No. 15, April 14, 1934, p. 697; No. 16, April 21, 1934, p. 771; No. 21, May 26, 1934, p. 1009; No. 22, June 2, 1934, p. 1053; No. 24, June 16, 1934, p. 1137.

In the letter to the President from Miss Perkins and Eastman, the President was urged to push the leaders in both houses to get Eastman's bill passed, there being a strong possibility that Congress, in the expiring days of the Seventy-third Congress, might adjourn without action. The passage of the labor amendments was not only a victory for Eastman in the sense that Congress acted, but also because the labor-sponsored amendments to which he objected were not adopted. It was a victory in still another sense, for the carriers had objected to it on the ground that Eastman had simply rewritten a similar measure sponsored by the Railway Labor Executives Association (*Railway Age,* 96:581–583, April 21, 1934), and the unions eventually opposed Eastman's bill because it granted too much "freedom of association" to workers in the railroad industry (*Railway Age,* 96:815–818, June 2, 1934). The original union bill had been stronger on the question of company unions than they thought Eastman's bill was.

After the bill had gone through the tortuous procedures of Congress, the final version was so close to the original proposed by Eastman that he was able to recommend it without reservation to the President. See letter from Eastman to M. H. McIntyre, June 20, 1934.

77. Letter, Eastman to Hon. Franklin D. Roosevelt, June 21, 1934.

78. Letter, Eastman to Hon. Franklin D. Roosevelt, May 17, 1935. In this letter Eastman said in part, "There is only one way to meet this issue, and that is to recognize that it is in reality an issue of *fact* and not of law, and to demonstrate, if possible by careful and painstaking marshaling of the evidence that the fact is not what the Court found it to be. Such a demonstration would go far to make the country realize, what many people fail to grasp, that many of these constitutional issues depend at bottom upon questions of fact, rather than of law, and upon the conclusions which a bare majority of the justices may reach as to such facts and regardless of the conclusions which the Congress and the President may have reached. It would also help to educate those who press for legislation, where a constitutional issue may be involved, in the need for laying an adequate factual foundation. The ordinary hearings before Congressional committees are not sufficient for this purpose because the witnesses are not under oath, nor are they subjected to any searching cross-examination."

79. Letter, Eastman to Hon. Franklin D. Roosevelt, August 6, 1935.

80. See *First Report,* pp. 69–70.

81. *New York Times,* September 9, 1933, p. 19, col. 7.

82. *New York Times,* October 5, 1933, p. 31, col. 1.

83. The proposal was criticized by rail executives, one of whom is reported to have said, "Suppose someone offered you a suit of clothes at a bargain, and you did not need the clothes, and you had to borrow money to buy them,

what would you do?" *New York Times,* September 26, 1933, p. 1, col. 5. Others felt that the government was entering the field of managerial discretion, or that carriers preferred to deal directly with the steel companies for the purchase of needed supplies. *New York Times,* September 27, 1933, p. 29, col. 2. Roosevelt and his advisers were reported, however, as being in favor of extending the rail plan to the purchase of rolling stock and other operating equipment. *New York Times,* September 28, 1933, p. 1, col. 1. See also "President Wants Prices of Rails Reduced," *Railway Age,* 95:417, September 16, 1933.

84. "Steel Companies Agree to Bid for Rail Orders," *Railway Age,* 95:474–475, September 30, 1933.

85. *Business Week,* October 7, 1933, p. 14.

86. "Competitive Bids Asked for Rail for 47 Roads," *Railway Age,* 95:504–505, October 7, 1933. "In most cases the commitments of the railroads are contingent upon loans from the Public Works Administration at 4 per cent interest, but a number of the roads expect to make the purchases without government loans." *Ibid.,* p. 504.

87. *New York Times,* October 29, 1933, p. 1, col. 6.

88. Letter, Eastman to Hon. Franklin D. Roosevelt, October 21, 1933. In his *First Report,* Eastman modified this judgment somewhat. He said, "Later it developed that the uniform price had been arrived at as follows: Counsel for the United States Steel Corporation advised that under the N.R.A. code no confidential prices could be sent to the Coordinator, notwithstanding that he was not to be the purchaser of the rails. Before the letter was sent, therefore, the American Iron and Steel Institute was informed that under the code, the company would file on October 30 a new price of $37.75 to take the place of the price of $40 which had been filed. The Institute at once advised the other companies and thereupon they followed the lead of the United States Steel Corporation in their letters to the Coordinator. While this may not have been 'consultation and collusion,' it had the result that prices arrived at independently were not submitted, as had been the intent of the Coordinator." *First Report,* p. 70.

89. *New York Times,* October 31, 1933, p. 1, col. 3. "Compromise Reached on Rail Price," *Railway Age,* 95:670–672, November 4, 1933.

90. *Steel,* Vol. 93, No. 19, November 6, 1933, p. 18. The column "Windows in Washington" reported: "Any fair umpire would rule that in his first test of authority — and he has plenty — Mr. Eastman was beaten. True, steel producers lowered their price a total of $3.625 while Mr. Eastman came up only $1.375 but producers did not issue any challenge and Mr. Eastman did. It was $35 or show your books, and steel has done neither. In quarters in Washington which are distinctly hostile to steel, the Eastman charge of collusion by railmakers in offering a $37.75 price has aroused much interest. It was collusion for the other three makers to follow the U.S. Steel Corporation in adopting this price, but not collusion when the industry agreed to $36.375 in the White House itself!"

91. Letter, Eastman to Louis Mc Howe, secretary to the President, September 23, 1933.

CHAPTER VIII. THE MORE PERFECT UNION

1. *Traffic World,* October 23, 1954, p. 5.

2. Address before the Democratic Women's Luncheon Club of Philadelphia, January 29, 1934.

3. December 1, 1934, p. 744.

4. *Modern Railroads,* June, 1950, p. 41.

5. *New York Times,* August 26, 1934, II, p. 7. And at that time a Class I railroad was one which had an annual gross revenue of at least $1,000,000. On January 1, 1956, this minimum revenue figure was raised to $3,000,000.

6. At the end of 1929, 14 major systems controlled 85 per cent of the total rail mileage. Included in this group were the VanSweringen companies, which subsequently fell apart as a system.

7. Among these independent service associations were the American Railway Engineering Association, Bureau of Railway Economics, Railway Accounting Officers' Association, and Railway Treasury Officers' Association.

8. Interview, Transportation Building, Washington, D.C., December 29, 1950. Mr. Fletcher became the general counsel for both the ARE and the ARA in April 1933, and, as has been said, worked on the Emergency Railroad Transportation Act of 1933 in behalf of the carriers. When the AAR was formed in 1934, he became vice president and general counsel for that organization. In 1944 he became vice president in charge of research, and in 1946 and 1947 he served as interim president. Since that time he has served as special counsel.

9. See *Fifteen Per Cent Case, Ex Parte No. 103,* 178 I.C.C. 539; *Duplication of Produce Terminals,* 188 I.C.C. 323; *45th Annual Report,* I.C.C. 1931, p. 119; *46th Annual Report,* I.C.C. 1932, p. 2.

10. Address at Harrisburg, Pennsylvania, October 20, 1933, before the Interstate Bus and Truck Conference.

11. Letter from W. R. Cole, president of the Louisville and Nashville Railroad, July 26, 1930, in U.S. Senate, *Investigation of Railroads,* Part 23. Hearings before a subcommittee of the Committee on Interstate Commerce, 74 Cong., on S. Res. 71 (Washington: Government Printing Office, 1940), p. 10375. This citation will hereafter be referred to as *Investigation of Railroads.*

12. A speech by John H. Hammond, quoted in *Exhibits Presented at Hearing before Lloyd K. Garrison* in *Georgia v. Pennsylvania Railroad,* Supreme Court of the United States, October Term, 1945, No. 11, August 29, 1946, pp. 50–51.

13. Letter from W. W. Colpitts of Coverdale and Colpitts, January 29, 1934, in *Investigation of Railroads,* p. 10413.

14. Letter from H. W. DeForest, May 1, 1934, in *Investigation of Railroads,* p. 10417.

15. The state of Georgia, in *Georgia v. Pennsylvania Railroad,* attempted to show that investors had played the dominant role in the establishment of the AAR but the special examiner appointed by the Supreme Court in the case concluded that they had had "no direct causal connection with either the fact or the form of the AAR's organization." Lloyd K. Garrison, *Exhibits,* p. 292.

16. From minutes of meeting of advisory committee, June 1, 1934, in *Investigation of Railroads,* p. 10422.

17. The committee consisted of W. W. Atterbury, president of the Pennsylvania Railroad and chairman of the committee; F. E. Williamson of the New York Central; J. J. Pelley of the New Haven; Hale Holden of the Southern Pacific; H. A. Scandrett of the Chicago, Milwaukee and St. Paul; and W. R. Cole of the Louisville and Nashville. *Railway Age,* July 28, 1934, p. 126.

18. Lloyd K. Garrison, *Exhibits,* p. 318.

19. From the file of A. J. County, vice president of the Pennsylvania Railroad, *Investigation of Railroads,* pp. 10435–10436.

20. Railway Accounting Officers Association, Presidents Conference Committee on Federal Valuation of the Railroads, Railway Treasury Officers Association, Bureau of Railway Economics. Lloyd K. Garrison, *Exhibits,* p. 327.

21. *Railway Age,* March 12, 1949, p. 529.

22. Association of American Railroads, *Plan of Organization* [1934], Article 21.

23. *Ibid.,* Article 18.

24. *Investigation of Railroads,* p. 9978.

25. Interview with R. V. Fletcher, December 29, 1950. *Plan of Organization* [1947], Article 23.

26. Lloyd K. Garrison, *Exhibits,* p. 324.

27. *Ibid.,* p. 325.

28. Interview with R. V. Fletcher, December 29, 1950.

29. *Ibid.*

30. Memorandum, October 18, 1934, in *Investigation of Railroads,* p. 10452.

31. Lloyd K. Garrison, *Exhibits,* p. 319.

32. *Ibid.,* p. 320.

33. *Ibid.,* pp. 320–321.

34. *Ibid.,* p. 322.

35. *Ibid.,* p. 411–412.

36. *Ibid.,* p. 413.

37. The case involved an alleged violation of a board resolution prohibiting the making of joint rates with trucks and buses where so doing would invade the territory of another railroad.

38. On both occasions, one railroad was opposing the use of buses by another railroad in direct competition with the competing carrier. *Ibid.,* pp. 406–407.

39. *Ibid.,* p. 408.

40. United States Senate, *Scientific and Technical Mobilization,* Part 15, hearings before a subcommitte of the Committee on Military Affairs, 78 Cong., 2 sess., on S. Res. 107 and S. 702 (Washington: Government Printing Office, 1944), p. 1739 (hereinafter cited as *Scientific and Technical Mobilization*). Besides the planning and policy-forming activities of the association, to which Mr. Fletcher referred, the AAR has important operating responsibilities.

41. Lloyd K. Garrison, *Exhibits,* pp. 323–326.

42. Resolution adopted by member roads, September 21, 1934, in *Plan of Organization* [1934], pp. 14–16.

43. *New York Times,* September 22, 1934, p. 21.

44. *New York Times,* September 25, 1934, p. 33.

45. *New York Times,* September 23, 1934, p. 33.

46. Letter from Joseph B. Eastman, September 12, 1934.

47. Address of the federal coordinator, Chicago, October 10, 1934, p. 15.

48. *New York Times,* September 25, 1934, p. 33.

49. Resolution adopted by Board of Directors, October 12, 1934, in *Plan of Organization* [1934], pp. 16–17.

50. Association of American Railroads, *The Railroads, A Statement of Policy* (Washington, D.C.: Association of American Railroads, October 1934), p. 1.

51. These three subjects were the very ones that mainly engaged the attention of the section of research of the federal coordinator.

52. *Railway Age,* April 17, 1948, p. 770.

53. *Investigation of Railroads,* p. 10075.

54. *Ibid.,* p. 10076.

55. Letter from R. V. Fletcher, January 16, 1932, in *Investigation of Railroads,* p. 10455.

56. ARE Resolution, July 15, 1934, in *Investigation of Railroads,* pp. 10458–10460.

57. *Investigation of Railroads,* p. 10077.

58. Letter from T. M. Hayes, June 8, 1935, *Investigation of Railroads,* p. 10464.

59. Letter, June 4, 1934, in *Investigation of Railroads,* p. 10501.

60. Letter from George B. Chandler, secretary of the Ohio Chamber of Commerce, June 4, 1935, in *Investigation of Railroads,* p. 10502.

61. Letter from P. H. Coleman, car service division of the AAR, March 1, 1935, in *Investigation of Railroads,* p. 10517.

62. 93 *Cong. Rec.* 6588–6592 (June 9, 1945).

63. *Time,* June 30, 1947, p. 83.

64. Letter from Mr. Ritchie, AAR, November 12, 1934, in *Investigation of Railroads,* p. 10471.

65. Letter from B. E. Dwinell, Law Department of the Chicago, Rock Island and Pacific Railway Co., January 6, 1933, in *Investigation of Railroads,* p. 10497.

66. Letter from O. W. Dynes, Chicago, Milwaukee, St. Paul & Pacific Railroad, January 5, 1934, in *Investigation of Railroads,* p. 10467.

67. *Railway Age,* November 17, 1934, p. 626.

68. *New York Times,* November 13, 1946, p. 28.

69. Interviews with Louis Stark and Felix Belair, Washington office of the *New York Times,* October 12, 1950.

70. Letter from James F. Wright, November 23, 1933, in *Investigation of Railroads,* p. 10504. The coordinator's staff received literally bales of answers on printed forms of various kinds, in which a hairdresser favored repeal of the fourth section and a chiropodist thought that motor carriers should be regulated.

71. Letter from Joseph B. Eastman, December 3, 1933.

72. *The Five Per Cent Case,* 31 ICC 351, pp. 425–426.

73. For another example, see *Fifteen Per Cent Case,* 45 ICC 303, p. 316.

74. E. Pendleton Herring, "Special Interests and the Interstate Commerce Commission," *American Political Science Review,* XXVII (December, 1933), p. 912.

75. E. Pendleton Herring, *Public Administration and the Public Interest* (New York: McGraw Hill, 1936), p. 192.

76. *Railway Age,* June 24, 1930, p. 1548D115.

77. *Modern Railroads,* June, 1950, pp. 57–62.

78. *Ibid.,* p. 81.

79. *Ibid.,* p. 186.

80. Transcript of Remarks, October 1, 1937, in *Investigation of Railroads,* p. 10219.

81. *New York Times,* October 16, 1946, p. 41.

82. Lloyd K. Garrison, *Exhibits,* p. 318.

83. U.S. Congress, Senate Committee on Interstate Commerce, *Some Educational, Legislative and Self-Regulatory Activities of the United States Railroads,* Senate Report No. 26, Part 2, Pursuant to S. Res. 71, 74 Cong. (Washington: Government Printing Office, 1941), pp. 59–60.

84. *Ibid.,* p. 69.

85. Hearings on *Investigation of Railroads,* p. 10182.

86. *Ibid.,* pp. 10083–10084.

87. *Ibid.,* p. 10194.

88. *New York Times,* April 17, 1943, p. 8.

89. *Railway Age,* October, 1943, p. 657.

90. *Scientific and Technical Mobilization Hearings,* Part 12, pp. 1349–1379.

91. *Railway Age,* August 26, 1944, p. 340. The case referred to is *U.S. v. AAR,* Civil No. 246 in the Nebraska District Court.

92. *Georgia v. Pennsylvania Railroad,* No. 10, original in the U.S. Supreme Court.

93. Hearings and floor debates on this bill were held from 1945 to 1948. The House passed a version of the bill on December 15, 1945; the Senate on June 18, 1947 and the House on May 11, 1948. President Truman vetoed the bill on June 12, 1948, but the measure was repassed by Congress.

94. *New York Times,* October 16, 1946, p. 41.

95. John M. Shott, *The Railroad Monopoly* (Washington, D.C.: Public Affairs Institute, 1950).

96. *Investigation of Railroads,* pp. 9975, 9989.

97. *Some Educational, Legislative, and Self-Regulatory Activities of the United States Railroads,* pp. 68–69.

98. Letter, August 17, 1934, in *Investigation of Railroads,* p. 10218.

99. *Investigation of Railroads,* pp. 9971–9972.

100. *Ibid.,* p. 9978.

101. *Ibid.,* p. 9979.

102. September 2, 1944, p. 362.

CHAPTER IX. REPORTS AND REPERCUSSIONS

1. In 1936, Eastman was saying that although the labor provisions of the Emergency Railroad Transportation Act of 1933 were troublesome, the failure to produce reductions in waste and other preventable expense was due primarily to the reluctance of the carriers to make them. In early 1936, he pointed out that the carriers by then had a leeway of 100,000 men a year who

could be counted in reductions without violation of the Act. *Railway Age*, 100:20, January 4, 1936.

2. Some of these topics had been stressed in the Commission's annual report for 1931 in passages undoubtedly written by Eastman. For a useful table of the reports and studies of the federal coordinator, arranged by subject and listed chronologically, see Earnshaw, "The Federal Coordinator of Transportation," pp. 312-313n.

3. The traffic reports were as follows: *Merchandise Traffic Report*, March 22, 1934; *Conclusions of the Federal Coordinator of Transportation on Merchandise Traffic*, May 29, 1936; *Passenger Traffic Report*, January 21, 1935; *Passenger Traffic Report Appendix I and II*, May 3, 1935; *Views of Passenger Traffic Officers on Short Haul Passenger Traffic*, May 1, 1936; *Conclusions on Passenger Traffic*, June 12, 1936; *Freight Traffic Report*, Vol. I and Vol. II, June 7, 1935; *Freight Traffic Report, Errata*, June 11, 1935; *Freight Traffic Report*, Vol. III, July 25, 1935; *Railway Traffic Organization*, August 2, 1935; *Freight Traffic Report, Appendix I*, November 2, 1935; Appendix III, May 20, 1936; Appendix II, June 1, 1936.

4. See, for example, the opinion of Pierre S. du Pont: "Mr. Eastman's report was to me distinctly disappointing in the fact that while much fault was found with existing conditions and most radical ultimate remedies prescribed, there was not one sentence to show any specific trouble or to suggest a remedy for any of the general ills complained of. In view of the important questions involved, I cannot imagine a less constructive report. My point of view may be distorted in view of the fact that I have read the conclusions, whereas the text may perhaps be more illuminating, though I doubt that such is the case." Letter, Pierre S. du Pont to Mr. Jeremiah Milbank, January 29, 1934, *Hearings on Investigation of Railroads, 1938*, Part 23, p. 1045.

5. "Willard and Eastman Address Traffic Clubs," *Railway Age*, 95:653–654, November 4, 1933.

6. Of this aspect, one of the trade journals said, "Combining in one universal service the handling of all merchandise traffic is the proposition which Transportation Coordinator Eastman offers to the railroads and trucks, so that they can both make money out of handling this kind of freight and the public can have better service." *Business Week*, March 31, 1934, p. 17.

7. A whole year later, Eastman said in a speech to the National Association of Mutual Savings Banks that he had shown that merchandise traffic was generally handled in a wasteful and inefficient way, that the railroads considered his views impracticable, but that he had seen no proof in a year's time that the proposals made by his staff were impracticable. *Speech to National Association of Mutual Savings Banks*, New York, May 8, 1935. He had said the same thing before the Chamber of Commerce of the state of New York on March 7, 1935, in these words, "We proposed new methods of handling this [merchandise freight] traffic . . . but the plan was bold and radical and it required country-wide cooperation on the part of the railroads. They will have none of it, but offer nothing in its place." *Address of Joseph B. Eastman, federal coordinator of transportation, before the Chamber of Commerce of the State of New York*, New York, March 7, 1935 (mimeo.), p. 6.

8. *Railway Age*, 98:469, March 23, 1935.

9. *Ibid.*

10. "Railroad Problems Not Complex," *Railway Age,* 98:859, June 1, 1953.

11. "Co-Ordinator Eastman Meets with Railroad Executives," *Railway Age,* 99:138, July 27, 1935.

12. *Conclusions,* p. 25.

13. *New York Times,* August 13, 1933, Sect. II, p. 8, col. 4.

14. "Experiment in Store-Door Service Welcomed by Coordinator," *Railway Age,* 95:495–497, October 7, 1933.

15. *Ibid.*

16. *New York Times,* September 29, 1933, p. 6.

17. *Address of Joseph B. Eastman, federal coordinator of transportation, before Associated Traffic Clubs of America at Baltimore, Md.,* October 24, 1933, p. 12.

18. "Radical Revision of Freight Handling Recommended," *Railway Age,* 98:885, June 8, 1953.

19. *New York Times,* June 8, 1935, p. 9, col. 1.

20. *Exhibits Presented at Hearing Before Lloyd K. Garrison, Special Master, the State of Georgia v. the Pennsylvania Railroad Company, et al., Volume D. prepared for Mr. Fletcher,* No. 100.

21. *Ibid.*

22. Railroads have been going strong for piggy-back operations in recent years. Hauling highway trailers on flat cars is a container-type operation using the smaller size load. Both these ideas were set out in the Freight Traffic Report. The plans differ from road to road. Some carry only their own trailers, others serve common and even other motor carriers. For a description of these operations, see Interstate Commerce Commission, 69th and 70th *Annual Reports,* pp. 3–5 and 9–10.

23. "The Coordinator's Freight Traffic Report," *Railway Age,* 99:267, August 31, 1935.

24. *Ibid.*

25. "Passenger Traffic Survey," *Railway Age,* 95:562, October 21, 1933.

26. "Eastman Issues Passenger Ballot," *Railway Age,* 95:798–799, December 2, 1933.

27. *Passenger Traffic Report,* prepared by section of transportation service, transmittal letter to the regional coordinating committees, January 17, 1935.

28. Turney, a lawyer, was unique among railroad officials in that he had held the post of vice president in charge of law *and* traffic with the St. Louis Southwestern Railway Company. He then practiced law in St. Louis from 1925 to 1933. Turney also served for a time, and at a financial sacrifice, with Eastman when the latter headed the office of defense transportation.

29. "Eastman Hails Passenger Revival," *Railway Age,* 100:985, June 20, 1936.

30. *Conclusions of the Federal Coordinator of Transportation on Passenger Traffic,* Washington, D.C., June 1936, p. iii.

31. *Ibid.,* p. iv.

32. *Passenger Traffic Report,* p. 26.

33. *Address of Joseph B. Eastman, federal coordinator of transportation, before the Railway Business Association,* November 9, 1933 (mimeo).

34. *New York Times,* April 7, 1934, p. 23, col. 5.

35. "Activities of the Purchases and Stores Division," *Railway Age*, 96:590, April 21, 1934.

36. "Talk Standards for Railway Buying at New York," *Railway Age*, 96:655–656, May 5, 1934, report on one of Mr. Lockwood's speeches before the New York Railroad Club.

37. "Organize to Study Purchases," *Railway Age*, 96:699–670, May 5, 1934.

38. "Eastman Investigates Sale and Handling of Scrap," *Railway Age*, 97:555, November 3, 1934.

39. Federal Coordinator of Transportation, Section of Purchases, *Report on Handling and Disposition of Scrap* (mimeo.), p. 54.

40. "Coordinator Proposes Scientific Research Plan," *Railway Age*, 95:570, October 21, 1933. The scientific committee included F. B. Jewett, chairman, president of the Bell Telephone Laboratories, C. F. Kettering, president of the General Motors Research Corporation, the directors of research for the United States Steel Corporation, and the Aluminum Company of America, Harold G. Moulton, president of Brookings Institution, and research people from the National Research Council and the coordinator's office.

41. " 'Scientific Research' — What and Why?" *Railway Age*, 95:750, Nov. 25, 1933.

42. "Plans Made for Research Study," *Railway Age*, 95:983, December 23, 1933.

43. "Centralized Scientific Research," *Railway Age*, 97:477–480, October 20, 1933.

44. *Address of Joseph B. Eastman, federal coordinator of transportation, before the Society of Automotive Engineers, White Sulphur Springs, W. Va.,* June 20, 1935, "Mechanical Progress in Transportation" (mimeo.), p. 3.

45. *Ibid.*, p. 4.

46. Report of the Mechanical Advisory Committee to the Federal Coordinator of Transportation, December 27, 1935.

47. Federal Coordinator of Transportation, *Report on Freight Car Pooling with Plan for Proposed Box Car Pool*, prepared by section of car pooling, October 23, 1934. See *New York Times*, October 25, 1934, p. 35, col. 8, and "Box Car Pool proposed in Report of Coordinator Eastman," *Railway Age*, 97:513–516, Oct. 27, 1934.

48. *Analysis of That Portion of the Report of the Car Service Division of the Association of American Railroads Released November 7, 1935 Dealing with the "Average Per Diem Plan" For the Settlement of Hire of Equipment (Box Cars) Made Effective May 1, 1935,* prepared by the section of car pooling, federal coordinator of transportation, December 17, 1935 (mimeo.).

49. *Grain Elevator Reports* (mimeo.).

50. Federal Coordinator of Transportation, *Report on The Leasing of Railroad Owned Grain Elevator Properties,* prepared by J. A. Little, Washington, D.C., May, 1936.

51. *First Report,* p. 63.

52. Most of the research reports were not finished until close to the expiration of the office of the federal coordinator, or after it. Among the important research products of the section of labor relations was *Annual Earnings of Railroad Employees, 1924–1933,* Washington, D.C., May, 1935. The informa-

tion for this report was derived by "direct examination of more than 300,000 individual employment histories," and was made possible by a grant to the coordinator of CWA funds made by the Federal Emergency Relief Administration. Other reports were *Employment Attrition in the Railroad Industry*, Washington, D.C., 1936; *Cost of Railroad Employee Accidents, 1932*, May 21, 1935 (mimeo.); *Unemployment Compensation for Transportation Employees*, Washington, D.C., March, 1936.

53. *Summary of the Work of the Federal Coordinator of Transportation under the Emergency Railroad Transportation Act, 1933*, June 1933–June 1935 (processed), p. 37.

54. *Hours, Wages, and Working Conditions in Scheduled Air Transportation*, Washington, D.C., March, 1936 (also printed as *Senate Document No. 208*, 74 Cong., 2 sess.); *Hours, Wages and Working Conditions in Domestic Water Transportation*, Washington, D.C., 1936 (two volumes); *Hours, Wages and Working Conditions in the Intercity Motor Transport Industries*, Washington, D.C., October-December 1936 (three parts); *The Extent of Low Wages and Long Hours in the Railroad Industry*, Washington, D.C., November, 1936; and *Comparative Labor Standards in Transportation*, Washington, D.C., March, 1937.

55. Discussed in Chapter X.

56. See especially, *What is Public Aid to Transportation?* Washington, D.C., 1940, pp. 213. This publication was not confined to the highway issue.

CHAPTER X. COORDINATING THE COMPETITION

1. *Second Report*, p. 4.

2. *Railway Age* kept its readers closely informed of the early steps taken by the coordinator to get the necessary background of information on which to base recommendations for legislation. See *Railway Age*, 95:413, September 16, 1933, "Eastman Investigates Truck Transportation"; "Eastman Studies Control of Water, Motor Transport," *Railway Age*, 95:437, September 23, 1933; "Eastman Inquires as to Subsidies in Air Transportation," *Railway Age*, 95:509, October 7, 1933; "Study of Labor Conditions in Motor Truck Industry," *Railway Age*, 95:535, October 14, 1933; "Eastman Seeks Shippers' Views on Water Transport," *Railway Age*, 95:569, October 21, 1933; "Joint Bus Traffic Survey Being Made by Coordinator and N.R.A.," *Railway Age*, 96:934–936, June 23, 1934.

3. *Address of Joseph B. Eastman before the Interstate Bus and Truck Conference, Harrisburg, Pa.*, October 20, 1933 (mimeo.).

4. His decision on this point was welcomed by some sectors of the business press. Of the coordinator's *Second Report*, which contained the recommendations for the federal regulation of the motor bus and truck and water transport industries, *Business Week* said that it had finally clinched an issue over which controversy had raged for some time. See issue of March 17, 1934, p. 24.

5. *Second Report*, pp. 37–41.

6. See, for example, speeches before the American Trucking Association, Chicago, Illinois, October 22, 1934; National Industrial Traffic League, New York, November 14, 1934; Mississippi Valley Association, St. Louis, Mo., November 26, 1934; Reading Traffic Club and Reading Chamber of Com-

merce, Reading, Pa., March 3, 1935; National Rivers and Harbors Congress, Washington, D.C., May 2, 1935; National Association of Credit Men, Pittsburgh, Pa., June 20, 1935; National Transportation Conference, Detroit, Michigan, March 19, 1936.

7. *Traffic World*, Vol. 52, No. 4, July 22, 1933, p. 138.

8. I. Leo Sharfman, *The American Railroad Problems* (New York: Century, 1921), p. 375n.

9. *Traffic World*, Vol. 52, No. 4, July 22, 1933, p. 138.

10. The organizations represented at the first session of the conference included: American Bankers Association; American Highway Freight Association; American Iron and Steel Institute; American Newspaper Publishers Association; American Short Line Railroad Association; American Railway Association; Association of Railway Executives; Association of Regulated Lake Lines; Mississippi Valley Association; Mississippi Valley Barge Line Company; National Association of Manufacturers; Railway Business Association; Security Owners Association; National Association of Mutual Savings Banks. For discussion, see "National Groups Joining in Transport Discussion." *Railway Age*, 95:197, July 29, 1933.

11. *Traffic World*, Vol. 52, No. 4, July 22, 1933, p. 138.

12. *Traffic World*, Vol. 52, No. 8, August 19, 1933, p. 313. The officers chosen for the conference, besides Wheeler as president and Sorrell as secretary, were vice chairmen representing the Bowery Savings Bank and the National Association of Manufacturers.

13. *Traffic World*, Vol. 52, No. 13, September 23, 1933, p. 506.

14. "Transportation Conference Now on Permanent Basis," *Railway Age*, 95:291, August 19, 1933.

15. "Transport Conference Meets," *Railway Age*, 95:572, October 21, 1933.

16. "Eastman Seeking Views of Business on Needed Transport Legislation," *Railway Age*, 95:673, November 4, 1933.

17. "Transport Conference Agrees on Motor Carrier Regulatory Principles," *Railway Age*, 96:234, February 10, 1934; "Transportation Conference Opposes Public Ownership," *Railway Age*, 96:451, March 24, 1934.

18. *Some Thoughts on the Railroad Future*, address of Joseph B. Eastman, before the National Association of Mutual Savings Banks, New York, N.Y., May 16, 1934 (mimeo.), p. 17.

19. *Second Report*, p. 58.

20. "Labor Executives Prepare Legislative Program," *Railway Age*, 95:640, October 28, 1933.

21. "Labor Leaders Discuss Legislation with Eastman," *Railway Age*, 95:800, December 2, 1933.

22. "Railroad Labor to Press Its Legislative Program," *Railway Age*, 96:208, February 3, 1934.

23. *Traffic World*, Vol. 53, No. 6, February 10, 1934, p. 267. The full-crew bill was S.2624; the train-length bill, S.2625; the six-hour bill, H.R.7648; the sleeping car and express companies amendment, H.R.7649; and the Railway Labor Act amendment, H.R.7650.

24. "Railroad Labor Questions Rapidly Coming to the Fore," *Railway Age*, 96:323, March 3, 1934.

25. "Unions' Bills Makes Progress," *Railway Age*, 96:741–742, May 19, 1934.

26. *Railroad Retirement Board v. Alton R.R.*, 295 U.S. 330 (1935). In this case, Mr. Justice Roberts stated the dubious proposition that the old age security of railroad workers could never have a close enough relation to interstate commerce to justify federal regulation. This holding was in the period when the Supreme Court was "saving" the country from the New Deal.

27. "Railroad Labor Leaders Plan Legislative Campaign," *Railway Age,* 97:810, December 15, 1934.

28. *New York Times,* January 13, 1935, p. 27, col. 1.

29. "Railroad Labor to Ask Limitation on Dismissals," *Railway Age,* 98:313, February 23, 1935.

30. *Address of Joseph B. Eastman before Railway Labor Representatives at the Morrison Hotel, Chicago, Illinois,* January 12, 1935 (mimeo.).

31. *Ibid.,* p. 10.

32. *Ibid.,* pp.10–11.

33. Although Eastman had said he was in favor of pensions, he opposed the measures proposed by the RLEA with the statement cautioning against "hastily drawn legislation which would lead to further disillusion and disappointment, especially among railroad employees." He did not oppose special retirement and annuity legislation but thought it desirable. He did say, however, that "the total volume of evidence, including the results of the comprehensive study by my staff, soon to be released, seems to me still insufficient to prove that a special retirement system for railroad employees is socially and economically sound." "Eastman Asks More Study of Pension Legislation," *Railway Age,* 99:109, July 27, 1935.

34. *New York Times,* January 13, 1935, p. 27, col. 1.

35. After setting up the railroad retirement board, the act provided for the appointment of an investigation commission of nine (three senators, three congressmen, and three presidential appointees) to make an investigation of pension systems and report their findings to Congress before January 1, 1936. For comments, see *New York Times,* August 27, 1935, p. 11, col. 8; August 30, 1935, p. 2, col. 8. Two months after the enactment of the legislation, Roosevelt had appointed neither the board nor the commission that was to make the investigation. Eastman's studies of pension systems were still going forward, and he was looking to the FERA for further funds to advance them. "Seek Funds to Administer Pension Act," *Railway Age,* 99:514, October 19, 1935. The pension acts of 1935 were contested in the courts but before a decision could be reached in the Supreme Court the carriers and the unions, at the instigation of the President, undertook in 1936 to iron out their disagreements about pension legislation, and new legislation was adopted in 1936 which superseded the acts of 1935.

36. Besides the central efforts of the carriers, the unions, and the coordinator to get enactment of their legislative programs, there were subsidiary, collateral, and separatistic movements to secure marginal advantages. One of these was the struggle over the long-and-short haul clause, which swirled in and out of the congressional committees during the tenure of the federal coordinator, but which was not resolved before the expiration of that office. On June 5, 1935, the House Committee on Interstate Commerce opened hearings on a bill introduced by Rep. Samuel Pettengill of Indiana to repeal Section 4 of the Interstate Commerce Act. This provision forbade higher charges for short hauls than long hauls when the shorter was embraced within

the larger, with certain exceptions if approved by the Interstate Commerce Commission. The railroad carriers felt that this provision prevented them from competing with the water carriers for long-haul traffic, since the railroads were forbidden to cut the long-haul rate below the short-haul rate. The move to repeal the long-and-short-haul provision was an attempt at self-help by the railroads to improve their competitive position in relation to the water carriers. The unions and some of the shippers joined the carriers in the move to repeal Section 4. For an account of the controversy, see *Traffic World,* Vol. 55, No. 23, June 8, 1935, p. 1101; No. 24, June 15, 1935, p. 1145; No. 25, June 22, 1935, p. 1193; *Traffic World,* Vol. 56, No. 1, July 6, 1935, p. 18; No. 3, July 20, 1935, p. 106; No. 4, July 27, 1935, p. 151; Vol. 57, No. 9, February 29, 1936, p. 383.

Eastman resisted the Pettengill Bill because he had his own program for regulating the competition between the railroad and water carriers. Of this resistance by Eastman, Pettengill tartly observed, "As is well known, Commissioner Eastman is an outright and honest advocate of government ownership of railroads, although he says that the time is not ripe for it. If, however, the railroads are to be kept handicapped while competing transportation agencies are free to slice them to pieces, the time for which Mr. Eastman hopes may come much earlier than anticipated." See *Traffic World,* Vol. 57, No. 9, February 29, 1936, p. 383. There were indications of a movement to push through comprehensive regulation of water carriers along the lines proposed by Eastman, as a means of blocking the Pettengill bill. It was thought that if the water carriers were regulated by the ICC, it would be unnecessary to eliminate the long-and-short-haul clause. But the Pettengill bill was eventually passed by the House, although this is as far as it got during the tenure of the coordinator. See *Traffic World,* Vol. 57, No. 10, March 7, 1935, pp. 439, 441.

37. Regulation by the federal government was made necessary by Supreme Court decisions depriving the states of the authority to regulate motor carriers in interstate commerce. *Buck v. Kuykendall,* 267 U.S. 307 (1925); *Bush v. Maloy,* 267 U.S. 317 (1925); *Michigan Commission v. Duke,* 266 U.S. 570 (1925); *Frost Trucking Company v. Railroad Commission,* 271 U.S. 583 (1926). As Sharfman points out, the effect of these decisions was similar to that of the *Wabash Case* in 1886 when the Supreme Court made federal regulation of the railroads inevitable. Sharfman, *Interstate Commerce Commission,* Vol. IV, pp. 99–101. The first proposals for federal regulation of motor carriers seem to have been made by the state regulatory commissions through the National Association of Railroad and Utilities Commissioners. In his review of the background of motor vehicle regulation, Eastman mentioned the two national investigations of the motor bus and truck industry by the ICC as laying a foundation of fact for legislative action. *Second Report,* pp. 24–25. These investigations led to the publication of two reports: *Motor Bus and Motor Truck Operation,* 140 ICC 685, decided April 10, 1928, and *Coordination of Motor Transportation,* 182 ICC 263, decided April 6, 1932. Recommendations for legislation of varying comprehensiveness emerged from these investigations.

38. H.R. 6836, 73 Cong., 2 sess., known as the Rayburn bill, then before Congress with the endorsement of the ICC, had been drawn up by the National Association of Railroad and Utilities Cmmissioners.

39. *Second Report,* p. 27.

40. *Ibid.*, pp. 14–15.

41. *Second Report*, p. 18.

42. *Coordination of Motor Transportation*, 182 ICC 263, at 328.

43. *Second Report*, p. 18.

44. *Second Report*, p. 29.

45. *Ibid.*, p. 37.

46. *Ibid.*, p. 38.

47. The suggestion that the Commission was "railroad-minded" and could not therefore be expected to do justice to other forms of transportation in competition with the railroads is one that recurs frequently. See, for example, Samuel P. Huntington, "The Marasmus of the ICC: The Commission, The Railroads, and the Public Interest," 61 *Yale Law Journal*, No. 4, April 1952, p. 467; Charles S. Morgan, "A Critique of 'The Marasmus of the ICC: The Commission, The Railroads, and the Public Interest,'" 62 *Yale Law Journal*, 171 (1953); Samuel Huntington, Charles S. Morgan, C. Dickerman Williams, "The ICC Re-Examined: A Colloquy," 63 *Yale Law Journal*, No. 1, November, 1953, p. 44. In the last of these three articles, Mr. Morgan, who worked with Eastman when he was federal coordinator, said of the Motor Carrier Act, 1935, "Part of the legislative work of the Federal Coordinator of Transportation undoubtedly could have been, and some of it would have been, carried out by the Commission if this special agency had not been set up. The Commission had made two nationwide investigations of the need for federal motor carrier regulation and had made recommendations to and appeared before Congress on this subject; the Coordinator's work in this respect was a follow-up." Charles S. Morgan, "The ICC Re-Examined: A Colloquy," 63 *Yale Law Journal*, 44, November, 1935, p. 61.

48. *Second Report*, p. 45. The Rayburn bill was H.R. 6836, 73 Cong., 2 sess. The Rayburn bill was drawn up by the National Association of Railroad and Utilities Commissioners, as indicated above. The NARUC measure in turn was worked out by that agency in cooperation with the Association of Railway Executives and a committee appointed by the American Highway Freight Association, a trucking organization. The AHFA became part of the new American Trucking Associations: which then opposed the bill on the ground that the trucking code provided as much regulation of motor carriers as was necessary at the time. The attitude of the American Trucking Associations Inc. caused a split in the haulers' ranks, and the group favoring the Rayburn bill withdrew, asserting that the ATA had become dominated by the motor truck manufacturers. See *Business Week*, January 27, 1934, pp. 18–19. The dissenters, organized as the National Highway Freight Association, joined the National Association of Railroad and Public Utilities Commissioners in asserting the need for regulation by statute on the ground that the codes are "here today, gone tomorrow." *Business Week*, February 10, 1934, p. 28. The National Highway Freight Association was formed after a preliminary meeting of truckers from the central western states, and J. L. Keeshin, of Keeshin Motor Express, Chicago, was elected president. *Traffic World*, Vol. 53, No. 3, January 20, 1934, p. 133.

49. Section 325 provided for an investigation of the need for regulation of the sizes and weight of vehicles and of the hours of service of all employees of all motor carriers, including private carriers. *Second Report*, p. 49, not changed in *Third Report*.

50. The initial opposition of ATA to motor carrier regulation by statute collapsed after the Supreme Court killed the codes, and it became a supporter of the Motor Carrier Act, 1935, and the ICC. The paper put out by the American Trucking Associations, Inc., self-described as the "only national newspaper in the trucking field," took a strong line against the failure of Congress to provide adequate funds for the enforcement of the Motor Carrier Act, 1935, after its passage on August 9, 1935. *Transport Topics*, Vol. 6, No. 5, September 2, 1935, p. 1.

51. During the period of the federal coordinator, the *International Teamster*, the official magazine of the International Brotherhood of Teamsters, Chauffeurs, Stablemen, and Helpers (AFL), seemed to be particularly worried by the competition they were getting from the United Brewers of America and the United Mine Workers of America and gave little space to the government's program. Although some labor action on the motor carrier bill was mentioned in an editorial, no further mention was made of the matter. *International Teamster*, Vol. 31, No. 9, August 1934, p. 12. The official organ of the Amalgamated Association of Street, Electric Railway and Motor Coach Operators of America (AFL) also exhibited little interest in the government's program but it did welcome regulation of the motor carriers because it would limit fly-by-nights and help to stabilize labor conditions. *Motorman, Conductor, and Motor Coach Operator*, Vol. 43, No. 21, November 1935, p. 3.

52. The railroad carriers watched the split among the truckers with attention. See "Asks Truck Code Trial in Lieu of Regulation," *Railway Age*, 95:889, December 23, 1933; "Highway Freight Association Opens Washington Office," *Railway Age*, 96:589, April 21, 1934; "NRA Code No Substitute for Regulation," *Railway Age*, 96:1, January 6, 1934.

53. The bus operators watched the railroads with great suspicion. One of the leading trade journals early spoke against "legislation initially sponsored by competitive interests and drawn with malevolent ingenuity to accomplish annihilation rather than stabilization through regulation," *Bus Transportation*, Vol. 12, No. 1, January 1933, p. 1. Before the introduction of Eastman's proposals, the operators were urged to give the codes "a chance." *Bus Transportation*, Vol. 13, No. 11, November 15, 1934, p. 409. But when the proposals were laid before Congress, the bus operators did what they could to obtain passage. *Bus Transportation*, Vol. 14, No. 3, March 15, 1935, p. 112.

54. *Address of Joseph B. Eastman before the National Association of Motor Bus Operators at Cleveland, Ohio*, September 21, 1934 (mimeo., 17 pp.). He distinguished between the motor bus and the motor truck operators and said that the opinions of the latter had "been shaped too much by those who build trucks rather than by those who operate them." *Ibid.*, p. 11.

55. *Address of Joseph B. Eastman before the Motor Truck Club of Massachusetts at Boston, Massachusetts*, June 11, 1935 (mimeo.), p. 10.

56. *Second Report*, p. 26.

57. *Traffic World*, Vol. 53, No. 1, January 6, 1934, p. 9.

58. *Business Week*, July 27, 1935, p. 15.

59. "New Bill Would Regulate Bus and Truck Service," *Railway Age*, 96:80, January 20, 1934.

60. "Hearings Begun on Motor Bus and Truck Legislation," *Railway Age*, 96:83, January 20, 1934.

61. "I.C.C. Approves Rayburn Bus and Truck Bill," *Railway Age*, 96:222, February 10, 1934. The hearings were closed on February 2, 1934.

62. "Hearings Begun on Motor Carrier Regulation Bill," *Railway Age*, 98:313, February 23, 1935; "Final Hearings on Motor Carrier Regulatory Bill," *Railway Age*, 98:368, March 9, 1935.

63. The measure was the Eastman bill, H.R. 5262.

64. Some of the agricultural shippers organizations favored the bill but suggested that itinerant truck peddlers be included in the plan for regulation.

65. "Final Hearings on Motor Carrier Regulatory Bill," *Railway Age*, 98:372, March 9, 1935.

66. "Motor Carrier Bill Reported by Senate Committee," *Railway Age*, 98:577, April 13, 1935. Motor common carriers of passengers are required to establish reasonable through rates with other such carriers, but there is no such requirement in the case of property carriers.

67. "Senate Passes Motor Carrier Bill," *Railway Age*, 98:611, April 20, 1935.

68. "Bus-Truck Bill before House Committee," *Railway Age*, 99:27, July 6, 1935.

69. "Bus-Truck Bill Referred to New Sub-Committee," *Railway Age*, 99:93, July 20, 1935.

70. The doctrine of *The Shreveport Case*, 234 U.S. 342 (1914), was that the ICC had jurisdiction to correct intrastate rates that burdened interstate commerce unreasonably.

71. "House Committee Reports Eastman Bus-Truck Bill," *Railway Age*, 99:135, July 27, 1935.

72. The bill passed the House on August 1, the Senate accepted the House amendments on August 5, and the Senate passed the amended bill on August 16. The fight against the bill in the House was led by Wadsworth of New York. "Motor Carrier Bill Passed," *Railway Age*, 99:187, August 10, 1935.

73. *Business Week*, March 9, 1935, p. 25.

74. *Business Week*, August 10, 1935, p. 11.

75. "Fifteen-Year Campaign Wins Motor Carrier Regulation," *Railway Age*, 99:214, August 17, 1935.

76. *New York Times*, August 11, 1935, Section III, p. 1, col. 4. Williamson proved to be quite right. The phenomenal growth of motor transport since 1935 has been attributed in considerable part to regulation. Its growth is shown at p. 44, Interstate Commerce Commission, 70th *Annual Report*.

77. *Address of Joseph B. Eastman before the American Association of Motor Vehicle Administrators, Chicago, Illinois*, October 10, 1935 (mimeo.), p. 1.

78. Introductory Statement of Joseph B. Eastman at round table discussion of "The Regulation of Motor Vehicle Carriers Using the Public Highways." National Association of Railway and Utilities Commissions, Nashville, Tennessee, Oct. 16, 1935 (mimeo.), p. 1.

79. *Address of Joseph B. Eastman before the American Trucking Associations, Inc., Chicago, Illinois*, October 14, 1935 (mimeo.), p. 1. The President signed the new act on August 9 with a pen provided by the American Trucking Association, Inc.

80. "Long Ties Up Funds for Motor Law Enforcement," *Railway Age*, 99:285, August 31, 1935.

81. "Motor Carrier Act Effective October 1," *Railway Age*, 99:407, September 28, 1935.

82. The *New York Times* carried an inaccurate account of the reorganization when it referred to Eastman as the head of the new bureau rather than division. *New York Times*, Sect. III, p. 1, col. 3.

83. Argument of Joseph B. Eastman, member of Interstate Commerce Commission before Civil Service Commission, November 2, 1935 (mimeo.).

84. *New York Times*, October 25, 1935, p. 43, col. 6.

85. *Business Week*, November 16, 1935, p. 27.

86. "Railway and Truck, Co-Partners," *Railway Age*, 99:677, November 23, 1935.

87. *New York Times*, December 31, 1935, p. 23, col. 6.

88. "Railroads, Truckers and Shippers Seek to Harmonize," *Railway Age*, 100:90, January 4, 1936. Eastman "met with the conferees at their invitation and expressed approval of the effort being made by the three groups represented to dispose of controversial matters to the fullest extent possible through conference rather than by litigation," *Ibid.*

89. *Ibid.*

90. *Business Week*, January 4, 1936, p. 20.

91. *Second Report*. The section on water carriers took about 8 full pages, that is, pp. 5–13. The section on motor carriers took about 22 pages, that is, pp. 13–35. The water carrier appendix was 72 pages long. The motor carrier appendix was 65 pages long.

92. *Second Report*, p. 37. The ICC had jurisdiction over domestic water carriers so far as they "participate in joint interstate service with the railroads, and it has complete jurisdiction over such water carriers as are controlled by the railroads."

93. *Second Report*, p. 6.

94. *Second Report*, p. 9.

95. *Ibid.* Of these conferences, Eastman said, "The results have been periodic breakdowns of the agreements, rate wars, heavy losses, a recognition of the futility of such competition, and finally a repetition of the process of getting together and falling apart."

96. *Second Report*, p. 11.

97. *Business Week*, December 2, 1933, p. 24. The water carriers were represented by spokesmen for coastwise, intercoastal, Great Lakes and inland waterway carriers. They took action to establish committees to maintain "contact" with the railroads and the federal coordinator of transportation. For a description of the organization of these committees, see *Traffic World*, Vol. 52, No. 13, September 23, 1933, p. 510.

98. "Gen. Ashburn Advocates Transport Co-ordination," *Railway Age*, 95:571, October 21, 1933.

99. A special committee of the House of Representatives on government competition with private business had recommended that the government get out of the barge line business. 72 Cong., 2 sess., House of Representatives, House Resolution 235, May 31, 1932. The committee reported February 8, 1933. *Traffic World*, Vol. 51, No. 6, February 11, 1933, p. 287–288.

100. *Address of Joseph B. Eastman before National Rivers and Harbors Congress, Washington, D.C.*, April 30, 1934 (mimeo.), p. 7.

101. *Address of Joseph B. Eastman before the National Industrial Traffic*

League, New York, N.Y., November 14, 1934 (mimeo.). He thought that the ICC might be given discretion to make exceptions from the rule against giving to a carrier more than one kind of license to operate. He thought that the "commodities clause," forbidding carriers to transport commodities produced by them, might be moderated slightly by giving the ICC authority to make exceptions.

102. *New York Times,* February 5, 1935, p. 29, col. 1.

103. This fear had been voiced often in the debate over the motor carrier bill. The Maritime Association advocated regulation of shipping by the Shipping Board Bureau because of apprehension about the influence of the railroads in the Interstate Commerce Commission. *New York Times,* March 20, 1935, p. 43, col. 1. Industrial shippers as well as agricultural shippers expressed the same view. *New York Times,* February 22, 1935, p. 43, col. 1.

104. It was reported that the members of the Merchant Marine Committee were "too waterway minded" to expedite a bill bringing water carriers under the ICC. *New York Times,* June 30, 1935, Section IV, p. 11, col. 7.

105. Nine American flagship lines supported the Eastman bill on the ground that it would stabilize rates, eliminate unfair practices among the lines, and guard against destructive competition with its consequences of eventual high rates and the bankruptcy of the weaker lines. *New York Times,* April 16, 1935, p. 45, col. 1.

106. *Address of Joseph B. Eastman before the Propellor Club of the United States, Port of Philadelphia, Philadelphia, Pa.,* April 27, 1935 (mimeo.), pp. 6–7.

107. *Ibid.,* p. 11.

108. *Ibid.,* p. 14.

109. *Fourth Report,* pp. 14–21.

110. I. L. Sharfman, *The Interstate Commerce Commission,* Vol. IV, pp. 319–341, for a useful statement of the changes proposed by Eastman in 1935 and 1936 and the reaction of the Commission to them.

111. *Third Report,* p. 22.

112. See *Third Report,* Appendix VIII, for the detail of the bill proposed by Eastman for the reorganization of the Commission.

113. *Third Report,* p. ix.

114. *Third Report,* p. viii–ix.

115. *Business Week,* February 2, 1935, p. 18.

116. *Address of Joseph B. Eastman before the Propellor Club of the United States, Port of Philadelphia, Philadelphia, Pa.,* April 27, 1935 (mimeo.), p. 9.

117. *Ibid.*

118. *Fourth Report,* p. 24ff.

119. In his *Second Report,* p. 53, Eastman thought that the need for added regulation of the air lines was clear enough to justify a bill, but Congress had certain short run controls in mind that made it desirable to postpone a specific recommendation for regulation. He was clear, however, that any comprehensive regulation should be centered in the Interstate Commerce Commission. President Roosevelt at the time showed himself to be sympathetic to the idea that the ICC should regulate commercial aviation. *New York Times,* February 1, 1935, p. 1, col. 7. But the regulation of the air lines was eventually lodged in agencies outside the ICC.

In the same *Report,* p. 58, Eastman said that he had no recommendations to make for the regulation of natural gas because the subject was then under study by the House Committee on Interstate and Foreign Commerce. He had no recommendations for the further regulation of pipe lines in view of powers already vested in the ICC and the Department of the Interior, pp. 53–58.

120. *Fourth Report*, p. 33.

CHAPTER XI. END OF THE LINE

1. See *New York Times*, July 13, 1935, p. 17, col. 1. Eastman approved the suggestions, saying that they would be difficult of adoption but greatly worthwhile. He added, "Communities must be shown that they have more to gain than to lose from anything which will improve the financial and competitive health of the railroads and enable them to build up their traffic. The projects should not be inaugurated without consultation with the communities. The legal rights and welfare of the railroad employees must be considered and respected."

2. *New York Times*, July 20, 1935, p. 17, col. 1.

3. *New York Times*, November 8, 1935, p. 33, col. 1.

4. *New York Times*, February 1, 1936, p. 19, col. 6. The order was to apply to Worcester, Mass.; Mechanicsville, New York; Grand Rapids, Mich.; Jacksonville, Florida; Montgomery, Ala.; Meridian, Miss.; Freeport, Ill.; Des Moines and Council Bluffs, Iowa; Beaumont, Texas; and Ogden, Utah.

5. *Business Week* reported the announcement, and then said that Eastman's office might expire before the order could be enforced, "in view of the opposition churned up by railroads and shippers, with the moral support of his fellow members of the Interstate Commerce Commission." *Business Week*, February 8, 1936, p. 7.

6. See Cunningham, "The Federal Coordinator's Contribution to Coordination," p. 272. Cunningham also pointed out that the coordinator on July 17, 1934, had requested the regional coordinating committees to work out arrangements with the carriers in three terminals — Kansas City, Detroit, and Birmingham (Indianapolis was later substituted for Detroit) — to try some terminal unification to see what the concrete problems might be. The Indianapolis test was not finished in July 1935 when the coordinator recommended a broader program. In Kansas City eight of twelve roads were willing to go along and four were not, and in Birmingham "the lines were unwilling to proceed on any basis tending to change present control over individual operations," p. 270.

7. Eastman was, of course, not unaware of the interest of the unions in preventing the dismissal of workers and sought to work out an equitable scheme that would take care of such workers, and at the same time make it possible for the carriers to go ahead with the much needed rationalization of the railroad industry. He had legislation introduced in 1935 to provide a system of dismissal compensation for displaced workers. 74 Cong., 1 sess., S.1630 and H.R. 5378. After the bill was drafted, the Supreme Court declared the Railroad Retirement Act unconstitutional, and there was some feeling that the reasoning in *Alton Railroad Company v. Railroad Retirement Board*, 295 U.S. 330, might lead the court to declare the dismissal compensation bill unconstitutional also, although Eastman was optimistic that the court could be shown that dismissal compensation and the safety and efficiency of the

railroad service were connected. Eastman's conclusion was that "the best way of solving this problem would be by agreement, after negotiations, between the managements and the labor organizations." For a discussion of this matter, see *Fourth Report,* p. 50–58. The suggestion about negotiations appears at p. 57.

8. See account in *New York Times,* March 5, 1936, p. 33, col. 4.

9. *Ibid.*

10. The reaction of the carriers may be gathered from the way in which the development of the bill was reported to them: "Bill would Create New Labor Protection Set-up," *Railway Age,* 100:411, March 7, 1936; "Hearings on Wheeler-Crosser Bill," *Railway Age,* 100:621, April 11, 1936; "Wheeler-Crosser Bill Before Senate Committee," *Railway Age,* 100:657, April 18, 1936; "Consider Changes in Job-Freezing Measure," *Railway Age,* 100:690, April 25, 1936; "Rigor Mortis for the Railroads," *Railway Age,* 100:731, May 2, 1936.

11. "Eastern Terminal Orders Expected About March 31," *Railway Age,* 100:412, March 7, 1936.

12. *Address of Joseph B. Eastman before Chicago Traffic Club, Chicago. Ill.,* March 9, 1936 (mimeo.).

13. *Ibid.,* p. 6.

14. Eastman said that much could be done collectively that could not be done individually and then, "The Association of American Railroads was formed for that very purpose and is founded on that principle. It is the self-same principle that is embodied in the Emergency Railroad Transportation Act, which the railroads themselves supported and helped to originate and which imposes the same duty on them with respect to these matters that it imposes on me. They are committed thoroughly and irretrievably to the principle, both by the Emergency Act and by the formation of their own Association." *Ibid.,* p. 10.

15. "Government Management of Railways Being Attempted," *Railway Age,* 100:235, February 8, 1936. The mood of this piece may be gathered from the comment: "The government has the effrontery to hold the railroads up to the public as wasters because of duplications of their facilities and service the cost of which is not a spit in the ocean compared with the transportation wastes being caused by its own reckless and idiotic expenditures."

16. The unions' proposals do not seem to have included any meeting of minds on the proposed unification orders but rather action to avoid or to nullify their effects. The strategy for opposition to the orders was put on two grounds: that the unions and management might work out an agreement which would replace the Emergency Railroad Transportation Act; and if negotiations broke down, the unions would present legislation to Congress to take care of displaced workers. *New York Times,* February 18, 1936, p. 33, col. 1. This strategy was worked out between the RLEA and the members of the three labor advisory committees appointed under the Emergency Railroad Transportation Act of 1933. See "Labor Committees Consider Eastman's Proposed Orders," *Railway Age,* 100:337, February 22, 1936.

17. *Business Week,* March 14, 1936, pp. 24–26.

18. For text of the letter see *New York Times,* March 9, 1936, p. 1, col. 3. Quoted in Eastman to Franklin D. Roosevelt, May 25, 1936.

19. *New York Times,* February 4, 1936, p. 31, col. 4, contains an account

of the initial conference with a list of all the persons conferring. *Railway Age,* putting the most generous interpretation on carrier aims in the negotiations said, "The objective of the conference was the obtaining of the economies for which the Emergency Railroad Transportation Act of 1933 was enacted, but which, because it prohibits the reduction of employees through consolidations or unification below the number existing in May 1933, have not been realized." See "Committee is Established to Negotiate With Labor," *Railway Age,* 100:195, January 25, 1936.

20. *Ibid.*

21. *New York Times,* February 5, 1936, p. 27, col. 5. Some 80,000 employees had been added to the rolls since 1933.

22. *New York Times,* February 26, 1936, p. 36, col. 1.

23. *New York Times,* March 11, 1936, p. 7, col. 1. The unions were working for an agreement that would provide two-thirds pay for temporary displacement and dismissal wages or pensions for those permanently dismissed. Management agreed in principle but failed to mention any specific figures on which it was prepared to agree in detail.

24. *New York Times,* March 14, 1936, p. 23, col. 8.

25. *Ibid.* See also above, Chapter VII, for a discussion of the 1934 negotiations referred to by Phillips.

26. *New York Times,* March 17, 1936, p. 31, col. 1.

27. *New York Times,* March 18, 1936, p. 33, col. 8.

28. *New York Times,* March 19, 1936, p. 37, col. 4.

29. *New York Times,* March 20, 1936, p. 35, col. 4.

30. *New York Times,* March 25, 1936, p. 33, col. 8.

31. *New York Times,* March 27, 1936, p. 33, col. 4; March 28, 1936, p. 23, col. 1.

32. *New York Times,* March 27, 1936, p. 33, col. 4.

33. *New York Times,* March 31, 1936, p. 31, col. 1.

34. *New York Times,* April 10, 1936, p. 35, col. 8.

35. At a meeting of the Railway Labor Executives Association in Washington on December 5, 1935, it was reported that they favored a federal system of unemployment insurance throughout the transportation industry instead of separate systems for separate transportation agencies, such as the railroads, buses, trucks, air carriers, and water lines. Because the transportation companies themselves covered so many states, it was argued that the inclusion of transportation workers within the state systems of their residence would be impractical. *New York Times,* December 6, 1935, p. 37, col. 8. This view was in accord with the position that Eastman himself had expressed earlier, although it was his opinion that a scheme for a transportation unemployment insurance system should follow the enactment of legislation bringing all the principal transportation agencies under federal regulation. *Third Report,* pp. 75–76. With the enactment of the Social Security Act of 1935, the labor relations division of the coordinator's office (under Otto S. Beyer) drew up a transportation unemployment compensation plan that would take the form of an amendment to the Social Security Act and be administered by the Social Security Board. *New York Times,* December 31, 1935, p. 2, col. 5. It was this plan that Eastman formally recommended on April 6, 1936. The administration of the scheme was to be in the hands of a division of the Social Security Board. The Interstate Commerce Commission said that it approved

the idea of a national rather than a state system for transportation workers, but said that it was not familiar enough with the problems of unemployment compensation to make an intelligent recommendation on Eastman's proposal. *New York Times,* April 7, 1936, p. 22, col. 1.

36. *New York Times,* April 10, 1936, p. 35, col. 8.

37. *New York Times,* May 2, 1936, p. 23, col. 4. The unions were able to take advantage of a split among the carriers, some of which were willing to enter into the desired agreement. The unions then argued that the Wheeler-Crosser bill should be changed so as to apply *only* to those carriers that did not reach a voluntary agreement on displacement. *New York Times,* May 3, 1936, Sect. III, p. 8, col. 3.

38. *New York Times,* May 7, 1936, p. 35, col. 5.

39. *New York Times,* May 19, 1936, p. 40, col. 6.

40. *Report of the Railway Labor Executives' Association Covering Their Legislative Activities and Conferences with a Committee Representing Carriers in the United States on the Subject of Protection of Rights and Interests of Railway Employees Involved in the Coordination of Railroads or Their Facilities, Agreement Reached in Conference at Washington, D.C., May 21, 1936* (45 printed pages, n.d.).

41. "Labor-Management Pact on Dismissal Allowances," *Railway Age,* 100:849, May 23, 1936.

42. See also, "Agreement on Coordination Allowances," *Railway Age,* 100:885, May 30, 1936, where it was said, "in spite of the efforts of the railroads, no reference was made in it to the question of the continuation of Mr. Eastman's office. They had sought to have included a provision that agreement should not be binding in the event of any legislation covering the subject matter."

43. See account of the agreement in *Monthly Labor Review,* 42:1503–1507, June, 1936.

44. D. B. Robertson, "The Stake of Railroad Labor in the Transportation Problem," 187 *Annals of the American Academy of Political and Social Science* 92, September, 1936.

45. *New York Times,* May 22, 1936, p. 1, col 1.

46. *New York Times,* May 20, 1936, p. 2, col. 4. See also "Continuation of Coordinator Eastman's Office Proposed," *Railway Age,* 100:850, May 23, 1936.

47. See "Seeks Three More Years for Coordinator Office," *Railway Age,* 100:891, May 30, 1936.

48. Eastman, Letter to Hon. Franklin D. Roosevelt, May 25, 1936. In this letter Eastman said also that it was true that many of the railroads were "opposed to the continuance of the Emergency Act and the Coordinator. They want to be left to their own devices and to be allowed to work out coordinations in their own way. It is natural for them to feel this way about it."

49. Although Eastman was willing to address himself thus to Roosevelt, he did not help his friends to help him. A letter to Eastman from Fisher G. Dorsey, vice president and treasurer of the Lone Star Package Car Company, dated March 10, 1936, said, "Can you think of any other spots where I might be able to strike a blow in your behalf?" (National Archives, 0 — 26 — 17). Eastman replied to him under date of March 14, 1936, thanking him for his efforts but ignoring the request. The files of the National Archives contain

several such letters to Eastman but no record of his doing more than thanking the correspondents for their interest.

50. Memorandum from Franklin D. Roosevelt to Eastman, May 27, 1936 (National Archives, 0 — 26 — 17).

51. Letter, Eastman to Hon. Franklin D. Roosevelt, June 4, 1936.

52. "Continuation of Federal Coordinator Office Doubtful," *Railway Age,* 100:950, June 13, 1936. The shippers helped to inter the coordinator's office when the carriers and the unions in opposition to extension were joined by the National Industrial Traffic League.

53. "Continuation of Coordinator's Office Uncertain," *Railway Age,* 100:928, June 6, 1936.

54. The proposed resolution would have continued the coordinator but with little authority other than to continue studies "to encourage action on the part of carriers and other subsidiaries" towards reduction of costs, improvement, stabilization of employment, rehabilitation of the industry, and financial organization. *New York Times,* May 26, 1936, p. 39, col. 4.

55. *Business Week,* June 27, 1936, p. 34. It was also said that Eastman had foreborn "to push for government ownership of railroads at a time when that might have been brought to pass. The explanation may be that the radical young member of the commission had grown too old by the time the opportunity arrived. But the railroads have never forgotten his 'young' ideas and what he was able to do has been over their protest in almost every instance." The general conclusion was that there had been little action but much research.

56. *New York Times,* February 2, 1936, Section III, p. 4, col. 2.

57. Quoted in *Conclusion of the Federal Coordinator of Transportation on Passenger Traffic,* June 12, 1936, pp. 54–56.

58. Virgil D. Cover, "Three Years of Attempted Transportation Coordination," *Public Utilities Fortnightly,* February 4, 1937. The author reviews some of Eastman's recommendations with respect to merchandise traffic and passenger traffic and says that railroad opposition was sometimes "based on the strategic advantage of one road as opposed to another" and sometimes "on the basis of railroads against competitors." *Ibid.,* p. 140.

59. William J. Cunningham, "The Federal Coordinator's Contribution to Railroad Coordination," *Harvard Business Review,* Spring, 1937, p. 269.

60. *Railway Age* took the view that "management has now been restored to railway directors and executives" and felt that the passing of the coordinator meant that the AAR would have to show that it could accomplish the purposes of the Coordinator, inasmuch as it had been organized to show that there was no need for governmental coordination." "Opportunity for Association of American Railroads," *Railway Age,* 100:1017, June 27, 1936. The editorial said that most of Eastman's definite recommendations had been regarded by railway officers as impractical but thought that they had stimulated investigation and action. Its conclusion was that Eastman's work had probably done the railroads more good than harm, which was not what one might call a wildly enthusiastic judgment.

61. *Railway Age* thought that the failure of the Congress to renew the authorities of the coordinator showed the power of labor unions. *Ibid.*

62. Cunningham, "The Federal Coordinator's Contribution to Coordination," p. 266.

63. See *New York Times,* December 21, 1935, p. 4, col. 3, for report on consent of AAR to meet with union heads to discuss worker displacement plan. It was said that this probably meant the end of the Emergency Railroad Transportation Act because management had consistently opposed the act after the first year and unions probably would not press for extension if a displacement agreement could be reached. The initiative in the talks appears to have come from the unions. "Committee to Confer with Labor on Protection of Displaced Employees," *Railway Age,* 99:877, December 28, 1935.

64. "Eastman Finds Employees Entitled to Pay for Transfer," *Railway Age,* 95:222, August 5, 1933.

65. *New York Times,* August 10, 1933, p. 27, col. 1; August 19, 1933, p. 16, col. 3.

66. *Address of Joseph B. Eastman, federal coordinator of transportation, before National Association of Commercial Organization Secretaries, Washington,* May 2, 1934 (mimeo.). In this talk, he said, "I was opposed to the amendment then, but in view of what has happened since, I am inclined to think that it was wise" (p. 2).

67. *Address of Joseph B. Eastman, federal coordinator of transportation, before the New York Bond Club, at New York City,* June 5, 1934 (mimeo.), p. 10.

68. *Address of Joseph B. Eastman, federal coordinator of transportation, before Railway Labor Representatives at the Harrison Hotel, Chicago, Illinois,* January 12, 1935 (mimeo.). Similar advice was given to the Brotherhood of Railway and Steamship Clerks (*New York Times,* November 10, 1935, Section III, p. 5, col. 1).

69. "Baltimore and Ohio to Pay Dismissal Compensation," *Railway Age,* 98:277, February 16, 1935.

70. "Eastman Inquires Into Company Unions," *Railway Age,* 95:405, September 16, 1933.

71. *New York Times,* October 6, 1933, p. 27, col. 2.

72. See summary of questionnaire returns in *New Republic,* December 20, 1933, p. 156.

73. *New York Times,* December 9, 1933, p. 23, col. 1. See also "Eastman Warns Roads on Labor Relations," *Railway Age,* 95:849, December 16, 1933.

74. "Regional Committees to Make Recommendations on Company Unions," *Railway Age,* 96:50, January 13, 1934.

75. "Craftsmen Plan Eastman Protest," *Railway Age,* 96:50, January 13, 1934.

76. "Progress in Settling the Company Union Question," *Railway Age,* 96:170, January 27, 1934.

77. On March 31, 1934, Eastman submitted his proposal for revision of the Railway Labor Act of 1926 to House Commerce Committee Chairman Sam Rayburn and to Senate Commerce Committee Chairman Dill. On April 10, Senator Dill began hearings on S.3266 (Eastman's bill) and on May 21 the bill was reported favorably. On May 22, Congressman Rayburn began hearings on H. R. 9686, which was identical with S.3266, but on June 11 the House committee reported favorably a measure which included some union-sponsored amendments unacceptable to Eastman. On June 18, the House accepted S.3266, and Eastman's bill was enacted. On June 21, 1934, the President signed the act and appointed three members to the National Mediation Board

for which the act made provision. For a running and detailed account of the revision of the Railway Labor Act of 1926, see *Traffic World*, Vol. 53 (Eastman's message to Congress on the act), No. 14, p. 644, April 7, 1934; (Senate hearings) No. 15, April 14, 1934, p. 697, and No. 16, April 21, 1934, p. 771; (House hearings), No. 21, May 26, 1934, p. 1009, No. 22, June 2, 1934, p. 1053, and No. 24, June 16, 1934, p. 1137. On June 14, Secretary of Labor Frances Perkins and Eastman wrote to President Roosevelt urging that the leaders in both houses be requested to take necessary action. The letter concluded, "If this is done, it will not only forestall almost certain railroad labor difficulties in the near future, but will progressively improve railroad labor relations, thus furnishing a worthy object lesson to other industry." *Traffic World*, Vol. 53, No. 25, June 23, 1934, p. 11184.

78. See *New York Times*, April 1, 1934, p. 24, col. 1; "Revised Labor Act Proposed by Eastman," *Railway Age*, 96:510–512, April 7, 1934; "Senate Committee Hearing on Eastman Labor Bill," *Railway Age*, 96:555–556, April 14, 1934; "Eastman Again Urges National Adjustment Board," *Railway Age*, 96:611–612, April 28, 1934; "Senate Committee Considers Railway Labor Bill," *Railway Age*, 96:703, May 12, 1934; "Labor Bill Reported by Senate Committee," *Railway Age*, 96:777, May 26, 1934; "Bill to Amend Labor Act Reported," *Railway Age*, 96:872, June 16, 1934; "Railway Labor Act Amendments Passed," *Railway Age*, 96:924, June 23, 1934; "President Signs Railway Labor Act," *Railway Age*, 96:994, June 30, 1934. For specific positions of the carriers and the unions against the measure, see "Both Sides Oppose Labor Act Amendments," *Railway Age*, 96:815–818, June 2, 1934.

79. *Labor*, Vol. 14, No. 34, April 18, 1933, p. 2.

80. *Labor*, Vol. 14, No. 43, June 20, 1933, p. 3.

81. *Labor*, Vol. 16, No. 12, November 13, 1934.

82. There was early editorial disagreement with Eastman's interpretation of the Emergency Railroad Transportation Act, that the labor provisions did not apply to layoffs instituted in the ordinary course of management. *Labor*, Vol. 14, No. 49, August 1, 1933, p. 1.

83. *Labor*, Vol. 17, No. 44, June 23, 1936, p. 4.

84. *Labor*, Vol. 25, No. 32, March 18, 1944, p. 3.

85. *Ibid.*

86. "Coordinator's Office Expires," *Railway Age*, 100:1000, June 20, 1936.

87. These comments were reported in *New York Times*, June 18, 1936, p. 40, col. 1.

88. Memorandum, Eastman to Franklin D. Roosevelt, "Further Transportation Program in re Coordination," July 25, 1936.

CHAPTER XII. A MATTER OF ADMINISTRATIVE STYLE

1. Claude M. Fuess, *Joseph B. Eastman* (New York: Columbia University Press, 1952), 285.

2. "Getting More Good from the AAR," July 8, 1957, p. 58.

3. Marver H. Bernstein, *Regulating Business by Independent Commission* (Princeton: Princeton University Press, 1955), p. 258.

4. *Ibid.*, p. 282.

INDEX